*The Problem of Immigration in a*
*Slaveholding Republic*

# The Problem of Immigration in a Slaveholding Republic

*Policing Mobility in the Nineteenth-Century United States*

KEVIN KENNY

OXFORD
UNIVERSITY PRESS

Oxford University Press is a department of the University of Oxford. It furthers
the University's objective of excellence in research, scholarship, and education
by publishing worldwide. Oxford is a registered trade mark of Oxford University
Press in the UK and certain other countries.

Published in the United States of America by Oxford University Press
198 Madison Avenue, New York, NY 10016, United States of America.

CIP data is on file at the Library of Congress

ISBN 978–0–19–758008–0

DOI: 10.1093/oso/9780197580080.001.0001

Printed by Sheridan Books, Inc., United States of America

*To my teachers*

# Contents

# Acknowledgments

WRITING A BOOK is a collaborative process. The author draws on the expertise and generosity of others and tries to share something useful in return. In the ten years I spent writing *The Problem of Immigration in a Slaveholding Republic*, I was fortunate to receive advice, criticism, and encouragement from many friends and colleagues. My editor at Oxford University Press, Susan Ferber, pushed me hard and patiently to clarify my argument. The three anonymous reviewers assigned by the Press provided detailed and demanding critiques of the manuscript. I would also like to thank Jeremy Toynbee and India Gray. Rosanna Crocitto, Michael Crocitto Kenny, Ciaran Kenny, and Brian Malone read successive drafts and offered invaluable suggestions and emotional support. I am deeply grateful to Hidetaka Hirota for his insightful commentary and criticism at every stage of the writing. Particular thanks go to Tyler Anbinder, Katherine Carper, Eric Foner, Amanda Frost, Andrew Gerstenberger, Steven Hahn, Kate Masur, Lucy Salyer, and Michael Schoeppner, all of whom generously took the time to read my work and offer detailed comments. Bryan Willits, my research assistant, edited drafts of each chapter, checked the citations, collected the illustrations, read the proofs, and provided sound intellectual advice. For their help with various aspects of the book, I thank Eugenio Biagini, Marion Casey, Enda Delaney, Hasia Diner, Owen Dudley-Edwards, Elizabeth Ellis, Philip Erenrich, Gary Gerstle, Miriam Nyhan Grey, Caroline Heafey, Martha Hodes, Madeline Hsu, Owen Crocitto Kenny, Patrick Kenny, Anna Law, Erika Lee, Heather Lee, June Lloyd, Maddalena Marinari, Mae Ngai, Maureen O'Leary, Guy Ortolano, Ann Ostendorf, Virginia Reinburg, Franziska Seraphim, and Nicholas Wolf.

I started writing *The Problem of Immigration in a Slaveholding Republic* at Boston College and finished writing it at New York University. I would like to thank the students in my US immigration classes at both universities. We worked through a lot of the ideas in this book together. I would also like to acknowledge the generous support of the Advisory Board of Glucksman Ireland House and Deans Susan Antón, Thomas Carew, Una Chaudhuri, Caroline Dinshaw, and Antonio Merlo of the Faculty of Arts and Science at NYU.

While I was writing this book, I presented papers at seminars at Cambridge University, Edinburgh University, New York University, and Oxford University, and on panels organized by the Organization of American Historians and the Immigration and Ethnic History Society. I am grateful to everyone who attended these events. Parts of the argument appeared in a different form in the *Journal of American History* and the *Journal of the Civil War Era*, whose editors—Ben Irvin, Kate Masur, and Gregory Downs—helped me understand the issues at stake and how to write about them. *The Problem of Immigration in a Slaveholding Republic* was completed with the support of a Summer Stipend from the National Endowment for the Humanities, which gave me valuable time to write.

I dedicate this book to the historians who taught me about the nineteenth-century United States when I came to New York City as an immigrant.

As ever, my deepest debt, and not one I will try to express in words, is to the Crocitto Kennys – Rosanna, Michael, Owen, and Luna.

*The Problem of Immigration in a
Slaveholding Republic*

# *Introduction*

IN THE UNITED States today, the federal government controls immigration by deciding who to admit, exclude, or remove. Yet in the century after the American Revolution, Congress played only a very limited role in regulating immigration. The states patrolled their borders and set their own rules for community membership. In the Northeast, they imposed taxes and bonds on foreign paupers. In the Old Northwest (today's Midwest), they used the same methods to exclude and monitor free black people. Southern states policed the movement of African Americans, both free and enslaved, and passed laws imprisoning black sailors visiting from other states or abroad. These measures rested on the states' sovereign power to regulate their internal affairs. Defenders of slavery supported fugitive slave laws but resisted any other form of federal authority over mobility across and within their borders. If Congress had the power to control immigrant admissions, they feared, it could also control the movement of free black people and perhaps even the interstate slave trade. Immigration, in other words, presented a political and constitutional problem in a slaveholding republic.

The Civil War and the abolition of slavery removed the obstacles to a national immigration policy. In two cases heard in 1875, *Henderson v. New York* and *Chy Lung v. Freeman*, the Supreme Court declared that the era of state immigration control was at an end. Yet it would be a mistake to think that, in the absence of slavery, Congress would have regulated—let alone restricted—European immigration earlier. Following the example set by the states, Congress might have excluded vulnerable newcomers, just as it did when it passed the first general immigration act in 1882. But nobody before the end of the nineteenth century—not even the Know-Nothings in the 1850s—wanted to restrict European immigration numerically. Some nativists in the antebellum era called on Congress to extend the waiting period for naturalization or to regulate migration by paupers, but to no avail. Admission was the norm for Europeans, and it remained so until the 1920s. Even though the abolition of slavery cleared a path for the emergence of a national immigration policy, in other words, it did not make that policy inevitable.[1]

The catalyst was the arrival in the United States of significant numbers of immigrants from China. Starting in the 1870s, the federal government excluded Chinese laborers on antislavery grounds, deploying techniques of registration, punishment, and deportation first used to police free black people in the antebellum South. To justify these measures, the Supreme Court ruled in the *Chinese Exclusion Case* of 1889 that the federal government's power over immigration was inherent in national sovereignty and required no constitutional justification. This book explains how the existence, abolition, and legacies of slavery shaped immigration policy as it moved from the local to the federal level over the course of the nineteenth century. In so doing, it reveals the tangled origins of the national immigration policies we take for granted today.[2]

—•—

Although the federal government did not regulate admissions before the Civil War, it controlled three other kinds of population movement that intersected with immigration in important ways: the return of fugitive slaves, the removal of free black people overseas, and the expulsion of Native Americans to the continent's interior. The fugitive slave clause of the US Constitution required that persons "held to service" who escaped from bondage must be "delivered up on Claim of the Party to whom such Service or Labour may be due." Congress passed legislation to this effect in 1793. In *Prigg v. Pennsylvania* (1842), the Supreme Court ruled that the 1793 federal statute took precedence over a state law that made it a felony to remove "any negro or mulatto" with a view to enslaving them. Northern states responded by passing more stringent "personal liberty" laws to protect free black people and escaped slaves, while southern slaveholders demanded stronger federal legislation to secure their property rights. Congress then passed a sweeping new law in 1850, allowing enslavers or their agents to arrest suspected fugitives and take them before a wide range of officials who issued certificates of removal. No fugitive was allowed to testify in any trial or hearing under this law. With its system of forced and arbitrary removal and its lack of due process or judicial oversight, the Fugitive Slave Act of 1850 prefigured the mechanism for deporting immigrants introduced at the federal level in the postbellum era.[3]

The federal government supported the removal of free African Americans overseas. Some left voluntarily, for Haiti, Canada, or Africa, but most were removed through the so-called colonization movement. Colonization was not emigration. Even when voluntary, its purpose was to expel free black people on the grounds that they could never achieve civil or political equality in the United States. In other words, the colonization movement was a form of social engineering based on race. The American Colonization Society, founded in 1817 as a semi-public enterprise funded in part by the Monroe administration, transported about 11,000 people, most of them formerly enslaved, to Liberia. Some African Americans initially saw advantages in voluntary departure; none supported compulsory removal.[4]

The federal government also forcibly relocated Native Americans. The Indian Removal Act of 1830 created the machinery that expelled more than 80,000 people from the Southeast to locations beyond the Mississippi River. For a moment, it looked as though Chief Justice John Marshall might halt the process. In *Worcester v. Georgia* (1832), Marshall defined Native American nations as "distinct, independent political communities," subject to the jurisdiction of the federal government but not the states. Marshall's decision, however, lacked an enforcing mechanism and did nothing to prevent the expulsion of Native Americans from their homelands. In *United States v. Rogers* (1846), Roger Taney's Court rejected Marshall's position, ruling that Native tribes were not sovereign communities but collections of individuals bound together by race, endowed only with those rights the federal government chose to confer on them. These two principles—tribal autonomy versus minority status—operated in uneasy tension until the 1870s, when Congress discontinued the practice of making treaties with Native tribes and nations. The *Rogers* decision gave Congress a plenary power largely immune from judicial review, laying the groundwork for immigration policy as well as Native American policy in the postbellum era.[5]

When it came to admitting or removing immigrants, Congress played almost no role before the Civil War. Towns and states controlled admissions and expulsions. Under the Constitution, each state retained sovereignty over matters on which it had not surrendered power to the national government, including mobility within and across its borders. Towns and states used their police power to regulate admissions and expulsions. Today the term "police" refers to a body of people charged with keeping public order and investigating crimes. In the nineteenth century, police had a related but broader meaning, referring to the right of local communities to regulate the health, safety, morals, and general welfare of their residents. State and local governments passed laws and ordinances that prohibited the arrival of foreign convicts; required ship captains to post bonds or pay taxes for foreign paupers and others who might require public support, such as the mentally or physically disabled; ordered the deportation of foreign paupers to their states or countries of origin; quarantined both native-born and foreign passengers who carried contagious diseases; patrolled the movement of free and enslaved black people within and between the states; and confined free black sailors to jail for the duration of their stay in southern ports. They insisted that it was their right and obligation to protect public health and safety in this way. As Justice Philip Pendleton Barbour put it in 1837, in the first immigration case to reach the Supreme Court, states had the same authority and duty to protect themselves against "the moral pestilence of paupers, vagabonds, and possibly convicts" as they did to protect against "the physical pestilence" arising from infectious disease.[6]

State-level policies regulating immigration and other kinds of mobility emerged from the poor law system. Local laws requiring bonds or taxes for alien passengers were designed, for the most part, not to exclude immigrants but to raise revenue for the upkeep of the poor. Poor laws provided for the removal of paupers out of state or even—in the case of Massachusetts—out of the country. Only very rarely, however, did these laws exclude immigrants from entry. Nearly all immigrants were admitted, as long as ship captains paid the required taxes or fees (which they transferred to the passengers by raising fares). States in the South and the Old Northwest, meanwhile, used their poor laws to monitor free black people or to bar their entry altogether. European immigrants, while they might be removed as paupers, confronted no such restrictions on their interstate movement.[7]

When challenges to state immigration laws made their way to the US Supreme Court, it was by no means clear on what grounds these laws could be evaluated. Strangely for a country that attracted so many immigrants, the Constitution says nothing about their admission, exclusion, or expulsion. Its sole provision concerning immigration gives Congress the power to establish a uniform rule for naturalizing foreigners—after they have been admitted to the United States. Congress acted on this power immediately, passing four naturalization laws between 1790 and 1802 that laid down the system still in place today—citizenship after a probationary period of residence, accompanied by evidence of good character and an oath renouncing foreign allegiance. Yet, to be eligible for citizenship, an alien had to be a "free White person." Not until 1870 was the right to naturalize extended to people of African origin. Asian immigrants remained barred from citizenship until the middle of the twentieth century.[8]

Other than naturalization, the Constitution offers no guidance on immigration policy. It contains several provisions indirectly related to the subject, but none of them provided the basis for a national policy. Congress could claim authority over admissions via the taxing and spending clause, to the extent that immigrants were classified as imports—a question that remained disputed throughout the nineteenth century. It could also claim authority over enemy aliens via the war powers clause. More significantly, the treaty power clause enabled the president to craft immigration policy through diplomacy. Treaties with Great Britain and China in the nineteenth century, for example, guaranteed free trade and free migration, two questions that were always closely related. The meaning of the migration or importation clause, which prevented Congress from prohibiting the importation of slaves for twenty years, was more controversial. Some contemporaries argued that it applied to voluntary migration as well as the external slave trade. By this logic, Congress could regulate neither the slave trade nor immigration before 1808, but it could regulate both thereafter. Opponents of the John Adams administration insisted, on these rather shaky grounds, that the provision for deporting immigrants from noncombatant countries in the Alien Friends Act of 1798 was unconstitutional. Some warned that the act might even empower the executive branch to remove enslaved people from the United States. Most contemporaries, however, insisted that the migration or importation clause had no relevance to free immigration. When Congress duly passed legislation in 1807 marking the end of the twenty-year moratorium, it limited the prohibition to the external slave trade. Nonetheless, claims that Congress had authority to regulate voluntary immigration under the migration or importation clause persisted until the Civil War.[9]

A final part of the Constitution—and the one the Supreme Court turned to most frequently in evaluating laws controlling immigration in the nineteenth century—was the commerce clause. This provision gave Congress the power "To regulate Commerce with foreign Nations, and among the several States, and with the Indian Tribes." In *Gibbons v. Ogden* (1824), John Marshall defined commerce very broadly to cover "commercial intercourse between nations, and parts of nations, in all its branches," including navigation. Although states could enact quarantine laws and other measures to protect public health and safety, Marshall ruled, power over interstate and foreign commerce rested ultimately with Congress. Marshall's opinion laid the groundwork for thinking about immigration as a form of commerce, but

it also raised the prospect—in theory, if not as a practical political matter—
that the federal government could use its commerce power to regulate the
internal slave trade or even the institution of slavery.[10]

The constitutional battle over immigration authority in the nineteenth
century pitted federal commerce power against local police power. Which
level of government had authority? Throughout the antebellum era, the
Supreme Court danced around this question rather than confronting it
squarely because any decision concerning immigration affected the institution of slavery, and especially the movement of free black people. If the courts
invalidated the right of Massachusetts to impose taxes or bonds on foreign
paupers, what would become of similar laws in South Carolina punishing
free black seamen, laws in southern states mandating the expulsion of freed
slaves, or laws in both the North and the South excluding free black people? If
Congress had power over immigrant admissions under the commerce clause,
how far would that power extend when it came to other forms of mobility?
In the *Dred Scott* case (1857), the Supreme Court identified one set of rules
for white people, including European immigrants, and another for African
Americans. Given the political constraints on federal power in a slaveholding
republic, however, any sweeping assertion of federal power over mobility was
fraught with peril.

In *New York v. Miln* (1837), six of the seven justices upheld a New York
statute requiring captains to file passenger reports, on the grounds that it
was "not a regulation of commerce, but of police." The sole purpose of the
law, Justice Barbour explained for the Court, was to protect the citizens of
New York from foreign paupers. "There can be no mode," he wrote, "in which
the power to regulate internal police could be more appropriately exercised."
Citing Emer de Vattel's treatise on international law, *The Law of Nations*
(1758), Barbour held that each state in the Union had the same sovereign
power as any foreign nation to admit and exclude foreigners. Barbour avoided
the question of whether a state police measure requiring bonds for passengers
intruded on Congress's power to regulate interstate or foreign commerce. The
Court's affirmation of police power in *Miln* reassured southern states that federal power would not be used to regulate the movement of free black people,
though it fell short of recognizing their claim to hold power over commerce
concurrently with the federal government.[11]

When the Supreme Court directly considered state laws imposing taxes
and bonds on passengers in the *Passenger Cases* of 1849, the result was discord
and confusion. By a contentious 5 to 4 majority, the Court ruled that the laws
of New York and Massachusetts violated federal commerce power. Anyone

who reads the *Passenger Cases* today, however, will emerge bewildered by the eight separate opinions unless they realize that much more was at stake than the arrival of passengers in Boston and New York. The four dissenters, led by Chief Justice Taney, warned that overturning state immigration laws would lead to federal "tyranny"—a codeword for any threat to the interests of the slave states. Admittedly, a majority of the justices in the *Passenger Cases* upheld federal commerce power over state police power, yet their opinions were equivocal and often contradictory. The decision, moreover, had little practical impact, as New York and Massachusetts converted passenger taxes, deemed unconstitutional, into nominally optional commutation fees in the same amount (as a less expensive alternative to posting bonds). The *Passenger Cases* are important not for their impact on policy but as a set of arguments about sovereignty and federalism that reveal the inextricability of immigration and slavery. If Congress could control mobility to the extent claimed by the majority in the *Passenger Cases*, Taney warned, it could decide for each state "who should or should not be permitted to reside among its citizens." Black people, he believed, were not entitled to move freely within the United States. In the *Dred Scott* case, Taney pushed this logic to its awful conclusion, ruling that no African American descended from slaves could ever be a citizen of the United States.[12]

But what did citizenship mean in the antebellum era? The Constitution used the word citizen several times, but it offered no definition before the Fourteenth Amendment in 1868. In the antebellum era, states and local governments defined their own rules for civil and political membership. Country of birth was less important than race and gender. Native-born white male householders were citizens, but their wives—even when they came from the same social backgrounds—were prohibited by state coverture laws from owning property, making contracts, and earning wages. Suffrage was not a necessary attribute of citizenship, but women's inability to vote or hold elected office undermined their civil as well as their political status. Free black people, even in northeastern states that recognized them as citizens, faced restrictions on voting, serving in the militia, attending public schools, holding office, and testifying in court. Southern states, meanwhile, denied the very possibility that black people could be citizens. Male immigrants of European origin, by contrast, could move freely throughout the United States, naturalize as citizens, exercise the vote, and hold office.[13]

The Fourteenth Amendment defined national citizenship by two simple criteria: birth on the soil or naturalization. Birthright citizenship, written into the Constitution in 1868, had deep roots in American history. Throughout the antebellum era, black people claimed both state and national citizenship by virtue of birth on the soil, organizing conventions, submitting petitions, and initiating lawsuits to assert their rights. It was not until Reconstruction that their struggle to make birthright the basis of citizenship reached fruition. Since the Fourteenth Amendment, it has been customary to think of citizenship as membership in a centralized nation-state, with rights defined and protected by the federal government. But it took a civil war to create this kind of citizenship and to extend it to everyone born within the jurisdiction of the United States—the children of immigrants as well as Americans born on the soil who had once been enslaved.

Forged in a war to end slavery, the Fourteenth Amendment became a powerful force for assimilating immigrants and their children, regardless of their background or status. In the United States, the principle of birthright citizenship has been the bedrock of civil and political membership since Reconstruction. That principle is under threat today, with nativists questioning—implausibly but persistently—whether the American-born children of unsanctioned immigrants owe their allegiance to the United States or to a foreign power.[14]

⎯•⎯

As the balance of power shifted from the local to the federal level during the Civil War and Reconstruction, so too did authority over immigration. Reconstruction had a double-edged impact on immigration. On the one hand, the civil rights acts and the Fourteenth Amendment equipped not just citizens but also unnaturalized immigrants, including those ineligible for naturalization, such as the Chinese, with federally protected rights. On the other hand, the new national state that emerged after the Civil War could regulate and exclude immigrants much more effectively than any individual state. State laws were subject to judicial review under the commerce clause and the Fourteenth Amendment in ways that national laws were not.

In *Henderson v. New York* and *Chy Lung v. Freeman*, considered simultaneously in 1875, the Supreme Court unanimously invalidated state laws requiring bonds, taxes, or fees for passengers. Transportation of passengers from Europe, Justice Samuel Miller noted in *Henderson*, was an essential part of American trade and required a uniform rule. That rule, he concluded, was provided by the commerce clause. In *Chy Lung*, the Court invalidated a California law directed at Chinese immigrants, which required bonds for "lewd and debauched women" arriving in the state. Authority over admissions belonged exclusively to Congress, Miller reiterated, based on its "power to regulate commerce with foreign nations." If it were otherwise, a state could "embroil us in disastrous quarrels with other nations." In both cases, the Court conceded that states could continue to police public health and safety internally—but not in ways that infringed on domains where Congress held exclusive power, including external commerce and foreign affairs. If *Chy Lung* was a short-term victory by Chinese immigrants, it also signaled that the federal government could control admissions if it chose to act. Officials in the Northeast, alarmed that they would have to pay the costs of sustaining paupers once state laws were invalidated, pressured Congress to assume control of immigration. Politicians in the American West, realizing that national laws would be more effective and durable than their own, urged Congress to exclude the Chinese. In March 1875, before *Henderson* and *Chy Lung* were decided, Congress passed the Page Act, the first in a series of anti-Chinese laws that heralded the emergence of national immigration policy.[15]

Chinese immigrants faced severe and often violent discrimination in the American West, but until the 1870s they also enjoyed some fundamental protections. The Coolie Trade Prohibition Act of 1862, which outlawed American involvement in the transportation of Chinese contract workers to foreign destinations (with Cuba and Peru in mind), correctly classified the Chinese laborers who came to the United States as voluntary immigrants. It therefore had no immediate effect on American immigration. The Burlingame-Seward Treaty of 1868 recognized the right of Chinese workers to migrate to the United States. The Fourteenth Amendment extended due process and equal protection to foreigners who had not acquired citizenship—including Chinese immigrants, who were barred from naturalizing. Aware of their rights and supported by powerful merchants, Chinese immigrants challenged laws that tried to exclude them or discriminated against them after entry. Under the principle of birthright citizenship, moreover, their American-born children were automatically citizens of the United States. This definition of national citizenship generated a racial backlash. A twisted reading of the Thirteenth Amendment, which prohibited slavery in the United States, produced the syllogism that coolies were slaves, Chinese laborers were coolies, and Chinese laborers must therefore be excluded as an antislavery measure.[16]

Legislation in the 1870s and 1880s, at both the state and federal level, rested on this antislavery logic, with a particular emphasis on gender. Restrictionists targeted male laborers and female prostitutes, placing both in the category of unfree. California, for example, passed laws in 1870 to "Prevent the Establishment of Coolie Slavery" and to prevent "the Kidnapping and Importation of Mongolian, Chinese, and Japanese females, for Criminal or

Demoralizing Purposes," adding the category "lewd and debauched women" in 1874. At the federal level, the Page Act, passed as an extension of the Coolie Trade Prohibition Act, criminalized the importation of prostitutes and required Asian women to undergo consular inspection and obtain certificates demonstrating that they were not immigrating for "lewd or immoral purposes." All Chinese women outside the upper class came under suspicion. By establishing gender and marriage as mechanisms for federal immigration control, the Page Act significantly reduced the number of Chinese women immigrants, prevented Chinese men from starting families in the United States, and impeded the growth of the Chinese-American population. In 1890, partly as a result of the Page Act, Chinese men outnumbered women by 27 to 1 in the United States.[17]

The Page Act, however, was ineffective in controlling migration by male laborers. It criminalized the importation of coolies as well as prostitutes, yet Chinese migrant workers in the United States were classified as free under federal law. Led by Denis Kearney and other Irish immigrants, California workers demanded protection against Chinese labor competition. By the mid-1870s, both the Democratic Party and the Republican Party supported Chinese exclusion. Building on the Page Act, Congress passed legislation in 1882 excluding Chinese laborers, both skilled and unskilled, for ten years based on the antislavery argument that all Chinese workers were unfree. Known as the Chinese Exclusion Act, the 1882 law discriminated by class as well as race, banning workers while exempting merchants, teachers, students, and diplomats. Together, the Page Act and the Chinese Exclusion Act marked a decisive step in the transition from state to federal immigration control, placing Chinese immigrants into a special category with its own system of law.[18]

That kind of law had precedents in the antebellum South. In most southern states before the Civil War, free black people were required to register to demonstrate their status and their entitlement to residency. They had to carry papers and produce them on demand, could be banished for certain offenses, and were often denied reentry if they left their states. As control over immigration shifted to the national level in the 1870s, federal anti-Chinese laws followed a similar pattern to these earlier local laws—restrictions on migration (into the national territory rather than between the states), prohibitions on the right to return, and requirements to register and carry proof of legal status under pain of corporal punishment and expulsion. Fears that American labor could not compete with Chinese coolie labor also evoked antebellum

Free-Soil arguments that free or enslaved black labor would degrade the condition of white workers.[19]

Directed initially at Chinese immigrants, federal policy quickly expanded to cover immigrants more generally. In *Henderson* and *Chy Lung*, the Court asserted national authority over immigration for both economic reasons (immigration as a huge form of international commerce) and security reasons (state-level immigration decisions could embroil the nation in diplomatic conflict or war). Officials and politicians in the Northeast called for national legislation to replace the old state-level system and pay for the upkeep of the immigrant poor. The Immigration Act of 1882, modeled on the antebellum state laws and designed and implemented by officials from New York and Massachusetts, levied a head tax on all foreign passengers and excluded those likely to become a public charge. A second general immigration act, passed in 1891, shifted the administration of national policy away from the states and toward the federal government and expanded the list of excludable and deportable classes. The elements of a federal immigration regime were now in place, supported by a new conception of national sovereignty.[20]

The Supreme Court clarified the nature of national sovereignty in the *Chinese Exclusion Case* of 1889. Under the exclusion laws of the early 1880s, Chinese laborers already in the United States could travel abroad and return if they had proper documentation. Congress unilaterally discontinued return certificates in the Scott Act of 1888 and barred all Chinese laborers who had left the country, even if they held valid documentation issued previously. One such laborer, Chae Chan Ping, challenged the new act. Chae had left the United States to visit China in 1887. When he came back to San Francisco on October 8, 1888, seven days after the Scott Act became law, he was refused permission to land. Denied a writ of habeas corpus on the grounds that he had not been deprived of his liberty unlawfully, Chae Chan Ping took his case to the Supreme Court.[21]

Chae Chan Ping's lawyers did not challenge Congress's power to control immigrant admissions. After all, the Supreme Court had ruled unanimously in *Henderson* and *Chy Lung* that admissions lay under the control of the federal government. Instead, Chae Chan Ping's lawyers argued that he had a vested right to reside in the United States, where he had lived since 1875, and was being expelled without due process. The US government contended that because Chae Chan Ping was outside the country, Congress had a clear right to bar his entry, based on the nation's sovereign power to control its borders. The Court agreed, ruling that residency in the United States was a privilege rather than a right. Congress had granted that right to certain immigrants and could revoke it through legislation. Authority to regulate the nation's borders, the Court found, was inherent in the sovereignty of the United States. As a matter of national security, this authority lay with the legislature and executive, which had a plenary power over immigration largely immune from judicial review.[22]

Federal control over immigration, based on powers inherent in national sovereignty, developed in tandem with Native American policy. Immigration control rested on the claim that the United States had exclusive power over the national territory. Yet hundreds of Native nations living within the borders of the United States also made claims to territorially bounded political status. In the late nineteenth century, as it consolidated control over immigration, the federal government also terminated treaty-making with Native nations, allotted individual landholdings to break up tribal territory, and extended or imposed national citizenship. Some Native Americans welcomed US citizenship because it provided access to work, education, and the vote. Others—especially those belonging to tribes and nations that had retained their land against threats of dispossession and removal—resisted citizenship as a negation of their sovereignty. The plenary power articulated by the Supreme Court in *United States v. Rogers* (1846) provided the underpinning for federal policy in both immigration and Indian affairs from the 1880s onward.[23]

Postbellum federal immigration policy rested on the same principle that the antebellum states had invoked during the era of slavery when policing mobility within and across their borders. National authority over immigration, as defined by the courts, was a version of local police power writ large. The lawyers and jurists who defined federal immigration authority in the postbellum era cited the same theories of international law that supported state sovereignty before the Civil War. In *Nishimura Ekiu v. United States* (1892), the Court extended federal power to all forms of immigration, not just Chinese. In *Fong Yue Ting v. United States* (1893), the Supreme Court ruled that the federal government had the same power to deport as to exclude. Congress, the justices concluded, had the power to admit, exclude, or expel foreigners to protect the national interest, with minimal interference by the courts. This doctrine of power inherent in sovereignty laid the basis for US immigration policy in the twentieth century.[24]

———

This book explains how a national immigration policy emerged in the context of slavery. The four chapters in Part One, "Sovereign States," examine the tensions between local and federal power before the Civil War. State laws regulating the mobility of foreigners and free black people clashed with federal commerce power, the treaty-making power of the United States, and the privileges and immunities of black citizens. In considering these laws, local and federal courts grappled with a series of closely related issues: state-level taxation of immigrant paupers, the interstate slave trade, movement by free black people within and between the states, the nature of citizenship and comity, the property rights of slaveholders, and the return of fugitive slaves. The Civil War and Reconstruction resolved the problem of immigration in a slaveholding republic. The three chapters in Part Two, "Immigration in the Age of Emancipation," examine the development of a federal policy based on a new claim to national sovereignty. With state immigration laws invalidated, restrictionists realized that the national government could exclude foreigners much more effectively than the states. Congress excluded Chinese prostitutes and laborers, while introducing harsh new mechanisms of registration, punishment, and deportation. The Supreme Court upheld its power to do so as an attribute of national sovereignty.

Historians approach sovereignty as a contested claim to authority rather than a form of power whose meaning can be determined a priori. Sovereignty in this sense cannot be grasped in the abstract, only in its particular and evolving contexts. Claims to authority over immigration were always contingent and dynamic. They were part of an ongoing political and constitutional argument, a set of questions and answers about who had the right to control borders, mobility, political allegiance, and community membership in the age of slavery and emancipation. The process of state formation puts sovereign claims into practice by building and operating administrative institutions, but the emphasis here is on the arguments about sovereignty that justified laws, policies, and political action.[25]

The primary focus throughout this book is on the logic of sovereignty and race as expressed in judicial opinions and decisions, legislative debates, statutes, and official reports. The book examines ideas, laws, and policies that were used to justify control over the mobility of immigrants and black people. For this reason, the argument focuses mainly on the articulation of power rather than resistance. While most of my writing has been social history "from the bottom up," this current book takes a largely top-down approach because of the nature of the problem it seeks to explain. Black people and immigrants, as several historians have demonstrated, created rights and defined citizenship for themselves in the nineteenth century, taking legal action, writing petitions, and organizing meetings and protests. In doing so, they confronted deeply ingrained convictions about white racial supremacy that originated in slavery and conquest. This book excavates the origins of these convictions in an attempt to explain the terrible power of what people were resisting.[26]

For similar reasons, *The Problem of Immigration in a Slaveholding Republic* examines laws as debated and written by legislatures, and as interpreted by courts, more than laws as applied in practice. The book focuses on the ideas and politics that gave rise to these laws and to a lesser extent on their implementation as policy. This approach differs from, but also complements, a trend in scholarship that can be referred to as the institutional and social history of immigration policy. Recent historians have shown how quotidian enforcement practices by local officials on the ground often diverged—to the benefit or detriment of immigrants—from laws and policies devised at the central level. My approach focuses on the legal and political arguments that gave rise to these laws and policies, in order to clarify who claimed authority over mobility and on what grounds. The book thereby contributes to an integrated understanding of the social, legal, and political history of mobility and sovereignty in the nineteenth-century United States.[27]

Generations of historians laid down the classic narrative of immigration—dislocation from a homeland, adjustment in a new host country, upward social mobility, and eventual assimilation—at a time when most Americans confidently expected their country to grow and prosper. These historians wrote mostly about immigration from the 1890s through the 1920s. The periods before and after this classic era demand their own approaches. Historians today, living in an era pervaded by inequality and a sense of decline, and often focusing on the entrenched forms of racism endured by Asian, Latino, Afro-Caribbean, and African immigrants in the twentieth century and beyond, have rightly discarded older models of assimilation. The century before Reconstruction also differed radically from the Ellis Island era. Any understanding of this earlier period must examine European and Asian immigration in the same historical context as African American and Native American history. Connecting these histories, which are usually told separately, reveals the foundations of present-day border control, incarceration, deportation, and the ongoing tension between state and federal sovereignty in immigration policy.[28]

States and cities today play a double-edged role in immigration policy, depending on their location and politics. The federal government controls admissions, but states and cities continue to regulate the lives of immigrants once they have entered the country. Many local jurisdictions pass laws restricting immigrants' access to public welfare, educational tuition, driver's licenses, and employment, along with measures enhancing cooperation with federal law enforcement. Others, however, pass pro-immigrant laws facilitating access to benefits, education, and work. Some provide sanctuary against federal surveillance, complementing grassroots efforts by faith-based organizations and other activists. The states' rights tradition in American history has a deep association with racism, in the form of slavery and Jim Crow. Yet, just as the antebellum states enacted personal liberty laws to resist fugitive slave laws, local jurisdictions across the United States today refuse to act as agents of federal immigration enforcement and play a vital role in protecting immigrants' rights. This trend suggests a revival of local sovereignty, not simply as autonomy from the national government, but as a counterweight to federal power and an affirmative commitment to the welfare of all residents. Given the issues at stake, the debates over immigration when the United States was a slaveholding republic remain of critical importance to understanding the present.[29]

# PART ONE

*Sovereign States*

# I

## *Foundations*

THE DECLARATION OF Independence begins with the "self-evident" truths that all men are created equal and "endowed by their Creator with certain unalienable Rights." Less well-known is the list of twenty-seven grievances against George III that follows. One of these grievances concerned immigration. "He has endeavoured to prevent the population of these States," the Declaration stated, by refusing to pass laws to encourage immigration and obstructing "the Laws for Naturalization of Foreigners." In a draft of the Declaration, Thomas Jefferson also included a passage blaming the king for slavery: "He has waged cruel war against human nature itself, violating it's [*sic*] most sacred rights of life & liberty in the persons of a distant people who never offended him, captivating & carrying them into slavery in another hemisphere or to incur miserable death in their transportation thither." King George, according to Jefferson, had suppressed every attempt "to prohibit or to restrain this execrable commerce," and now he was encouraging American slaves "to rise in arms among us." Years later, in his autobiography, Jefferson attributed the omission of this passage from the final version of the Declaration to the intransigence of South Carolina and Georgia, the two southern states that depended most heavily on continued importation of enslaved people. This explanation hardly does credit to the importance of slavery in the revolutionary era—one-third of the signatories of the Declaration of Independence were slaveholders, and the institution existed in all of the American colonies.[1]

Most of the architects of the American Revolution and the Constitution saw the country they were founding as a refuge for "the oppressed of all nations," or at least all European nations. Thomas Paine declared in his pamphlet *Common Sense* (1776) that freedom had "been hunted round the globe" and America must "receive the fugitive and prepare in time an asylum for mankind." Other revolutionary leaders were equally accepting of liberty-seeking immigrants, provided they were of the right sort. As George Washington put it in a letter to Irish immigrants in New York City in 1783: "The bosom of America is open to receive not only the Opulent and respectable Stranger, but the oppressed and persecuted of all Nations and Religions; whom we shall wellcome to a participation of all our rights and previleges, if by decency and propriety of conduct they appear to merit the enjoyment." At the Constitutional Convention in Philadelphia in 1787, James Madison expressed his desire "to invite foreigners of merit and republican principles among us" on the grounds that America "was indebted to emigration for her settlement and prosperity." Those parts of the country that had encouraged immigration, Madison noted, "had advanced most rapidly in population, agriculture, and the arts." Immigrant labor, he predicted, would be essential to America's expanding economy. If the United States was a haven for immigrants, however, it was also a slaveholding republic. What would it mean for the country to be both of these things at once? How would citizenship be defined? Who would control the slave trade, the mobility of free black people, and the admission of immigrants in a federal system with sovereignty divided between the national government and the states?[2]

## Immigrants and Citizens

J. Hector St. John de Crèvecoeur left his native Normandy for New France in 1755 and settled in New York in 1759. In his *Letters from an American Farmer*, published in 1782, Crèvecoeur offered an early rendition of the melting pot ideal. A surveyor and farmer, he celebrated American diversity and democracy in a series of distinctively horticultural metaphors. Migrants were like plants, he wrote: "the goodness and flavour of the fruit proceeds from the peculiar soil and exposition in which they grow." In Europe, they lacked "vegetative mould and refreshing showers; they withered, and were mowed down by want, hunger, and war." In America, "by the power of transplantation, like all other plants they have taken root and flourished!" They became "men." Switching metaphors, Crèvecoeur formulated the most enduring American image of assimilation: "Here individuals of all nations are melted into a new race of men, whose labours and posterity will one day cause great changes in the world." By "all nations," he meant Europeans only. The American people, for Crèvecoeur, were a "mixture of English, Scotch, Irish, French, Dutch, Germans, and Swedes. From this promiscuous breed, that race now called Americans have arisen."[3]

Some of Crèvecoeur's contemporaries were skeptical about the supposed benefits of immigration. Jefferson, in his "Notes on the States of Virginia" (1787), argued against encouraging the "servile masses of Europe" to cross the Atlantic. The new American system of government, he noted, was "a composition of the freest principles of the English constitution, with others derived from natural right and natural reason. To these nothing can be more opposed than the maxims of absolute monarchies." Because of this liberty, America would inevitably attract many immigrants, who would either bring with them the oppressive principles of the countries they left behind or throw off these principles "in exchange for an unbounded licentiousness, passing, as is usual, from one extreme to another." They and their children would turn American society into "a heterogeneous, incoherent, distracted mass" incapable of self-government. Jefferson did not object to immigrants coming to America voluntarily nor to the recruitment of skilled workers, but he saw no need for the national government to encourage immigration in general. Based on an analysis of colonial records, he calculated that the American population had doubled every twenty-seven years and predicted that it would continue to grow at that rate through natural increase and desirable immigration, resulting in a society that would be "homogeneous, more peaceable, more durable."[4]

In Massachusetts, the anti-Federalist pamphleteer Agrippa voiced similar concerns in stronger terms. Like other anti-Federalists, Agrippa was suspicious of placing too much power in the hands of the national government proposed by the Constitutional Convention in 1787. In a letter to the people of Massachusetts on December 28, he addressed the question of authority over immigrant admissions. Congress should not have "the sole power to regulate the intercourse between us and foreigners," he argued, "for though most of the states may be willing for certain reasons to receive foreigners as citizens, yet reasons of equal weight may induce other states, differently circumstanced, to keep their blood pure." As a negative counterpart to Massachusetts, Agrippa held up the example of Pennsylvania, which had "acquired her present extent and population at the expense of religion and good morals." By contrast, the New England colonies, other than Rhode Island, "by keeping separate from the foreign mixtures, acquired their present greatness in the course of a century and a half," and had preserved their religion, morals, and "manly virtue."[5]

Long before the Revolution, colonial legislatures had decided for themselves which foreigners to incorporate into their communities. The Plantation Act of 1740 recognized the power of local American courts to naturalize foreigners after a seven-year waiting period, followed by an oath of allegiance to the British monarch, without the need for a separate act of Parliament in each case. Naturalized aliens attained the same rights as English colonial subjects by pledging their allegiance to the community that admitted them. The colonies controlled the naturalization process, which amounted to a contract between the foreigners and the community that agreed to accept them as members. This form of naturalization, based on practical rather than doctrinal considerations, allowed immigrants to cast off one allegiance in favor of another. In England, by contrast, the allegiance of subject to monarch was considered an unbreakable bond within a hierarchy of fixed social and individual ranks rooted in the laws of nature. If English law operated on the principle of immutable allegiance—once a subject, always a subject—American naturalization policy rested on mutual consent. Colonial policy recognized the advantages of immigration in labor-scarce settings and provided an easy method for assimilation. Legislation passed in 1773, however, prohibited colonial governments from naturalizing citizens, leading to Jefferson's complaint in the Declaration of Independence.[6]

The American Revolution, at least in principle, extended the contractual understanding of allegiance from naturalization to citizenship per se. If government rested on the consent of the governed, citizens could theoretically renounce their allegiance to that government and form a new one if they wished. Whereas subjectship in English law entailed a social hierarchy with varying privileges and disabilities, all citizens of the United States were nominally equal under the law. The Constitution structured relationships between the federal government and the states, but it did not define citizenship. It took for granted that citizenship existed at both the state and national level, yet it did not say what either form of citizenship meant or explain the relationship between them. Article II assumed the existence of national citizenship by stating that only a natural-born citizen of the United States or a citizen of the United States at the time of the adoption of the Constitution could be elected president. Article III, in giving the federal courts jurisdiction over disputes between the citizens of different states, affirmed the existence of state citizenship. So, too, did the privileges and immunities clause in Article IV ("The Citizens of each State shall be entitled to all Privileges and Immunities of Citizens in the several States"). But none of these provisions clarified what citizenship meant or the rights that came with it.[7]

The privileges and immunities clause built upon and modified a similar provision in the Articles of Confederation (1777–1789), the loose system of national government that the Constitution replaced. In order "to secure and perpetuate mutual friendship and intercourse among the people of the different states in this union," one article provided that "the free inhabitants of each of these states, paupers, vagabonds and fugitives from Justice excepted, shall be entitled to all privileges and immunities of free citizens in the several states" and that "the people of each state shall have free ingress and regress to and from any other state." The ambiguity of language here—with its slippage between the terms "people," "inhabitants," and "citizens"—opened the possibility that unnaturalized aliens who were inhabitants of one state might be entitled to the rights and privileges of citizens if they moved to another state. The privileges and immunities clause in the Constitution, also known as the comity clause, removed the reference to paupers, vagabonds, and fugitives, and referred solely to "citizens" rather than to "people" or "inhabitants." In *Federalist* no. 80, Alexander Hamilton declared this clause "the basis of the Union," claiming it would allow the national judiciary to preside impartially "in all cases in which one State or its citizens are opposed to another State or its citizens." Yet the meaning of comity remained ambiguous: the privileges and immunities clause referred to "the citizens of each State," but nowhere did the Constitution define national citizenship or its relationship to state citizenship. These questions remained unresolved until Reconstruction.[8]

The states did not clearly define local citizenship, any more than the Constitution defined national citizenship. White male householders born in the United States were generally regarded as citizens. Their wives were citizens too, but in the antebellum era they could not own property, make contracts, earn wages, vote, or hold elected office. Free black people faced restrictions not only on voting but also on militia service, school attendance, officeholding, and testifying against white people in court, and had to register and carry proof of identity. Black activists claimed citizenship for themselves, attending political conventions, submitting petitions, pursuing legal suits, securing their lives and property, and protesting in the streets. In a context where the meaning of citizenship was fluid and contested, they secured rights by acting like citizens. The Fourteenth Amendment eventually established two simple criteria for citizenship—birth on the soil or naturalization—and guaranteed that the federal government would protect the rights of due process and equal protection for all people under its jurisdiction. This momentous transformation did not emerge from a vacuum: for almost a century before Reconstruction, African American activists had been defining citizenship by asserting rights derived from birth on American soil.[9]

The Constitution also assumed the existence of national citizenship by giving Congress the power to set a uniform rule for naturalization. Remarkably for a country that attracted so many immigrants, this is the only part of the

Constitution that refers directly to the subject. Rather than granting power over admission or exclusion, the provision on naturalization applied to foreigners after they had entered the United States. Congress passed four naturalization acts between 1790 and 1802, introducing a policy with stark racial limits. The Naturalization Act of 1790 confined the right to become a citizen to "any Alien being a free white person" who had lived in the United States for two years. It did not mention sex. Women did not automatically acquire citizenship through marriage until a law to that effect was passed in 1855. Before that, white women could apply for naturalization, but they often had little incentive to do so, as they could not vote and, if married, could not hold property. Widows could protect their property by naturalizing and were able to do so by swearing an oath of allegiance without a formal application if their husbands had been citizens. Children of naturalized immigrants aged twenty-one years or under and residing within the United States were also citizens, as were children of US citizens born abroad (who were classified as "natural born citizens" under the Constitution). People of African origin could not naturalize until 1870, and Asian immigrants could not do so until the mid-twentieth century.[10]

Contemporaries saw the probationary period for naturalization as essential. Living in the United States for a few years prior to receiving citizenship, they believed, would allow immigrants to form a civic and political attachment to the country by learning the rules and customs of republican democracy. Madison warned that without this residence requirement, "aliens might acquire the right of citizenship and return to the country from which they came, and evade the laws intended to encourage the commerce and industry of the real citizens and inhabitants of America, enjoying at the same time all the advantages of citizens and aliens." Beyond the two-year requirement, all the 1790 law required was that immigrants furnish proof of good character in a court in any state where they had resided for at least one year and take an oath to support the Constitution. This "easy mode of naturalization," Madison predicted, would encourage immigration in an economy short of labor.[11]

Critics of the 1790 law, however, demanded more stringent regulations. In the politically turbulent decade that followed the first Naturalization Act, Congress revised the law three times. The Federalist Party, suspicious of radical immigrants from Ireland, England, and France, favored a longer waiting period for naturalization. An act passed in 1795 extended the residence period to five years and required declarations of intent to be filed three years in advance. Prospective citizens had to renounce titles of nobility along with "all allegiance and fidelity to any foreign prince, potentate, state, or sovereignty whatever." Some found the five-year probationary period too short. In the House debates on the 1795 bill, Thomas Hartley, a Federalist from Pennsylvania, proposed seven and his Federalist colleague, William Vans Murray of Maryland, proposed ten. Irish-born Thomas Fitzsimons of Pennsylvania, a Federalist and one of three Catholics to sign the Constitution, argued that immigration and an easy path to naturalization should be encouraged. "Nature seems to have pointed out this country as an asylum for the people oppressed in other parts of the world," he declared. "It would be wrong, therefore, to first admit them here, and then treat them for so long a time so hardly." A ten-year waiting period, he warned, "would make this class of people enemies to your Government."[12]

In 1798, amid fears of immigrant radicalism and war with France, Congress passed a new naturalization act extending the probationary residency period to a minimum of fourteen years. Immigrants had to have lived in the state where they filed their application for at least five years, and they had to file their declaration of intent at least five years before admission to citizenship. Courts were required to furnish the secretary of state with a list of these declarations. In an important, though at the time ineffective, precedent for later federal immigration law, "all white aliens" arriving in the United States were supposed to report to a designated officer within forty-eight hours and receive a registration certificate from the office of the secretary of state. Those already residing in the country had to register within six months. Persons who failed to register were subject to a fine and could be compelled to sign bonds guaranteeing their future behavior. The certificates were to count as mandatory evidence in naturalization proceedings, though in practice most foreigners ignored this requirement. The fact that state rather than federal courts administered the naturalization process left enforcement to local discretion, and, at a time when mere suspicion of radicalism became grounds for deportation, immigrants had little incentive to file declarations of intent for fear of exposing their alien status.[13]

The 1802 Naturalization Act reintroduced a five-year residency requirement, with declarations of intent to be filed three years before admission to citizenship. Hamilton, citing "Notes from Virginia" against Jefferson, opposed this move. "The safety of a republic," he argued, depended on a common national sentiment, uniform principles and habits, the protection of citizens from foreign bias and prejudice, and "the love of country, which will almost invariably be found to be closely connected with birth, education, and family." How likely was it that foreigners would "bring with them that temperate love of liberty, so essential to real republicanism?" Admitting immigrants of every description to the privileges of American citizenship, Hamilton concluded, would "break down every pale which has been erected for the preservation of a national spirit and a national character." Jefferson, despite his earlier reservations about an open immigration policy, objected that the fourteen-year waiting period for naturalization denied hospitality and asylum to "oppressed humanity." The 1802 act discontinued the requirement for compulsory registration by all immigrants within forty-eight hours of arrival, yet it attempted to retain registration, as proof of residency, as a requirement for naturalization. Once again, however, immigrants did not comply with this provision, which was left unenforced (and was repealed in 1828). The requirements laid down in 1802 provided the basis of American naturalization policy thereafter.[14]

Other than naturalization, the Constitution is silent about immigration. Some of its provisions could be construed as implying that Congress had authority in this area, but nowhere did the Constitution directly grant power over admission or removal to the federal government. The taxing and spending clause gave Congress the "power to lay and collect taxes, duties, imposts and excises" and "to pay the debts and provide for the common defense and general welfare of the United States." During the controversy over the Alien and Sedition Acts in 1798, some critics of the Adams administration interpreted the words "common defense and general welfare," by a rather tortured argument, as giving Congress the power to exclude or deport aliens perceived as a threat to national security. The clear purpose of the taxing and spending clause, however, was to permit Congress to raise revenue to provide for defense and welfare, not to provide a general mandate to protect the nation through the arrest or deportation of immigrants. The power to collect taxes and duties, meanwhile, was relevant if immigrants were legally classified as imports, as indentured servants and other poor migrants were in the colonial era. Whether passengers were persons or articles of commerce remained disputed in constitutional law throughout the nineteenth century.[15]

The war powers clause and the treaty power clause offered firmer grounds for federal authority over immigration. The first of these provisions gave Congress the power to declare war "and make Rules concerning Captures on Land and Water," a provision that supporters of the Alien and Sedition Acts took to cover the arrest or deportation of enemy aliens. More significantly, the treaty power clause authorized the president to make treaties with the advice and consent of the Senate—including treaties regulating the related questions of trade and migration. State and national laws regulating the arrival of foreigners in the nineteenth century, whether black British sailors in the South or Chinese migrants in the West, came into conflict with treaties, forcing the Supreme Court to address these conflicts. When the federal government restricted Chinese immigration in the 1880s it did so in large measure by moving away from diplomacy toward a unilateral assertion of national sovereignty. For almost a century before that, however, the United States lacked a national policy for regulating its borders. Control over immigrant admissions rested with the states.[16]

## Slavery and the Constitution

In ratifying the Constitution and joining the Union, no slaveholding state surrendered its sovereign power to control slavery within its borders. Created by the individual colonies, and later by the states, slavery rested on local rather than national law. Nowhere in the text of the Constitution did the words "slave" or "slavery" appear; the document was intended, after all, as a model for republican democracy. Yet, while the Constitution did not create slavery, it directly recognized and protected the institution by preventing Congress from prohibiting the external slave trade for twenty years, boosting the representation of southern states in Congress by counting each slave as three-fifths of a person, and mandating the return of fugitives.[17]

The Constitution required a census of the US population to be taken within three years of the first Congress and at ten-year intervals thereafter. In 1790, the first census takers counted the number of free white males aged sixteen or older (in order to assess the country's industrial and military potential), along with free white males under sixteen, free white females, "other free persons" (i.e., free black people), and slaves. Native Americans were not included as part of the population of the United States. The census enumerated a total population of 3,929,214, of whom 697,897 (just under 18 percent) were enslaved. An additional 59,150 people were listed in the category of "other free persons." People of African descent, in other words, made up one-fifth of the American population in 1790. This should come as no surprise, as they were the single largest migrant group to the British American colonies in the eighteenth century, outnumbering all European migrants combined. More than 600,000 people of African origin were forcibly transported to the mainland United States from Africa and the Caribbean before American involvement in the international slave trade was prohibited in 1808. Those who went to the colonies that formed the United States accounted for only a small proportion of the 12 million enslaved Africans transported to the Americas (most of them to the Caribbean and Brazil). But the slave system in the United States became the largest in the Western Hemisphere in the nineteenth century.

With sovereignty divided between the federal government and the states under the Constitution, who would control the importation of enslaved people? At the Constitutional Convention, northern opponents of slavery wanted an immediate ban on the trade, whereas the delegates from South Carolina and Georgia wanted to protect the importation of slave labor from federal interference. New Englanders, whose economies did not rest on enslaved labor to the same extent, favored strong federal control over commerce, including taxes on imported goods, to protect their mercantile interests. Southern slaveholders, who exported cash crops such as tobacco, rice, and indigo, demanded a two-thirds majority in Congress for the adoption of commercial legislation to prevent their exports or imports from being taxed. When Luther Martin, an anti-Federalist from Maryland, objected that importing slaves was "inconsistent with the principles of the revolution and dishonorable to the American character," South Carolina Federalist John Rutledge, chairman of the Committee of Detail that drafted the Constitution, replied that "Religion & humanity had nothing to do with the question— Interest alone is the governing principle with Nations." The "true question," for Rutledge, was whether the southern states "shall or shall not be parties to the Union."[18]

Charles Pinckney, Rutledge's fellow South Carolinian, warned that his state could never approve a constitution that prohibited the slave trade. "If slavery be wrong," Pinckney declared, "it is justified by the example of all the world" from ancient Greece and Rome to contemporary France, England, and Holland. "In all ages," he claimed, "one half of mankind have been slaves." Virginians, Pinckney pointed out, stood to gain by terminating the external trade, as the price of slaves would rise, allowing them to be sold at a profit to other states. If left to make the decision on their own, he claimed, South Carolina and Georgia would probably stop importations eventually. They would not join the Union, however, unless the Constitution set a time limit before which Congress could not prohibit the external slave trade.[19]

The compromise was to require Congress to wait until 1808 before acting. South Carolina conceded that a simple majority would suffice for commercial legislation, and the New England states joined the lower South and Maryland in voting to prohibit export taxes and to allow the importation of slaves for another twenty years. The Constitution's commerce clause gave Congress the power "To regulate commerce with foreign nations, and among the several states, and with the Indian tribes." Using this power, Congress could theoretically have passed a law immediately banning the importation of slaves. The next section of the Constitution imposed a temporary limitation on the commerce power, stating, "The Migration or Importation of such Persons as any of the States now existing shall think proper to admit, shall not be prohibited by the Congress prior to the Year one thousand eight hundred and eight, but a Tax or duty may be imposed on such Importation, not exceeding ten dollars for each Person." No such tax was ever enacted. As this twenty-year prohibition applied only to the existing states, Congress could have prohibited the importation of slaves into states created after 1789, though given the political realities, it never attempted to do so.[20]

Why did the Constitution use "migration" as well as "importation"? An initial draft of the clause used the phrase "migration and importation" twice—first in preventing Congress from imposing a ban for twenty years, and then in permitting Congress to impose a tax of up to ten dollars for each person who arrived in the interval. Federalist politician Gouverneur Morris of Pennsylvania, who wrote the Preamble to the Constitution, pointed out that using "migration" as well as "importation" in the second instance implied that "the Legislature may tax freemen imported." In light of Morris's objection, the Convention unanimously adopted an amendment dropping the word "migration" from the second part of the clause and allowing taxation only on the "importation" of persons—in other words, enslaved people brought into the country from abroad. The meaning of the word "migration" in the first part of the clause, however, remained unclear.[21]

In the Pennsylvania and North Carolina ratification debates, some delegates expressed concerns that the migration or importation clause would allow Congress to regulate free immigration as well as the external slave trade. In Pennsylvania, which attracted large numbers of immigrants, Federalist leader James Wilson, a signatory of both the Declaration of Independence and the Constitution, insisted that the clause referred only to slaves. Responding to an objection that the tax provision would inhibit the "introduction of white people from Europe," Wilson stated that the language in the second half of the clause confining taxation to "importation" meant that the clause as a whole referred only to unfree migration. In North Carolina, the influential anti-Federalist James Galloway declared that he wanted the "abominable trade" in slaves to end. Like Wilson, he rejected the idea that the tax on importation "extended to all persons whatsoever." As North Carolina needed immigrants, he believed it ought to provide a bounty "to encourage foreigners to come among us" rather than impose a tax on them. James Iredell, a strong supporter of ratification, responded to Galloway that, "The word *migration* refers to free persons; but the word *importation* refers to slaves because free people cannot be said to be imported. The tax, therefore, is only to be laid on slaves who are imported, not on free persons who migrate." Beyond these scattered exchanges at the Convention and during the ratification debates, nobody at the time seemed to doubt that the term "such persons" was simply a euphemism for "slaves." Nonetheless, the use of "migration" in the first half of the clause left open the possibility that Congress could regulate free immigration once the twenty-year moratorium was lifted. Arguments that the migration or importation clause gave Congress the power to regulate immigration, and not just the external slave trade, remained prominent in American jurisprudence for most of the nineteenth century.[22]

During the revolutionary era, a few political figures predicted hopefully but vaguely that ending the external slave trade would somehow lead to the end of slavery itself. James Wilson declared that Congress, within a few years of banning the trade, "will have the power to exterminate slavery within our borders." What he intended by this statement is unclear, as he also suggested that the most likely outcome would be gradual emancipation, of the kind already being pursued in Pennsylvania. Wilson may simply have meant that the example set by federal intervention would inspire more states to adopt emancipation schemes or inspire more individuals to free their slaves. Philadelphia physician and politician Benjamin Rush expressed much the same belief, informing New Hampshire clergyman and historian Jeremy Belknap that Pennsylvania's Quakers believed "the Abolition of slavery must be gradual in order to be effectual, and that the Section of the Constitution which will put it in the power of Congress twenty years hence to restrain it altogether, was a great point obtained from the Southern States." Prohibiting the foreign slave trade would somehow hasten the abolition of slavery—but it was not clear how.[23]

Madison tried to clarify the constitutional issues in *Federalist* no. 42. The Constitution, he explained, gave the federal government power to control relations with foreign nations through treaties and by regulating commerce. "This class of powers," he wrote, "forms an obvious and essential branch of the federal administration. If we are to be one nation in any respect, it clearly ought to be in respect to other nations." The federal commerce power covered trade between states, without which union would be impossible; it also covered foreign trade, including the external slave trade. The migration or importation clause merely prevented Congress from exercising its commerce power to regulate the external trade for twenty years. Madison claimed he would have preferred if the importation of slaves had been prohibited straight away. Yet it "ought to be considered as a great point gained in favor of humanity," he wrote, that the trade could be abolished within twenty years, and that it would "receive a considerable discouragement from the federal government" in the meantime. The migration or importation clause, Madison insisted, did not extend to free immigration. Anti-Federalists tried "to pervert this clause into an objection against the Constitution," he claimed, "by representing it on one side as a criminal toleration of an illicit practice, and on another as calculated to prevent voluntary and beneficial emigrations from Europe to America." Such arguments deserved no answer, as they were merely "specimens of the manner and spirit in which some have thought fit to conduct their opposition to the proposed government." The migration or importation clause, in short, applied only to the external slave trade. Madison's position, which represented the consensus, made good practical sense. After all, nobody before the late nineteenth century wanted to restrict immigration quantitatively—as distinct from targeting political radicals in the 1790s, setting space limits on passenger ships, or taxing foreign paupers in the antebellum era.[24]

What, then, did the words migration and importation signify? In the constitutional debates over immigration in the antebellum era, there were three contending answers. Those who defended the right of states to control the movement of people—free and enslaved black people as well as white immigrants—insisted that the clause was limited to curtailing the external slave trade. This was the dominant reading at the time of the Constitutional Convention and subsequently. Both "migration" and "importation," according to this interpretation, referred to slaves coming from abroad—as persons under the first heading and as property under the second.

A second, and radical, interpretation was that "importation" referred to the arrival of enslaved people from abroad, but "migration" referred to their movement across state lines. This raised the explosive question of whether the national government could regulate, or even prohibit, the internal slave trade under its interstate commerce power, just as it had terminated the external trade under its foreign commerce power. Abolitionists made this case forcefully in the 1830s.

According to a third interpretation, "migration" referred to free white immigrants and "importation" to enslaved people imported from abroad. The migration or importation clause was a temporary prohibition on Congress's power to regulate mobility under the commerce clause. But, while Congress could regulate neither immigration nor the external slave trade before 1808, it could potentially regulate both thereafter. A version of this argument featured prominently in the political crisis over the Alien and Sedition Acts, when critics of the Adams administration argued that the federal government's actions were unconstitutional because it lacked the power to regulate immigration before 1808.[25]

## The Alien and Sedition Acts

At the heart of the controversy over the Alien and Sedition Acts were two questions. To what extent did the president's prerogative prevail over the power of Congress? And to what extent did the national government have authority over the states in matters concerning immigration and slavery? The Alien and Sedition Acts consisted of three laws passed by the Federalist-controlled Congress during the Adams administration to prepare for a possible war with France and to weaken the Democratic-Republican opposition. First, and most controversially, the Alien Friends Act allowed the federal government to deport aliens of all backgrounds who were suspected of plotting against the government, even during peacetime. This act expired after two years and was not renewed. Second, the Alien Enemies Act, which remains in force today, authorized the deportation of unnaturalized aliens whose countries of origin were at war with the United States. Third, the Sedition Act severely restricted speech critical of the federal government and remained in force for three years. The Naturalization Act of 1798, with its extended residency period, shared the same reactionary impetus as the Alien Sedition Acts. These laws backfired against the Federalists, contributing to the Democratic-Republicans' victory in the 1800 elections, and provoked a major controversy over the nature of power in a federalist system.[26]

The least controversial of the three Alien and Sedition Acts was the Alien Enemies Act, which applied only when a war had been declared or an invasion was underway. In such cases, "all natives, denizens, citizens, or subjects" of hostile nations aged fourteen or older and not naturalized were "liable to be apprehended, restrained, secured, and removed, as alien enemies." During the debates over the bill, several congressmen denounced the provision requiring the removal of aliens at the president's pleasure as tyrannical. Nathaniel Macon, a Democratic-Republican from North Carolina, objected that the act "gave the President a very extraordinary power; it seemed that his proclamation, in all cases, was to be considered as law." Federalist James Bayard of Delaware found this "a principle contrary to all our maxims of jurisprudence, viz: to provide punishment for a crime by a law to be passed after the fact is committed." Albert Gallatin of Pennsylvania, the Swiss-born

Democratic-Republican who led the opposition to the Alien and Sedition Acts, found the provision that people could be apprehended and imprisoned simply for harboring aliens from enemy nations contrary not only "to every principle of justice and reason" but also to the Constitution, which stated that no person could be deprived of life, liberty, or property without due process of law. Gallatin could not "consent to punish any man on suspicion merely." Instead of defining an offense and assigning the punishment, he objected, the Alien Enemies Act ceded that power to the executive branch. The president could accomplish by proclamation what ought to be done by statute, determining when aliens were to be arrested and removed, and requiring officials and citizens to "perform a duty that is undefined." As a result, the people and the judiciary would be forced to obey the president rather than the law. The Alien Enemies Act, Gallatin concluded, "leaves not only alien enemies but citizens of the United States to the will of the president."[27]

Critics of the Adams administration found the Alien Friends Act even more alarming. This law authorized the president, purely at his discretion, to deport any alien he suspected of plotting against the federal government or judged dangerous to the security of the United States. Those who refused to leave and remained "at large" within the United States without a license from the president could be imprisoned for up to three years and were banned from naturalization. Aliens who received a license had to sign a bond, in a sum to be determined by the president, with one or more sureties to guarantee their good behavior. Those who returned without the president's permission were subject to imprisonment for as long as he deemed necessary. The Alien Friends Act also required the captain of every vessel arriving in the United States to file a report of all aliens on board, specifying their names, ages, occupations, countries of birth and allegiance, the countries from which they had arrived, and their physical description. Ship captains who failed to file a report faced a fine of $300, subject to the forfeiture of their vessels.[28]

During the debates over the Alien Friends bill, Albert Gallatin raised a series of constitutional objections. He saw the bill as arbitrary and tyrannical as well as unconstitutional. The power to expel alien friends resident in the United States, he insisted, could not be derived from the commerce clause. The federal government certainly had the authority to punish and remove alien enemies engaged in seditious practices, but alien friends posed no such threat. If Congress passed a bill based on "a supposed necessity which did not exist," Gallatin warned, it could pass a similar measure "removing citizens of the several States." The Constitution provided protections against such

abuses of power, he explained, and these protections applied to "persons," including aliens, not just to "citizens."[29]

Gallatin recognized the "power inherent in every independent nation" to
admit or exclude foreigners from friendly nations. He insisted, however, that
this power belonged solely to the states, not to "the General Government." The
migration or importation clause, Gallatin argued, prohibited Congress from
regulating immigration until 1808. The term "migration," he claimed, "must
refer to free emigrants" and the term "importation" to "slaves." Congress,
therefore, could not interfere with the "migration of persons" for twenty
years. The Alien Friends bill violated this provision by giving the president
the power to remove aliens. Congress, in short, was exercising a power that it
could not exercise until 1808, if even then. The Constitution gave Congress
no power, either explicitly or implicitly, to remove alien friends. The states
reserved this power for themselves.[30]

Gallatin was an early abolitionist, but other critics of the Alien Friends bill
feared that if the federal government was equipped with a general power over
migration, it might interfere with slavery. Robert Williams, a Democratic-
Republican from North Carolina, challenged the contention that the migration or importation clause gave Congress the right "to prevent the migration
of foreigners, or remove them after they arrive." If Congress could remove
one person, he asked, was there "anything in the Constitution to prevent
them from sending all aliens from the country"? If Congress had the power
to remove aliens, he feared, it could also remove enslaved people. Although
Southerners might be willing to grant that slaves were "a dangerous property
and an evil in their country," Williams declared, they certainly would "not
consent to Congress assuming the power of depriving their owners of them,
contrary to their will." Yet the national government could do precisely that,
he warned, if it received the powers proposed by the Alien Friends bill, which
mandated removal not for any particular crime but at the discretion of the
president. Abraham Baldwin of Georgia, a moderate Democratic-Republican,
predicted that if the Alien Friends bill passed, "Congress would again be
appealed to by the advocates for an abolition of slavery, with requests that the
President may be authorized to send these persons out of the country." The
only bulwark against that form of tyranny was "federalism" (with a lower-case
f ), which he defined as the "idea that there are State Governments who divide
the powers of Government with the Federal Government."[31]

Proponents of the Alien Friends bill claimed that Congress had the authority to regulate migration under the taxing and spending clause. James
Bayard of Delaware and Samuel Dana of Connecticut insisted that the power

to "provide for common defence and general welfare" entailed the power to deport friendly aliens, an argument that Gallatin and Baldwin dismissed as specious. The references to defense and general welfare, they explained, were taken out of context. Far from providing a source of substantive legislative power, they merely qualified the preceding words in the clause, explaining the purpose of levying taxes for the common good rather than conveying a general authority over the national welfare and defense. They certainly implied no "general power" over immigration. To adopt the meaning Bayard and other Federalists put upon these words, Baldwin warned, would mean that "all the State Governments must fall prostrate" before the federal government.[32]

Supporters of the Alien Friends bill responded that federal control over admissions and expulsions was necessary to national sovereignty. Inherent in any national government, in Samuel Dana's words, was "the power of preserving itself, which implies all the necessary power of making all laws which are proper for this purpose." The current bill, he pointed out, did not seek to restrict free white immigration but only to remove unnaturalized foreigners whose presence appeared dangerous. It would allow the government to remove undesirable aliens without interfering with the right of states to admit foreigners. Admission and expulsion, in other words, were different powers. Dana's Federalist colleague, William Gordon of New Hampshire, saw the ability to deport aliens as integral to "the very existence of Government" and located the authority to do so in both the "power of making war" and the power of "providing for the general welfare." Harrison Gray Otis of Massachusetts, likewise, insisted that Congress had the right to protect the general welfare, which the states had no right to resist when aliens endangered the country. If aliens were left to plot treason, and Congress was unable to remove them without the states' permission, Otis warned, the new Constitution would be no better than the old Confederation. Robert Goodloe Harper of Maryland also rejected the notion that deporting a few foreigners would lead to excessive power over immigration. What, he asked with some exasperation, "had banishment to do with migration?" He found it difficult "to believe that the objections to this measure, on Constitutional grounds, were serious."[33]

From a Federalist perspective, the least "serious" objection to federal authority was the argument that the migration or importation clause prevented Congress from regulating free immigration in addition to the external slave trade. This argument rested on the assumption that expelling alien radicals intruded on the power of the states to regulate the arrival of immigrants, which the Federalists denied. More fundamentally, it depended on the assertion that the migration or importation clause applied to immigration as well as the external slave trade. Gallatin made precisely this claim, saying that the clause covered "free emigrants" as well as "slaves brought into the United States without their consent." Abraham Baldwin recalled that, when the delegates to the Constitutional Convention chose the euphemism "such persons," they realized "that this expression would extend to other persons besides slaves." Jonathan Dayton of New Jersey, the Federalist speaker of the house, disagreed with Baldwin on this point.

Dayton and Baldwin were the only two members of the current Congress to have sat in the Constitutional Convention, but their memories of the proceedings diverged sharply. Dayton "could only ascribe either to absolute forgetfulness, or to willful misrepresentation" the assertion that the delegates understood the migration or importation clause to cover voluntary immigration as well as the slave trade. Its sole and express purpose, he insisted, was to prevent Congress from interfering with the external slave trade before 1808. No question at all had arisen concerning the admission of other foreigners. In order "not to stain the Constitutional code," the word "slaves" was changed to "such persons," just as the Constitution used "the circuitous expression of 'three fifths of all other persons'" in another section. Not until the current debate over the Alien Friends bill, Dayton claimed, had he heard the clause applied to free immigrants.[34]

With the Federalists in control of both houses, it was inevitable that the Alien Friends bill would pass. The vote split on sectional lines, with southern congressmen heavily opposed and representatives from New England almost unanimously in favor. The anti-Federalist argument that the migration or importation clause applied to free immigration, thereby preventing Congress from imposing regulations until 1808, was clearly expedient, as the true object of this clause was the external slave trade. Yet this argument was potentially powerful. In claiming that Congress was temporarily prohibited from regulating voluntary migration as well as the importation of slaves, opponents of the Adams administration hoped to prevent the national government from assuming a general power over the movement of people. This power, they believed, was fundamental to the sovereignty of the states.[35]

In response to the Alien Friends Act and the Sedition Act, Thomas Jefferson anonymously drafted the Kentucky Resolutions, an extreme articulation of the theory of states' rights. The states composing the United States of America, Jefferson explained, were "not united on the principle of unlimited submission to their General Government." They had yielded only certain powers to that government, reserving the rest. Each state was "an integral party" to the national compact and, under the Constitution, could judge whether the central government created by this compact exceeded the powers it had been given. The Constitution delegated to the federal government the power to punish certain crimes, such as treason, but the government could not punish other crimes. The First Amendment, moreover, prohibited Congress from restricting freedom of religion, speech, and the press, the way the Sedition Act attempted to do. As for immigration, newcomers from friendly nations remained under the jurisdiction and protection of the states that admitted them, rather than that of the federal government. Jefferson took for granted that the migration or importation clause prevented the federal government from restricting free immigration as well as the slave trade. Ordering the removal of aliens, he contended, was equivalent to restricting their immigration, which the Constitution had prohibited Congress from doing before 1808. The Alien Friends Act, like the Sedition Act, therefore violated the Constitution.[36]

For Jefferson, the Alien Friends Act also violated the doctrine of separation of powers, paving the way to tyranny by transferring judicial power to the executive branch, which already held a veto on legislative power. As the Kentucky Resolutions noted, the Alien Friends Act authorized the president to remove people from the United States "on his own suspicion, without accusation, without jury, without public trial, without confrontation of the witnesses against him, without hearing witnesses in his favor, without defence, without counsel." For a state to imprison a person because of his failure to obey a president's order to depart the United States, the Kentucky Resolutions observed, was contrary to the Fifth Amendment's guarantee that "no person shall be deprived of liberty without due process of law" and the Sixth Amendment's provisions regarding fair and impartial criminal trials. The Alien and Sedition Acts required the states to submit to undelegated power, Jefferson warned, and undelegated power was unlimited. The legitimate response to such an abuse of power was for the people to change its government. Jefferson's initial draft of the Kentucky Resolutions went so far to say that "a nullification of the act is the rightful remedy," though the version adopted by the state legislature dropped this claim. Every state, for Jefferson, had "a natural right in cases not within the compact . . . to nullify of their own authority all assumptions of power by others within their limits." Without this right, the states "would be under the dominion, absolute and unlimited, of whosoever might exercise this right of judgment for them." Like Gallatin, Jefferson warned that the "friendless alien" was merely "the safest subject of a first experiment." The Sedition Act made clear that citizens could also be targeted. Such measures, unless prevented at the outset, would drive the states "into revolution and blood," undermining republican government and providing "new pretexts for those who wish it to be believed that man cannot be governed but by a rod of iron."[37]

Jefferson found no support for this extreme position outside Virginia, where Madison anonymously authored a similar set of resolutions adopted in December 1798. Of the other fourteen states, four did not respond to Jefferson's call for support and ten opposed the resolutions, invoking the supremacy clause to acknowledge the primacy of federal law over state laws. Neither Jefferson nor Madison mentioned slavery in their resolutions, any more than the Constitution used that word, but the theory of nullification (or what Madison called "interposition") became a rallying cry for proslavery states' rights advocates in the antebellum era. Lurking behind all objections to federal authority over immigration in this era was the fear that empowering Congress to regulate immigration would threaten the institution of slavery. As for the deportation of immigrants, President Adams never tried to assert the authority given to him by the Alien Friends Act, which expired on March 3, 1801. It would be another eighty years before Congress passed a law authorizing deportation of noncitizens. In the interval, state and local governments controlled immigration, with the federal government playing a limited role by crafting policy through diplomacy and treaties.[38]

The one form of migration that the federal government did control was the external slave trade. Although the Constitution postponed any federal law prohibiting that trade until 1808, Congress retained the power to impose regulations. A law passed in 1794 banned the use of American shipyards for fitting or building ships for the slave trade and the use of American ports as embarkation points. In 1800, Congress increased the fines for US citizens and resident aliens participating illegally in the trade and imposed prison terms on those working on slave ships. Vessels involved in the trade were subject to confiscation, with informants receiving a share of the value. Given the twenty-year moratorium on prohibiting the external slave trade, these laws were designed to regulate American participation in the trade to or between foreign countries rather than importation to the United States. Congress did, however, pass an act in 1803, in response to pressure from Southerners concerned about free and enslaved black people arriving from the Caribbean after the Haitian Revolution, prohibiting the importation of any "negro, mulatto, or other person of color, not being a native, a citizen, or registered seaman of the United States" to states that had already banned the importation of enslaved people. Significantly, this language acknowledged that some black people at this time were citizens of the United States. Because the 1803 act directly controlled admissions into the United States, moreover, it was the first federal immigration law.[39]

In March 1807, as the moratorium provided by the Constitution approached expiration, Congress passed legislation prohibiting the external slave trade, effective January 1, 1808. The Constitution did not require that such a law be passed, but most Americans outside of South Carolina and Georgia supported curtailment of the trade. The act was passed nine months before it went into effect to give slave traders time to wind down their operations. It imposed large fines and long prison terms on Americans and foreigners participating in the trade and provided for the forfeiture of vessels and their human cargo. What would become of enslaved people seized under the law remained unclear. The federal government was not prepared to spend money returning them to Africa, but neither was it prepared to grant them freedom. Persons seized under the 1807 law were initially treated as confiscated property and sold as slaves. State governments could choose to sell rather than expel them, thereby boosting their revenue and increasing their slave population. Congress passed a law in 1819 stipulating that such captives must be returned to their place of origin at the expense of the federal government—an early if distinctive example of deportation. Liberia became the favored destination for these deported slaves from the 1820s onward, even though none of them came from that part of Africa. In 1822, Congress declared slave trading a form of piracy, confirming that enslaved people brought to the United States illegally were persons rather than property. These slaves were deported but, in the interval between capture and removal, US marshals often rented them out to perform uncompensated labor. If they remained in the United States, having been imported into the country contrary to the law, these several thousand captives became—through no fault of their own—America's first "illegal immigrants." These assertions of federal sovereignty over the external slave trade aside, the states continued to control both immigrant admissions and the institution of slavery within their borders.[40]

## *The Expansion of Slavery*

Despite the expectations of many Americans during the revolutionary era, the institution of slavery expanded and flourished in the early republic rather than gradually dying away. Northerners found it easier than Southerners to agree to emancipation, albeit gradually. By 1787, five northern states and the republic of Vermont (which joined the Union as the fourteenth state in

1791) had banned slavery or passed gradual emancipation laws. Within three decades of American independence, every northern state had introduced measures for immediate or gradual emancipation, usually stipulating that people born enslaved after a certain date would be freed when they reached adulthood. By 1810 three-quarters of northern black people were free and by the 1840s nearly all were. Congress restricted the geographical scope of slavery with the Northwest Ordinance of 1787, which outlawed the institution in the area north of the Ohio River that includes present-day Ohio, Indiana, Illinois, Michigan, and Wisconsin, though forms of slavery survived in some parts of the region for several decades.[41]

Slavery not only survived in the South but grew on a colossal scale, giving rise to a new economy based primarily on the mass production of cotton. More than 800,000 enslaved people—almost twice as many as crossed the Atlantic to the mainland American colonies—moved south and west from the Upper South between 1790 and 1860. The number of slaves in the United States almost doubled from 697,897 in 1790 to 1,191,354 in 1810. By 1860 it had reached 3,953,760. With the external slave trade prohibited, most of this increase came through natural means rather than importation. Almost everywhere else in the Americas, the institution depended on continued imports, and when the external slave trade ended, the population declined. Cuba banned importation as late as 1862 and abolished slavery in 1886. Brazil banned importation in 1850 and, after a series of incremental steps, abolished slavery in 1888. In both Cuba and Brazil, Africans made up the majority of adult slaves until the abolition of the slave trade. In the United States, by contrast, most enslaved people were American born even before the Revolution and virtually all by the time of the Civil War.[42]

Given that Congress could abolish the external slave trade via its power to control foreign commerce, did its power over interstate commerce imply an analogous power to regulate or prohibit the interstate slave trade? Put another way, did the framers of the Constitution intend the commerce clause to regulate the interstate slave trade? Although it is notoriously difficult to discern original intent, the answer to this question is plainly no. About 2,000 men were involved in the framing and ratification of the Constitution, and very few of them left clues about their intentions. But the southern states would not have ratified the Constitution if they believed it gave Congress power to regulate, restrict, or perhaps even eventually prohibit, the interstate slave trade. Throughout the antebellum era, nonetheless, a persistent strain of antislavery thought maintained that the commerce clause gave Congress the power to regulate the trade between the states if it chose to do so.[43]

Congress's power over the internal slave trade became an urgent political question with the crisis over the admission of Missouri as a slaveholding state in 1820. On December 18, 1818, Whig politician and Speaker of House Henry Clay of Kentucky presented Missouri's request to be admitted to the Union. James Tallmadge Jr., Democratic-Republican of New York, responded with a surprise amendment proposing the prohibition of further entry by slaves into Missouri and gradual emancipation by freeing all enslaved children born in the state after its admission to the Union (restrictions that did not apply to any other state). The congressional debate over the Missouri crisis focused on the migration or importation clause rather the commerce clause. Timothy Fuller of Massachusetts, Tallmadge's fellow Democratic-Republican, insisted that the clause gave Congress the power to prohibit not only the importation of slaves from abroad but also their sale between the states. "Hitherto," he declared, "it has not been found necessary for congress to prohibit the migration or transportation from State to State. But now it becomes the right and duty of congress to guard against the further extension of the intolerable evil and the crying enormity of slavery." For the first time, a congressman had openly declared that the national legislature could regulate the interstate slave trade.[44]

This was a new interpretation of the migration or importation clause. Opponents of the Adams administration had claimed in 1798 that the clause applied to free migration as well as the importation of enslaved people, and that the Alien Friends Act was therefore unconstitutional. In 1818, however, some Northerners contended that the word "migration" applied to the slave trade between the states, not just the external trade. The migration or importation clause barred Congress from interfering with the importation of slaves for twenty years, but once that temporary limitation expired, these congressmen argued, Congress had power under the commerce clause not only to prohibit the external slave trade but also to regulate or prohibit the interstate trade. Tallmadge's amendment received majority support in the House but was rejected by the southern-dominated Senate. Southern politicians continued to argue, as they had in 1798, that the word "migration" referred to white foreigners only. In doing so, however, they were no longer challenging laws concerning immigration but responding to a threat that the commerce power might be used to control the movement of enslaved people within the United States.[45]

In the midst of the Missouri crisis, Madison clarified his position on the interstate slave trade. In a letter to Robert Walsh, a journalist and editor who taught at the University of Pennsylvania, Madison reiterated his long-standing conviction that the words "migration" and "importation" in the Constitution referred to slaves in their dual capacity as people and property. He told Walsh that he had always foreseen "the difficulties that might be started" if power over interstate commerce was confused with power over foreign commerce. The interstate commerce power, he insisted, was intended only "as a negative & preventive provision against injustice among the States themselves; rather than as a power to be used for the positive purposes of the General Government." In other words, the federal government could prevent states from taxing commerce with other states, but it should not interfere in interstate commerce beyond that. It would be "safer," Madison wrote, to leave the interstate commerce power in this limited form than "to extend to it all the qualities & incidental means belonging to the power over foreign commerce." Walsh refuted Madison's position in a 116-page monograph arguing that, because Congress had the power to prohibit the external slave trade under the commerce clause, it also had the power to regulate the domestic trade. The real issue for Walsh was one "of keeping the territory of the union, and the new states, free from this pestilence; and ultimately of suppressing altogether the diabolical trade in human flesh, whether internal or external."[46]

By a compromise struck in 1820, Missouri entered the Union as a slave state alongside Maine as a free state. Missouri was admitted without any restrictions on slavery or the internal slave trade, but slavery was prohibited elsewhere within the vast territory of the Louisiana Purchase acquired from France in 1803. Yet the crisis was not over. Missouri proceeded to draft a constitution instructing the state legislature to pass whatever laws might be necessary to prevent "free negroes and mulattos" from entering or settling in the state. Virginia, Maryland, Kentucky, South Carolina, and Georgia had passed similar laws. Missouri, however, needed Congress to approve its Constitution as a condition for its admission to the Union. Because many northern states considered free black people to be citizens, the provision calling for their exclusion from Missouri came into conflict with the US Constitution's privileges and immunities clause. Southern congressmen, however, insisted that each state retained the sovereign power to define citizenship and to exclude and expel people as it saw fit. In the House, Philip Pendleton Barbour, Democratic-Republican of Virginia, argued that a state had the same right to bar or remove free black people as it did to exclude "vagabonds and fugitives from justice." The Constitution, he declared, did not apply to "Indians, free negroes, mulattoes, slaves." It was framed by "the descendants of white men," who never intended that it should confer rights on the "colored class" or interfere with the power of the states to control them.[47]

Charles Pinckney of South Carolina, who served four terms as governor of his state after the Constitutional Convention, insisted that Congress was prohibited from interfering with slavery in any way. Reiterating the argument

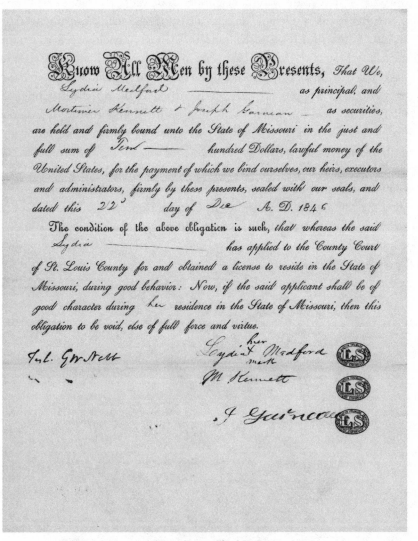

FIGURE 1.1 "Free Negro Bond for Lydia Medford." St. Louis County Court, Missouri, December 22, 1846. Many southern and midwestern states required free black migrants to enter into bonds backed by white guarantors as a condition of their entry and as an indemnity against public expenditure for their upkeep. Lydia Medford, described as a thirty-year-old "washer," entered into a bond of $10 with the State of Missouri in 1846, with two men providing security for her good character and behavior. Washington University in St. Louis, Freedom Bonds Collection.

he had made at the Convention, Pinckney insisted that the word "import" in the migration or importation clause applied only to slaves, while the term "migration" applied "wholly to free whites." Without the twenty-year limitation imposed by this clause, he pointed out, Congress might have prohibited the external slave trade even sooner, under its power to regulate foreign commerce. But it was "a solemnly understood compact," once the southern states agreed to the termination of the trade, that Congress could never "touch the question of slavery." On this basis, "the property of the Southern States in slaves was to be as sacrally preserved, and protected to them" as rights to land or any other kind of property were to the citizens of the Northeast. Congress, for Pinckney, had the power to prohibit both the importation of enslaved people and the arrival of free immigrants after 1808—but not the movement of slaves between the states.[48]

The Missouri debate continued through the spring of 1821, when Henry Clay devised another compromise. This compromise allowed Missouri to enter the Union without amending its Constitution, on condition that it not enact the provision requiring a law excluding free black people or use that

FIGURE 1.2 "Am I Not A Woman and A Sister?" Seal of the Philadelphia Female Anti-Slavery Society, founded in 1833 as an integrated women's chapter of the American Anti-Slavery Society (AASS). Like the AASS, the PFASS petitioned Congress to prohibit the interstate slave trade and abolish slavery, and it supported the Underground Railroad. Reproduced with permission from the Historical Society of Pennsylvania.

provision in any way to deny the privileges and immunities of citizens of other states. When Missouri passed a law in 1825 prohibiting the entry of black people, it duly exempted those who were considered citizens of other states. Yet because Congress recognized the right of states to exclude paupers and vagabonds as potential public charges, Missouri was able to exclude free black people through its poor law system. States throughout the Midwest also used their poor laws for the same purpose. What the privileges and immunities of citizens amounted to under these circumstances remained unclear, though the Missouri crisis did at least affirm that, in the eyes of many Northerners, free black people were citizens of their states and, on that basis, of the United States.[49]

In the decades following the Missouri Compromise, some abolitionists continued to argue that Congress had jurisdiction over the interstate slave trade under the commerce clause and could regulate or even ban the trade on that basis. The American Anti-Slavery Society, founded in 1833, declared its intention "in a constitutional way, to influence Congress to put an end to the domestic slave trade." At its founding convention, the Society endorsed a Declaration of Sentiments affirming that Congress had the power and the obligation "to suppress the domestic slave trade between the several States." In the late 1830s, abolitionists organized petitions to Congress signed by more than 20,000 men and women calling for the prohibition of the interstate slave trade. When Congress introduced a gag rule suppressing these petitions and passed resolutions declaring all attempts to prohibit the trade unconstitutional, the abolitionist movement split. William Lloyd Garrison and his followers renounced conventional politics on the grounds that the US Constitution was a sinful document that endorsed slavery, while the political abolitionists who coalesced in the Liberty Party argued that the Constitution authorized the federal government to abolish slavery. The movement to prohibit the internal slave trade never regained the force it achieved at its peak in the late 1830s. By this time, the age of mass immigration from Europe was underway. Who would control the admission of immigrants into the United States in this new era?[50]

# 2

## Police Power and Commerce Power

IN JUNE 1824, Amos Daley, a citizen of Rhode Island, was charged with the crime of illegally entering the state of South Carolina. Daley had been jailed in April after arriving in Charleston on the schooner *Fox*, under Captain Rose. A state law passed in 1822 (the first Seamen Act) provided that "free negroes or persons of color, as cooks, stewards, mariners, or in any other employment" could be seized and confined in jail until their vessel was ready to depart from the state. Captains could remove these seamen from jail when their ships were ready to leave if they paid the expenses for their detention. Jailed seamen not redeemed by their captain could be "taken as absolute slaves, and sold." Amos Daley was released from jail when the *Fox* was ready to depart on May 3, 1824, with a warning not to come back to South Carolina on pain of corporal punishment. When he returned to Charleston on the same vessel in June, he was arrested and jailed.[1]

South Carolina had passed a second Seamen Act on December 20, 1823, reinforcing the provisions of the 1822 act but exempting "free American Indians" and seamen forced to land by shipwreck or bad weather. Captain Rose testified at Amos Daley's trial that the law did not apply to him as he was a member of the Narragansett Indian nation. A certificate in Daley's possession, signed by the town clerk of Kingston, Rhode Island, on December 27, 1823, stated that he was "a man of color," born in the town of Warwick in 1800, the son of William Daley, who owned a farm in Warwick, and Susannah Daley. Captain Rose and other witnesses confirmed that William and Susannah Daley were Narragansetts and testified that Amos Daley's features were those of that tribe. One witness conceded that Daley's hair was "rather against him" because it was not as straight as that of most Narragansetts, but said "he had seen genuine squaws of that tribe, who were old, with very curly hair." It was "not uncommon," this witness explained, "to call Indians men of color."[2]

Leaving aside the question of whether Amos Daley was exempt from the South Carolina law as a Native American, three constitutional questions were at stake. Daley's lawyers argued that, as a citizen of Rhode Island, he was entitled by the privileges and immunities clause of the Constitution to all the rights enjoyed by citizens of South Carolina. They also argued that South Carolina's laws violated federal power under the commerce clause. Interstate and foreign navigation—of the kind in which Daley was employed—were commercial matters, they insisted, under the control of the national government rather than the states. Finally, Daley's lawyers argued that the Seamen Acts violated the treaty-making power of the United States. None of these arguments, however, carried much weight in antebellum South Carolina, which did not regard free black people as citizens and zealously protected its sovereignty against federal power.

Rejecting Amos Daley's claim to be Native American, the court convicted him of violating South Carolina's laws by returning to the state. The prosecuting attorney called two witnesses (including state legislator Robert J. Turnbull, the author of the 1822 act), who explained that long straight hair, rather than complexion, was "the test of genuine blood" among the Narragansetts. The prosecution produced as evidence a log of Amos Daley's physical description from his first arrest, which revealed that "the prisoner's hair was wooly." On these grounds, the judge ruled that Amos Daley was a free colored seaman and therefore guilty. As the *Fox* had been blown back into port by a storm, he agreed that Daley had returned involuntarily, rather than in direct defiance of the law, and therefore "only sentenced him to receive twelve lashes on his bare back the same afternoon, at 5 o'clock in the work-house."[3]

South Carolina's seamen laws offer a stark example of how the antebellum states used their police power to regulate the admission and expulsion of foreigners. Under the Constitution, each state reserved substantial powers over their internal affairs, which they deployed to control public health, safety, and welfare and to promote what they saw as a well-regulated society based on the common good. Towns and states used their police power to quarantine sick and diseased passengers; to prohibit the admission of foreign convicts; to regulate the admission of paupers by imposing taxes, fees, and bonds; to control the movement of free and enslaved black people within and across their borders; and to imprison free black sailors, both foreign and native born, who visited southern ports. In a federal republic where power was divided between the national and local levels, towns and states asserted their sovereignty by policing mobility. Their police power repeatedly came into conflict with federal commerce power.[4]

How far did federal commerce power extend, and to what extent was Congress willing or able to exert that power in a slaveholding republic? If commerce covered navigation as well as trade—the transportation of people as well as the transportation of goods—could Congress regulate the mobility of free black people and aspects of the interstate slave trade as well? If immigration was a form of commerce, could Congress regulate the admission or exclusion of foreigners? Did the states hold power over commerce concurrently with the federal government? Or, if power over interstate and foreign commerce was exclusive to Congress, could the states use their internal police power to protect their residents against immigrants, just as they controlled the mobility of free black people? Where did the line between local and federal authority over migration begin and end? State and federal courts considered these questions repeatedly throughout the antebellum era. The tension between local police power and national commerce power, like the conflict over the rights of free black people provoked by the Seamen Acts, could not be resolved before the institution of slavery was abolished.

## Policing Free Black Sailors

In June 1822, Denmark Vesey, a free black sailor and carpenter, was arrested in Charleston on suspicion of plotting a slave revolt. Born around 1767, probably in St. Thomas in the Dutch West Indies, he was sold to a Bermuda slave trader named Joseph Vesey in 1781 and assumed his name. Denmark Vesey accompanied Joseph on several voyages and spent some time in Haiti before settling in Charleston, where he purchased his freedom and helped found the city's African Methodist Episcopal Church. Influenced by the Haitian Revolution, Vesey was suspected of laying plans for a similar revolt in South Carolina. The plot—if indeed there was a plot—was betrayed, and in the ensuing hysteria, the authorities arrested 130 black people and convicted sixty-seven of planning an insurrection. Thirty-two were deported, and the remaining thirty-five—including Vesey—were hanged. The authorities claimed to have discovered evidence of a massive conspiracy, involving thousands of free and enslaved African Americans in the Charleston area, even though no uprising took place and no white people were killed. The presence of free black people, and black seamen in particular, opened the port city to the radical ideas of the Atlantic world, posing a direct threat to slavery. Rumors circulated that black sailors were conduits for revolutionary schemes connecting Charleston with Haiti and West Africa.[5]

South Carolina responded by passing an act in December 1822 regulating the entry of "free negroes and persons of color." The act declared that, henceforth, "no free negro or person of color, who shall leave the State, shall be suffered to return," and subjected those who did return to corporal punishment. It imposed taxes on free black people who were not natives or longtime residents of South Carolina, required them to have guardians who could certify their good character, and prevented enslaved people from hiring out their labor. One provision stipulated that "free negroes or persons of color" employed on vessels entering South Carolina's harbors from foreign ports or other American states must be confined in jail while their ship was in port. When the ship was ready to leave, the captain could free the prisoners, for a fee. If he refused to do so, they could be sold into slavery. The first of several measures passed by South Carolina and other states to regulate black seamen, this law provoked a bitter constitutional controversy and a protracted diplomatic dispute with Britain that remained unresolved before the Civil War.[6]

In January 1823, the British sloop *Bob* arrived in Charleston under Captain John McKee, with an entirely black crew who were immediately arrested and imprisoned. McKee and his partner James Calder appealed to the sheriff, Francis G. Deliesseline, who refused to release the men. When the *Bob* was ready to depart, Calder paid the fees required to free the crew and the ship left port. Calder appealed to the South Carolina Constitutional Court, where he made an extraordinary revelation: his crew was actually enslaved but had claimed to be freeborn British subjects to evade South Carolina's slave codes. The court ruled that while the 1822 law was a legitimate exercise of state power, it applied only to "free persons of color." Since the crew was enslaved, they should not have been arrested. By the peculiar logic of South Carolina's racial laws, seafaring slaves had greater freedom of movement than free black sailors. Calder received a refund of the fees he had paid to redeem the imprisoned sailors.[7]

Justice William Johnson of the US Supreme Court, who was openly critical of South Carolina's seamen laws, agreed to hear a test case. For much of the nineteenth century, Supreme Court justices rode circuit, presiding over US courts in their home states. Johnson was assigned to the circuit court for South Carolina. Henry Elkison, a British subject born in Jamaica, had been arrested and confined in Charleston in the summer of 1823 after arriving on a British ship trading from Liverpool. The British consul in Charleston hired an attorney, who petitioned for a writ of habeas corpus to bring Elkison before the court and justify the reason for his detention. Writs of habeas corpus were normally heard before state courts rather than federal courts, but given that a South Carolina court had implicitly validated the Seamen Acts in the *Calder* case, Elkison's attorney felt sure that a state court would reject the petition. He therefore filed in the federal court, knowing that Justice Johnson was critical of South Carolina's policy.[8]

Elkison's lawyer argued that his client was a freeborn British subject protected by the commercial treaty between Britain and the United States signed in 1815. This treaty protected the movement of British subjects engaged in commerce with the United States, prohibiting the enactment of laws abridging their rights to enter or leave the country and to use warehouses and other buildings for purposes of trade. As Elkison was engaged in commerce, his attorney argued that South Carolina's law violated both the commercial treaty and the supremacy clause, as the treaty took priority over any state law. The two lawyers representing South Carolina, Isaac E. Holmes and Colonel Benjamin F. Hunt, defended the 1822 Seamen Act as a local police measure beyond the reach of federal power. The law was the equivalent of a quarantine measure, they claimed, designed to protect the state from the "moral pestilence" of free black sailors. Quarantine laws paid no heed to nationality or legal status: every person deemed "infected" could be prevented from interacting with those on shore. That free black sailors were "infected"—in other words, they posed a threat to public safety—was a conclusion in need of no demonstration. Faced with the "moral pestilence which a free intercourse with foreign negroes will produce," Hunt declared, South Carolina had every right to take measures for its "self-preservation." The state had not surrendered its sovereignty by ratifying the Constitution. On the contrary, it retained the right to resume full independence if necessary. Holmes, likewise, concluded his argument by declaring "that if a dissolution of the Union must be the alternative, he was ready to meet it." The confrontation between state and federal authority was starkly drawn.[9]

William Johnson delivered his opinion on August 7, 1823. He began by flatly rejecting the idea that the South Carolina law was a legitimate quarantine measure. If the purpose of the law was to protect slaves from the "contagion" carried by free black people, Johnson asked, why were the sailors being put in a jail for "delinquent, domestic slaves"? State officials, aware of complaints that the law violated the Constitution and treaties with Britain, had "shown every disposition to let it sleep," Johnson noted, but "a voluntary association of gentlemen, who have organized themselves into a society" were determined "to see the laws carried into effect." He was referring to an extralegal society called the South Carolina Association. Composed of prominent Charlestonians, including Holmes and Hunt, the Association was dedicated to enforcing the laws against black seamen.[10]

The central issue at stake was which form of government had authority to regulate movement between the states and into the United States. Did this authority lie with Congress under its commerce power or with the states under their police power? Johnson had no doubts about the answer. The words of the commerce clause, he ruled, "sweep away the whole subject, and leave nothing for the States to act upon." Even in the absence of specific legislation, Johnson insisted, federal power over foreign and interstate commerce was paramount. The South Carolina law also violated the treaty-making power, which the Constitution assigned to the national government. If South Carolina could prohibit British seamen from engaging in commerce, he asked, what would prevent other states from passing laws prohibiting British vessels from employing people of Irish or Scottish birth? If skin color was grounds for exclusion, why not eye color or hair color? If the Union was to survive, no state could act unilaterally in these ways. On matters of commerce, and on migration as a subset of commerce, Johnson insisted, the federal government was sovereign. South Carolina's law, he concluded, was "altogether irreconcilable with the powers of the General Government . . . and tends to embroil us with, if not separate us from, our sister States." It directly challenged "the sovereignty of the United States" and would lead to "a dissolution of the Union." If each state could "throw off the Federal Constitution at its will and pleasure, like the old Confederation, the Union becomes a mere rope of sand."[11]

Despite the force of Johnson's rhetoric, this ruling had no practical impact. Under the Judicial Act of 1789, as Isaac Hunt had pointed out for the defense, a federal judge could issue a writ of habeas corpus for a person incarcerated under a state's criminal law only in exceptional circumstances. Johnson reluctantly concluded that he lacked the authority to issue the writ for Henry Elkison. Only Congress, he ruled, "could give a uniform and national operation to this provision of the Constitution." Johnson was also careful to note that the South Carolina law applied only to "free persons of color" and that the court was not encroaching on the state's power over its enslaved population. In the end, his arguments that the South Carolina act violated the commerce clause and the supremacy clause, powerful as they were, were dicta with no binding force.[12]

Nonetheless, Johnson's opinion provoked a backlash in South Carolina. When local newspapers refused to publish the opinion, Johnson arranged to have it distributed as a pamphlet. Writing under the pseudonym "Caroliensis," Isaac Holmes of the South Carolina Association and state legislator Robert

J. Turnbull published a dozen articles in the *Charleston Mercury* criticizing Johnson. Another correspondent, writing under the pseudonym "Zeno," objected that any free black person from the northern states could enter South Carolina if the state legislature was "divested of its right to control him by its police laws" and could reside there "without any other control than that which applies to our white population." In response, Johnson conceded that the privileges and immunities clause merely extended "the rights of citizens mutually, to those only who can by any possibility become citizens of the State, to which they emigrate." Free black citizens who entered southern states from the North, in other words, were entitled to the privileges and immunities enjoyed by citizens in those states. If South Carolina did not recognize its own free black residents as citizens, it was not obliged to extend the rights of citizenship to black people visiting from other states. Such were the limits of comity in a slaveholding republic. On the other constitutional issues, however, Johnson held firm: South Carolina's law violated the federal government's power to make treaties and to regulate foreign and interstate commerce.[13]

## *Defining Commerce*

Chief Justice John Marshall found William Johnson's position on the Seamen Acts extreme. He did not disagree with Johnson on the nature of federal power over commerce, but he found it untactful to confront the political implications so directly. As Marshall put it in a letter to Justice Joseph Story: "Our brother Johnson, I perceive, has hung himself on a democratic snag in a hedge composed entirely of thorny State-Rights in South Carolina, and will find some difficulty, I fear, in getting off into smooth, open ground." South Carolinians, Marshall noted, saw Johnson's ruling on the Seamen Acts "as another act of judicial usurpation," and they were threatening to disrupt the Union in response. Just as "the massacres of St. Domingo" (Haiti) had originated in French republican theories, Southerners feared that federal policies might encourage a slave revolt. South Carolina's law, Marshall explained, was by no means exceptional. Massachusetts regulated the arrival of immigrant paupers, and Virginia regulated the mobility of free black people through laws "not very unlike in principles to that which our brother has declared unconstitutional."[14]

Marshall, indeed, had considered the Virginia law in a circuit court case in 1820, when he evaded the constitutional issues on a technicality. The *Wilson*, an armed privateer from Venezuela manned by a crew that included eighteen free "people of color," arrived in Norfolk, Virginia, in October 1819, carrying a cargo of liquor. Many of the crew had boarded at the island of St. Thomas; others were taken from Spanish and British ships captured on the high seas. On arrival, the *Wilson* was declared forfeit to the United States for violating two federal laws: the Internal Revenue Act of 1799, which required import duties, and the 1803 statute prohibiting the "importation" of any "negro, mulatto, or other person of color" to states that had enacted laws barring their entry. As Virginia had passed one such law, violating it would be a federal offense. The Virginia statute, however, applied only to "free negroes and mulattoes," without mentioning the category "other persons of color." It was not proven, Marshall found, that the sailors who had landed in the state were "free negroes and mulattoes," let alone that they had been "imported." Congress had the authority to pass the 1803 act under the commerce clause, which included power over navigation, but because the seamen on the *Wilson* did not seem to fall into the categories covered by this act, Marshall felt no need to delve into the constitutional issues further. He might have done so, he told Justice Story, but he was "not fond of butting against a wall in sport." Marshall's ruling avoided conflict with a foreign nation and affirmed the power of Congress to legislate on the slave trade, without challenging the sovereign police power of the states.[15]

Marshall tried to steer a similarly moderate course in the better known case of *Gibbons v. Ogden* (1824) while formulating a clearer definition of the commerce power. In 1808 the New York legislature had granted a monopoly to politician Robert R. Livingston and inventor Robert Fulton to operate steamboats carrying passengers within the jurisdiction of the state. Livingston and Fulton assigned to Aaron Ogden, the former governor of New Jersey, the right to navigate the waters from Elizabethtown (today's Elizabeth), New Jersey, to the port of New York City. Thomas Gibbons, a one-time business partner of Ogden who operated two steamboats on this route, claimed that he had the right to trade in these waters as his vessels were licensed under the federal navigation act of 1793. The New York courts ruled in Ogden's favor, finding that the state law did not violate the Constitution and upholding an injunction restricting Gibbons from operating his vessels. The case made its way to the US Supreme Court, which reversed this decision and clarified the nature of authority over commerce in a federalist system.[16]

Daniel Webster, a Boston-based constitutional lawyer and Whig congressman, opened the oral arguments in *Gibbons v. Ogden* on February 24, 1824, with a strong claim for federal sovereignty. A principal reason for the adoption of the Constitution, Webster explained, was to prevent obstacles to commerce between the states. Rather than each state regulating interstate commerce independently, the framers wanted a uniform system controlled by the federal government. Under the Constitution, Webster insisted, the national government's power over interstate and foreign commerce was exclusive. State quarantine laws were legitimate police regulations, he conceded, but they violated the Constitution if they were passed with the purpose of regulating national or foreign commerce, or if they intruded on these forms of commerce in a way that was unnecessary for the exercise of state power. Ogden's lawyers, New York State Attorney General Thomas Oakley and Irish revolutionary exile Thomas Addis Emmet, countered that the states were sovereign entities that, in signing the Constitution, had relinquished only certain limited powers to the national government. Federal power over commerce, they insisted, did not preexist its expression in legislation; it came into being only if Congress passed laws specifically divesting states of their commercial power, which it had not done. Until Congress acted, a state could regulate its commerce with other states to protect the public good.[17]

The Supreme Court ruled unanimously in favor of Thomas Gibbons on March 2, 1824, with John Marshall writing the opinion. Marshall agreed with much of Webster's argument. Congress, he found, had ultimate power over interstate and foreign commerce, while the states controlled internal commerce that did not conflict with that power. Marshall defined commerce broadly to include navigation and intercourse, not just traffic in goods. "Commerce, undoubtedly, is traffic," he wrote, "but it is something more: it is intercourse. It describes the commercial intercourse between nations, and parts of nations, in all its branches, and is regulated by prescribing rules for carrying on that intercourse." The word "commerce" includes "navigation," Marshall explained, and "power over commerce, including navigation, was one of the primary objects for which the people of America adopted their government." Marshall held that the word "migration" in the migration or importation clause "applies as appropriately to voluntary as importation does to involuntary arrivals," and "the power to regulate commerce applies equally to the regulation of vessels employed in transporting men, who pass from place to place voluntarily, and to those who pass involuntarily." He did not go so far as to say that the power lay dormant even if it had not been enacted in legislation, but he insisted that a state that tried to regulate commerce with foreign nations or among the various states "is exercising the very power that is granted to Congress, and is doing the very thing which Congress is authorized to do." States could enact their own quarantine and public health laws, insofar as these laws were intended to protect the welfare of citizens, but they could not do so with the intention of intruding on foreign or interstate commerce. This compromise struck a precarious balance between national and local power.[18]

Ultimately, however, Marshall did not rest his decision on the commerce clause. His definition of commerce was so broad that, in theory at least, it might allow Congress to regulate the interstate movement of free black people, the slave trade, and even the institution of slavery within the states. States retained control over internal commerce, Marshall conceded, but federal power did not "stop at the external boundary of a State." This power was "general" and could be used to regulate commerce not only between states but also within states if their laws infringed on Congress's power. As someone who bought and sold hundreds of enslaved people in his lifetime, Marshall was aware that many Southerners would find so sweeping an assertion of federal commerce power alarming. He therefore invoked (without directly citing) the supremacy clause, whereby any state law must yield to an existing federal law on the same subject. The New York statute granting exclusive rights of navigation to Aaron Ogden conflicted with the federal Navigation Act of 1793 under which Gibbons held his license. To deny the priority of federal law, Marshall warned, would "explain away the Constitution of our country and leave it a magnificent structure indeed to look at, but totally unfit for use."[19]

William Johnson concurred with the majority in *Gibbons v. Ogden*, though on quite different grounds. Johnson agreed that the New York law was unconstitutional but rested his decision squarely on Congress's exclusive power under the commerce clause. For Johnson, the state law would have violated the Constitution even if Congress had not passed the Navigation Act of 1793 or any other commercial legislation. Congress had power over interstate and foreign commerce regardless of which measures, if any, it took to enact that power. The states had no power in this domain. Just as he had done in the *Elkison* case in South Carolina the previous year, Johnson insisted that the power granted by the commerce clause "must be exclusive; it can reside in but one potentate; and hence the grant of this power carries with it the whole subject, leaving nothing for the State to act upon." Marshall's opinion, by contrast, was deliberately ambiguous, obscuring the potential implications of the commerce power for the slave states. Nor did Marshall's ruling provide any guidance on the legitimacy of the Seamen Acts.[20]

Southern politicians and newspapers, sensing a threat to slavery, condemned Marshall's expansive view of federal commerce power. Thomas Jefferson, nearing the end of his life, cautioned against "the rapid strides with which the Federal branch of our Government is advancing towards the usurpation of all the rights reserved to the States, and the consolidation in itself of all powers, foreign and domestic; and that too by constructions which, if legitimate, leave no limits to their power." Jefferson did not mention slavery, a topic on which he was generally circumspect in his correspondence, but he saw the implications of Marshall's position clearly. "The power of Congress comprehends navigation within the limits of every state in the Union," Marshall wrote in *Gibbons v. Ogden*, "so far as that navigation may be connected with 'commerce with foreign nations, or among the several states, or with the Indian tribes.'" Representative Robert S. Garnett of Virginia warned in Congress of "the usurpation on the part of Congress of the right to legislate on a subject, which, if you once touch [*sic*], will inevitably throw this country into revolution—I mean that of slavery."[21]

*Gibbons v. Ogden*, in short, had important implications for slavery. Ogden's lawyer, Thomas Addis Emmet, arguing that the states shared a concurrent commerce power with Congress, insisted that the Constitution treated slaves as articles of commerce and that many states had prohibited their importation on this basis. By passing the 1803 act outlawing the importation of people of color into states that had prohibited their entry, Congress had recognized the sovereign power of the states to ban the external slave trade—in other words, to regulate a form of commerce. Marshall responded that, if Emmet's inference was correct, any state "might now import African slaves into its own territory," despite Congress's prohibition of the external slave trade. The power retained by the states over that trade prior to 1808, he explained, was merely a temporary restraint on Congress's ability to regulate foreign commerce. During this period, states could decide for themselves whether to import enslaved people from abroad, but they could not do so after 1808. Two months after *Gibbons v. Ogden*, Emmet declared that "State-Rights" were "the bulwarks of individual and personal liberty," and he warned that consolidating federal power as Marshall proposed "will be the euthanasia of our Constitution."[22]

Enslavers' fears about federal power intensified when US Attorney General William Wirt of Virginia delivered an opinion in 1824 affirming that South Carolina's Seamen Acts violated the commerce clause and treaty obligations with Britain. The section of South Carolina's 1822 law mandating imprisonment of free black seamen, he wrote, amounted to "a regulation of commerce, of a highly penal character, by a State" and was therefore unconstitutional. Wirt also found that the South Carolina statute violated the laws of the United States as established by treaty. The national government, not the states, had the power to make treaties with foreign nations, and these treaties constituted part of "the law of the land." The commercial treaty of 1815 with Great Britain permitted commerce "without any restriction as to the color of the crews by which it shall be carried on." Foreign and domestic ships entering American ports had "a right to remain there, unmolested in vessel and crew, for the peaceful purposes of commerce." The South Carolina law, Wirt concluded, was "incompatible with the rights of all nations which are in amity with the United States." Yet, like William Johnson's ruling in the *Elkison* case a year earlier, Wirt's opinion had no practical impact. From Charleston on July 3, 1824, Johnson wrote to Secretary of State John Quincy Adams that he was "obliged to look on and see the Constitution of the United States trampled on by a set of men" who took pleasure in "bringing its functionaries into contempt." Only the Supreme Court could invalidate South Carolina's Seamen Acts, and the Court was not about to do so.[23]

Seven years after Wirt's opinion, in response to pressure from British diplomats, Secretary of State Martin Van Buren asked the new US Attorney General John M. Berrien of Georgia to revisit the question. In sharp contrast to Wirt, Berrien found that the South Carolina laws violated neither the commerce clause nor the treaties with Great Britain. "The general right of a State to regulate persons of color within its own limits," Berrien wrote, "is one too clearly recognised by the tenth amendment to the Constitution to be drawn into controversy." The South Carolina law, designed to protect the interests of the state, was "a justifiable exercise of the reserved powers of that State." Each state, as Berrien noted, retained "an undisputed power to regulate its own internal police." In a strong defense of states' rights, he insisted that asserting "the absolute and unqualified supremacy" of federal laws would not comport with the intentions of the framers of the Constitution. Nor, he warned, would it "tend to the perpetuity of the Union, which it is their object to uphold and preserve."[24]

The national government had the power to regulate commerce and make treaties, Berrien conceded, but this power was not unlimited. States reserved the right to regulate their internal affairs even if, in doing so, their laws intruded incidentally on national laws or treaties. But Berrien was not convinced that South Carolina's laws conflicted with the laws or treaties of the United States. Under the Constitution, the legislative branch could undoubtedly regulate foreign and interstate commerce, and state laws that conflicted with the "rightful exercise of this power must necessarily yield." But, for Berrien, the Constitution restricted Congress's power to laws that are "necessary and proper." The states regulated their own internal affairs, and national laws controlling commerce could not impinge on their sovereignty except insofar as they were necessary and proper to the regulation of national commerce. The admission of "colored" seamen to ports of the United States was a matter of convenience rather than necessity, as trade could just as well be carried on without them. If excluding these seamen damaged commerce, moreover, it would be only South Carolina's commerce that suffered.[25]

Just as every state had a right to control its borders against foreigners bearing diseases, Berrien insisted, the slaveholding states had the right to pass laws protecting themselves against the moral threat posed by free black seamen. Foreigners who had commercial rights under the laws of the United States or under treaties between the United States and other nations, he pointed out, were subject to state quarantine laws. These laws impinged on national and interstate commerce, yet as Justice Marshall had explained in *Gibbons v. Ogden*, they were legitimate exercises of police power that did not violate the Constitution. The federal government would not deny any state the right to protect its citizens against contagious disease. The slaveholding states, by the same token, must be allowed to protect themselves against the "moral contagion" caused by the introduction of "colored people," which made "physical pestilence" trivial by comparison.[26]

Nor did Berrien agree that the South Carolina law conflicted with the commercial treaty guaranteeing British subjects free and secure entry into American ports to engage in trade. These privileges, he noted, were granted with the significant qualification that they were "'subject to the laws and statutes of the two countries, respectively.'" What would happen, Berrien asked, if an American captain sailed from Charleston to Liverpool with an enslaved person employed as a cook? The captain would find that his property was not protected by the commercial treaty, as Britain had its own local laws on slavery. So, too, did the sovereign American states. If Britain could enforce its own laws, there was no reason why black seamen should be exempt from state laws when they arrived in South Carolina. Laws passed by the states, Berrien insisted, were part of "the laws and statutes" of the United States referred to in the treaty with Britain. If those laws were passed after the treaty, they took precedence.[27]

Berrien wrote this opinion in 1831, but political circumstances the following year made his position problematic for the Jackson administration. Congress had enacted a law in 1828 designed to protect American manufacturers by imposing heavy taxes on industrial imports. While most New Englanders favored this law, many Southerners found it inequitable because their economies, oriented toward agricultural exports, depended on the importation of industrial goods. By February 1829, five southern states had adopted resolutions protesting what they called the "tariff of abominations." The South Carolina legislature printed a document, secretly drafted by Vice President John C. Calhoun, claiming that the tariff was unconstitutional and that a state could nullify it within its own borders. By the middle of 1831, ousted from the Democratic Party by Andrew Jackson, Calhoun came out openly in favor of nullification, or what he called "state interposition." When Jackson purged his cabinet in 1831, Berrien returned to his native Georgia, and Roger B. Taney agreed to become the US attorney general. In this volatile context, Secretary of State Edward Livingston, responding to British protests and the passage of a Seamen Act in North Carolina, asked Taney to review Berrien's opinion. Rejecting Berrien's position that the Seamen Acts were legitimate police regulations might drive Georgia into the nullification camp. Accepting that position, however, might validate the principle of nullification more generally. In seeking to resolve this crisis of sovereignty, Taney offered a forthright defense of the Seamen Acts, building on Berrien's position on police power but adding a chilling new argument concerning citizenship.[28]

Taney's views on free black people in 1832 directly prefigured his position in the *Dred Scott* case twenty-five years later. As a resident of Baltimore, home to the largest free black community in the country, Taney was acutely aware of the contradictions posed by the presence of free African Americans in a slave state. "The African race in the United States even when free," he wrote, "are everywhere a degraded class—& exercise no political influence. The privileges they are allowed to enjoy, are accorded to them as a matter of kindness & benevolence rather than of right. They are the only class of persons who can be held as mere property—as slaves." Taney claimed, as he would do again in the *Dred Scott* case, that Americans of African descent "were not looked upon as citizens by the contracting parties who formed the constitution. They were evidently not supposed to be included by the term *citizens*." In an early draft of his opinion, Taney also applied this doctrine of original intent to free black Britons. The commercial treaty of 1815, he believed, did not provide protections and privileges to British free black people because at that time nobody thought of them as full-fledged British subjects.[29]

On the question of sovereignty, Taney distinguished between legitimate resistance to inappropriate judicial decisions, on the one hand, and illegitimate interference with constitutionally sound federal laws, on the other hand. As an example of the first, he cited Andrew Jackson's defiance of the Supreme Court's ruling in *Worcester v. Georgia* (1832), which invalidated Georgia laws infringing on the sovereignty of the Cherokee nation. For Jackson, the idea that a Native American tribe could exist as a politically autonomous entity within a state violated the Constitution. In his first State of the Union address, in December 1829, he quoted the Constitution that "no new State shall be formed or erected within the jurisdiction of any other State" without the consent of its legislature. Taney saw the tariff act of 1828, by contrast, as a constitutionally valid regulation of foreign commerce that no state could defy. Congress undoubtedly had power over foreign commerce, but the Seamen Acts, Taney found, did not violate that power, as they were legitimate exercises of police power. Every slaveholding state, Taney wrote, had "a right to guard itself from the danger to be apprehended from the introduction of free people of colour among their slaves." In joining the Union, they had not surrendered that right. Inherent in each state's sovereignty was the power to regulate mobility in order to protect the public good.[30]

In his opinion on the Seamen Acts, Taney flatly denied that the privileges and immunities clause was "intended to include the colored race." When the slaveholding states adopted the Constitution, he insisted, they had not agreed to grant to free black people visiting from New England the same rights and privileges enjoyed by white citizens of these states. They did not regard their own free black population as citizens and had no obligation to extend that privilege to black visitors from other states. Every slaveholding state, Taney noted, restricted the migration and settlement of free black people within its limits, forbade them to keep or carry arms, and presumed them to be enslaved unless they could prove they were free. These states could not surrender their power to enact such regulations "without bringing upon themselves inevitably the evils of insurrection & rebellion among their slaves." They reserved the power to protect themselves against the introduction of free black people, and their legislatures had the right to determine the necessary means. Taney could find no power conferred on the federal government by the Constitution "to restrict either by Legislation or Treaty the absolute & unlimited power of legislation by the several states in relation to the people of colour coming within their limits." If the commercial treaty with Great Britain conflicted with laws subsequently passed by South Carolina, such as the Seamen Acts, the treaty had no bearing on those laws. The power reserved by the states to exclude people from their territory was inherent in their sovereignty.[31]

## Regulating Immigration

In the eighteenth century, merchants saw the servants they transported as a source of profit, articles of merchandise to be imported and sold along with others. Chiefly Irish, Scottish, or English, these servants signed contracts (indentures) in exchange for their transatlantic passage, binding themselves to service for a set number of years. A second, related category of servants known as redemptioners, most of them from the German principalities, redeemed (i.e., paid off) the debt for their passage shortly after arrival with the help of friends or relatives. Those who failed to do so were sold into servitude by the captain to recover the debt. Transported convicts comprised a third, entirely involuntary, category of servants in colonial America. Until the early nineteenth century, immigration control operated on the assumption that the passenger trade was a form of commerce. By the mid-1830s, however, there were no European indentured servants in the United States. The legal status of passengers was called into question.[32]

The termination of the external slave trade and the decline of indentured servitude meant that most passengers who came to the United States in the century after 1830 were free migrants from Europe (though sailors remained subject to very harsh labor discipline). But were these passengers "imports" or "persons"? Their status was much disputed in constitutional law throughout the nineteenth century. Proslavery justices insisted that passengers were persons and could not be treated as articles of merchandise—even as they defended the proposition that enslaved people were a form of property. Classifying immigrants as merchandise, they realized, might allow Congress to use its commerce power to regulate the movement of people in general and the mobility of African Americans in particular.[33]

The Passenger Act of 1819, the first federal law of its kind, signaled the shift to free migration that was taking place. This act set basic standards to protect against overcrowding and stated minimal dietary requirements for ships departing (but not entering) the United States. It required captains of ships arriving in the United States to submit a list of all those on board, noting their age, sex, and occupation, place of origin, and intended residence, along with the number that had died on the voyage, which the collector at the port of arrival forwarded to the US secretary of state. From these reports emerged the first federal records of immigration and the foundations of a bureaucratic apparatus for later national policy. No conflict over state versus federal power arose in this instance, as the legislation referred strictly to shipboard conditions. With the rise of mass immigration over the next two decades, however, the question of where international voyages ended and state sovereignty began assumed increasing importance.[34]

Between 1820 and 1880, some 10 million immigrants came to the United States from Europe. The Irish were the dominant group until the 1850s, when they were surpassed by immigrants from the German principalities. Large

numbers of immigrants also continued to arrive from Britain. When a foreigner arrived in the United States in the nineteenth century, admission was
the expected outcome. Exclusion was very rare. Some paupers were removed
out of state or overseas after arrival, but almost nobody was turned away at
the docks. The main purpose of state immigration laws was to raise money
for the upkeep of poor immigrants through taxes and bonds, not to exclude
them from entry. As long as ship captains paid these fees, nearly all European
immigrants were admitted. Not until the 1870s and 1880s did federal laws
begin to exclude people for the first time, including Chinese laborers and
immigrants likely to become a public charge. This did not mean, however,
that the United States simply had open borders before the onset of federal immigration control. Throughout the antebellum period, the states passed laws
regulating the admission and expulsion of foreigners, as well as the mobility
of free black people and the poor. These local and disparate laws comprised
the immigration policy of the United States before the Civil War.[35]

Local policies regulating immigration and other kinds of mobility
emerged in part from the poor law system. Under the English poor laws,
relief was the responsibility of the parish in which paupers had their legal
residence or "settlement." Towns could refuse entry to transient people who
might require support, warn them not to remain, or deport them. A poor
law passed in Massachusetts in 1794 replaced the system of "warning out"
unwanted strangers, granting settlement subject to permission by the town
government. To acquire legal settlement, however, a person had to be a citizen of the state. Towns were responsible for providing relief to the poor, but
they could claim reimbursement from a transient pauper's place of settlement
elsewhere in the state or from the Commonwealth for paupers who did not
have legal settlement in any Massachusetts town. If a town chose not to provide relief, it could remove the individual "by land and water, to any other
State, or to any place beyond sea [sic], where he belongs." This deportation
provision made the Massachusetts system uniquely harsh in its treatment of
immigrant paupers. The poor laws were even more discriminatory toward
free black people, especially in the Old Northwest, where states and territories routinely excluded African Americans, or restricted their entry, under the
pretext of poverty. European immigrants, by contrast, were free to move between the states.[36]

With the onset of mass immigration, the system in Massachusetts un-
derwent several revisions. In 1820, drawing on colonial precedents, the state
passed a law requiring bonds as security against passengers deemed likely to
become a public charge. Captains had to sign a bond for each such passenger

lacking a legal settlement in Massachusetts, to indemnify against expenses arising for their upkeep within three years of arrival. In 1831, the legislature amended this act to apply only to alien passengers, thereby placing foreign-born paupers in a special class. Captains could choose between entering into a bond for each alien passenger considered likely to become a public charge or paying a head tax of five dollars for every alien passenger landed. In 1837, with the number of indigent immigrants increasing, Massachusetts eliminated the choice between bonds and taxes. Captains were required both to sign a bond of up to $1,000 for each alien passenger likely to become a public charge and to pay a head tax of two dollars for every alien passenger who was not in a high-risk category. Shipping companies passed the cost of the taxes along to the passengers by raising fares but resented the intrusion in their business.[37]

In New York, immigration policy built on similar colonial origins. A law passed in 1788 required captains of vessels arriving in New York City to file a report on the passengers they landed. Captains had to post bonds for passengers considered likely to become public charges or return them to their place of embarkation. Unlike Massachusetts, New York law had no provision for deporting alien paupers overseas after they landed. New York's 1824 passenger law required captains of vessels arriving from foreign ports to post a bond of up to $300 for each alien passenger in case they became a public charge. By a separate ordinance, the mayor of New York City had the authority to commute the bonding requirement into a head tax (initially three dollars per alien passenger, lowered incrementally thereafter, and set at one dollar in 1847). In addition to these bonds or taxes, New York City levied a separate head tax to support its quarantine center at the Marine Hospital on Staten Island. For ships arriving from foreign ports, this tax was $1.50 per cabin passenger and one dollar per passenger in steerage. Passengers arriving on domestic coastal vessels were charged twenty-five cents each, with the proviso that no vessel arriving from New Jersey, Connecticut, or Rhode Island had to pay for more than one voyage a month. The marine tax applied to citizen passengers as well as aliens. Once again, the passengers bore the brunt of the costs.[38]

This system of passenger control was inefficient and corrupt. Initially, captains favored posting bonds over paying head taxes, knowing that the money would be difficult to collect. A bond market developed whereby brokers assumed the obligation from captains in return for a fee. In the words of New York's Emigration Commissioner Friedrich Kapp, "the entire business became a private traffic between a set of low and subordinate city officials, on the one hand, and a band of greedy and unscrupulous brokers, on the other."

The system, for Kapp, "was a sort of legalized robbery, the headquarters of which was at the City Hall." City officials pocketed commutation money rather than using it to defray expenses for the upkeep of the immigrant poor. When shipping companies or bondsmen agreed to meet their responsibility to provide relief, some of them opened their own private facilities rather than paying money to the city. An investigation into one of the most notorious of these poor houses, run by Tapscott & Co., found that dinner consisted of "salt fish" and bread "totally unfit for use," and "at other times of refuse grease with other mixtures collected from the ships during their trips across the Atlantic." Inmates were "lying sick and in the most pitiful and wretched condition of suffering, quite unable to help themselves, and compelled to eat the food above described."[39]

Shipping merchants challenged the constitutionality of state laws imposing charges on the passenger trade. In August 1829, the *Emily* arrived in New York City with one hundred passengers on board. Under New York's 1824 law, the captain of every ship arriving in the city from a foreign port had to furnish within twenty-four hours a written report of the name, age, occupation, place of birth, and last legal settlement of each passenger. On this basis, the city assessed the fees or bonds due on alien passengers. For every person not reported, or falsely reported, the captain faced a seventy-five-dollar fine. George Miln, a Scottish merchant who served as consignee for the *Emily*, decided to test the New York law by instructing the captain, William Thompson, to submit a passenger list with only one name. The city sued Miln, and the case was argued before John Marshall's Supreme Court in 1834 without a decision. By the time the Court heard the case again in 1837, Marshall was dead, Roger Taney had replaced him as chief justice, and Andrew Jackson had appointed four new justices to the Court: John McLean of Ohio, Henry Baldwin of Connecticut, James Wayne of Georgia, and Philip Pendleton Barbour of Virginia. All but McLean either owned slaves as property or strongly supported the institution of slavery.[40]

In *New York v. Miln* (1837), the justices upheld the New York statute by a majority of 6 to 1. The first case involving foreign immigration to reach the Supreme Court, *Miln* was also the first case involving commerce heard by Roger Taney's Court. Abolitionists at this time were submitting petitions to Congress with tens of thousands of signatures, demanding that the interstate slave trade be curtailed via the commerce clause. In this context, any judicial decision on a state immigration law had significant implications for southern police laws regulating black people. George Miln's lawyers argued that the New York law was unconstitutional because it violated the commerce clause.

Counsel for New York countered that the states retained sovereign power over commerce, which they had exercised before the Constitution and held concurrently with Congress. The New York law, by this logic, would have been valid even if it were considered a regulation of foreign commerce rather than a police law. The state's lawyers denied, however, that the law regulated commerce. Instead, as Justice Barbour summarized New York's argument, they saw it as "a mere regulation of internal police, a power over which is not granted to congress" but reserved to the states. The majority opinion considered only the portion of the law requiring a report on the passengers, which they upheld as a matter of internal police. By choosing not to discuss the law's requirement for bonds on passengers, the justices avoided the larger constitutional question of what happened when a state law infringed on federal commerce power.[41]

Justice Barbour, who had defended the black exclusion clause of the Missouri Constitution as a congressman in 1820–1821, wrote the majority opinion. The Court evaded the controversial question of what would happen if a state police measure infringed on federal commerce power. "We shall not enter into any examination of the question whether the power to regulate commerce, be or be not exclusive of the states," Barbour explained, "because the opinion which we have formed renders it unnecessary." He found that the New York law was "not a regulation of commerce, but of police; and that being thus considered, it was passed in the exercise of a power which rightfully belonged to the states." In the case of *Brown v. Maryland* (1827), Barbour noted, the Supreme Court had invalidated a state law requiring importers of foreign goods to take out a license if they intended to trade these goods wholesale. In laying a duty on imports, the Court had ruled, the law interfered with the power of Congress to regulate commerce. Imported goods were clearly subjects of commerce, Barbour conceded, but passengers, "not being imported goods," did not fall within the power of Congress to regulate foreign commerce.[42]

The purpose of the New York law, Barbour explained, was not to regulate commerce but to prevent the state from being burdened by an influx of immigrants who might become paupers. Both the end and the means, he found, were justified. Barbour cited Madison's *Federalist* no. 45 on the "numerous and indefinite" powers reserved to the states to regulate the "lives, liberties, and properties" of the people and to preserve "internal order." In *Gibbons v. Ogden*, Barbour reminded the Court, John Marshall had identified laws concerning public health, internal commerce, and turnpike roads and ferries as among the range of powers reserved by the states.

New York had the sovereign power to regulate its internal affairs, and there was no collision between state and federal power in this case. The 1824 law, Barbour concluded, operated only within the territory and jurisdiction of the state. It was passed for the benefit of "the people of New York, for whose protection and welfare the legislature of that state is authorized and in duty bound to provide."[43]

The states, in short, had the right to use their police power to exclude undesirable people for the public good. They had possessed this power at the time of the Constitution, and they had not surrendered it to Congress by joining the Union. Barbour cited Emer de Vattel's treatise on international law to support this argument: "The sovereign may forbid the entrance of his territory, either to foreigners in general, or in particular cases, or to certain persons, or for certain particular purposes, according as he may think it advantageous to the state." And "since the lord of the territory may, whenever he thinks proper, forbid its being entered, he has no doubt a power to annex what conditions he pleases, to the permission to enter." Each state in the Union, Barbour explained, had the same jurisdiction over persons within its territorial limits as a foreign nation did over people within its territory, provided it had not yielded that jurisdiction to Congress under the Constitution. In matters of internal police, he wrote, "the authority of a state is complete, unqualified, and exclusive."[44]

Alien immigrants, Barbour pointed out, were subject to state criminal laws in just the same way as citizens. If the captain, a crew member, or one of the passengers on the *Emily* had committed an offense the moment they came on shore in New York, they would have been subject to the state's criminal law because they were within its territory and jurisdiction. Immigrant passengers were subject to the state's police power in the same way. The requirement for a report on the passengers, designed to protect the citizens of New York from foreign paupers, was a valid exercise of that power. "There can be no mode," Barbour wrote, "in which the power to regulate internal police could be more appropriately exercised." New York was more likely than any other state to be "exposed to the evil of thousands of foreign emigrants" and the expense of maintaining them. Every state must "protect its citizens from this evil." Under their existing inspection laws, states could examine imported goods—articles of commerce—and remove or destroy them if they were unsound or infectious. Under their quarantine and health laws, they could regulate navigation—a form of commerce—by inspecting cargo, delaying the landing of ships, and detaining passengers. The New York law did not interfere with commerce nearly as extensively as these laws did. It merely operated on persons already within the territory and jurisdiction of the state, as a matter of internal police.[45]

Justice Smith Thompson of New York was equally forthright. "Can any thing fall more directly within the police power and internal regulation of a state," he asked, "than that which concerns the care and management of paupers or convicts, or any other class or description of persons that may be thrown into the country, and likely to endanger its safety, or become chargeable for their maintenance?" The New York law, Thompson concluded, was an exercise of police power that neither violated any federal legislation nor infringed on any matter necessary to the execution of federal power. The report on passengers, he pointed out, was required only after a ship had arrived within the limits of the state. Insofar as the law concerned commerce, therefore, it affected only the internal commerce of the state. Thompson went further than the other justices by suggesting that, in the absence of explicit legislation, Congress had no dormant power over foreign commerce. Because Congress had "not legislated on this subject, in any manner to affect this question," states were not prohibited from doing so. Thompson did not consider the Passenger Act of 1819 in making this argument.[46]

Barbour drew a direct analogy with the Seamen Acts. The states had the same power and duty to protect themselves against "the moral pestilence of paupers, vagabonds, and possibly convicts" as they did to ward off "the physical pestilence" arising from infectious disease. They had an indisputable right to protect their residents against external threats, whether in the form of immigrant paupers in the North or free black seamen in the South. That right was based on the same kind of power in both cases—the states' sovereign police power to secure and protect the public welfare. This argument rested, once again, on a distinction between commerce and persons whereby neither immigrants nor free black people could be classified as merchandise subject to federal control, but slaves could be held and traded as property. Only Barbour and Taney fully endorsed this position, yet Taney insisted that it was the official opinion of the Court.[47]

Joseph Story of Massachusetts, the late John Marshall's closest ally on the Court, was the lone dissenter in *Miln*. Unlike the other justices, Story based his opinion on the New York statute in its entirety, not just the section requiring a report on passengers. In *Gibbons v. Ogden*, he noted, Marshall had ruled that commerce referred to "the commercial intercourse between nations, and parts of nations, in all its branches." If Congress had passed a law containing the provisions of the New York statute, Story observed, no one would doubt that it was a regulation of passenger ships engaged in foreign commerce. The states could pass quarantine laws and laws preventing the arrival of paupers, provided these measures did not violate statutes legitimately passed by Congress, but they had no authority to enact laws affecting subjects beyond their territorial limits or laws within those limits that impinged on the power of Congress to regulate commerce. Even if the lawyers for New York were correct that the state law was not a regulation of commerce but a police measure akin to the health and quarantine laws Marshall had identified in *Gibbons v. Ogden*, Story insisted, no state could enforce any of these measures by regulating external commerce in ways that intruded on federal power.[48]

The New York law, for Story, expressly regulated owners, captains, and passengers engaged in foreign commerce. He saw no reason to revisit the question of whether the states shared a concurrent commerce power with Congress, as he believed Marshall had settled this matter in *Gibbons v. Ogden*. Congress had exclusive power over foreign commerce, and this would be true even if it passed no legislation (which, in any case, it had done in the Passenger Act of 1819). For a state to pass its own laws in this domain, Story insisted, would be to subject "all our trade, commerce and navigation, and intercourse with foreign nations, to the double operations of distinct and independent sovereignties." A strong believer in national government, Story had no doubts as to where sovereignty on this matter resided. The power to regulate commerce with foreign nations and among the states was exclusive to Congress.[49]

Story emphasized that the New York law affected US citizens as well as aliens. Although the law required bonds only for alien passengers, the reporting requirement applied to all passengers who arrived either from foreign ports or from other American states. If this law was constitutional, Story warned, it would "justify the states in regulating, controlling, and, in effect, interdicting the transportation of passengers from one state to another in steamboats and packets." Any state could levy a charge on all such passengers, require bonds to protect against them becoming public charges, and authorize their removal. States would then retaliate against one another in a way that would threaten "the safety and security of the Union." It was for this very reason that the Constitution had granted power over commerce exclusively to Congress. Immigrants, for Story, were articles of foreign commerce, and any local restraint on their introduction into the United States, whether through bonds or taxes, interfered with Congress's power over commerce. The New York act was therefore unconstitutional and void. Story noted in closing that he had "the entire concurrence" of the late Chief Justice Marshall, who had said to him before his death that "the present case fell directly within the principles established" in *Gibbons v. Ogden* and *Brown v. Maryland*. Story, however, found no support among the other justices.[50]

The Court's ruling in *Miln* reassured Southerners that Congress would not interfere with state sovereignty when it came to regulating the movement of free or enslaved black people, yet it left some niggling doubts. By upholding state control over immigrant admissions, the ruling indirectly affirmed the constitutionality of the Seamen Acts and other state measures regulating the mobility of free black people. If passengers were not imports, they could not be controlled by Congress under the commerce power, and state laws were valid exercises of police power. Yet, because the majority confined its opinion to the reporting requirement, without directly addressing whether bonds and fees were constitutional, the Court neither upheld nor questioned state laws that regulated the mobility of free black people through similar means. Proslavery Southerners would have preferred a ruling explicitly upholding measures of this kind based on a concurrent power over commerce, even when Congress had passed legislation. In their arguments before the Court, New York's lawyers warned that if Congress claimed jurisdiction over the admission of immigrants from Europe, it would also have the power to regulate the internal movement of people by land. Vagrancy laws, poor laws, and other police measures protecting the public welfare would thereby come under federal jurisdiction, including the "class of laws peculiar to the southern states prohibiting traffic with slaves, and prohibiting captains from bringing people of colour in their vessels." The question of which form of government controlled these various kinds of mobility remained unresolved.[51]

## Regulating Free Black People

The presence of free black people in the American South contradicted the racial logic that held slavery to be the natural condition of people of African descent. It also raised fears of discontent and rebellion. Throughout the antebellum era, free black people had to register, carry papers, and sometimes wear badges, proving their status and their right to residency. Although "free papers" ostensibly offered protection from enslavement, they also allowed states to monitor their free black populations and raise revenue by charging registration fees. Virginia banned free black people from migrating into the state as early as 1793. Maryland passed a law in 1806 imposing a fine of ten dollars per day on any free black person who entered. Failure to pay could result in being sold as a slave. Mississippi passed a law in 1831 expelling all free black people under sixty and over sixteen within sixty days, unless they could prove their good character and obtain a certificate from the courts, at a cost of three dollars. Mississippi, Virginia, and North Carolina passed laws excluding their own free black residents if they traveled without permission to unapproved locations. Kentucky, Alabama, Virginia, and Louisiana required that emancipated slaves leave the state on pain of reenslavement. Arkansas went so far as to pass a law in 1859 requiring all free black people (of whom there were about 700) to leave the state by January 1, 1860, or face sale into slavery for one year, with the proceeds from their labor financing their subsequent deportation. Unlike British seamen or immigrant paupers, the free black people targeted by these laws had been born on American soil and were treated like foreigners in their own country.[52]

In the North, the status of free black people varied by location. Social customs supplemented by vigilante surveillance restricted the mobility of free African Americans, and de facto segregation was standard. Black people in the Northeast endured considerable prejudice and discrimination, but the presumption under the law was that they were citizens of the states where they resided. They could travel without passes, seek employment, buy and sell property, make contracts and take legal suits, and in most cases testify against white people in court. Throughout New England, except in Connecticut, male black residents could vote.

The territories and states of the Old Northwest, by contrast, restricted or prohibited the entry of free black people. The Northwest Ordinance of 1787 prohibited slavery, and some states formed from this territory tried to exclude free black people as well, fearful that emancipated slaves would move north from Maryland and Virginia. The Ohio Constitution of 1803 outlawed slavery. The legislature passed laws in 1804 and 1807 requiring free black migrants to provide proof of their freedom and to register, for a fee, with county officials who provided certificates that also served as work permits. Employers who hired black people without certificates were fined. Like foreign immigrants arriving in eastern seaboard ports, every free black migrant had to find two guarantors who would sign bonds of $500 each to cover expenses in case the migrant became a public charge. From 1807 onward, Ohio implemented this system through its poor laws, mandating expulsion for black migrants who violated the registration requirements or could not support themselves. In practice, this system was not as rigorous as it seemed on paper. Finding sureties was not easy, though abolitionist and antislavery leaders—especially in Ohio and Illinois—sometimes filled this role. Because the bond-surety system lacked an enforcement mechanism, the money was hard to collect if the bonds fell due. States lacked the administrative apparatus to control their borders beyond a certain point, allowing free black migrants to enter undetected. Yet the presence of these anti-black laws on the statute books achieved much of its effect by imposing stigma and generating fear.[53]

Indiana and Illinois passed the most draconian laws. On its admission to the Union in 1816, Indiana prohibited slavery and, like Ohio, required bonds for free black migrants and prevented them from voting or testifying against whites in court. The Indiana Constitution of 1851 required the legislature to prohibit free black people from entering the state, a provision enacted the following year and stringently enforced. Illinois, after its admission to the Union in 1818, permitted compulsory long-term indentures for African Americans, severely curtailed the rights of free black people, and discouraged their migration by requiring certificates of freedom under pain of a fine or sale into labor to the highest bidder. The Illinois Constitution of 1848 called for legislation prohibiting the migration of free black people to the state. The resulting legislation, passed in 1853, made it a crime for any African American, free or enslaved, to enter. Those who were unable to pay a fine could be sold at public auction to perform uncompensated labor for any person who paid the fine and the court costs.[54]

In *Moore v. Illinois* (1852), the US Supreme Court upheld measures of this kind. The main issue before the Court was the constitutionality of a state law punishing people who harbored fugitive slaves. The Court invalidated this law but found police laws regulating mobility justified. Justice Robert Grier, a Jacksonian Democrat from Pennsylvania, delivered the opinion. The states, he wrote, had the right "to make it a penal offence to introduce paupers, criminals, or fugitive slaves, within their borders, and punish those who thwart this policy by harboring, concealing or secreting such persons." Some states bordering the slave South, Grier noted, had "found it necessary to protect themselves against the influx of either liberated or fugitive slaves, and to repel from their soil a population likely to become burdensome and injurious, either as paupers or criminals." For the Court to deny free black people the right to travel and settle in this way was, in effect, to exclude them from citizenship. As late as 1864, the Illinois Supreme Court upheld the conviction of a "mulatto" who, after illegally entering the state, was sentenced to forcible indenture.[55]

If free black people endured regulation, humiliation, and punishment when moving between the states, the so-called colonization movement proposed sending them out of the country altogether. Some black leaders initially saw potential in voluntary emigration to Haiti, Canada, or Africa. The Quaker businessman Paul Cuffee, son of a Ghanaian father, brought

**TEARING UP FREE PAPERS.**
In the Southern States, every colored person is presumed to be a slave, till proved to be free; and they are often robbed of the proof.

FIGURE 2.1 "Tearing Up Free Papers." Woodcut from the *Anti-Slavery Almanac* (1838), published by the American Anti-Slavery Society. An enslaver restrains a free southern black woman as her child stands beside her and another man destroys the papers that attest to her freedom. Library Company of Philadelphia.

1839] *Anti-Slavery Almanac.* 19

**A NORTHERN FREEMAN ENSLAVED BY NORTHERN HANDS.**
Nov. 20, 1836, (Sunday,) Peter John Lee, a free colored man of Westchester Co., N. Y., was kidnapped by Tobias Boudinot, E. K. Waddy, John Lyon, and Daniel D. Nash, of N. Y., city, and hurried away from his wife and children into slavery. One went up to shake hands with him, while the others were ready to use the gag and chain. See Emancipator, March 16, and May 4, 1837. This is not a rare case. Many northern freemen have been enslaved, in some cases under color of law. Oct. 26, 1836, a man named Frank, who was born in Pa., and lived free in Ohio, was hurried into slavery by an Ohio Justice of the Peace. When offered for sale in Louisiana, he so clearly stated the facts that a *slaveholding* court declared him FREE—thus giving a withering rebuke to northern servility.

FIGURE 2.2 "A Northern Freeman Enslaved by Northern Hands." Woodcut from the *Anti-Slavery Almanac* (1839), published by the American Anti-Slavery Society. A free black man from Westchester, New York, is kidnapped by four men who gag and chain him before sending him into slavery. Library Company of Philadelphia.

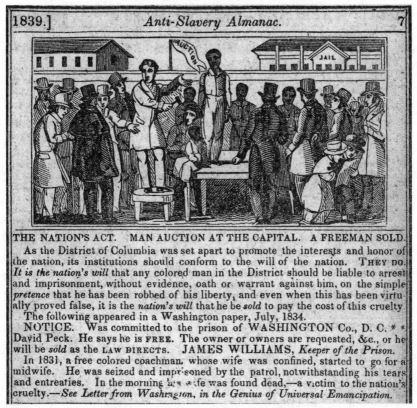

[1839.]       *Anti-Slavery Almanac.*      7

THE NATION'S ACT.   MAN AUCTION AT THE CAPITAL.   A FREEMAN SOLD.

As the District of Columbia was set apart to promote the interests and honor of the nation, its institutions should conform to the will of the nation. THEY DO. *It is the nation's will* that any colored man in the District should be liable to arrest and imprisonment, without evidence, oath or warrant against him, on the simple *pretence* that he has been robbed of his liberty, and even when this has been virtually proved false, it is the *nation's will* that he be *sold* to pay the cost of this cruelty.

The following appeared in a Washington paper, July, 1834.

NOTICE. Was committed to the prison of WASHINGTON Co., D. C. ✱ ✱ David Peck. He says he is FREE. The owner or owners are requested, &c., or he will be *sold* as the LAW DIRECTS.   JAMES WILLIAMS, *Keeper of the Prison.*

In 1831, a free colored coachman, whose wife was confined, started to go for a midwife. He was seized and imprisoned by the patrol, notwithstanding his tears and entreaties. In the morning his wife was found dead,—a victim to the nation's cruelty.—*See Letter from Washington, in the Genius of Universal Emancipation.*

FIGURE 2.3 "The Nation's Act. Man Auction at the Capital. A Freeman Sold." Woodcut from the *Anti-Slavery Almanac* (1839), published by the American Anti-Slavery Society. A kidnapped free black man is auctioned before a crowd of white bidders in Washington, DC, a major center of the slave trade. Library Company of Philadelphia.

thirty-eight African Americans to West Africa in 1816. Richard Allen of the African Methodist Episcopal Church also supported emigration in this form. So did the abolitionist John Russwurm, who moved to Liberia in 1829. The colonization movement, however, should not be confused with voluntary emigration. Colonizers wanted to remove free black people because they believed they could never achieve equality in the United States. This idea won the support of the Virginia legislature, which passed a law in 1816 requiring freed slaves to leave the state within the year. Virginia Congressman Charles Fenton Mercer hoped to win federal funding for colonization with the same purpose in mind. The Rev. Robert Finley, a Presbyterian clergyman from New Jersey, supported colonization in the belief that it would encourage manumissions and lead to the gradual demise of slavery.[56]

Supporters of Mercer and Finley came together in 1817 as the American Colonization Society (ACS), a semi-public enterprise funded in part by the Monroe administration. In 1821–1822, with help from the US Navy, the ACS purchased land adjacent to Sierra Leone and founded Liberia, with its capital Monrovia named in the president's honor. Supreme Court Justice Bushrod Washington served as the first president of the ACS. James Madison and Henry Clay later presided over the society, and other prominent supporters of colonization included John Marshall, Roger Taney, Daniel Webster, Stephen Douglas, and Abraham Lincoln. The ACS transported about 11,000 people, mostly former slaves, from the United States to Liberia, which declared its independence in 1847. White supporters of the ACS defended colonization as a compromise between slavery and abolition. Henry Clay and his colleagues admitted that slavery might be morally wrong, but they insisted that free black people could never become independent citizens and feared that their presence would destabilize the institution of slavery. The colonization movement held certain attractions in the Upper South, where state-level agencies augmented ACS efforts by funding the removal of emancipated slaves abroad, but the expansion of cotton production gave slaveowners in Virginia and Maryland the opportunity to sell their slaves to planters in the Lower South as a profitable alternative. Politicians in the Lower South, meanwhile, resisted colonization as a form of outside interference with slavery.[57]

Very few free black people wanted to leave their country. And if they left, they wanted to do so on their own terms. African American activists suspected the motives of the ACS from the outset and strongly rejected the idea of compulsory removal. As early as 1817, the year of Paul Cuffee's death, Richard Allen began to question the emerging movement. David Walker's *Appeal to the Coloured Citizens of the World* (1829), a rallying cry for black freedom, forcefully condemned "the colonizing trick." "Do they think to drive us from our country and homes," Walker asked, "after having enriched it with our blood and tears, and keep back millions of our dear brethren, sunk in the most barbarous wretchedness, to dig up gold and silver for them and their children?" Black opposition continued to mount in the 1830s with the rise of the abolitionist movement. Among the most vocal opponents of colonization were James W. C. Pennington and Frederick Douglass, both of whom were born into slavery. Some black leaders, including Martin Delany and Henry H. Garnet, advocated voluntary migration to new homelands in the Caribbean, Latin America, or Africa in the 1850s while continuing to condemn the colonization movement.[58]

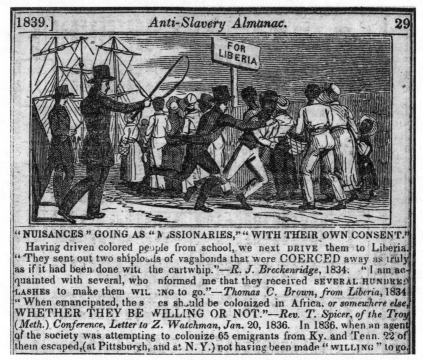

"NUISANCES" GOING AS "MISSIONARIES," "WITH THEIR OWN CONSENT."

Having driven colored people from school, we next DRIVE them to Liberia. "They sent out two shiploads of vagabonds that were COERCED away as truly as if it had been done with the cartwhip."—*R. J. Breckenridge*, 1834. "I am acquainted with several, who nformed me that they received SEVERAL HUNDRED LASHES to make them WILLING to go."—*Thomas C. Brown, from Liberia*, 1834. "When emancipated, the s es should be colonized in Africa, *or somewhere else*, WHETHER THEY BE WILLING OR NOT."—*Rev. T. Spicer, of the Troy (Meth.) Conference, Letter to Z. Watchman, Jan.* 20, 1836. In 1836, when an agent of the society was attempting to colonize 65 emigrants from Ky. and Tenn. 22 of them escaped,(at Pittsburgh, and at N. Y.) not having been made "WILLING" to go.

FIGURE 2.4 "'Nuisances' Going as 'Missionaries,' 'with Their Own Consent.'" Woodcut from the *Anti-Slavery Almanac* (1839), published by the American Anti-Slavery Society. Supporters of the "colonization" movement classified free black people as nuisances to society who could never achieve civil or political equality. They also cast them in the role of missionaries leaving the United States for Africa voluntarily. "Having driven colored people from schools," the *Almanac* acerbically commented, "we next drove them to Liberia." Library Company of Philadelphia.

Black and white abolitionists also protested the Seamen Acts. Between 1822 and the beginning of the Civil War, eight states—South Carolina, North Carolina, Georgia, Florida, Alabama, Mississippi, Louisiana, and Texas— passed such laws. At a meeting of "colored citizens of Boston" in October 1842, black activists led by Benjamin Weeden and Charles A. Battiste passed resolutions declaring the Seamen Acts "manifestly unconstitutional; inasmuch as the Constitution declares that all the citizens of each State shall be entitled to all the rights and immunities of citizens of the several States." Calling on Congress and the Massachusetts state legislature to act, these black citizens expressed their hope that the Supreme Court would find the laws unconstitutional. Their petition, published in William Lloyd Garrison's *The Liberator* on November 4, 1842, gained the support of white abolitionists.

A group of 155 Boston citizens, including many captains and shipowners who did business in southern ports and employed "free persons of color," sent a memorial to Congress arguing that the Seamen Acts both violated the constitutional rights of free black people and damaged American commerce. The memorial protested that crew members were taken from their vessels in Charleston, Savannah, Mobile, and New Orleans, thrown into prison, and detained at the shipowners' expense, a practice they found "greatly to the prejudice and detriment of their interests, and of the commerce of the nation." Both petitions went to the House Committee on Commerce, chaired by the Massachusetts Whig Robert Winthrop, which conducted an inquiry and presented majority and minority reports.[59]

The majority report, written by Winthrop and supported by seven of the nine committee members, found the Seamen Acts unconstitutional on three grounds. First, the laws violated the privileges and immunities clause. In Massachusetts, the report noted, black men had enjoyed "full and equal privileges of citizenship" since the abolition of slavery by the state constitution in 1780. Under the US Constitution, colored seamen who were citizens of Massachusetts were entitled to the privileges and immunities of citizens in all the states. Second, the laws violated federal power over interstate and foreign commerce. The Constitution assigned power over these kinds of commerce exclusively to Congress, "leaving nothing in reference to it for the States to act upon." Third, the laws violated the treaty-making power of the federal government, as they were in direct conflict with commercial conventions signed between the United States and Britain. The report noted that application of these laws to foreign vessels appeared to have been suspended in recent years. Yet that made it all the more objectionable that they were being applied to US citizens. "The idea that foreign seamen are treated with greater clemency in our own ports than native American seamen," as the report put it, "can only serve, on the contrary, to increase the impatience, and aggravate the odium, with which such laws are justly regarded."[60]

The majority report conceded that states could regulate their internal affairs but denied that the Seamen Acts were "within the legitimate purview of police power." Free black crew members, "charged with no crime, and infected with no contagion," were being incarcerated "without any other examination than an examination of their skins," subjected to corporal punishment, and sold into slavery for life. The targets included American-born as well as foreign-born seamen. No state, the report insisted, could "be permitted to abrogate the constitutional privileges of a whole class of citizens, upon grounds, not of any temporary moral or physical condition, but of distinctions which originate in their birth, and which are as permanent as their being." The power of the states to regulate their internal affairs could "never justify enactments or regulations, which are in direct, positive, and permanent conflict with express provisions or fundamental principles of the national compact." Citing *Prigg v. Pennsylvania* (1842), in which the Supreme Court ruled that a state's police power could not interfere with the rights of an enslaver to reclaim a fugitive as property, the report insisted that, by the same token, police power could not "divest a free citizen of his constitutional right over himself, his own actions, and his own motions."[61]

Congressman Kenneth Rayner, a Whig from North Carolina, wrote a minority report dissenting from all of these arguments. Pointing out that South Carolina had passed its first Seamen Act as a direct response to Denmark Vesey's conspiracy, Rayner claimed that the sailors who instigated the rebellion "were agents of certain fanatics, who thus sought to gratify their vengeance against Southern institutions, by kindling the flames of a servile war." South Carolina had not only the right but also the duty to protect itself against "these leagued bands of incendiaries." Southern police regulations were "not the result of unfriendly feeling towards the North, but of stern necessity."[62]

Rayner also offered an alternative reading of the privileges and immunities clause. Even admitting, for the sake of argument, that free black people could be citizens of the United States, he argued, the privileges and immunities of citizenship "must refer to those of the States *in* which, and not to the State *from* which, the citizen happens to be." Just as citizens of slaveholding states could not bring their human property with them into Massachusetts, citizens of Massachusetts must comply with the laws of the states in which they found themselves. If a northern state decided by its own laws which rights and privileges citizens visiting from other states enjoyed, then a southern state could decide which rights to extend to black visitors. That certain states recognized "no distinction of color, in relation to citizenship" could have no effect on the laws of South Carolina or Louisiana. Rayner denied, in any case, that free black residents of Massachusetts were full citizens of that state. A citizen enjoyed all the "privileges and immunities" conferred by that status—and this was not true of free black people in Massachusetts, let alone in South Carolina.[63]

For Rayner, the Seamen Acts were straightforward police regulations rather than a question of commerce. In *Gibbons v. Ogden*, the Supreme Court had ruled that, while Congress had the power to regulate foreign and interstate commerce, the states reserved powers to protect public health and safety and to regulate commerce within their borders. Every state, for Rayner, also had the power to punish offenses against its authority, including offenses by "those who disseminate seditious and insurrectionary doctrines among the slaves." He cited Justice Barbour's finding in *New York v. Miln* that a state law requiring reports on passengers was a valid police measure to protect residents not just from "the physical pestilence" arising from infectious disease but also from "the moral pestilence of paupers, vagabonds, and possibly convicts." This ruling, for Rayner, applied even more clearly to free black seamen, given the threat they posed to the institution of slavery.[64]

Although a strong majority of the House Committee on Commerce viewed the South Carolina Seamen Acts as unconstitutional, the best they could hope for was that Congress might pass a resolution to this effect. When Winthrop introduced resolutions of this kind, however, the House tabled them. Only the judicial branch, he concluded, could resolve the matter. Yet any case concerning the Seamen Acts would ultimately have to be heard before Roger Taney, who had strenuously endorsed South Carolina's laws as the US attorney general. No such case ever came before the Supreme Court. At least 20,000 free black sailors were imprisoned under the Seamen Acts. An unknown number were sold into slavery.[65]

In the spring of 1844, Massachusetts appointed two prominent attorneys as agents to protect the rights of its black citizens in southern ports. Samuel Hoar was sent to Charleston and Henry Hubbard to New Orleans. Their goal was to initiate federal lawsuits against the Seamen Acts that would make their way to the Supreme Court. Over the previous eight years, the Massachusetts legislature had passed a series of resolves against the acts, provoking an increasingly angry response in the South. In December 1842, the Georgia assembly issued a resolution declaring that "Negroes, or persons of color, are not citizens under the Constitution of the United States, and that Georgia will never recognize such citizenship." Just as Hoar and Hubbard were being appointed, the Massachusetts legislature petitioned Congress to consider a constitutional amendment revoking the three-fifths clause. Under these circumstances, the decision to send agents to the South could only prove inflammatory.[66]

Governor James Hammond of South Carolina refused to receive Samuel Hoar, even though the two men were acquainted, and called on the state assembly to expel him. The assembly's Committee on Federal Relations issued a report denouncing Hoar "as the emissary of a Foreign Government, hostile to our domestic institutions," who was sent to South Carolina "with the sole purpose of subverting our internal police." The power to exclude "conspirators against the public peace, and disaffected persons whose presence may be dangerous to their safety," the state assembly noted, "is essential to every Government." This power was "everywhere exercised by independent States." South Carolina had never ceded to the federal government its "right of internal government and police," and nothing in the US Constitution prevented the state from exercising its power or relieved it from "the duty of providing for the public safety." Following Georgia's lead, the assembly resolved that "free negroes and persons of color are not citizens of the United States, within the meaning of the Constitution, which confers upon the citizens of one State the privileges and immunities of citizens in the several States." The assembly also passed a law proclaiming that no person imprisoned under the Seamen Acts was entitled to a writ of habeas corpus. Threatened with mob violence, both Hoar and Hubbard fled for Boston just days after their arrival in the South.[67]

The Massachusetts legislature responded to Hoar's expulsion with a nineteen-page "Declaration." South Carolina tried to justify its actions, the Declaration noted, under "the plea of necessity of police regulations to her own safety." Massachusetts denied that any other state could claim jurisdiction over its ships, imprison and whip its citizens, force captains to redeem the captives and pay the expenses for their detention, or sell them into slavery. "These acts are acts of war," the Declaration stated. "They have no justification in the recognized intercourse of Christian or civilized nations intending to remain at peace. They lead to the last appeal between sovereigns, and to nothing else." The US Constitution, Massachusetts pointed out, guaranteed to "the citizens of each State," rather than the citizens of the United States, "all Privileges and Immunities of Citizens in the Several States." Citizens of Massachusetts, in other words, deserved the protections of the Constitution as citizens of their state in the first instance rather than as national citizens. Every sovereign state was obliged to protect those who owed it allegiance. Failure to challenge the Seamen Acts would undermine a state's sovereign status. This conception of sovereignty rested not simply on a state's autonomy from the federal government but also on its duty to protect its citizens.[68]

There was, however, a contradiction in this argument that exposed the bankruptcy of comity in a slaveholding republic. "The citizens of Massachusetts," the Declaration pointed out, "are entitled in South Carolina to the privileges which citizens of South Carolina themselves enjoy." Yet, unlike Massachusetts, South Carolina did not recognize free black people as citizens. Free black visitors from another state, the South Carolina assembly insisted, could not have "greater rights, immunities and privileges, within our territories, than are enjoyed by persons of the same class in South Carolina."

In response to South Carolina's treatment of its visiting black seamen, the Declaration noted, Massachusetts could just as well decide "that none but the free negro of South Carolina should be considered by her as a citizen of that State, entitled to the privileges and immunities of citizens, within her limits." As South Carolina refused to recognize the authority of the Constitution, why should Massachusetts remain bound by its comity obligations to South Carolina? Abolitionists led by Charles Francis Adams urged the state legislature to sever legal relations with both South Carolina and Louisiana altogether. Conscious of financial ties with the plantation South, the legislature called for federal legislation and lawsuits instead.[69]

Without South Carolina's cooperation and a federal judiciary and legislature willing to act, Massachusetts's protest could have no practical effect. The Georgia assembly passed a resolution supporting the right and duty of South Carolina and Louisiana to protect their citizens, whose "peace and safety were almost daily endangered by the machinations of unscrupulous emissaries, operating secretly though actively, under the pretence and guise of business occupations." These states had responded justly to Massachusetts's attempt to "interfere with their sovereign rights and constitutional domestic legislation," and Georgia would support all such efforts "should a similar indignity be offered to the sovereignty and safety of our own or any other sister State of the Union." The Alabama assembly responded to Massachusetts's interference with the "domestic police of the South," along with its call to amend the three-fifths clause, by affirming the right of every state "to exclude from her borders all persons whose admission would endanger her security." Citing *New York v. Miln* and echoing Rayner's minority report, Alabama insisted that South Carolina had the same authority to enact seamen laws as it did "to provide precautionary measures against the moral pestilence of paupers, vagabonds, or convicts" or "to guard against the physical pestilence which may arise from a ship, the crew of which may be laboring under an infectious disease." A state's right to guard its citizens against danger, the Alabama assembly declared, was "higher and deeper than the constitution." Any state could leave the Union to preserve its sovereignty.[70]

# 3

## *The Threat to Slavery*

IN JUNE 1837, three months after the Supreme Court upheld New York's immigration law in the *Miln* case, the schooner *Union Jack* arrived in Boston from St. John, New Brunswick, with nineteen alien passengers on board. Under Massachusetts law, captains were required to report the name, birthplace, last legal residence, age, sex, and occupation of each passenger, as well as specify if any were deaf, dumb, blind, maimed, or mentally disabled. The state required a bond of $1,000 for every alien passenger deemed likely to become a public charge and a tax of two dollars for every alien passenger who was not in a high-risk category. Captain James Norris paid the required tax under protest and brought suit against the city to recover his money. After the Massachusetts Supreme Judicial Court ruled in favor of Boston in 1842, Norris appealed to the US Supreme Court.

Meanwhile, the *Henry Bliss* had arrived in New York City from Liverpool in June 1841, carrying 295 alien passengers in steerage. The New York passenger act of 1824 upheld by the Supreme Court in *Miln* required a bond of up to $300 for each alien passenger considered likely to become a public charge. A separate ordinance allowed the mayor of New York to commute the bonding requirement if captains paid a head tax, set in 1847 at one dollar for each alien passenger in steerage. To support its quarantine center at the Marine Hospital on Staten Island, New York City levied a separate head tax of $1.50 per alien cabin passenger; one dollar per alien passenger in steerage; and twenty-five cents per passenger, whether citizen or alien, arriving on a domestic coasting vessel. When Captain George Smith refused to pay the marine tax for the steerage passengers on the *Henry Bliss*, the New York City health commissioner, William Turner, brought an action against him for $295. The state Supreme Court ruled against Smith in 1842. The US Supreme Court heard *Smith v. Turner* and *Norris v. City of Boston* together in the *Passenger*

*Cases* in 1849 and, by a bare majority, found the two state laws unconstitutional as violations of federal commerce power.[1]

The *Passenger Cases* involved much more than the constitutionality of two state immigration laws. At stake were fundamental questions concerning states' rights, slavery, the mobility of free black people, and the balance of sovereignty in a federal republic. Faced with the complexity of these issues, the nine justices delivered eight separate opinions. Five of them ruled—on various grounds and with varying degrees of attention to the two statutes under review—that state regulations of immigrant admissions infringed on Congress's power under the commerce clause. The four dissenting justices, by contrast, saw these laws as legitimate exercises of police power. Led by Chief Justice Roger Taney, the dissenters warned that invoking the commerce clause over state sovereignty was a path to tyranny, directly threatening the interests of the slave South. By the majority's reasoning, Justice Levi Woodbury warned, passengers "in vessels, boats, wagons, stages, or on horseback are as much connected with commerce as if they come in by sea, and they may consist of paupers, slaves, or convicts, as well as of merchants or travelers for pleasure and personal improvement." As a result, the laws of Ohio, Mississippi, and several other states "either forbidding or taxing the entrance of slaves or liberated blacks" could be nullified, not just the laws of Atlantic seaboard states taxing immigrant paupers.[2]

The *Passenger Cases* marked the culmination of a long debate about local versus national control over mobility. In the 1830s and 1840s, state and federal courts confronted a series of issues concerning the movement of free black people between the states, the privileges and immunities of citizens, the property rights of sojourning slaveholders, and the role of the federal and state governments in capturing and returning fugitive slaves. Three cases in particular provide the background for understanding the *Passenger Cases* and why they were so divisive—the Massachusetts case of *Commonwealth v. Aves* (1836), along with two others that reached the US Supreme Court, *Groves v. Slaughter* (1841) and *Prigg v. Pennsylvania* (1842). The constitutional questions about slavery, sovereignty, and mobility raised by these cases remained unanswered before the Civil War. The *Passenger Cases*, far from resolving the problem of immigration in a slaveholding republic, hardened the lines of sectional disagreement.[3]

## *Regulating the Movement of Enslaved People*

If a southern state could deny, within in its own jurisdiction, the rights enjoyed by a citizen visiting from a northern state, the opposite was also true. Just as South Carolina refused to recognize free black sailors from Massachusetts as citizens, Massachusetts refused to recognize the property rights of slaveholders unless obliged by federal law to do so, as in the case of fugitives. What, then, was the legal status of enslaved people brought to the North by their enslavers? English legal tradition suggested they were free the moment they entered a polity where slavery did not exist under local law. In 1765, English jurist William Blackstone wrote that the "spirit of liberty is so deeply implanted in our constitution, and rooted even in our very soil, that a slave or negro, the moment he lands in England, falls under the protection of the laws, and with regard to all natural rights becomes *eo instanti* a free man." Seven years later, in the *Somerset* case, Lord Mansfield arrived at the same conclusion. A resident of Virginia named Stewart had traveled to England on business with the intention of returning. He took with him a slave named Somerset, his personal servant, who absconded while in London but was captured and put on board a vessel lying in the Thames bound for Jamaica. Lord Mansfield issued a writ of habeas corpus, and the Court of King's Bench ruled unanimously that Somerset was held illegally and should be discharged. "The state of slavery," Mansfield allegedly declared, "is of such a nature that it is incapable of being introduced on any reasons, moral or political, but only by positive law. . . . It is so odious, that nothing can be suffered to support it, but positive law." Mansfield was no abolitionist. His decision did not free any of the 14,000 enslaved people then resident in England; it merely stated that no law existed to sanction holding Somerset against his will with the intention of sending him out of the country. Slavery could not exist in the absence of positive law (i.e., man-made or statute law), and no such law created or sustained the institution in England. Although this decision concerned relations between different parts of the British Empire rather than comity between sovereign states, it proved influential in antislavery and abolitionist circles in the antebellum United States, providing a precedent for the Massachusetts case of *Commonwealth v. Aves* in 1836.[4]

In May 1836, Mary Slater left New Orleans for Boston to visit her father, Thomas Aves. Mary's husband, Samuel Slater, remained in New Orleans, where she intended to rejoin him after a few months. She brought with her an enslaved girl, Med, aged about six, whom she left with her father while absent from Boston for a few days. On August 17, 1836, Thomas Aves was served a writ of habeas corpus claiming that Med "was unlawfully restrained of her liberty." Summoned to show the cause of the child's detention, Aves explained that his son-in-law, Samuel Slater, had purchased Med and her mother, and that they were enslaved in New Orleans at the time of Mary Slater's departure for Boston. The question before the Massachusetts Supreme Court was whether Med could be held as a slave in a state whose constitution and laws prohibited slavery.[5]

Benjamin R. Curtis, the Boston lawyer who served as Aves's counsel, argued that a citizen of a slaveholding state who came to Massachusetts temporarily, for business or pleasure, with an enslaved person, could restrain that person for the purpose of carrying her out of Massachusetts. Lord Mansfield had ruled in *Somerset* that slavery could exist only by positive law, but he had done so in an English court. American issues, Curtis insisted, must be decided in American courts. Louisiana was not a foreign nation; all states in the Union must respect the rights of its citizens. "We are bound up with her and the other slave-holding states, by the constitution, into a union," Curtis reminded the court, "upon the preservation of which no one doubts that our own peace and welfare depend." The implication was that, under the principle of comity, the property rights of slaveowners were valid everywhere—and not just in the case of fugitive slaves.[6]

For the Commonwealth, Boston abolitionist Ellis G. Loring, one of the leading lawyers of the New England Anti-Slavery Society, saw comity quite differently. When it came to slavery, he pointed out, there was no reciprocity: "We have no slaves in Massachusetts, in regard to whom we can ask the same comity which is claimed of us." The slaveholding states, where "color furnishes a presumption of slavery, and a free colored citizen may be called on to prove affirmatively his freedom, or be sold into slavery," denied comity to black citizens of other states. In direct violation of the privileges and immunities clause, black citizens from the North—seamen and others—were forbidden by law from entering many southern states, on pain of imprisonment and corporal punishment. Conversely, when Southerners traveled to the North with slaves, no state was obliged to enforce "any contract or law, which offends their morals, or contravenes their policy, or violates a public law, or offers a pernicious example." Humans could be held as property under the local law of states that recognized slavery, but there could be no slavery where freedom prevailed. Yet, by the same logic, what could prevent southern states from enacting measures like the Seamen Acts if they did not recognize free black people as citizens? Loring did not raise, and could not have answered, this question. Nor could anyone else resolve this contradiction in a context where some states sanctioned slavery and others denied its possibility.[7]

Chief Justice Lemuel Shaw delivered the opinion of the court. Although slavery was contrary to natural right, Shaw pointed out that, it was not contrary to the law of nations. As Lord Mansfield had noted in *Somerset*, the institution could exist in places that had laws upholding it. Nations could choose to recognize slavery if they wished and create customs and laws accordingly. What was true of nations, Shaw argued, was also true of the sovereign states that made up the American Union: each state could declare that persons were property to be bought, sold, and mortgaged. Yet these laws did not make persons into slaves in states that did not recognize slavery or had outlawed the practice. Shaw cited a ruling in Louisiana "that if a person with a slave, goes into a State to reside, where it is declared that slavery shall not exist, for ever so short a time, the slave *ipso facto* becomes free, and will be so adjudged and considered afterwards in all other States." He also cited, without naming, an Ohio Supreme Court decision by John McLean in 1817 that an enslaved man residing in Kentucky whose owner sent him to work in Ohio became free once he crossed into that free state. "In Kentucky, as in every other state where slavery is tolerated," McLean noted, "a presumption may perhaps arise that every black man is a slave unless the contrary appear." But in Ohio, "the presumption is different. Every man is supposed to be free, until his obligation to servitude be clearly shown." Except in the case of fugitives, McLean concluded, "the right of a citizen of a sister state to possession and control of his slave is governed by the law of the sister state."[8]

Enslavers, in other words, did not automatically carry their rights in human property with them, and no person could be held as property if local law did not permit slavery to exist. Slavery could not exist in Massachusetts, Justice Shaw explained, not only because it was contrary to natural right but also because its existence violated the state's laws and constitution. Shaw was no abolitionist; he emphasized that his opinion had no bearing on fugitives who entered a free state, as the states remained bound by the Fugitive Slave Act of 1793. The slave girl Med, however, was not a fugitive; her owner's wife brought her to Massachusetts and, because there could be no slavery there, Med was free as soon as she entered the state. Given that Med's mother was in New Orleans and she was too young to take care of herself, Justice Shaw made her a ward of the court.[9]

With individual states making their own laws on slavery and citizenship, and refusing to recognize the laws of other states, what role did the federal government have to play? The Fifth Amendment of the Constitution protected the property rights of slaveowners. The fugitive slave clause required any "person held to service or labor" who fled to another state to be returned to the state from which they had escaped. Building on this provision, the Fugitive Slave Act of 1793 allowed owners of enslaved people and their agents to search for escapees within the borders of free states, capture runaways and bring them before a magistrate, and take custody of them in order to carry them out of the state if the magistrate approved the evidence presented. Any person who helped harbor or conceal a fugitive faced a fine of $500. In these ways and others, the Constitution recognized and supported slavery. Yet some abolitionists continued to argue that Congress also had the authority to regulate or prohibit the interstate slave trade under the commerce clause. The Supreme Court considered this question directly only once, in *Groves v. Slaughter* (1841), but avoided the main issues on a technicality.[10]

In December 1836, a slave trader named Robert Slaughter took a group of slaves to Mississippi, where he sold them on credit to John W. Brown. In partial payment, Brown signed two promissory notes endorsed by Moses Groves and others and payable at the Commercial Bank at Natchez one year later. When these notes fell due, Groves and his associates refused to pay, claiming that the contracts violated the Mississippi Constitution of 1832, which prohibited the importation of slaves into the state by outsiders "as merchandise or for sale" from May 1, 1833 onward. This provision targeted out-of-state commercial traders, in part because enslaved people imported by outsiders were considered more likely to cause discontent or rebellion. Residents of the state could still bring in slaves, as could new settlers. Slaughter received no payment for the slaves he had sold nor were they returned to him. The case made its way on appeal to the US Supreme Court. At stake were three related questions: Did Congress have exclusive power to regulate commerce? To what extent did commerce include the movement of persons? And were slaves considered persons or property?[11]

In his argument before the Court, Mississippi Senator Robert J. Walker defended his state's right to regulate the slave trade. Congress had exclusive power over interstate commerce, he acknowledged, but using that power to control the slave trade was tantamount to regulating the institution of slavery, which was strictly under state control. If Congress could interfere in states' rights in this way, Walker warned, it could also prevent free states like Massachusetts from forbidding the entry of slaves. Representing Slaughter, Henry Clay argued that Mississippi could not prohibit the introduction of slaves as merchandise without violating the commerce clause. For Clay, Congress could regulate aspects of the interstate slave trade under its commerce power, but it could not prohibit that trade. As Daniel Webster explained, the Constitution recognized slaves as property through the fugitive slave clause, and Congress was obliged under the Fifth Amendment to protect that property. While southern states controlled slavery within their borders as a matter of local sovereignty, non-slaveholding states must yield to federal laws that supported the institution.[12]

By a majority of 5 to 2, with Justice Smith Thompson writing the opinion, the Court ruled in favor of Robert Slaughter. The provision in the Mississippi Constitution calling for the importation of enslaved people to be prohibited, he found, was not self-executing. In other words, it did not go into effect until the legislature acted—which it had not done until 1837. As the enslaved people in question were imported before this legislation was passed, their purchasers must pay for them. Thompson concluded that it was unnecessary to inquire whether the requirement in the Mississippi Constitution "was repugnant to the Constitution of the United States." By finding a way around the question of whether Mississippi's protectionism violated federal power over interstate commerce, the Court evaded the problem of sovereignty raised by the transportation of enslaved people across state borders as property for sale.[13]

The divisions among the justices, even those in the majority, reflected how intractable that problem had become. John McLean of Ohio followed his typical antislavery line in *Groves*. Yet in concurring with the majority, he wrote a separate opinion denying that the interstate slave trade amounted to commerce. Congress had the power to regulate the importation of slaves from foreign countries under the commerce clause, McLean noted, before the prohibition of the external slave trade in 1808. The migration or importation clause demonstrated this point conclusively, as it merely qualified the commerce clause with a twenty-year moratorium. But selling enslaved people between the states, McLean insisted, was not a form of commerce, as people could not be articles of merchandise. Some states classified enslaved persons as property under local law, to be sure, but "the Constitution acts upon slaves as persons, and not as property." The three-fifths clause and the fugitive slave clause, McLean noted, referred to "persons" and "person" respectively. Any state, whether Mississippi or Ohio, could prohibit the importation of slaves without infringing on Congress's commercial power, which referred to property rather than persons. Any such prohibition fell within the police powers of a state: "Its power to guard against, or to remedy the evil, rests upon the law of self-preservation; a law vital to every community, and especially to a sovereign state." States, in short, could prohibit the entry of enslaved people at their own discretion, in ways that had nothing to do with commerce. This rule applied not just to Mississippi but also to antislavery states in the North.[14]

McLean's antislavery logic provoked Justice Roger Taney to write his own proslavery opinion on why the power to regulate the slave trade lay exclusively with the states. The issue before the Court was whether a state could prevent the entry of enslaved people, not whether Congress could regulate the interstate slave trade, yet these two questions were closely related. Like McLean, Taney insisted that the federal government had no power to control the slave trade. Yet, while McLean's argument led to the free-soil conclusion that all states could therefore prohibit the entry of slaves, Taney's protected the states against federal intrusion. For Taney, power over the movement of enslaved people between the states lay exclusively with the states, each of which had a right to decide for itself whether to permit slaves to be brought within its limits for sale or any other purpose. Congress could not control the action of the states on this subject, neither by its commerce power nor by any other power conferred by the Constitution. On this point, Taney and McLean agreed, but whereas McLean argued on antislavery grounds that all states could exclude slaves as persons, Taney argued that Congress could not prevent human property from being imported into a state.[15]

Justice Henry Baldwin of Pennsylvania agreed with Taney that no state could prevent enslavers from moving their property across state borders as they wished. Not only did Congress lack authority over slavery as a local institution, Baldwin emphasized, it was obliged by the Constitution to protect the property rights of enslavers. If a slaveowner transported slaves from the slave state of Maryland to the slave state of Kentucky via Pennsylvania or Ohio, no law in either of the two free states could "take away or affect his right of property." Slave traders entering Mississippi, Baldwin insisted, had the same rights as traders resident in the state. Under the privileges and immunities clause, Mississippi could not deny to citizens of other states a right—in this case the right to import human property for sale—that it guaranteed to its own citizens. A state could regulate the slave trade under its internal commerce power but not if the regulation put the citizens of other states on a different footing. "The direct tendency of all such laws," Baldwin concluded, "is partial, antinational, subversive of the harmony which should exist among the states, as well as inconsistent with the most sacred principles of the Constitution which on this subject have prevailed through all time, in and among the colonies and states." Thus, for Baldwin, even if the contract between Groves and Slaughter had been invalid under the Constitution of Mississippi (which, the Court ruled, was not the case until the state legislature passed the required laws), it must be upheld under the privileges and immunities clause. No state could violate the property rights of slaveowners entering from other states. The federal principle of comity protected the slave trade.[16]

Not surprisingly, the justices had failed to arrive at a coherent position on slavery and commerce in *Groves v. Slaughter*. The Court dodged the main constitutional issues by ruling that the provisions of the Mississippi Constitution required legislation to come into effect. Justices McLean, Taney, and Baldwin agreed with Thompson that the contract with Slaughter was valid, but on different grounds and with different intentions. McLean argued, from an antislavery perspective, that every state could exclude slaves as they were persons, not property. Taney, aware that classifying slaves sold between states as merchandise might bring them under the federal commerce power, agreed with McLean that they could not be excluded as persons, yet he did so in order to protect the interstate state slave trade. Baldwin argued that enslaved people were a form of property and, on those grounds, that no state could violate the comity rights of citizens by restricting the importation of slaves for sale. None of the justices adopted the position that the federal government could regulate or prohibit the internal slave trade as a form of interstate commerce. On the contrary, the Court successfully avoided this politically explosive question.[17]

The one area where the federal government had unequivocal power over slavery concerned fugitives. This question came before the Supreme Court in *Prigg v. Pennsylvania*. In 1832, Margaret Morgan moved from Maryland to Pennsylvania, with her husband, a free black man named Jerry Morgan. Born enslaved, Margaret Morgan assumed she was free, as she and her parents lived as free people, although her owner, John Ashmore, had never formally liberated her. In 1837, Ashmore's wife, Margaret Ashmore, claimed Margaret Morgan as a slave and sent Edward Prigg, a citizen of Maryland, to Pennsylvania to capture her. Under the 1793 Fugitive Slave Act, an alleged fugitive could be seized and handed over to a claimant on the basis of evidence presented to any federal, state, or local magistrate. Prigg obtained a warrant and had Morgan arrested as a fugitive and taken before a magistrate, who refused to grant certificates for the removal of Morgan and her children, one of whom had been born in Pennsylvania. Prigg abducted the family, took them back to Maryland, and delivered them to Margaret Ashmore.[18]

Prigg was indicted in York County for violating a Pennsylvania law, passed in 1826, that made it a felony to carry away "any negro or mulatto" from the Commonwealth with the intention of selling them into temporary or permanent servitude. The Pennsylvania statute was one of a series of "personal liberty laws" passed in the North to ensure that free black people and fugitive slaves had procedural rights. Extradited from Maryland and facing a fine and prison time with hard labor, Prigg pleaded not guilty on the grounds that Pennsylvania's law violated the fugitive slave clause and the Fugitive Slave Act of 1793. A jury in York County delivered a special verdict seeking guidance

from the Supreme Court of Pennsylvania, and the case made its way from
there to the US Supreme Court. Both the attorney general of Pennsylvania
and Prigg's counsel, who represented Maryland, wanted to test the constitutionality of the 1826 law.[19]

The Supreme Court ruled in Prigg's favor by a majority of 6 to 1, finding that
the Pennsylvania law infringed on the federal government's authority over the
return of fugitive slaves. Justice Joseph Story of Massachusetts delivered the
opinion of the Court. Story had been the lone dissenter in *Miln* (1837), when
he ruled that a New York immigration statute violated the commerce clause.
In *Prigg,* he once again upheld federal sovereignty, this time in the name of
slavery. Even though he claimed to find the institution of slavery abhorrent,
Story pointed out that the Constitution and federal legislation required the
return of fugitives. Without the fugitive slave clause, he claimed, the Union
"could not have been formed." Its purpose was to secure the human property
of citizens of the slaveholding states in every state into which fugitives might
escape. The right to seize and retake fugitive slaves, and the duty to deliver
them up, were absolute and uncontrollable by state legislation. The laws of
Congress, as long as they were constitutional, superseded and prohibited all
state legislation on the subject. The Fugitive Slave Act therefore took precedence over the Pennsylvania statute of 1826, which punished "the very act
of seizing and removing a slave by his master which the Constitution of the
United States was designed to justify and uphold." The majority in *Prigg*
also agreed that the Pennsylvania statute, by prohibiting the extradition of
fugitives, violated the obligation of the states to protect and enforce the property rights of slaveowners under the privileges and immunities clause. "The
owner of a fugitive slave," Story wrote, "has the same right to seize and take
him in a State to which he has escaped or fled that he had in the State from
which he escaped, and it is well known that this right to seizure or recapture
is universally acknowledged in all the slaveholding States." Margaret Morgan
and her children remained enslaved in Maryland and vanished from the historical record.[20]

Despite upholding federal power in *Prigg*, Story acknowledged a degree of
state sovereignty. The states, he emphasized, could not oppose federal law on
fugitive slaves, but neither were they required to execute that law. They were
not "bound to provide means to carry into effect the duties of the National
Government." Chief Justice Roger Taney and Justice Peter Daniel of Virginia,
although they concurred with the majority opinion, disagreed strongly with
this view, arguing that enforcement of the fugitive slave clause required state
officials to participate. Antislavery justice John McLean dissented, arguing

in favor of personal liberty laws such as Pennsylvania's on the grounds that, without these laws, states could not prevent slave catchers from seizing free black people.[21]

The Court's decision in *Prigg*, by clarifying that enforcement of the fugitive slave clause was entirely a federal responsibility, opened two divergent paths. The same section of the Constitution that mandated the return of fugitive slaves guaranteed that citizens of all states would enjoy the privileges and immunities of citizens in the states they visited. But why should Massachusetts comply with the fugitive slave clause, lawmakers had asked after the expulsion of their agent Samuel Hoar from Charleston in 1844, if South Carolina refused to comply with the privileges and immunities clause? Massachusetts, from this perspective, had a duty to protect both its own black citizens traveling in the South and enslaved people who entered the state with their enslavers. Northern states responded to the ruling in *Prigg* by passing more stringent personal liberty laws, prohibiting local officials from cooperating in the capture and return of fugitives. Southerners, inspired by *Prigg* and outraged by the personal liberty laws, demanded that Congress pass a stronger fugitive slave law. Although supporters of slavery invoked states' rights to insist that the national government could not interfere with the institution or with the interstate slave trade, they invoked federal power

FIGURE 3.1 "Fugitives Escaping from the Eastern Shore of Maryland" (1851). A group of twenty-eight fugitive slaves who successfully escaped to the North. Wood engraving in William Still, *The Underground Railroad* (Philadelphia, Porter & Coates, 1872). Library of Congress Prints and Photographs Division, LC-USZ62-75975.

when it came to capturing and returning fugitives. The result was a new fugitive slave act.[22]

The Fugitive Slave Act of 1850 was part of a compromise over slavery following the Mexican-American War. Congress passed legislation allowing California to enter the Union as a free state, with the other territories acquired from Mexico making their own decisions about slavery. Congress also banned the slave trade in Washington, D.C. and, most controversially, passed a law permitting slaveholders or their agents to arrest suspected fugitives and take them before a much broader array of federal officials than before, including judges, postmasters, and customs collectors, who issued certificates of removal upon presentation of evidence. The federal commissioners created under the act earned a fee of ten dollars if they found in favor of the claimant, but only five dollars if they ruled that the evidence did not justify return (on the specious grounds that processing the paperwork for removal was more demanding). The commissioners could deputize citizens to enforce the law, with those who refused facing stiff fines. Many free black people in the North had to acquire "free papers" for the first time in order to prove that they were not fugitives from slavery. No fugitive was permitted to testify in any trial or hearing under the act. This system of forced and arbitrary removal, with its lack of judicial oversight and due process, set a precedent for the deportation of immigrants in the postbellum era.[23]

## Passengers as Commerce

In the months leading up to the Compromise of 1850, sectional tensions were enflamed by the *Passenger Cases*, when authority over immigration collided directly with the interests of the slave states. In *Prigg v. Pennsylvania*, the Supreme Court had conceded that the states retained a police power to regulate their internal affairs. They could arrest and remove runaway slaves, as well as "idlers, vagabonds, and paupers," provided their police measures did not interfere with the constitutional rights of owners to reclaim their property or with federal laws upholding these rights. In *New York v. Miln*, likewise, the Court had upheld a New York law regulating immigration as a legitimate exercise of police power. In *Miln*, however, the Court had carefully avoided the larger question of whether passenger taxes imposed at the state level clashed with federal commerce power. In the *Passenger Cases* (1849), the Court confronted this question directly. Daniel Webster, in his last argument before the Supreme Court, argued strenuously that the laws of Massachusetts and New York violated the commerce clause. Five of the nine justices—John

FIGURE 3.2 "Effects of the Fugitive Slave Law." The Fugitive Slave Act of 1850 empowered federal commissioners to issue warrants for the arrest of alleged fugitive slaves and to enlist civilian bystanders in their apprehension. Here, four black men—possibly free—are ambushed by six armed whites in a cornfield; two of them are hit, while the other two react with horror. Below the image, the artist included the proclamation of universal equality and rights from the Declaration of Independence, along with a verse from Deuteronomy: "Thou shalt not deliver unto the master his servant which has escaped from his master unto thee. He shall dwell with thee. Even among you in that place which he shall choose in one of thy gates where it liketh him best. Thou shalt not oppress him." Published by Hoff & Bloede, New York, 1850. Library of Congress Prints and Photographs Division, LC-DIG-ds-14484.

McLean of Ohio, James Wayne of Georgia, John McKinley of Alabama, Robert Grier of Pennsylvania, and John Catron of Tennessee—agreed with Webster. Taken as a whole, their opinions addressed four critical aspects of the problem of immigration in a slaveholding republic: the point at which state passenger laws came into operation, the relevance of the migration or importation clause, the nature and extent of federal commerce and local police power, and the implications for the Union as a whole.[24]

The first question was where and when state laws came into operation. Justice McLean, referring to the Boston case, insisted that because the captain had to pay two dollars for each non-pauper alien passenger before they were permitted to land, this tax amounted to a regulation of foreign commerce. Justice Catron found, with regard to the New York law, that the *Henry Bliss* was engaged in foreign commerce when Commissioner Turner demanded the tax of $295, as the passengers and their baggage were still on board and

FIGURE 3.3 "The Fugitive Slave Law in Operation." Two armed men forcibly remove a black man from his home while a kneeling black child begs for mercy. Engraving by Albert Bobbett in Benjamin Perley Poore, *Perley's Reminiscences of Sixty Years in the National Metropolis* (Philadelphia: Hubbard Brothers, 1886). Library Company of Philadelphia.

the voyage had not ended. For Justice McKinley, likewise, the voyage ended only when the passengers landed and became "a portion of the population of the state, temporarily or permanently." Before that, they could not be subject to state laws. Justices Wayne and Grier cited John Marshall's opinion in *Gibbons v. Ogden* (1824) that the power of Congress over commerce "does not stop at the jurisdictional lines of the several states" and that it would be "a very useless power" if it did. When a foreign voyage commenced or terminated at a port within a state, Marshall had ruled, Congress could exercise its power to regulate commerce within that state. The power applied once a journey began and until it had ended.[25]

The second question concerned the migration or importation clause. For the justices in the majority, this provision gave Congress the power to regulate both free migration and the external slave trade. Justice Wayne insisted that the clause included "the migration of other persons, as well as the importation of slaves." Both free migrants and enslaved people, therefore, "may be the subjects of importation and commerce." Justice McLean cited Marshall's opinion in *Gibbons* that the migration or importation clause "certainly seems to class migration with importation," along with Justice William Johnson's opinion in the same case that "although the leading object of this section undoubtedly was the importation of slaves, yet the words are obviously calculated to comprise persons of all descriptions." Justice McKinley also emphasized that the clause gave Congress power over free migrants as well as the external slave trade. If the clause applied only to the importation of enslaved people, he asked, why had the framers used the phrase "a tax or duty may be imposed on such importation" in the second half of the clause, omitting the word "migration"? If they had omitted "migration" from the clause entirely, it would have applied only to the slave trade, but retaining that word in the first half of the clause distinguished migration from importation. Delegates at the Constitutional Convention had amended the clause by striking out the word migration in the second half, in an effort to make the clause apply to slaves exclusively. Yet, for McKinley, the clause meant what it said. It referred to two different kinds of population movement, by free immigrants as well as enslaved persons. Congress had power over immigration and the states could not intrude on the lives of passengers until they had landed.[26]

If free immigrants and imported slaves were both "subjects of commerce" under congressional control, that did not make them identical. Enslaved migrants, McKinley explained, were "the subject of trade and importation," but they were not "immigrants" as they were transported involuntarily. Their importers had to report them at the custom house like "any other article of commerce or importation." Free immigrants, by contrast, were subjects of commerce in the broad sense defined by John Marshall. They could move voluntarily "from one place to another," and when they migrated from a European country to the United States, they voluntarily dissolved their allegiance to their home sovereign and assumed temporary or permanent allegiance to the government of the United States. If transported on an American ship, they were subject to and protected by the laws of the United States during their voyage, which ended only after the passengers had landed. States could not intervene before that.[27]

This raised the third and central question in the *Passenger Cases*, the balance between commerce power and police power. All five justices in the majority agreed that portions of the two state statutes under review violated the commerce clause by imposing taxes or fees on passengers. The states had the power to regulate their internal affairs, including trade, but they could not infringe on Congress's authority to regulate commerce between the states or with other nations. As Marshall had established in *Gibbons v. Ogden*, commerce included not only the exchange of commodities but also "navigation" and "intercourse." Power over interstate and foreign commerce was exclusive to Congress; the states had no concurrent power in this domain. "A tax or duty on tonnage, merchandise, or passengers is a regulation of commerce," Justice McLean wrote in the *Passenger Cases*, "and cannot be laid by a state, except under the sanction of Congress and for the purposes specified in the Constitution." A state law imposing a tax on passengers arriving from foreign ports, even when passed as a police measure with the intention of protecting residents against foreign paupers, could not intrude on federal commerce power in pursuing that goal.[28]

What, then, was the nature and extent of police power? Although the states had delegated power over foreign and interstate commerce to the federal government, the justices in the majority conceded that they retained substantial powers over their internal affairs. They could regulate commerce within their borders and use their police power to protect public health and safety, provided these measures did not infringe on federal power. Every state, Justice Wayne observed, had "the right to turn off paupers, vagabonds, and fugitives from justice," just as "the states where slaves are have a constitutional right to exclude all such as are, from a common ancestry and country, of the same class of men." State quarantine and health laws, although they affected commerce, were not regulations of commerce per se but "precautionary regulations to prevent vessels engaged in commerce from introducing disease into the ports to which they are bound." Massachusetts had an undeniable right to protect itself from foreign paupers and others who might become a public charge, but the nineteen alien passengers who had arrived in Boston on the *Union Jack* in 1837 did not come under this heading. "The fund thus raised was no doubt faithfully applied for the support of foreign paupers," McLean wrote, "but the question is one of power, and not of policy." As the power to regulate foreign commerce belonged to the federal government rather than the states, the Massachusetts law was unconstitutional.[29]

The final question was how the New York and Massachusetts laws affected other states and the Union as a whole. These laws, Justice Grier noted, assumed that foreigners who arrived in Boston and New York and later became paupers would remain in these port cities. The bonds or taxes required at entry would pay for their upkeep. Yet tens of thousands of immigrants left the cities where they arrived, continuing their journeys to the interior—or at least they might have done so, Grier suggested, if the taxes added to their fares had not depleted their resources. By imposing these charges, the states where America's great ports were located potentially excluded immigrants from access to the interior or set the conditions on which they were allowed to proceed. Twelve American states lacked a seaport at this time and were therefore subject to the policies of states that had ports and imposed taxes on immigrants. The police powers of the eastern seaboard states, Grier concluded, could not be "perverted into weapons of offense and aggression upon the rights of others." A state could impose taxes on passengers who chose to become residents or citizens, but it was not necessary to its safety or welfare that it should, in effect, "exact a transit duty on persons or property for permission to pass to other states."[30]

The justices in the majority found the policies of Massachusetts and New York incompatible with what they believed to be the intended national policy of the United States. Encouraging immigration "was a cherished policy of this country at the time the Constitution was adopted," Justice McLean wrote. "As a branch of commerce, the transportation of passengers has always given a profitable employment to our ships, and within a few years past has required an amount of tonnage nearly equal to that of imported merchandise." Was this "great branch of our commerce" to be left open to state regulation on the grounds that "a man is not an import"—and hence that immigration could not be taxed—as the dissenting justices argued? Justice Wayne feared that allowing a state, "by taxation or otherwise," to direct the terms on which foreigners could enter "may defeat the whole and long-cherished policy of this country and of the Constitution in respect to immigrants coming to the United States." For Justice Grier, it was "the cherished policy of the general government to encourage and invite Christian foreigners of our own race to seek an asylum within our borders" and to convert "waste lands into productive farms, and thus add to the wealth, population, and power of the nation." How could the framers of the Constitution have intended that two or three states could "thwart the policy of the Union, and dictate the terms upon which foreigners shall be permitted to gain access to the other states?"[31]

Moreover, Justice Grier pointed out, if immigrants intending to move to the western states were compelled on arrival to contribute to the revenue of Massachusetts or New York, they could be subjected to the same restrictions in every city or state through which they passed. And if foreigners were subject to taxation or exclusion in the seaboard states, on the pretext that they might become paupers, states could impose the same policies on the citizens of other states. Indeed, the New York statute did precisely that by levying a tax of twenty-five cents per passenger on coasting vessels. For Grier, the primary purpose for forming the Union was to prevent states from enforcing conflicting commercial regulations. The Constitution conferred on Congress the power to control commerce among the states and with foreign nations for precisely that purpose. From its inception in 1789, Justice Catron noted, the policy of the United States was to attract immigrants through the prospect of becoming citizens. "By this policy," he wrote, "our extensive and fertile country has been, to a considerable extent, filled up by a respectable population, both physically and mentally, one that is easily governed and usually of approved patriotism." No state, for Grier, could hinder immigration of this kind. To do so would be to disrupt the Union and subvert the national interest.[32]

## Passengers as Persons

The decision in the *Passenger Cases* had little practical impact. New York and Massachusetts responded with the simple expedient of replacing immigrant taxes with commutation fees in the same amount in lieu of posting bonds. In practice, ship captains paid the fees, as bonds were more expensive if they fell due, and they became easier to redeem over time. The historical significance of the cases lies not in their impact on policy but in the insights they provide into the inextricability of immigration and slavery. This is especially true of the dissenting opinions. Four of the justices, led by Roger Taney, disagreed with the majority on each of the fundamental points at stake in the *Passenger Cases*. Taney wrote a lengthy opinion, as did Peter Daniel of Virginia and Levi Woodbury of New Hampshire, while Samuel Nelson of New York affirmed the judgments by Daniel and Taney without writing his own opinion. The dissenters insisted that the states had the right to regulate passengers under their sovereign police power, just as they had the right to regulate the movement of free black people. State control over mobility, they contended, did not interfere with foreign or interstate commerce. Ceding control over borders to Congress would lead to tyranny—a codeword for the perceived threat to the institution of slavery. Despite Justice Wayne's reassurance that the majority ruling had no bearing on the constitutional right of slaveholding states to exclude free black people, the dissenters feared that the federal government, once authorized to regulate immigration as a matter of commerce, would use the same power to regulate interstate movement by African Americans to the detriment of the South.[33]

The first point of contention was where the voyage ended and state control began. Unlike the majority, the dissenting justices saw state immigration laws as valid because the taxes were paid after the voyage was over. Captains paid the amount due on board ships at the ports of arrival, which lay within the states' control. The Massachusetts law, Roger Taney wrote, "meets the vessel after she has arrived in the harbor, and within the territorial limits of the state, but before the passengers have landed and while they are still afloat on navigable water." The voyage was complete, he insisted, "when the entry was made at the custom house and the proper list delivered." At that point, the passengers were under the jurisdiction and protection of the state, which had the right to tax them in return for the protection it afforded them. Nothing in the Constitution could prohibit this right. Ships carrying passengers were undoubtedly engaged in commerce, but Congress did not have the power to prevent states from taxing commerce "in their own ports and within their own jurisdiction." Justice Woodbury, likewise, held that the Massachusetts law applied only to a local matter after the voyage had ended. It was "not a matter of commerce or navigation, but rather of police, or municipal, or taxing supervision." Any effect on foreign commerce was incidental. Federal commerce power and local police power were two different kinds of power, exercised separately by two different forms of government. The captain was required to pay the tax only if the immigrants landed, as the condition on which the state permitted them "to come on shore and mingle with its citizens and to reside among them." Moreover, Taney reminded the Court, although the captain paid the tax, he transferred the cost onto the passengers, either as part of their fare or as a fee paid before landing. If a captain recovered the sum in question through a legal suit, Taney objected, he would be receiving money from the state that he had already taken from the passengers. If the Court invalidated these taxes, the money ought to be refunded to the passengers, not the captain. But Taney saw nothing wrong in states taxing foreign passengers to guard against them becoming paupers.[34]

Taxing American citizens traveling between states was another matter. New York's hospital money law taxed passengers arriving on domestic coasting vessels as well as passengers arriving from foreign ports. "The provisions contained in that law relating to American citizens who are passengers from the ports of other states is a different question, and involves very different considerations," Taney observed. "It is not now before us; yet, in order to avoid misunderstanding, it is proper to say that in my opinion it cannot be maintained." Taney proceeded to articulate an early defense of the constitutional right of citizens to travel throughout the United States. In a federal union with "a common government," he argued, every citizen of the United States was entitled to free access to all federal offices and courts in states and territories throughout the Union. "For all the great purposes for which the federal government was formed, we are one people with one common country," Taney wrote. "We are all citizens of the United States, and as members of the same community must have the right to pass and re-pass through every part of it without interruption, as freely as in our own states." Taney did not rest this conclusion on the commerce clause, as doing so would have undercut his position on immigration and raised the prospect of Congress overriding state laws restricting the mobility of free black people or even regulating the interstate slave trade. Instead, he listed various other parts of the Constitution—the privileges and immunities clause, the right to sue in a federal court in another state than one's own, the provision that vessels traveling between states need not pay duties, and the right to retrieve pro-perty under the fugitive slave clause—to support freedom of movement for citizens. As free black people did not enjoy this freedom, Taney's position im-plied that they were not citizens of the United States—a conclusion he would push to its terrible extreme in the *Dred Scott* case eight years later.[35]

On the second major point of contention, the dissenting justices found that the migration or importation clause applied only to the external slave trade, not to free immigration. As Justice Daniel put it, the clause "was in-tended to apply to the African slave trade, and to no other matter whatever." European passengers—"rational beings, freemen carrying into execution their deliberate intentions"—could never be classed with "the subjects of sale, barter, or traffic—or, in other words, with imports." Roger Taney, like-wise, insisted that the clause "was intended to embrace those persons only who were brought in as property." Citing Madison's papers and *Federalist* no. 42, Daniel and Taney argued that suggestions that the migration or importation clause applied to "voluntary and beneficial emigrations from Europe" had merely been pretexts for opposing the Constitution. The claim that the word "migration" embraced free immigrants as well as slaves, for Taney, was "so evidently founded on misconstruction as to be unworthy of serious reply." All the states at the time the Constitution was ratified, he pointed out, wished to encourage "voluntary and beneficial migration from Europe." The migration or importation clause, Taney explained, "was introduced and adopted solely to prevent Congress, before the time specified, from prohibiting the introduction of slaves from Africa into such states as should think proper to admit them." Including the word "mi-gration" had caused some confusion, he conceded, but the Constitution used this word alongside "importation" to recognize that slaves were both persons and property. Unwilling to use the word "slaves" in the founding charter of the republic, the framers used the euphemism "persons" instead, but the clause as a whole showed "that it was intended to embrace those persons only who were brought in as property."[36]

For the dissenting justices, the idea that Congress had a general power to regulate admissions was a dangerous fallacy. There would have been no reason for the Constitution to expressly grant Congress the power to prohibit the entry of slaves after 1807, Justice Woodbury observed, if Congress already had the power under other parts of the Constitution "to forbid the entry of everybody, as of aliens generally." As Congress did not possess this power to admit and exclude, it necessarily belonged to the states, "as the power must exist somewhere in every independent country."[37] If the states lacked this power, by what authority had most of them forbidden the importation of slaves between 1789 and 1808? Congress could not transfer such a power to the states; it belonged to them as sovereign entities, and they had not delegated it to the national government. Their right to exclude enslaved people was recognized in both the migration or importation clause and the federal act of 1803 prohibiting the importation of "any negro, mulatto, or other person of color" to states that had passed laws to that effect. Congress had never attempted to regulate immigration, as distinct from the external slave trade, Woodbury pointed out, whereas the states had "been in the constant habit of prohibiting the introduction of paupers, convicts, free blacks, and persons sick with contagious diseases, no less than slaves, and this from neighboring states as well as from abroad." The right of states to control their borders was inherent in their sovereignty.[38]

The dissenting justices all agreed on the third and central point at issue in the *Passenger Cases*, ruling that the state laws under review were not regulations of foreign commerce. That the Constitution gave Congress general authority over foreign and interstate commerce, Taney explained, did not prohibit states from making commercial regulations within their own territorial limits, provided these laws did not conflict with federal laws. The Massachusetts statute conflicted with no act of Congress or treaty that gave, or attempted to give, aliens the right to land in a state. Congress had passed legislation concerning passengers, to be sure, but only to regulate conditions on board vessels, not to determine how states could admit immigrants. Nor did the Massachusetts law impose tonnage duties or a tax on either the captain or the passengers simply for entering state waters. It merely refused permission to land "until the security demanded by the state for the protection of its own people from the evils of pauperism has been given." Neither the commercial treaty of 1815 with Britain nor the Passenger Act of 1819, Taney pointed out, had attempted to compel states to receive immigrants without security of this kind. If either measure had done so, the question would have gone far beyond commerce to affect the power of deciding who was permitted to reside among the citizens of a state.[39]

To support his argument against federal power, Taney insisted that passengers could not be classified as imports. Head taxes, therefore, were not taxes on commerce imposed by states in violation of the Constitution. Taney claimed that the opinions of the justices forming the majority in the *Passenger Cases* were "in direct conflict" with the Court's decision in *New York v. Miln* (1837) that "passengers clearly were not imports." In both England and the United States, Taney argued, the words "imports" and "importation" as used in statutes, official reports, and public debates, applied only to "articles of property, and never to passengers voluntarily coming to the country in ships." It was in that sense that these words had been used in the debates at the Constitutional Convention. The argument that passengers were imports, therefore, was "most evidently without any reasonable foundation."[40]

Justice Wayne, a member of the majority, strongly disagreed with Taney's reading of *Miln*. Of the seven justices who heard that case, four had since died, including Philip Pendleton Barbour, who wrote the majority opinion. Wayne claimed that Barbour's opinion, although it was reported as the opinion of the Court, did not have the concurrence of the majority except in one particular—that the requirement for a report on passengers was a police regulation and did not violate Congress's power to regulate commerce. Beyond this particular issue, Wayne insisted, the majority who concurred in the judgment did not agree with Barbour's opinion, especially his declaration that passengers could not be subjects of commerce. Only Taney and Barbour, Wayne recalled, had endorsed the opinion as a whole. Taney, however, insisted in the *Passenger Cases* that Barbour had spoken for the Court in *Miln*: all seven justices had taken part in the deliberations, which was delivered openly from the bench, and only Justice Story had dissented. By Taney's reading of *Miln*, passengers could not be commerce, and he drew on that supposed precedent to reach the same conclusion in the *Passenger Cases*.[41]

Proslavery and antislavery justices took opposite positions on this critical question. The dissenters insisted not only that African Americans could be held as property as slaves but also, with equal vehemence, that passengers—as "persons"—could not be articles of commerce. In Justice Daniel's words, "the term imports is justly applicable to articles of trade proper,—goods, chattels, property, subjects in their nature passive and having no volition,—not to men whose emigration is the result of will; it would be a 'perversion' to argue otherwise." Southern states' rights advocates, fearful that Congress might extend a general power over mobility to free black people or the interstate slave trade, insisted that the states reserved the power to admit, exclude, and remove people as they saw fit. State laws regulating the movement of passengers as persons were exercises of sovereign police power immune from congressional interference. The justices in the majority, by contrast, argued that passengers were a form of commercial merchandise whose movement was subject to control by Congress rather than by the states. From their perspective, immigration was a matter of national rather than local sovereignty.[42]

The dissenters also insisted that no treaty between the United States and Britain could oblige any state to surrender power over its borders. British subjects had equal and reciprocal rights to engage in commerce with the United States. These rights, however, were subject to the laws of both countries, and the laws of the United States included laws placing foreign passengers under the "decision and control" of the states. "I cannot believe," Roger Taney wrote in the *Passenger Cases*, "that it was ever intended to vest in Congress, by the general words in relation to the regulation of commerce, this overwhelming power over the states." Neither treaties nor federal laws, Justice Daniel agreed, could "arbitrarily cede away" the rights of states and their citizens. No treaty could deprive a state of its right to tax aliens entering its territory. Nor did state taxes violate the treaty with Britain, which simply allowed for "free, but regular, legitimate commercial intercourse between the people of the contracting nations, and exemption from burdens or restrictions inconsistent with such intercourse." If a treaty extended beyond this point by preventing states from taxing the property or persons of alien passengers, the national government would be exerting a power over internal affairs beyond the limits set by the Constitution. "It would be difficult," Daniel concluded, "to limit or even to imagine the mischiefs comprised in such an interpretation of the treaty stipulations above mentioned." No state had surrendered its sovereignty in this way.[43]

## State Sovereignty

The dissenters in the *Passenger Cases* feared that if Congress could control mobility to the extent claimed by the majority, southern states might lose control over the movement of free black people. Justice Daniel claimed, wildly, that British merchants would be able to bring "cargoes of negroes from Jamaica, Hayti, or Africa" to any of the states, which would lack the power "to prevent this invasion of their domestic security." Justice Taney, likewise, warned that allowing the treaty of 1815 to overrule state laws would give "the emancipated slaves of the West Indies" the right to settle throughout the southern states, "producing the most serious discontent and ultimately leading to the most painful consequences." The framers of the Constitution, Taney insisted, "were too wise and too well read in the lessons of history and of their own times" to confer such unnecessary authority. He could not imagine any power "more dangerous and full of peril to the states."[44]

For the dissenters, the obvious counterbalance to federal intrusion was the police power of the states to protect themselves by excluding persons as they saw fit. Justice Woodbury observed that police laws concerning paupers or criminals, like those imposing quarantine or banning obscene literature, destructive poisons, and liquors, were not intended to regulate commerce and should not be considered as doing so. Some states were "much exposed to large burdens and fatal diseases and moral pollution" from immigration, while others were almost exempt. Massachusetts, New York, Louisiana, and Maryland all needed to protect themselves from poor immigrants, whereas it was "a subject of indifference to a large portion of the rest of the Union not much resorted to from abroad." State laws protecting against the threat of immigration, unlike "duties, or imposts, or taxes on tonnage," were a noncommercial form of legislation and did not require a uniform rule applied by the federal government. These laws were a matter of self-defense.[45]

The purpose New York's immigration law, Taney explained, was to protect its citizens from contagious diseases and foreign paupers. If this law was deemed invalid as a regulation of commerce, how could the state protect itself from pestilence and pauperism? Each state had the sovereign right to protect its residents from sick and poor foreigners, and it must have the means to do so; poverty and disease, as subjects of local police rather than commerce, did not lie within the power granted to Congress. States not only had the right to protect their citizens, Taney insisted, they also had a duty. When there were rumors of cholera in European ports, for example, New York was obliged to place vessels and passengers in quarantine. Likewise, states had the power and the obligation to tax passengers to raise revenue for their upkeep. Thousands were arriving daily "in the great commercial emporium of New York," many of them carrying infectious diseases. Providing for them required a hospital with suitable grounds, staff, and supplies. Thousands more were indigent or infirm, and the Marine Hospital looked after them too. Poor and sick immigrants must pay for their own upkeep, Taney continued, and it was only equitable that they pay taxes for this purpose. The New York law, he reiterated, expressly secured to captains who landed such passengers and paid a tax, the right to recover the cost from the passengers. Without these taxes, Taney warned, the states could not support "the immense mass of poverty and helplessness which is now pressing so heavily upon property in Europe, and which it is endeavoring to throw off."[46]

New York's immigration policy, for Taney, was a model of local sovereignty and efficiency. It benefited the passengers, the captain, and the people of the city alike. Raising funds by a passenger tax to support a hospital where the city took care of sick and poor immigrants, he found, was much better suited to "the free, speedy, and extended intercourse of modern times" than the harsh quarantine methods that prevailed before the birth of the modern passenger trade. Those who denied the constitutionality of state immigration laws, Taney insisted, must point to another policy consistent with the rights and safety of the states, the interests of commerce, and "the obligations of humanity." This matter must be left to local discretion, as making the health and lives of the citizens of each state "altogether dependent upon the protection of the federal government" would deny the states the sovereign powers affirmed by the Court in *Gibbons v. Ogden* and *Brown v. Maryland*.[47]

Justice Woodbury, who served on the First Circuit Court in Boston, made a similar argument in the *Norris* case. The section of the Massachusetts act requiring an indemnity for the support of "lunatics, idiots, and infirm persons" required no discussion, he found, as it was an exercise of the acknowledged power of the states to defend themselves against "the ruinous burdens that would otherwise be flung upon them." Woodbury also found Massachusetts's two-dollar tax on all other alien passengers justified as a legitimate exercise of its power to determine who should be admitted and to raise funds for the support of foreign paupers. Like Taney, Woodbury contended that the impulse to provide for these paupers sprang from humanitarian motives. Rather than whipping the immigrant poor or driving them back to their places of settlement, the state treated them with kindness, relieved their distress, and housed them when necessary. It seemed only reasonable to Woodbury that captains or shipowners who profited from transporting passengers should pay a tax on arrival, to indemnify against expenses for their relief. Intended neither as a regulation of commerce nor as a source of general revenue, the tax was transferred to the state treasury with the sole purpose of supporting the poor. The cholera outbreak of the previous year, Woodbury noted, provided "a strong illustration that the terms required are neither excessive nor inappropriate." In *Prigg v. Pennsylvania* (1842), the Court had affirmed a state's right to exclude paupers as a police measure, and Woodbury found the "milder measure" of a passenger tax even more justifiable. It was a matter of "state rights," which did "not conflict with any constitutional provision."[48]

The power to control borders applied not just to immigrants but also to native-born paupers and to free black people (some of them classified as paupers) moving between the states. If regulating these groups did not conflict with the federal commerce power, the dissenters insisted, then neither did regulating immigrant admissions. Just as Mississippi and Ohio could prohibit or tax enslaved black people moving across state lines, Massachusetts and New York could regulate and tax passengers coming from foreign ports. Several state constitutions enabled their legislatures to control or prohibit entry by free black people or to prevent traders from bringing in enslaved persons as merchandise. If the Court deemed state immigration laws unconstitutional, it could also invalidate laws prohibiting the entry of free and enslaved African Americans. "These affairs," Woodbury wrote, "are a part of the domestic economy of states, belong to their interior policy, and operate on matters affecting the fireside, the hearth, and the altar."[49]

The main constitutional question at stake in the *Passenger Cases* was who controlled admission into the states. The justices in the majority, Roger Taney noted, believed that Congress had "the power to compel the several states to receive and suffer to remain in association with its citizens every person or class of persons whom it may be the policy or pleasure of the United States to admit." But the states had reserved the power to admit and expel persons they deemed dangerous to the public welfare. Any treaty or federal law authorizing the admission of persons against the consent of a state, therefore, "would be an usurpation of power which this Court could neither recognize nor enforce." If a state had the power to expel people, it could "meet them at the threshold and prevent them from entering." Neatly turning the tables on Justice McLean's formulation that "the question is one of power, and not of policy," Taney insisted that the states had the power to protect themselves against aliens and could do so by adopting whatever policies they saw fit. It was a question of "sovereignty" and "self-preservation." Justice Woodbury, citing the Court's decisions in *Prigg* and *Miln*, pointed out that "this power of excluding emigrants exists in all states which are sovereign." The word "emigrants," he explained, might include voluntary migrants, refugees, exiles, slaves, convicts, revolutionaries, people carrying infectious diseases, and paupers. No state could be compelled to admit such people.[50]

Proponents of state sovereignty invoked the principles of international law, particularly those enunciated by Swiss theorist Emer de Vattel, to support their arguments. The Massachusetts law, Woodbury concluded, is "not so unreasonable, and finds vindication in the principles of public law the world over." He quoted Vattel that "since the lord of the territory may, whenever he thinks proper, forbid its being entered, he has, no doubt, a power to annex what conditions he pleases to the permission to enter." Vattel had acknowledged that exclusionary laws could become dangerous "in excited times . . . if perverted to illegitimate purposes." But Woodbury maintained that it was "essential to sovereignty to be able to prescribe the conditions or terms on which aliens or their property shall be allowed to remain under its protection, and enjoy its municipal privileges." Congress could restrain a state's power to admit and exclude only to the extent that the state had surrendered such power to the federal government. The states had chosen to retain this power, however, and they could therefore exclude aliens, convicts, paupers, "or, what is still more common in America, in free states as well as slave states, exclude colored emigrants, though free."[51]

In the Alien Friends Act of 1798, Woodbury recalled, the federal government had tried to expel immigrants during peacetime. Critics denounced this act as unconstitutional on the grounds that "if such a power existed at all, it was in the states, and not in the general government, unless under the war power, and then against alien enemies alone." The only other federal measure that regulated admissions was the 1803 act prohibiting the introduction of slaves or free black persons into states that had already outlawed their admission. This act, however, explicitly recognized the power of the states to control admissions, thereby supporting rather than challenging that power. The act prohibiting the external slave trade from January 1, 1808, onward, meanwhile, "was aimed solely at the foreign slave trade," Woodbury wrote, and it had no bearing on free immigration or "the domestic slave trade, either before or since 1808."[52]

The states, then, retained control over the admission or expulsion of undesirable aliens. If they surrendered this power, Woodbury warned, local authorities in Europe would proceed to "inundate them with actual convicts and paupers, however mitigated the evil may be at times by the voluntary immigration . . . of many of the enterprising, industrious, and talented." Granted, the states could not carry their immigration policies so far as to "exclude rival artisans, or laborers, or to shut out all foreigners, though persecuted and unfortunate, from mere naked prejudice." This course of action "would be open to much just criticism." Yet, because the power to admit and exclude existed "absolutely in a state," it was up to each state to set the conditions—whether for economic reasons, such as the danger of pauperism, or for reasons related to public health, safety, or morality.[53]

The dissenting justices concluded with a warning that the majority decision would open the way to tyranny. For Justice Daniel, the majority trampled down "some of the strongest defenses of the safety and independence of the states of this confederacy." He expressed his alarm "at the approach of power claimed to be uncontrollable and unlimited." The assertion that the states needed permission from the national government to admit or expel aliens denied their sovereignty, yielding to the federal government a power incompatible with its status as "the creature of the states." The states had delegated no power over the admission of aliens to Congress, and any attempt to claim such a power could only result in "jealousy, ill feeling, and dangerous conflict" between the states and the federal government.[54]

At stake was the balance of power in a federal republic. If national laws and treaties were allowed to take precedence over state laws, Daniel warned, "then state sovereignty, state rights, or state existence even must be less than empty names." The Constitution, supposedly based on limited and delegated federal powers, would become "a falsehood or an absurdity." Rather than comprising a set of powers delegated by the people and the states, it would become "a power transcending that which called it into existence—a power single, universal, engrossing, absolute." Everything concerning "civil or political right" would be "engulfed" in federal legislation and treaties. A government supposedly based on charter rather than monarchy, Daniel warned, was asserting not only "absolute control of civil and political rights" but also the power to regulate "the private and personal concerns of life." Federal power was being extended to cover "personal intercourse," a domain well beyond the scope of any authority based on commerce. The word "intercourse" was nowhere to be found in the Constitution, Daniel observed, yet under the majority's position, Congress could claim control over every form of intercourse "between the individuals of our own country and foreigners, and amongst the citizens of the different states." Congressional power would extend not only to the right of foreign travel, by requiring passports for that purpose, but also "the right of transit for persons and property between the different states of the Union, and the power of regulating highways and vehicles of transportation."[55]

More than anything else, the dissenting justices feared the implications of the *Passenger Cases* for the institution of slavery. In using the words "persons" and "property," Daniel was referring to slaves in their dual capacity as people and chattel. He sensed a threat not simply to state laws regulating the mobility of free black people but also to the interstate slave trade. Woodbury, like Daniel, warned that the majority decision would render the states "mute and powerless." Congress, he pointed out, had already approved at least five state constitutions that prohibited enslaved persons from being introduced for sale. If Congress had exclusive power over interstate commerce, it could compel the states to exclude or admit black people, both enslaved and free, regardless of their laws. The national government could thereby "force upon the states slaves or criminals, or political incendiaries of the most dangerous character." The *Passenger Cases*, in short, had as much to do with slavery as with foreign immigration.[56]

This explains why the proslavery justices argued that passengers were persons, whereas the antislavery justices described them as articles of commerce. To concede that passengers were commerce yielded power over mobility to Congress and threatened the right of states to regulate free black people and to operate the interstate slave trade. Despite Roger Taney's fears, the southern states retained control over the mobility of free and enslaved black people, and their authority to do so was never tested in the courts. The Fugitive Slave Act, passed the year after the *Passenger Cases*, was a major concession to slaveholders. With the failure of the Compromise of 1850, however, the United States entered a decade of political crisis.

# 4

## The Boundaries of Political Community

ON SEPTEMBER 26, 1838, Harriet and Dred Scott boarded the steamboat *Gypsey* in St. Louis, Missouri, and set out on a month-long journey. They passed through the free state of Illinois to Fort Snelling, located within the boundaries of the Louisiana Purchase, where slavery was prohibited by the Missouri Compromise. The Scotts were owned as slaves by Dr. John Emerson, a US Army surgeon, who had been assigned to Fort Snelling. Harriet Scott gave birth to the couple's first child, Eliza, in free territory north of Missouri, as the *Gypsey* was traveling up the Mississippi River. This was not Harriet and Dred Scott's first journey to Fort Snelling; they had met and married there two years earlier. In 1843, the Scotts returned to Missouri to live with Dr. Emerson's widow, Irene Sanford Emerson. They claimed to be free on the grounds that they had lived in free territory. Under Missouri law, people claiming to be unlawfully enslaved could file a charge of assault based on false imprisonment and were entitled to a state-appointed attorney. Harriet Scott filed a suit against Mrs. Emerson in the St. Louis circuit court in 1846. Dred Scott filed an identical suit. Harriet had the more compelling case, given that her owner had relinquished all interests in her when she married Dred Scott. Under the principle of matrilineal descent, the status of the Scotts' two children depended on the status of their mother. Under prevailing gender norms, however, the courts soon consolidated Harriet's case with her husband's. A clerk misspelled the name Sanford in the official transcripts, and the case became known as *Dred Scott v. Sandford*.[1]

The Scotts fought for their freedom for eleven years. They lost their case on a technicality in 1847, but the following year the Missouri Supreme Court agreed to a new trial. In 1850, a jury of twelve white men in St. Louis freed

Harriet and Dred Scott. Two years later, the Missouri Supreme Court reversed the decision. Rather than appealing, the Scotts' lawyers filed a new suit in the federal courts in 1853 against Irene Emerson's brother, John Sanford, naming him as their current owner. Because the Scotts lived in Missouri and Sanford lived in New York, the US circuit court for Missouri accepted jurisdiction based on diversity of state citizenship. Sanford's lawyer argued that Dred Scott, as a descendant of slaves brought from Africa, was not a US citizen and therefore could not sue in federal court. The US circuit court upheld Scott's right to sue but, after a trial in 1854, rejected his claim to freedom. Scott's lawyers then appealed to the US Supreme Court, which heard arguments on the case twice. In a 7 to 2 decision delivered on March 6, 1857, the Court found that Dred Scott (and by extension his family) was not free by virtue of having resided in a free territory or state and therefore had no right to sue in federal court. The Scotts, in other words, were still slaves.[2]

In a long, dogmatic, and confusing opinion, Roger Taney then set out to resolve the most divisive political question of the day: the power of Congress to control slavery in the territories. In the Supreme Court's first invalidation of a major statute, Taney held that Congress had no power to prohibit slavery in the territories. This ruling invalidated the part of the Missouri Compromise (1820) that had prohibited slavery in the Louisiana Purchase and it repudiated the central plank in the Republican Party platform. Yet the *Dred Scott* decision was no triumph for the principle of "popular sovereignty" introduced by the Kansas-Nebraska Act of 1854, which allowed people in the territories to make their own decision on slavery. Taney insisted that, as Congress had no authority to regulate slavery in the territories, it could not authorize any territorial government to do so. Republican critics of the *Dred Scott* decision claimed that Taney's comment on this point was dictum, rather than part of the Court's holding. But Taney, whose opinion was widely accepted as the decision of the Court, clearly intended to prevent any law prohibiting slavery in the territories.[3]

In addition to invalidating the Missouri Compromise, Taney issued a sweeping declaration on the ineligibility of African Americans for national citizenship. With the explicit support of two justices in the majority, and the tacit support of the others, he insisted that African Americans, even those who were free, could not be citizens of the United States. The Constitution, according to Taney, had drawn a "line of division" between "the citizen race, who formed and held the Government, and the African race, which they held in subjection and slavery and governed at their own pleasure." No person consigned to the latter group could become "a member of the political community formed and brought into existence by the Constitution of the United States, and as such become entitled to all the rights, and privileges, and immunities, guarantied by that instrument to the citizen." Native Americans, Taney acknowledged, could become citizens under certain circumstances at the discretion of Congress. Naturalization law, however, was designed for European immigrants as members of what Taney referred to as the "dominant race," which constituted the people of the United States. Throughout the antebellum era, the Court had avoided drawing a clear line between laws regulating immigrant admissions and laws regulating the movement of free black people, for fear that congressional authority over the first might entail authority over the second. In seeking to settle the slavery question in *Dred Scott*, however, Taney drew a racial line with brutal clarity, including Europeans as part of the American people and placing African Americans outside the political community altogether.[4]

## *European Immigrants*

During the 1840s and 1850s, immigration to the United States reached one of its three historical peaks. An average of 300,000 immigrants per year entered the country, mainly from Ireland, Germany, and England. The population of the United States in 1860 was only 31 million, compared to 75 million in 1900. In proportional terms, therefore, the impact of the first wave of immigration was roughly equivalent to the second great wave at the turn of the twentieth century, when about 1 million foreigners entered the country each year. The foreign-born share of the population stood at 13 percent on the eve of the Civil War, about the same as today, compared to 15 percent in the early twentieth century. The Irish were the largest immigrant group before the Civil War, accounting for one-third of all arrivals in the 1830s and almost half in the 1840s. By midcentury, one in every four New Yorkers was Irish born. Nativists saw Irish immigrants wherever they looked, especially in the cities, and they did not like what they saw. They objected to how the Irish dressed and smelled, how they spoke and drank, and how they worshipped and voted. Underlying these sentiments was alarm over the immigrants' poverty, reflected in a series of petitions to Congress from states and cities in the Northeast. Given that Congress was extremely unlikely to regulate immigration, the main purpose of these petitions seems to have been to justify local actions by exerting pressure on the federal government.[5]

The petitions to Congress emerged with the onset of mass immigration by Irish Catholics, many of them desperately poor. On May 2, 1836, the Senate

Committee on Commerce considered a resolution from the Massachusetts legislature instructing its senators and representatives in Congress "to use their endeavors to obtain the passage of a law to prevent the introduction of foreign paupers into our country." The Senate responded by passing a resolution requesting information from the secretary of the treasury, who sent circulars to consuls and commercial agents in Europe, most of whom denied any knowledge of pauper emigrants or schemes to assist their departure. The Senate received the report from the Treasury Department in December 1836 but took no action. A petition from the inhabitants of Sullivan County, New York, the same year, protesting Catholic immigration was referred to the House Committee on the Judiciary, which commented that although Congress could not refuse admission to immigrants, it might consider revising the naturalization laws. Petitions demanding that Congress control the transportation of convicts and paupers to the United States or extend the waiting period for naturalization continued to arrive in Washington in the late 1830s as Irish immigration intensified but produced no legislative response.[6]

Congress conducted its first investigation into immigration in 1838, when the House adopted a resolution calling on the secretary of state to supply information on foreign paupers and other undesirable immigrants. A select committee sent a series of questions to the mayors of Boston and New York City, to the inhabitants of several other towns in Massachusetts and New York, and to an anti-immigrant organization called the Native American Association, in Washington, DC. This association submitted an unusually detailed petition calling for repeal or revision of the naturalization laws and the introduction of a system whereby US consuls would issue passports abroad, at a fee of twenty dollars each, certifying that prospective emigrants were not criminals or paupers. The select committee submitted a report accompanied by two bills, proposing fines for captains who transported foreign paupers or criminals and an extension of the waiting period for naturalization. Congress, however, took no action.[7]

Another wave of petitions demanding revision of the naturalization laws arrived in Congress in the mid-1840s. Many of them came from Philadelphia, where nativist mobs attacked Irish immigrants in the Kensington riots of 1844. Again, Congress did not act. On December 17, 1845, the House received a resolution from the Massachusetts legislature calling for immediate revision of the naturalization laws, which the Committee on the Judiciary firmly rejected. Congress reacted unfavorably to all requests to revise immigration or naturalization laws in this period, especially those from Massachusetts, where intense hostility to slavery coexisted with intense hostility to Irish immigrants. As the leading center of nativism as well as abolitionism, Massachusetts passed deportation laws to remove alien paupers alongside personal liberty laws to resist the return of fugitive slaves.[8]

With Congress playing no role in regulating immigrant admissions, New York and Massachusetts developed new apparatuses to manage the massive influx during the Irish famine. New York created a Board of Commissioners of Emigration in 1847, moving control over admissions from the municipal to the state level. The governor appointed this board, with the presidents of the city's Irish and German emigrant societies serving *ex officio*. The commissioners were authorized to board ships and conduct inspections. They also offered advice on housing, employment, and transportation once passengers had landed. Not until 1855—in an event of decisive importance for future immigrants but too late for the famine Irish—did New York open Castle Garden as its "Emigrant Landing Depot" and the home of the Commissioners of Emigration. Located on landfill at the southern tip of

FIGURE 4.1  "Riot in Philadelphia July 7, 1844." In May 1844, crowds of Irish Catholic immigrant workers and native-born Protestant workers battled each other for four days in Kensington, a manufacturing suburb of Philadelphia, in the worst nativist riot of the antebellum era. Protestant rioters burned down several private dwellings; a Catholic seminary; and two Catholic churches, St. Michael's and St. Augustine's. Riots erupted again in July in Southwark, just south of the city, as nativists—depicted here as gentlemen in top hats and coats—attacked Irish Catholics and the militiamen attempting to protect them, culminating in an attack on a third church, St. Philip de Neri (the building at top right with the inscription "I.H.S. A.D., 1840"). Lithograph by H. Bucholzer, 1844. Reproduced with permission from the Historical Society of Pennsylvania.

Manhattan, this facility processed as many as 8 million immigrants between 1855 and 1890 before being replaced by the federal clearing center on Ellis Island. Massachusetts, meanwhile, administered immigration through the Superintendent of Alien Passengers, appointed by the governor, until 1851, when it created the Commissioners of Alien Passengers and Foreign Paupers (popularly known as the Alien Commissioners) on the New York model.[9]

In January 1855, Mayor Fernando Wood of New York City wrote to President Franklin Pierce about the problem of immigration in his city. The port of New York, Wood claimed, had become "a sort of penal colony for felons and paupers" transported by European nations. Every community, he insisted, had an "inherent right to protect itself from dangers arising from such immigration." Wood requested the "interference of the general government" in combating these dangers. Just as it was "the duty of government to protect us from foreign aggression with ball and cannon," he declared, "it surely must also be within the scope of its duty to protect an enemy more insidious and destructive, though coming in another form." Far from calling on the federal government to wrest control over immigration from the states, however, Wood was seeking funding and political support for existing state efforts. As a leading Democratic politician and a product of Tammany Hall, he depended on immigrant support.[10]

Anti-immigrant nativists, by contrast, wanted the naturalization laws revised because they knew most Irish immigrants would vote for Wood's Democratic Party. The Democrats were one of the few national institutions that welcomed all immigrants, including the Irish. From 1840 through 1856, the party pledged in its national platform to support "the liberal principles embodied by Jefferson in the Declaration of Independence, and sanctioned in the constitution, which makes ours the land of liberty, and the asylum of the oppressed of every nation" and declared that any "attempt to abridge the present privilege of becoming citizens, and the owners of soil among us, ought to be resisted with the same spirit which swept the alien and sedition laws from our statute-books." Whereas the Whigs, and later the Know-Nothings and to a lesser extent the Republicans, were associated with nativism, the Democrats assiduously courted the Irish vote.[11]

Deciding who can vote is a fundamental power of any sovereign government. Suffrage and citizenship are interconnected, yet the connections are neither self-evident nor static. Just as citizenship remained undefined in the antebellum era and varied by state, so too did the criteria for exercising the vote. Article I, Section 2 of the Constitution left the eligibility requirements for voting at the discretion of the states: "The House of Representatives shall be composed of Members chosen every second Year by the People of the several States, and the Electors in each State shall have the Qualifications requisite for Electors of the most numerous Branch of the State Legislature." In effect, this provision disenfranchised women and most black men. Article I, Section 4 gave Congress a potential veto power over the states, specifying, "The Times, Places and Manner of holding Elections for Senators and Representatives, shall be prescribed in each State by the Legislature thereof; but the Congress may at any time by Law make or alter such Regulations, except as to the Places of chusing Senators." Before the Fifteenth Amendment in 1870, however, Congress did not seek to redress state limitations on voting.[12]

Several state constitutions in the antebellum era required that voters be citizens, while others conferred the right to vote on "inhabitants." Extending suffrage was a way for sparsely populated territories and states to attract settlers. For this reason, the Northwest Ordinance of 1787 enfranchised foreign-born men who had not yet naturalized. Male aliens could vote during the passage from territory to statehood in Ohio (1803), Indiana (1816), Illinois (1818), and Michigan (1837). Allowing foreigners to vote—or, more accurately, allowing unnaturalized European men to do so—reinforced the idea that suffrage was based on distinctions of race and gender. Foreign birth or allegiance was no impediment to voting if a man was white.[13]

Most of the eastern seaboard states, in contrast to the Midwest, took measures to limit the vote between 1800 and 1830 even as they extended it to white male citizens. The abolition of property qualifications led to universal suffrage for native-born white men, but, in tandem with this expansion, many free black men lost the right to vote. White women could vote, if at all, only on local matters. States in the Northeast replaced the word "inhabitant" with "citizen" in their voting requirements, limiting suffrage to native-born or naturalized residents. They also excluded paupers, vagrants, transients, and felons from voting, while introducing registration laws to screen out ineligible voters. Officials who registered voters by visiting households often overlooked the poor and foreign born, in part because middle-class dwellings were easier to identify, but also intentionally at times. Like the eastern seaboard states, most of the states that joined the Union between 1800 and 1830 also conferred the right to vote exclusively on citizens, with the exception of Illinois, which permitted aliens to vote until 1848.[14]

Even as eastern and midwestern states restricted suffrage, states and territories in the interior extended the vote to white foreigners. Wisconsin entered the Union in 1848 with a new system that gave the vote to "declarant aliens" who had lived in the United States for two years and filed their intent to naturalize. Taking out "first papers" did not deprive alien immigrants of their existing nationality nor require them to complete the naturalization process or swear an oath of allegiance to the United States. But it did qualify them to vote. Between 1848 and 1859, Minnesota, Michigan, Indiana, and Oregon, along with the territories of Kansas and Washington, followed the Wisconsin model. All were thinly populated, primarily agricultural, and eager to attract settlers. Congress authorized pre-citizen voting in most territories organized in the 1840s and 1850s (though not in Utah, New Mexico, and California, acquired via the Mexican American War). During the debates over the Kansas-Nebraska Act in 1854, Senator John Middleton Clayton, Whig of Delaware, presented a motion to exclude declarant aliens from voting in territorial elections or holding office, for fear that they would oppose the extension of slavery. The Senate narrowly approved the amendment, with all southern senators voting in favor. The northern-dominated House, however, omitted the amendment and the act eventually passed without it.[15]

The Kansas-Nebraska Act threw the political party system into crisis. Overriding the Missouri Compromise, which had outlawed slavery in most of the Louisiana Purchase, this act allowed residents of unorganized territories to decide whether or not slavery should exist, by the principle of popular sovereignty. The already disintegrating Whig Party went into terminal decline, and, for a while, it looked as though a new coalition known as the American Party (or "Know-Nothings") might become the main opposition to the Democrats. The Know-Nothings rose to prominence in the North as a reform movement opposing the expansion of slavery and supporting public schools, mechanics' lien laws (a way of guaranteeing payment to craftsmen), and property rights for married women. They were hostile to immigrants, especially Irish Catholics, and called for a federal law mandating a twenty-one-year waiting period for naturalization or, failing that, an equally lengthy postnaturalization residence period before voting. Between 1854 and 1856, Know-Nothing politicians controlled the legislative branches in six states and won gubernatorial elections in nine. They were strongest in states with sizeable immigrant populations, especially Massachusetts, where the Irish-born percentage of the population was highest and nativist sentiment most severe.[16]

With the rise of political nativism, the possibility of congressional control over immigration resurfaced in the form of renewed calls to legislate against the transportation of paupers and criminals into the United States. On January 25, 1855, James Cooper, Whig of Pennsylvania, introduced resolutions in the Senate calling on the secretaries of state and treasury to furnish information on the transportation of foreign convicts and paupers into the United States by European governments and asking the Committee on the Judiciary to consider appropriate legislation. "We have our quarantine laws to protect us against the introduction of small pox, cholera, and other kinds of pestilence; and these laws we enforce to the detriment of commerce," Cooper declared. "But hitherto we have neglected to guard ourselves against a more destructive pestilence than the small-pox or cholera." America had closed its ports against contagious disease, but not against "the more fatal contagion" of pauperism and crime. "We dread fever and the plague, and endeavor to exclude them," Cooper concluded, with a quote from Psalm 91:16, "while 'the pestilence which walketh in darkness and blighteth at mid-day,' has been suffered to enter without let or hindrance."[17]

Cooper's Democratic counterpart from Pennsylvania, Richard Brodhead, demanded to know what practical measures Cooper had in mind. What kind of bill, Broadhead asked, "could comply with the Constitution and not interfere with State sovereignty?" The states, after all, controlled immigrant admissions; Congress had the power only to establish a rule for naturalization. It could pass no bill that "would not conflict with State authority, State rights, and State jurisdiction." Despite Brodhead's objections, the Senate proceeded to pass a bill designed to prevent the assisted immigration of foreign criminals and paupers. The House Committee on Commerce considered this bill and agreed to move it forward but, as with all previous proposals, no further action was taken.[18]

On March 4, 1856, William Russell Smith, Democrat of Alabama, introduced another bill in the House. This measure, like all the others, failed to pass, but it was significant in that it prefigured a law passed by Congress in 1862 prohibiting American involvement in the transportation of Chinese laborers known as "coolies." Smith's bill, much like the 1862 act, would have required US consuls abroad to grant certificates stating the name, birthplace, age, and place of residence of prospective immigrants, confirming that they were not paupers or convicts and had not been sent involuntarily to the United States. Captains who transported emigrants without certificates would be subject to fines or imprisonment, and vessels that carried twenty or more such aliens would be forfeited to the United States. No such measure against immigrants, however, could pass in Congress before the Civil War.[19]

The Committee on Foreign Affairs issued a report on August 16, 1856, providing abundant documentation on criminals and paupers, along with some reflections on how Congress ought to proceed. "Our duty is a plain one," the report stated. "Let us manfully and faithfully perform it." But how could immigration be restricted? To the critical question, "Has Congress power over immigration?," the report could only answer that the national legislature had some kind of power, up to a point. It was "the inherent right of every community to protect itself against all public evils," including convicts and paupers sent by foreign governments. "The power exists somewhere," the report noted, "either in the States, or in the general government, or in both of them." To the extent that Congress possessed this power, it was provided by the migration or importation clause. Yet this clause, the report conceded, was "generally understood" at the time of its adoption "as applying altogether to slaves." As evidence that the clause provided authority over free immigration as well, the report cited sporadic references from the Constitutional Convention and the ratification debates, along with the arguments of John Marshall and William Johnson in *Gibbons v. Ogden* (1824) and William McKinley and James Wayne in the *Passenger Cases* (1849). This was hardly a strong argument.[20]

Ultimately, the committee had no choice but to acknowledge that the "internal police power" of the states enabled them "to exclude entire classes of persons" whenever they deemed it necessary. This power, as recognized by Justice Philip Pendleton Barbour in *New York v. Miln* (1837) and Justice Joseph Story in *Prigg v. Pennsylvania* (1842), was "complete, unqualified and conclusive." The only question was how far it could be exercised without coming into conflict with Congress's power over commerce. "This is a question not definitely or clearly settled," the report noted with considerable understatement, "for it involves unfortunately a principle in relation to which a difference of opinion has existed, and still exists, among the judges of the Supreme Court." Until the question was resolved, each level of government should exercise its authority "within its own sphere and the limits of its constitutional power." Sovereignty over immigration, in other words, remained divided.[21]

In this context, the states continued to pass their own laws regulating admissions and the post-entry rights of immigrants. In 1857, the Massachusetts legislature passed a literacy act requiring voters to demonstrate their ability to write their own names and read the Constitution, with a grandfather clause exempting citizens over sixty who had previously voted. The same year, the state legislature approved a fourteen-year waiting period before naturalized citizens could vote, but this measure failed to become law because any amendment to the state constitution had to be approved by a two-thirds' majority in two successive legislatures. In 1859, Massachusetts Republicans joined the Know-Nothings in passing an amendment imposing a two-year waiting period. Abraham Lincoln condemned this measure in a letter to the German-American leader Dr. Theodore Canisius of Springfield, Illinois. "Massachusetts," Lincoln wrote, "is a sovereign and independent state; and it is no privilege of mine to scold her for what she does." But he would oppose its adoption in Illinois, or in any other place, where he had a right to oppose it. "Understanding the spirit of our institutions to aim at the elevation of men, I am opposed to whatever tends to degrade them," Lincoln told Canisius. "I have some little notoriety for commiserating the oppressed condition of the negro; and I should be strangely inconsistent if I could favor any project for curtailing the existing rights of white men, even though born in different lands, and speaking different languages from myself." Canisius published this letter in his *Illinois Staats-Anzeiger* and the *Illinois State Journal* on May 18, 1859. The Massachusetts electorate proceeded to ratify the two-year waiting period by a large majority. Radical Republicans repealed the law during the Civil War, but literacy tests for voting remained in place in Massachusetts and Connecticut.[22]

Like many national institutions, the Know-Nothing Party was eventually torn asunder by slavery, the dominant political question of the day. Northern nativists saw Irish immigrants as agents not only of popery but also of what contemporaries called the Slave Power. Irish Americans voted for the Democratic Party, and their church—of which Roger Taney was a prominent member—took a conservative position on slavery. The idea of a Catholic plot against American liberties was grist to the mill of antislavery nativists, but southern Know-Nothings defended the institution of slavery. The Know-Nothing Party could not hold its proslavery and antislavery wings together. Running on a stridently nationalist anti-immigrant platform in 1856, Millard Filmore placed a distant third in the presidential election. The new Republican Party placed second to the victorious Democrats, who consolidated their position as the party of immigrants and slaveholders. The following year, in the notorious case of *Dred Scott v. Sandford*, supporters of slavery celebrated what appeared to be their greatest victory.[23]

## *The* Dred Scott *Case*

In *Dred Scott v. Sandford*, Roger Taney tried to settle the two biggest constitutional questions raised by slavery: whether Congress could prohibit the institution in the territories, and whether African Americans could be citizens of the United States. Under the Missouri Compromise, people who brought slaves into the Louisiana Territory north of the 36° 30' parallel were violating the law. The Kansas-Nebraska Act of 1854 overrode the Missouri Compromise line in the name of popular sovereignty, and in *Dred Scott* the Court invalidated the legislation passed in 1820 prohibiting slavery in the relevant territories. Taney ruled, implausibly, that the section of the Constitution granting Congress broad powers over the territories applied only to lands held or controlled in 1789. Congress, he claimed, therefore had no general power to prohibit the introduction of slavery into the territories. Nor, contrary to Stephen A. Douglas's notion of popular sovereignty, did any territorial government have the power to prohibit slavery.[24]

Congress had the power and the obligation to protect property rights, including property in slaves, Taney ruled, but it could not subvert those rights by preventing enslavers from carrying their property into the territories. Under the Constitution, Taney insisted, the federal government's sole power concerning slavery was "the power coupled with the duty of guarding and protecting the owner in his rights." Justice Peter Daniel, a vociferous supporter of slavery, went even further. The "only private property which the Constitution has specifically recognised, and has imposed it as a direct obligation both on the States and the Federal Government to protect and enforce," Daniel wrote, "is the property of the master in his slave." No other form of property, he claimed, was "placed by the Constitution upon the same high ground, nor shielded by a similar guaranty." Prohibiting slavery in a territory, Taney suggested, violated the Fifth Amendment's protection against the deprivation of property without due process of law. He did not, however, pause to discuss whether a law prohibiting slavery in a territory necessarily entailed, in itself, a loss of property.[25]

Taney also held that African Americans could not be citizens of the United States because the Constitution did not intend them to be so. In seeking to establish the boundaries of the American political community, he used citizenship as the dividing line between those who belonged and those who did not. "The words 'people of the United States' and 'citizens,'" Taney wrote, "are synonymous terms." Both words described "the political body who, according to our republican institutions, form the sovereignty and who hold the power and conduct the Government through their representatives." Every citizen of the United States was "one of this people, and a constituent member of this sovereignty." The question for Taney was whether African Americans belonged to the political community. He concluded that "they are not included, and were not intended to be included, under the word 'citizens' in the Constitution." When the Constitution was ratified, Taney claimed, Africans slaves and their descendants were "considered as a subordinate and inferior class of beings

FIGURE 4.2 "Dred and Harriet Scott." In *Dred Scott v. Sandford* (1857), the Supreme Court ruled that Congress lacked the power to exclude slavery from the territories, that Congress was obliged to protect the property rights of slaveowners, and that African Americans—free as well as enslaved—were not citizens of the United States, as the framers of the Constitution had not intended them to be so. Engraving, 1887. Library of Congress Prints and Photographs Division, LC-DIG-ds-12470.

who had been subjugated by the dominant race, and, whether emancipated or not, yet remained subject to their authority, and had no rights or privileges but such as those who held the power and the Government might choose to grant them." They could never be citizens of the United States, even if they were born free and considered citizens of the states in which they lived. Dred Scott, Taney concluded, had no rights or privileges under the Constitution and was not entitled to take a suit in federal court.[26]

Throughout his opinion, Taney always qualified the phrase "African race" with the words "imported into this country and sold and held as slaves." Strictly speaking, this formulation suggested that he did not reject citizenship for all people of African origin, only those who were enslaved or descended from slaves. Under the Constitution, Taney acknowledged, Congress could "authorize the naturalization of anyone, of any color, who was born under allegiance to another Government." In raising this point, however, his purpose was to emphasize that Congress chose not to extend naturalization to black people in the 1790 Naturalization Act. Taney cited this law as proof that "citizenship at that time was perfectly understood to be confined to the white race; and that they alone constituted the sovereignty in the Government."[27]

The most chilling dimension of Taney's opinion was his insistence that the stain of exclusion passed down through the generations, even to the minority of African Americans who were free. If a black person or their ancestor had once been a slave, Taney held, noncitizen status was permanent, and emancipation could not alter that fact. Although a state could confer local citizenship on any person, no person of African origin whose ancestor had been brought to the present-day United States as a slave could be a national citizen in the sense intended by the Constitution. African Americans, by this logic, were not part of the political community of the United States and they never could be. Taney had made much the same argument twenty-five years earlier in his opinion as attorney general on South Carolina's Seamen Acts. In that opinion, as in the *Dred Scott* case, he sought to place all black people—free and enslaved—outside the Constitution, which extended protections not just to citizens but also to persons. Doing so placed black people, free and enslaved, firmly under the control of the states, denying them the right to enjoy the privileges and immunities of citizens when they traveled. The reasoning here was strikingly illogical: the founding generation, according to Taney, intended to exclude all black people from citizenship; all enslaved people were black; therefore all black people were excluded from citizenship in perpetuity. But racism does not derive its force from logic.[28]

Taney rested his opinion on an extreme theory of original intent. He merged two kinds of originalism to make claims both about the intentions of the Constitution's framers and the common public understanding of the text at the time of ratification. The only parts of the Constitution referring to African Americans, Taney wrote, treated them as "persons who could morally and lawfully be held as property and as slaves." The framers had never intended slaves or their descendants to be citizens, he contended, and no "change in public opinion toward the African race since the adoption of the Constitution" could alter that. The Constitution must be construed in line with its original meaning. However unfair this interpretation might appear, Taney piously declared, there was nothing the justices could do about it, as they were bound by the intentions of the framers. The Court's duty was not to decide if the Constitution as written was just or unjust but to determine its original intent and interpret legislation accordingly. If the people of the United States found the Constitution unjust, the document contained provisions for how it could be amended. But "while it remains unaltered, it must be construed now as it was understood at the time of its adoption." Taney had no doubt about the correct construction: the Constitution, the laws of Congress, and the acts of the executive branch made it quite clear who was, and who could be, a citizen of the United States. African Americans were not included. Given that the founding charter of the republic protected slavery, and most Americans in 1789 did not regard free black people as citizens, Taney's opinion did not necessarily amount to a radical misreading of the Constitution. He distorted the facts of the past by claiming that no African Americans were citizens when the Constitution was ratified. Yet his arguments on citizenship reflected the majority sentiment in 1789, as well as the views of the governing Democratic coalition in 1857. Abolitionists and others disagreed with Taney on the citizenship question, and antislavery Republicans disagreed with him on congressional power over slavery in the territories, but the full force of his position in *Dred Scott* lay in how many Americans agreed with it, not how few.[29]

At the time of the American Revolution and the Constitution, Taney claimed, neither enslaved people nor their descendants—even those who had been freed—were acknowledged as part of the people of the United States. In this claim he was factually wrong. As Justice Curtis pointed out in dissent, some African Americans were citizens in 1789, and they were among the people who voted to ratify the Constitution. The main point of Taney's exaggerated claim, however, was that at the time of ratification, and for more than a century since, African Americans had "been regarded as beings of an inferior order, and altogether unfit to associate with the white race either in social or political relations." On this point, he expressed the racist sentiment of countless Americans at the time and earlier. In the colonial era, Taney wrote, black people were seen as "so far inferior that they had no rights which the white man was bound to respect." African slaves were bought and sold as articles of merchandise. Colonial laws to that effect demonstrated that "a perpetual and impassable barrier was intended to be erected between the white race and the one which they had reduced to slavery, and governed as subjects with absolute and despotic power." These laws made no distinction "between the free negro or mulatto and the slave." Rather, a "stigma of the deepest degradation was fixed upon the whole race."[30]

Taney found the language of the Declaration of Independence conclusive on this point. The equality and universal rights it proclaimed may have appeared to embrace all men, yet it was "too clear for dispute that the enslaved African race were not intended to be included, and formed no part of the people who framed and adopted this declaration." The men who wrote the Declaration understood the meaning of the words they used; they knew that their language did not "embrace the negro race, which, by common consent, had been excluded from civilized Governments and the family of nations, and doomed to slavery." Acting on "established doctrines and principles," they used "the ordinary language of the day, and no one misunderstood them." The "unhappy black race," Taney claimed, "were never thought of or spoken of except as property." Northern states emancipated their slaves after the Revolution, not out of any change of opinion but merely because slave labor was unsuited to their economies.[31]

The Constitution, for Taney, embodied the same principles as the Declaration of Independence. It referred to the people of the United States and the "citizens of the several States," without defining which kinds of persons were included under these terms. The meaning of the words "people" and "citizen," he claimed, were so well understood that no description or definition was necessary. The fugitive slave clause and the migration or importation clause pointed "directly and specifically to the negro race as a separate class of persons" who were not regarded as citizens of the United States. To Taney, African Americans were not part of the "people" who formed the Constitution nor of the "posterity" to whom it was dedicated. The Constitution, he noted, did not state that naturalization should be restricted to white people. Congress could have chosen to extend citizenship to all foreigners, yet the naturalization law of 1790 confined the privilege to free white persons. This language, for Taney, demonstrated how citizenship at that time was confined to "the white race," who constituted the people of the United States.[32]

Taney several times tried to clarify the murky distinction between state and national citizenship. States retained the right to confer citizenship on whomever they wished—including immigrant aliens or free black people— but only Congress had the power to confer national citizenship. Neither the states nor the federal government could bestow citizenship on people the framers intended to exclude from the "new political family" created by the Constitution. Dred Scott could not become a citizen of the United States, therefore, even if the state of Missouri declared him free and a citizen of that state. The southern slaveholding states, Taney insisted, would never have agreed to a Constitution that compelled them to receive black people from other states as citizens. If such visitors were entitled to the privileges and immunities of national citizens, he explained, they would be exempt "from the operation of the special laws and from the police regulations" of the southern states. They would be able to enter any state "without pass or passport, and without obstruction, to sojourn there as long as they pleased, to go where they pleased at every hour of the day or night without molestation, unless they committed some violation of law for which a white man would be punished." They would enjoy freedom of speech, could hold public meetings on political affairs, and could keep and carry arms. Just as in his opinion on South Carolina's Seamen Acts in 1832, Taney denied that any state could be forced to extend to black visitors any rights or privileges it denied to its own free black population.[33]

One potential mark of national citizenship, Taney noted, was possession of a US passport. Governments in nineteenth-century Europe introduced passports to regulate internal travel, using standardized documents to establish the bearer's personal and legal identity. The United States did not require registration or identification for internal purposes, though individual states policed the movement of African Americans with slave passes, free papers, and registration certificates. Persons entering or leaving the United States did not require passports before World War I, except briefly during the Civil War. The federal government provided passports for Americans traveling abroad, but not until 1856 did Congress give the State Department sole authority to issue these documents. Before that, local officials handled passport applications. Black activists in the North, seeing an opportunity to assert their citizenship, insisted that they were entitled to passports because, as citizens of their states, they were citizens of the United States. The federal government denied passports to free black people, however, on the grounds that their state citizenship was limited at best. Instead the government issued special certificates merely confirming that the bearers were American travelers. Taney cited this policy in *Dred Scott* to support his argument denying citizenship to African Americans.[34]

To reinforce this argument, Taney compared and contrasted Native American and African American history. Native Americans, he held, "were yet a free and independent people, associated together in nations or tribes, and governed by their own laws." These nations, he noted, "were regarded and treated as foreign Governments, as much so as if an ocean had separated the red man from the white." Governments in the colonial and national periods had repeatedly acknowledged this fact by making treaties with them. If a Native American left his tribe or nation and took up residence among the white population, Taney wrote, "he would be entitled to all the rights and privileges which would belong to an emigrant from any other foreign people." In this respect, Native Americans were "like the subjects of any other foreign Government." As citizens of their own nations, Native Americans—much like European immigrants—could cast off their allegiance and be naturalized as citizens of the United States. Their status stood in sharp contrast to Americans of African origin, who, Taney insisted, could never become citizens.[35]

In making this argument, Taney drew on precedents concerning the Cherokees in particular. In a letter to former Secretary of State Albert Gallatin in 1826, the Cherokee leader John Ridge captured the relationship between his nation and the United States: "Within the orbit of the U. States move the States & within these we move in a little circle, dependent on the great center." Just as Ridge feared, however, when the state of Georgia sought to extinguish the Cherokees' sovereignty, the "great center" did not protect them. Far from recognizing that the Constitution placed authority over Native affairs in the federal government, President Andrew Jackson rejected Cherokee autonomy as a violation of Georgia's sovereignty. He called on Native Americans to move west, warning that they were doomed to "weakness and decay" if they refused. Removal to the interior, Jackson claimed in his second State of the Union address in 1830, would "by a fair exchange, and, at the expense of the United States . . . send them to a land where their existence may be prolonged and perhaps made perpetual." Such were the euphemisms contemporaries used to describe the federally supported expulsion of Native Americans in the antebellum era.[36]

The Indian Removal Act of 1830 led to the expulsion of more than 80,000 Native Americans from the Southeast. Deceptively titled "an act to provide for the exchange of lands," this law authorized the president to make territory west of the Mississippi available "for the reception of such tribes or nations of Indians as may choose to exchange the lands where they now reside, and move there." Chief Justice John Marshall intervened in the case of *Worcester v. Georgia* (1832) to explain that Native Americans belonged to "domestic dependent nations" subject to the jurisdiction of the national government but not the individual states. They had always been considered "distinct, independent political communities, retaining their original natural rights, as the undisputed possessors of the soil, from time immemorial." Georgia's laws, therefore, could have no force in Cherokee territory. Yet, fearing a showdown with the Jackson administration, the Supreme Court made no provision for implementing this decision. In the winter of 1838–1839, the Cherokees joined the "Trail of Tears."[37]

An incident in the new Cherokee territory west of Arkansas led the Supreme Court to articulate a theory of sovereignty that would later become decisive in both Native American and immigration policy. In 1844, a man named William S. Rogers stabbed his brother-in-law Jacob Nicholson to death. Both Rogers and Nicholson were white, but they had married Cherokee women, thereby becoming citizens of the Cherokee nation. Prosecuted for murder by the federal authorities, Rogers argued that the US

Circuit Court had no jurisdiction because federal power did not extend to crimes committed between Native Americans inside their own territory. In 1846, the Supreme Court ruled against Rogers. As a white man, the Court found, he remained subject to federal jurisdiction and his affiliation with the Cherokees could not change this fact. By implication, Native tribes were not sovereign communities that could set their own rules of political member-ship but collections of individuals bound together by race. The decision in *United States v. Rogers* significantly expanded the scope of federal authority by defining Native communities as the equivalent of racial minorities rather than autonomous political communities. It set the precedent for the doc-trine of power inherent in sovereignty, and largely protected from judicial re-view, which would guide national policy after the Civil War. Although Taney delivered the opinion in *Rogers*, he reverted in *Dred Scott* to a conception of Native autonomy resembling John Marshall's. He did so to buttress his argu-ment against black citizenship by emphasizing that Native Americans, unlike African Americans, could become citizens.[38]

The two dissenting opinions, by John McLean and Benjamin Curtis, upheld the Missouri Compromise and sharply challenged Taney's racially exclusive vision of citizenship. McLean had taken an antislavery line since joining the Court in 1829. For McLean, everyone born in the United States was a citizen by birthright. "Being born under our Constitution and laws," he wrote, "no naturalization is required, as one of foreign birth, to make him a citizen." The belief that "a colored citizen would not be an agreeable member of society," McLean observed, was "more a matter of taste than of law." Several states had granted citizenship and suffrage to "persons of color," and under the 1848 treaty with Mexico the United States "made citizens of all grades, combinations, and colors. The same was done in the admission of Louisiana and Florida." These people, McLean pointed out, "exercised all the rights of citizens, without being naturalized under the acts of Congress."[39]

Benjamin Curtis, who joined the Court in 1851, was a less likely candidate for the role of antislavery advocate. Curtis had defended a slaveowner in the Massachusetts case of *Commonwealth v. Aves* in 1836; he detested abolitionists, vigorously supported the Fugitive Slave Act of 1850, and he went on to oppose the Emancipation Proclamation in 1863. Yet he also signed the 1842 petition to Congress from elite Bostonians protesting that the Seamen Acts violated the privileges and immunities clause by infringing on the citizenship rights of black sailors from Massachusetts. In *Dred Scott*, Curtis strongly defended the principle of birthright citizenship for all Americans. Ironically, Roger Taney, a states' rights supporter of slavery, had emptied out the content of state sovereignty in his heavy-handed attempt to resolve the riddle of national citizenship. He conceded that states could make citizens of anyone they wished, but he insisted that state citizenship did not confer national citizenship on people permanently ineligible for that status. Curtis, by contrast, insisted that national citizenship flowed from state citizenship. If Massachusetts granted citizenship to free black people, they were citizens of the United States as well as their own state. If Missouri recognized Dred Scott as a citizen, Scott was automatically a US citizen.

For Curtis, Dred Scott's African descent and the enslavement of his ancestors was in no way inconsistent with him being a citizen of the United States. All people recognized as citizens by a state, regardless of their skin color, had the right to sue in federal court. The Articles of Confederation had extended "all the privileges and immunities of free citizens in the several States" to the "free inhabitants" of every state, he noted, with the exception of "paupers, vagabonds, and fugitives from justice." At the Constitutional Convention, delegates from South Carolina moved to amend the language to apply only to "free white inhabitants," but only two states voted in favor. Eight states opposed this motion, with the vote of one state divided. The privileges and immunities clause, in its final form in the US Constitution, used the word "citizens" instead of "inhabitants," but for Curtis this word covered—and was intended to cover—free black people. As citizens of their states, they were citizens of the United States.[40]

Contrary to Taney's claim, some African Americans were state citizens, and therefore US citizens by Curtis's logic, at the time the Constitution was approved. All free native-born inhabitants of New Hampshire, Massachusetts, New York, New Jersey, and North Carolina, even if they were descended from African slaves, were citizens of those states. If they met the property qualifications, they could vote. Black people in these states, Curtis pointed out, were among those who voted to ratify the Constitution. "It would be strange," he observed, if the Constitution "deprived of their citizenship any part of the people of the United States who were among those by whom it was established." It would do no justice to the revolutionary generation to claim that "they intended to say that the Creator of all men had endowed the white race, exclusively, with the great natural rights which the Declaration of Independence asserts." The "people" of the United States and their "posterity" mentioned in the Preamble to the Constitution included free colored citizens. Naturalization law applied only to white people, to be sure, but Congress could extend that privilege to nonwhite people if it wished. Indeed, Curtis pointed out, Congress had already done so in treaties with the

Choctaws in 1830 and the Cherokees in 1836, as well as the treaty with Mexico in 1848.[41]

Yet, although Curtis powerfully rebutted Taney's argument on citizenship, he did not advance a radical antislavery position. Under the principle of comity, black citizens who traveled from one state to another were entitled only to the rights enjoyed by citizens of that state. If a state recognized its black residents as citizens, Curtis explained, they were also citizens of the United States and entitled to sue in federal courts. A black citizen of Massachusetts had comity rights if he traveled to another state, but each state had the power to determine which of its native-born members were citizens. A free black person from South Carolina who was not recognized as a citizen in that state, moreover, would not gain national citizenship by moving to Massachusetts. Nor, for Curtis, did citizenship entail civil, let alone political, equality; it merely provided access to federal courts. Each state could decide for itself "what civil rights shall be enjoyed by its citizens, and whether all shall enjoy the same, or how they may be gained or lost." If Curtis's arguments were conservative, his overall position nonetheless amounted to a sweeping rejection of Taney's facts and reasoning. Curtis resigned from the Court six months after the *Dred Scott* case, in large part because of his dispute with Taney, and for the time being the chief justice's racial definition of citizenship prevailed. In seeking to define the boundaries of the national political community, Taney insisted that citizenship carried rights and that those outside the circle of "the people" lacked all of these rights. The Fourteenth Amendment, which repudiated the *Dred Scott* decision eleven years later, rested on the same conception of the rights-bearing national citizen, broadening the circle to include African Americans. But it took a civil war to get there.[42]

Dred and Harriet Scott, meanwhile, gained their freedom through other means. In 1857, Irene Emerson's second husband, Congressman Calvin Clifford Chaffee of Massachusetts, transferred ownership rights to Peter Blow, the son of Dred Scott's former owner, who immediately freed the Scott family. But what did freedom mean for a former slave in Missouri? Free black people still had to register and post bonds guaranteeing their good character; if they did not, they could be arrested, hired out to employers, whipped, or expelled. As a condition of remaining in Missouri, the Scotts posted a bond of $1,000, with Taylor Blow (Peter's brother) acting as surety. Dred Scott, who was more than twenty years older than Harriet, died on September 17, 1858. Harriet Scott remained in St. Louis, where she found work as a washerwoman. She died there on June 17, 1876.[43]

# *A Second* Dred Scott *Case?*

Abraham Lincoln repudiated the *Dred Scott* decision. In a speech at Springfield, Illinois, on June 26, 1857, he believed that the authors of the Declaration of Independence "did not intend to declare all men equal in all respects. They did not mean to say all were equal in color, size, intellect, moral developments, or social capacity," but they did intend to "set up a standard maxim for a free society . . . for future use." Yet, now, in the name of "making the bondage of the negro universal and eternal," the Declaration was being "assailed, and sneered at, and construed, and hawked at, and torn, till, if its framers could rise from their graves, they could not at all recognize it." Republicans insisted that slavery was possible only when authorized by positive law: freedom was national, slavery a local aberration. The *Dred Scott* decision, however, threatened to make freedom local and slavery legal everywhere unless it was prohibited, while undermining the power of local legislation to outlaw the institution. In his "House Divided" speech at Springfield, Illinois on June 16, 1858, Lincoln warned of a conspiracy to nationalize slavery. "We shall lie down pleasantly dreaming that the people of Missouri are on the verge of making their State free," Lincoln predicted, "and we shall awake to the reality instead, that the Supreme Court has made Illinois a slave State." In particular, Lincoln and other Republicans feared that a "Second Dred Scott case" would prevent not just the territories but even the free states from excluding slavery.[44]

One such case, which had originated six years earlier, was drawing national attention as Lincoln issued these words. In November 1852, Louis Napoleon, a citizen of New York who had once been enslaved, filed a writ of habeas corpus for "eight colored persons, one man, two women and five children," who were being detained "under the pretence that they were slaves." Jonathan Lemmon and his wife Juliet, residents of Virginia, had arrived in New York City on the steamship *City of Richmond*, intending to embark for Texas on another ship. They brought with them eight enslaved people, comprising two related family groups, each headed by a young woman: twenty-three-year-old Emiline, with her brothers Lewis and Edward, aged sixteen and thirteen, and her daughter Amanda, aged two; and twenty-year-old Nancy, with her seven-year-old twin sons, also named Lewis and Edward, and her daughter Ann, aged five. While waiting for their ship to Texas, the Lemmons placed both families in a boarding house and stayed at a nearby hotel. Louis Napoleon, who was active in the Underground Railroad, learned of their captivity. The abolitionist John Jay, a long-time collaborator of Napoleon and a grandson of the first chief justice of the US Supreme Court, represented the captives at the hearing, along with the antislavery Whig and former Congressman Erastus D. Culver. Dozens of black men, women, and children observed the proceedings in the Superior Court of New York City.[45]

Jonathan Lemmon testified that the captives were the property of his wife, who was in transit from Virginia to Texas and never intended to stay in New York. A New York act passed in 1817 and renewed in 1830 declared that any non-fugitive slaves brought into the state were free, with the exception of those traveling with their owners and staying for less than nine months. In 1841, the legislature repealed this exception, stipulating that all enslaved people entering the state were free, even if they were merely passing through. Citing the *Somerset* case of 1772, Justice Elijah Paine Jr. ruled that there were no grounds for holding persons as property under the laws of New York. Slavery could exist only under positive law, and New York had no such law. Nor had it been necessary, Paine explained, for the Lemmons to travel via New York in order to bring their slaves to Texas. They chose to bring them to a free state, where slavery could not exist. Paine freed the captives, and Louis Napoleon brought them to a secret location, safe from the risk of arrest or kidnapping. With the assistance of Jay, Culver, and other abolitionists, they eventually made their way to Canada.[46]

The Lemmons continued to appeal the case for another eight years. "Immediately after the slaves were liberated," the *New York Times* reported, "a subscription was started, which was headed by Judge Paine, who gave a liberal sum, to reimburse Mr. Lemmon for the loss of his property, and the full value of the slaves was returned to him." Led by New York merchants seeking to forestall southern anger, this effort raised $5,000, which the Lemmons accepted. For antislavery activists, the appeal raised the terrifying prospect of another *Dred Scott* case, in which that the US Supreme Court might affirm the constitutional right of slaveowners to travel nationally with their slaves, into free states as well as territories. When the Lemmons appealed the Superior Court's verdict, Virginia Governor Joseph Johnson persuaded his legislature to pay the costs. New York's intermediate appellate court considered the case in October 1857, shortly after the *Dred Scott* case, and upheld Justice Paine's decision. With Virginia's continued support, the Lemmons then appealed to New York's highest court. By this time, Napoleon and Jay wanted to shut the case down, fearful that an eventual appeal to the US Supreme Court would backfire. If the case was dismissed for lack of controversy, the Lemmons would no longer have a straightforward path for appeal. John King, a Republican who served as governor of New York in 1857–1858, was sympathetic with the petitioners' position, but he preferred to defend his state's right to declare that all people brought into its territory were free. The case proceeded to the New York Court of Appeals.[47]

For the Lemmons, Charles O'Conor, the New York–born son of an Irish revolutionary exile, offered an opening argument that was extraordinary, even by the standards of the time, for its denigration of black Americans. He began by denying the relevance of the *Somerset* case to the issues at hand. Lord Mansfield had declared that slavery, being contrary to nature, could exist only by positive law. Without such law, no person who entered England could be a slave. But O'Conor dismissed this ruling as nothing more than "a bald inconsequential truism," which "might be equally well said of any other new thing not recognized in any known existing law." The *Somerset* ruling, for O'Conor, stemmed from "pride of learning and an ostentatious vanity," and came from a judge known as an enemy rather than a champion of liberty. The judicial department, in any case, had no right to declare slavery "to be contrary to the law of nature, or immoral, or unjust, or to take any measures or introduce any policy for its suppression founded on any such ideas." Judges should interpret the law of the land, not "promulgate or enforce their notions of general justice, natural right or morality." O'Conor rejected the theory of "freedom national" favored by prominent members of the antislavery movement, which saw liberty as the normal state in American society. "The proposition that freedom is the general rule and slavery the local exception," he insisted, "has no foundation in any just view of the law as science."[48]

In a distinctive reading of the Constitution, O'Conor maintained that any attempt by New York to prevent the Lemmons from passing through the state with their slaves violated both the commerce clause and the privileges and immunities clause. Citing *Gibbons v. Ogden* (1824) and the *Passenger Cases* (1849), he pointed out that Congress had exclusive power to regulate interstate commerce, "which includes the transportation of persons and the whole subject of intercourse between our citizens of different States as well as between them and foreigners." No state, therefore, could constitutionally enact any regulation of commerce between the states, regardless of whether Congress had exercised the same power over the question. O'Conor, in other words, invoked the federal commerce power in an effort to stymie a northern state's effort to exclude slavery from its soil. This was a remarkable twist, yet it was in keeping with southern invocations of federal power against states that harbored fugitive slaves. Likewise, O'Conor claimed that the purpose of comity was to exempt nonresident citizens from the laws of the states they entered, allowing them to retain the rights they enjoyed at home, chief among them the ownership of slaves as property. "No citizen," O'Conor insisted, "could be deprived of his privileges and immunities by the action of a State other than his own."[49]

O'Conor ended with a stark endorsement of the *Dred Scott* decision. The Declaration of Independence and the "free inhabitants" referred to in the Articles of Confederation, he insisted, included neither black people nor Native Americans living on tribal land. Nor was either group part of the sovereign "people" recognized at the Constitutional Convention as "the supreme original source of all political power." In a few places, O'Conor conceded, a small number of African Americans were permitted "by an overstrained liberality in the interpretation of laws, or by ignorance of them" to exercise some degree of political power. But "an inference fatal to the Republic should not thence be drawn." For O'Conor, like Roger Taney, African Americans were "forever excluded from social union by an indubitable law of nature" and could never be endowed with political equality. If the judiciary were to declare that free black people in the North were citizens of the states in which they lived, and hence entitled under the Constitution to the privileges and immunities enjoyed by citizens in the other states, O'Conor predicted, it would break the Union apart.[50]

District Attorney Joseph Blunt, a Republican, rebutted O'Conor on every point. Slavery, Blunt declared, was contrary to natural right. "It is not derived from any compact or consent of the slave," he explained. "It originates in force, and its continuance is maintained by force." But the law of slavery was local; it did not operate beyond the territory of the state where it was established. When an enslaved person moved beyond the jurisdiction of a state, the laws of that state did not apply. The laws of Virginia were not in force in New York. The states did have an obligation to return fugitive slaves under federal laws passed in 1793 and 1850, but in consenting to return them, they were merely performing their duty under the Constitution, rather than acknowledging the right of slavery to exist. The Lemmons' slaves were not fugitives, however, and they ceased to be property once they entered the state of New York, where state law expressly prohibited slavery.[51]

In March 1860, the New York Court of Appeals ruled against the Lemmons by a vote of 5 to 3. For the majority, Justice Hiram Denio explained that every sovereign state had the right to determine, by its own laws, the condition of all people within its jurisdiction and to exclude those whose introduction contravened its policies. Every state also had the right "to declare what subjects shall, within the State, possess the attributes of property, and what shall be incapable of a proprietary right." While the states constituted a single nation for all external purposes, and for certain domestic purposes as well, they retained sovereignty in matters not delegated to the general government or prohibited to them. Other than their obligation to return fugitives, free states had no obligation to recognize property in human beings. Nor, Denio found, did the Lemmons' transportation of their slaves have anything to do with commerce. In short, there was nothing in the Constitution or the laws of Congress to preclude a state from declaring enslaved persons introduced into its territory automatically free.[52]

The court roundly rejected O'Conor's claim that, under the principle of comity, citizens carried with them the rights and privileges of their home states when they traveled to other states. As national citizens, these travelers were entitled to the same rights and privileges, and subject to the same laws, as the citizens of the states they entered. They could hold property in these states only "by the same titles by which every other citizen may hold it." Justice William B. Wright offered a scathing rebuttal of O'Conor's argument on comity. "I think this is the first occasion in the juridical history of the country," he wrote, "that an attempt has been made to torture this provision into a guaranty of the right of a slave owner to bring his slaves into, and hold them for any purpose in, a non-slaveholding State." The purpose of the privileges and immunities clause, Wright explained, was to secure to the citizens of each state, within every other state, "the privileges and immunities (whatever they might be)" of the citizens of those states. A citizen of Virginia coming to New York was entitled to the rights enjoyed by citizens of New York. He was not entitled to hold slaves in New York, where no law upheld that status and specific laws denied the possibility of its existence. New York could not be required to permit acts by citizens of other states which, if performed by its own citizens, were illegal. That was not how comity worked.[53]

Three justices dissented, two of them without writing an opinion. The third, Justice Clerke, objected that much of the discussion was irrelevant to the legal questions at hand. Whether slavery agreed with or contradicted the law of nature, whether it was morally right or wrong, whether people of African origin were physically and morally suited to slavery and could be induced to work only by compulsion, whether tropical zones could be cultivated only by such slaves—these questions, for Clerke, were "very interesting within the domain of theology, or ethics, or political economy, but totally inappropriate to the discussion of the purely legal questions now presented for our consideration." The constitutional question was whether a state legislature had the power to declare all enslaved people entering the state instantly free. Was it consistent with the purpose of the Union, Clerke asked, that property brought from one state to another should be confiscated or declared not to be property? By the law of nations, the citizens of one government had the right to pass through the territory of another for business or pleasure, without any interference with their property rights. This principle was all the more important when it came to relations between the several states of the Union, Clerke observed, and it was part of the compact on which the United States was based. Like O'Conor, he pointed to "the celebrated Dred Scott case," with its recognition that the classification of slaves as property by the framers of the Constitution was "binding upon their posterity forever, unless that Constitution should be modified or dissolved by common consent."[54]

The decision by the New York Court of Appeals opened a path toward a final appeal to the US Supreme Court. Leading antislavery figures such as Abraham Lincoln, Charles Sumner, Salmon Chase, and Horace Greeley feared that if the Democrats won the presidential election of 1860, the Taney Court would use the Lemmon case to force the introduction of slavery into free states. But Virginia's governor, John Letcher, proved unwilling to press the matter and, in the end, the case died due to the outbreak of the Civil War. The successive antislavery rulings by the New York courts in the Lemmon case, combined with the antislavery stance of the state government, exacerbated tensions between North and South. It had not gone unnoticed that Lincoln's choice as secretary of state, William Seward, had signed the state's free-soil law of 1841 when he was governor of New York. Control over the movement of enslaved people featured prominently in the declarations of secession issued by southern states in 1860 and 1861.[55]

In his infamous "Cornerstone" speech delivered at Savannah, Georgia, on March 21, 1861, just three weeks before the outbreak of the Civil War, the vice president of the new Confederate States of America, Alexander H. Stephens, explained the meaning of secession. The formation of the Confederacy "put at rest, forever, all the agitating questions relating to our peculiar institution, African slavery as it exists amongst us—the proper status of the negro in our form of civilization. This was the immediate cause of the late rupture and present revolution." Jefferson and many leaders of the revolutionary generation, Stephens noted, believed "that the enslavement of the African was in violation of the laws of nature; that it was wrong in principle, socially, morally, and politically." They hoped that "somehow or other in the order of Providence," slavery would die out. Although the Constitution "secured every essential guarantee to the institution while it should last," Stephens believed that Jefferson and his contemporaries were fundamentally mistaken. "They rested upon the assumption of the equality of races," he declared. "This was an error. It was a sandy foundation, and the government built upon it fell when the 'storm came and the wind blew.'" The Confederate States of America, Stephens declared, was "founded upon exactly the opposite idea; its foundations are laid, its corner-stone rests, upon the great truth that the negro is not equal to the white man; that slavery subordination to the superior race is his natural and normal condition." The Confederate government was "the first, in the history of the world, based upon this great physical, philosophical, and moral truth."[56]

Stephens was quoting Matthew 24:27. A wise man once built his house upon the rock of truth, while a foolish man built his on sand. "And the rain descended, and the floods came, and the winds blew, and beat upon that house; and it fell: and great was the fall of it." In the storm that was about to engulf the United States, however, it was slavery rather than equality that was swept away. Enslaved people who fled the plantations, no longer captured and returned as fugitives, found refuge with an invading army. By 1865 American slavery was no more.[57]

# PART TWO

# Immigration in the Age of Emancipation

# 5

## *The Antislavery Origins of Immigration Policy*

IN 1853, GEORGE W. HALL, a "free white citizen" of California, shot Ling Seng, a Chinese miner at a camp in Nevada County. Convicted of murder on the testimony of three Chinese witnesses, Hall was sentenced to death. The California Supreme Court overturned the conviction, ruling that it violated an 1850 law stating that "No Black or Mulatto person, or Indian, shall be allowed to give evidence in favor of, or against a white man." This law applied regardless of whether the white man was a citizen or an alien. Race, rather than birthplace, was the measure. A similar prohibition applied in civil cases. It would be anomalous, the court declared in *The People v. Hall* (1854), to allow "a race of people whom nature has marked as inferior" and "whose mendacity is proverbial" to testify against white people. Because Hall had been convicted on the testimony of Chinese witnesses, he was set free.[1]

Chief Justice Hugh Murray, a prominent member of the California Know-Nothing Party, delivered the opinion of the court. The best recent science, he explained, had established that there were three races of men: white, black, and Indian. The Chinese fell into the last category, which included everyone of the "Mongolian type." As racial categories were fixed by nature, Murray explained, the California statute applied not only to those who were present in the state when the law was passed in 1850 but also to all subsequent interactions between the three "great types of mankind." If this were not so, people of African or Asian descent could testify against white people, who would have no protection from "the corrupting influences of degraded castes." Once allowed to serve as witnesses, they would demand "all the equal rights of citizenship," including the right to serve on juries and run for elected office. This prospect, Murray warned, was "an actual and present danger." It could hardly be supposed, he concluded, that the state legislature had intended merely to exclude "domestic negroes and Indians" from testifying against whites, while "turning loose upon the community the more degraded tribes of the same species, who have nothing in common with us, in language, country or laws." In prohibiting any "black or mulatto person, or Indian" from giving evidence, the legislature had protected white people from "the influence of all testimony other than that of persons of the same caste." The white "caste" excluded "black, yellow, and all other colors"—in other words, "all races other than the Caucasian." By "community," Murray meant white people only. Native Americans, African Americans, and Chinese Americans, regardless of birthplace, did not belong to the community that constituted the United States.[2]

Chinese migrants faced discrimination and calls for exclusion as soon as they began to arrive in the United States in significant numbers during the California gold rush of 1849. California and Oregon passed laws requiring miners ineligible for US citizenship—in other words, the Chinese—to pay monthly license fees. After the gold rush, Chinese migrants moved into railroad construction, agriculture, manufacturing, domestic service, and the laundry business. Most came on a temporary basis, and many made several journeys to the United States. As well as regulating the lives of Chinese migrants after they arrived, California tried unsuccessfully to prevent them from entering. An act passed in 1855 imposed an exorbitant fifty-dollar head tax on every Chinese person arriving in the state by sea. In *People v. Downer* (1857), counsel for California argued that the state had the authority to pass the law under its police power to safeguard the health, morals, lives, and property of its citizens. Just as southern states could restrict the migration of free black people, the lawyers insisted, California could restrict the entry of Chinese immigrants. The California Supreme Court rejected this analogy, ruling that the decision in the *Passenger Cases* (1849) "clearly controlled, and invalidated the fifty-dollar head tax." The state law, in other words, was unconstitutional because it violated federal power under the commerce clause. When California passed an act "to prevent the further immigration of Chinese or Mongolians to this State" in 1858, the court invalidated it on the same grounds.[3]

California responded to these setbacks by passing sweeping legislation directed at all its Chinese residents, not just those who were immigrants. "An Act to protect free white labor against competition with Chinese coolie labor, and discourage the immigration of the Chinese into the State of California," passed in 1862, imposed a charge of $2.50 per month on "every person, male and female, of the Mongolian race" over the age of eighteen residing in the state (with the exception of those involved in the production of sugar, rice, coffee, or tea who were not competing with white workers). In *Lin Sing v. Washburn* (1862), the California Supreme Court struck down the so-called Chinese Police Tax as a violation of federal commerce power. The court recognized California's right to protect itself against "obnoxious persons, such as paupers and fugitives from justice," and its right to tax its residents, but it ruled that the state could not impose a tax on immigrants without violating the commerce clause. Only Congress could regulate arrivals in this way, but Congress passed no legislation to this effect before secession triggered the Civil War and hastened the demise of slavery.[4]

This is not to say that Congress would have regulated, let alone numerically restricted, European immigration earlier. On the contrary, federal lawmakers had long rejected state-level calls to prohibit the introduction of paupers or to amend the naturalization laws, not simply because slave states opposed federal intervention but also because so few Americans supported immigration restriction. When Congress took its first significant restrictive action, during the Civil War, it targeted Chinese contract workers rather than European immigrants. The Coolie Trade Prohibition Act of 1862 banned American ships from transporting Chinese contract laborers to foreign destinations. This act classified Chinese migrant workers going to the United States as free rather than involuntary (unlike the anti-coolie law passed by California and invalidated by the state supreme court the same year) and therefore had no immediate effect on Chinese immigration to the United States. Over the next twenty years, however, critics of the Chinese expanded the term *coolie* to cover all Chinese laborers in the United States, justifying their exclusion on antislavery grounds. In sharp contrast to the Coolie Trade Prohibition Act, the Act to Encourage Immigration, passed in 1864, lent federal recognition to short-term contracts recruiting European workers. Importing contract labor sat poorly with the prevailing spirit of emancipation, however, and this act remained in force for only four years. These two measures—the first banning unfree migration by Chinese laborers and the second encouraging the migration of European contract workers—emerged from the politics of antislavery during the Civil War. Taken together, they laid the groundwork for a national immigration policy in the postbellum era.[5]

## *The Coolie Trade*

In the nineteenth century, Asian migrant workers throughout the Anglo-American world were known as *coolies*. This derogatory term referred to two separate migrant streams: Chinese contract workers who labored alongside or replaced slaves of African descent, especially in Cuba and Peru; and South Asian contract workers who went to Guiana, Trinidad, and Mauritius following the gradual emancipation of slaves by the British in 1833. Chinese migrants in the United States, by contrast, were not legally classified as coolies. Some of them signed contracts, but under federal law (until the 1870s) they were the just same as any other immigrants. Their enemies, nonetheless, described them as coolies in arguing for their exclusion. The figure of the coolie is best approached not as a literal description but as an ideological construct. Rather than arranging Chinese workers at various points along a line running between two extremes, "free" and "unfree," it is more useful to investigate the conditions under which they migrated and worked. Drawing too rigid a distinction between coolie and non-coolie, indeed, can result in a form of American exceptionalism based on a racial logic that cast the United States as free and the Caribbean, Latin America, and Asia as unfree. No Chinese worker anywhere was a coolie in the pure form of an enslaved laborer; by the same token, no migrant worker—or for that matter, no wage worker of any kind—was simply free.[6]

British merchants initiated the Chinese coolie trade, but American ships soon dominated. Emigration was formally illegal under Chinese law until 1893, yet many Chinese men, facing starvation or deprivation in the countryside, left voluntarily. Others, lured to cities with promises of work that never materialized, were coerced into emigrating to pay off the debt owed to transportation companies or to their employers overseas. The colonial enclaves of Macao and Hong Kong became the primary points of departure. In 1855, the Chinese government issued a proclamation prohibiting the coolie trade, and the British Parliament passed an act confiscating all British vessels engaged in transporting coolies to Cuba and Peru. The following year, the government of Peru temporarily restrained its citizens from engaging in the trade. The main effect of these measures was to drive the trade from the open ports of China into the smuggling port of Swatow, allowing American vessels to take over from the British.[7]

The arrival of Chinese contract workers in Cuba and Peru overlapped with the continuing importation of African slaves. Spain signed treaties with Britain in 1817 and 1845 curtailing the Atlantic slave trade, but these

**FIGURE 5.1** "Coolies Embarking at Macao." Most Chinese migrant workers who went to Cuba or Peru in the nineteenth century left from the port city of Macao, a Portuguese colony, enduring harsh conditions on long-term labor contracts. *Harper's New Monthly Magazine*, June 1, 1864. Wallach Division Picture Collection, The New York Public Library.

provisions were loosely enforced. Slavery was not abolished in Peru until 1854 and in Cuba until 1886. The first Chinese workers arrived in Cuba in 1847 and were sold on eight-year contracts to planters and a railroad company. As many as 125,000 Chinese laborers arrived over the next twenty-five years, mostly to work on sugar plantations alongside enslaved people of African birth or descent. About half of them died before completing their terms of service. In addition, some 95,000 Chinese came to Peru, where they worked on sugar and cotton plantations or in the guano mines on the Chincha Islands. Created by the accumulated excrement of seabirds and bats, guano was in demand globally as fertilizer. Mining it was one of the most unpleasant and dangerous jobs in the world. Given the nature of the work they performed, nearly all the

Chinese workers who went to Cuba and Peru were male. The Cuban census of 1872 recorded 58,400 Chinese people, of whom only thirty-two were female (two under contract and thirty free). In the United States, 93 percent of the Chinese population in 1870 was male.[8]

Chinese laborers came to the Americas under a wide variety of arrangements. Some were kidnapped, coerced into boarding ships, and forced to sign contracts they did not understand. These abuses were worst among those leaving Macao for Cuba and Peru. The great majority of Chinese migrants going to these two destinations, however, were not captives; they voluntarily signed long-term contracts, typically for five to eight years. Because they replaced or complemented slave labor, their working and housing conditions were especially harsh. Contracts were marketable, allowing workers to be bought and sold. Those who survived their first term often had little choice but to renew their service. Yet the existence of a contract—a legal arrangement setting a fixed term of labor, payment, food, and clothing—distinguished coolies from slaves. Chinese migrant workers in Cuba had rights, even if their employers routinely violated these rights. They sometimes brought lawsuits against their employers, and, even when forced to renew their contracts, they were making finite agreements. Coolies, therefore, occupied a distinct category between or beyond slave and free.[9]

Chinese labor migration to the United States differed in significant ways from its counterparts in the Caribbean and Latin America. The number of Chinese-born people in the United States rose from about 4,000 in 1850 to 34,933 in 1860 and 63,199 in 1870. Three-quarters of them lived in California, where about 9 percent of the population and 25 percent of wage earners were Chinese born in 1870. Despite stereotypes that they were uniquely exploited and degraded, Chinese miners in the American West worked in a wide variety of capacities, ranging from independent operators and profit-sharing cooperatives to wage labor and short-term contracts known as "tickets of credit." Contract workers had to pay off the cost of their passage but were otherwise free. In contrast to colonial settings around the world, the federal and state governments in the United States did not seek to enforce these labor contracts. Workers who absconded lost their wages, not their freedom or their lives.[10]

Many Americans described coolies in Cuba and Peru, by contrast, as equivalent to slaves because of the coercive nature of their passage, the length of their contracts, and the harsh conditions under which they worked. Ironically, both antislavery activists and proslavery ideologues argued that coolieism substituted one form of slavery for another, though for opposite reasons. From an abolitionist perspective, coolieism was slavery under a new name, and it must be terminated if emancipation was to mean anything. From a proslavery perspective, substituting bound Chinese laborers for slaves on plantations revealed the hypocrisy of abolitionism, and threatened to undermine the property value of slaves not only in the Caribbean but also potentially in the United States. Humphrey Marshall, a Kentucky planter who served as US commissioner to China from 1852 to 1854, warned Secretary of State Edward Everett that if Britain populated its colonies in the Caribbean and on the coast of South America with Chinese laborers, the effect on the American South would be disastrous. Not only would Chinese contract laborers replace slaves in the South, he added, they were already being used to promote British commercial and agricultural interests in Asia.[11]

The *New York Times* shared Marshall's belief that Chinese workers might displace slaves in the South, but in its initial coverage in the early 1850s it saw the coolie trade as a potential solution to the problem of slavery. Rehearsing the canard that non-European bodies were best suited to arduous labor in hot climates, an editorial on April 15, 1852, described the Chinese as "steady, sober laborers, thoroughly accustomed to tropical toil and the disadvantages of a tropical climate, . . . industrious and ambitious; capable of bearing an unparalleled amount of toil without fatigue." "The cost of a slave is much greater," the *Times* succinctly noted; "his labor worth much less." The newspaper predicted that a large proportion of sugar and tobacco cultivation in Cuba would soon be conducted by Chinese laborers. The value of slave labor in the American South would decline precipitously once Cuba's displaced slaves were "flung into the labor market" and American planters recognized the advantages of "celestial [i.e., Chinese] labor." Importing Chinese workers, the *Times* concluded, was "the true remedy for the disadvantages of Slavery."[12]

In its early reporting on the coolie trade, the *Times* found Chinese labor superior to slave labor in every way. The Chinese worker, according to an editorial on May 3, 1852, was "a shrewd handy-craftsman, fertile in inventive resources" and a skilled cultivator of the soil. He would "condense the reluctant toil of a slave for two days into one." The gain "from his superior aptitude" on the Cuban cane plantations, the *Times* found, "has been very nearly incredible." His only passion was "avarice," but that simply made him work harder. The expense of raising slaves in the American South, the *Times* concluded, could be spared by importing well-trained adult workers from China. The "real malady" of the South was "defective labor," and the remedy was the same as in Cuba—"the introduction of the Chinese Coolies." Early enthusiasm about the coolie trade soon gave way to skepticism, however, amid reports of abusive traveling and working conditions, shipwrecks, mutinies, and rebellions by Chinese passengers.[13]

On May 21, 1852, the interim chargé d'affaires to China, Peter Parker, a noted physician and missionary, sent a report to Secretary of State Daniel Webster concerning a "very aggravated case of piracy and murder." The American merchantman *Robert Bowne*, under Captain Lesley Bryson, had left Amoy (modern-day Xiamen), the island city in Fujian Province from which many Chinese workers emigrated, with 410 Chinese "coolies, so called," bound for San Francisco. On March 30, when the ship was about 300 miles off Formosa (today's Taiwan), the Chinese passengers—fearing that they might be headed for Peru rather than the United States—rose up and killed the captain, the first and second officers, and four crewmen. They took command of the ship, and when it ran aground near a small island on the Ryuku archipelago, between Taiwan and Japan, hundreds of them went ashore. The surviving crewmen seized and bound the twenty-three Chinese passengers who remained on board and brought the ship back to Amoy on April 18. Parker conceded that Captain Bryson had administered "injudicious treatment," including an order to cut off the coolies' queues (braids), but he suspected that the uprising was "premeditated before the vessel left port." Parker claimed that the United States had jurisdiction over the *Robert Bowne* affair as an act of piracy committed on the open seas on a ship sailing under the American flag, but he agreed to hand over seventeen passengers to the Chinese authorities for trial. Humphrey Marshall reported from Macao on March 8, 1853, that the Chinese court declined to hear testimony by American seamen and, comparing the abusive coolie trade to "buying pigs," found only one Chinese man guilty.[14]

The death of hundreds of Chinese workers on board the *Waverly*, bound for Peru in 1855, heightened concerns about the coolie trade. The *Waverly* left Amoy in September with 353 Chinese laborers on board and picked up ninety-seven more in Swatow (today's Shantou). Many of the passengers fell ill and four jumped overboard. When the captain died, the first mate, Mr. French, took command and changed course for the Philippines. The *Waverly* reached Manila on October 25, and the ship was placed in quarantine about six miles away from the city. When the Chinese passengers demanded to go on shore and attempted to take possession of the boats, the crew killed several of them, drove the rest below decks, and shut the hatches. On opening the hatches fourteen hours later, they found nearly 300 passengers dead from suffocation. Mr. French claimed he had no idea the ventilation below decks was inadequate and claimed the passengers had killed one another.[15]

Despite these incidents, demand for labor in Cuba was so high that the abusive trade in Chinese workers was bound to increase. In a letter to Secretary of State William Marcy on July 27, 1855, William H. Robertson, the acting consul in Havana, offered some insights into the coolie trade in Cuba. The *Hound*, out of Stonington, Connecticut, captained by Amos Peck, had arrived from Macao on July 22 with a cargo of Chinese laborers assigned to the Colonization Company. The company's agents, Pereda, Machado & Co., had made preparations, including provisions, wood, water, and accommodation, for 400 passengers. Captain Peck, they protested, had agreed to take only 230 on board, based on his calculation of what the passenger laws of the United States permitted, "even though the laws do not refer to passengers from one foreign port to another foreign port." The agents claimed damages for the losses incurred in providing for the passengers not loaded. "Captain Peck expressed himself as heartily ashamed of being concerned in such a trade," Robertson reported, "and states that, from information obtained from the passengers, on the passage, as to the manner of their being disposed of after arrival here, he cannot but consider the trade as bad, if not worse, than anything he has read or heard of the African slave trade."[16]

In this context, American commercial interests sought to clarify the legality of the coolie trade. On January 7, 1856, C. D. Mudgford, a shipping agent in Hong Kong, wrote to Peter Parker, who had been promoted to US commissioner to China the previous year, informing him that he had several ships ready to carry Chinese laborers to Peru and other destinations. Mudgford told Parker that he assumed the laborers were traveling voluntarily, like those who went to Australia and California, but the merchants he represented had ordered him "to abandon such trade if not strictly legal and moral." He therefore asked for Parker's opinion on whether the US government considered "the carrying of coolie emigrants in American ships as a lawful trade." Seeking to protect his commercial interests, Mudgford also asked whether American vessels pursuing this trade, when obliged to stop at foreign ports in the course of their journeys, could count on the assistance of the government if the Chinese passengers demanded to be released from their contracts.[17]

Acting on instructions from Secretary of State William L. Marcy, Parker issued a public notification on January 10, 1856, condemning the coolie trade. The traffic in Chinese workers, he declared, was "replete with illegalities, immoralities, and revolting and inhuman atrocities, strongly resembling those of the African slave trade in former years, some of them exceeding the horrors of the 'middle passage.'" The imperial government of China had communicated to the United States legation its strong disapproval of the traffic, which was conducted in localities where treaties prohibited foreign trade and was therefore illegal as well as immoral. Sending a copy of this notification to C. D. Mudgford, Parker enclosed a proclamation signed by a group of Chinese scholars and merchants in Amoy denouncing "the practice of buying people to sell again; subjecting those guiltless of crime to cruel punishment, and employing evil-disposed and traitorous natives to entice away peaceable people." Parker called on all American citizens to desist from this trade and warned that they would not only forfeit the protection of the American government but also render themselves liable to "heavy penalties." "This notification," he clarified, "respects the 'coolie trade' in contradistinction to voluntary emigration of Chinese adventurers; between these there exists a wide difference." He was referring, in other words, to the transportation of Chinese workers to Cuba and Latin America rather than their emigration to the American West.[18]

William R. Reed, who succeeded Peter Parker as US commissioner to China in 1857, also tried to restrict American involvement in the coolie trade. He found the trade "repugnant to the instincts of humanity, in contravention of the laws of the Chinese government, and as clearly a violation of the well-settled policy of the government of the United States." Yet the laws regulating the external slave trade and the European passenger trade could not be used to prohibit the coolie trade. The act criminalizing the importation of slaves to the United States on American or foreign vessels as of January 1, 1808, authorized the US Navy (but not other American ships) to seize American vessels involved in the trade. The act of 1820, making participation in the slave trade an act of piracy punishable by death, permitted all American ships, not just those of the Navy, to inspect American vessels suspected of carrying "any negro or mulatto" with the intention of enslaving them. Neither law mentioned Chinese migrants, however, as no Chinese were coming to the United States when they were passed. The Passenger Acts of 1819, 1847, and 1855, meanwhile, applied only to American vessels traveling from foreign ports to the United States and could not be used to regulate the passage of Chinese workers to Cuba or South America.[19]

Nonetheless, on January 5, 1858, Reed asked the US consul at Macao, S. B. Rawle, to inform the Spanish authorities that the transportation of coolies in American ships or by American captains was "expressly prohibited by law." He also instructed Rawle to inform Captain J. M. Cole of the American ship *Flora Temple*, bound for Havana from Macao with hundreds of Chinese workers on board, that if he was to transport "any Chinese coolie or laborer, for the purpose of disposing of such person as a slave, or to be held to service or labor in the United States or elsewhere," he would be liable to a fine, a term in prison, and forfeiture of his vessel. The deputy consul at Macao, William A. Macy, reported back to Reed on January 8 that the remonstrances in both cases had proved ineffectual. On a subsequent voyage, in October 1859, the *Flora Temple* struck a reef shortly after leaving Macao for Havana. The captain and crew abandoned ship and all 850 passengers on board were reported dead.[20]

## Regulating the Coolie Trade

On March 21, 1860, C. K. Stribling, the interim US chargé d'affaires at Hong Kong, wrote to Secretary of State J. S. Black in Washington concerning an uprising on the American ship *Leonidas*. On February 24, Stribling reported, the "coolie passengers" on board the *Leonidas*, then at anchor near Canton, rose up and badly wounded the captain and several of the crew. When Oliver Perry, the US consul at Canton, went on board, he found a number of Chinese passengers fastened to an iron bar, nearly all of them wounded. One man was dead, and another lay mortally wounded. Below deck everything was in confusion. The ship had embarked with 289 coolies on board; after the uprising, only 201 were found. An investigation led by the captain of the *Leonidas* concluded that the eighty-eight missing passengers had jumped overboard and most of them must have drowned, though the captain suspected pirates in the waters around the ship may have assisted some of them.[21]

That same month, the *Staghound*, out of Boston, left Swatow for Havana carrying 400 Chinese laborers contracted to work for eight years in Cuba. Along with Captain Samuel Hussey and three mates, the ship had a crew of thirty-two, a carpenter, two cooks, and "six quartermasters, whose duty appeared to be a special one of keeping guard over the cargo." By the time the *Staghound* reached Anjier (Anyer, in West Java, about eighty miles from Jakarta), the captain was sick with dysentery and the third mate had a broken collar-bone. The first officer and second officer (the captain's nineteen-year-old son) took command. The crew, of mixed European and American background, complained of short rations, overwork, and violent treatment by the officers. On March 3, they mutinied, mortally wounding the captain's son. The revolt was suppressed with assistance from a nearby British navy vessel, and twenty-four crew members were detained and sent to the United States for trial.[22]

The wreck of the *Flora Temple*, the uprising on the *Leonidas*, and the mutiny on *Staghound* were among a series of events that turned American public opinion against the coolie trade. Criticism intensified as American vessels stepped up their involvement in the illegal shipment of African slaves to Cuba in the late 1850s. The *New York Times*, which had initially hoped that importing Chinese workers might hasten the demise of slavery, denounced the coolie trade. "From the moment of his capture," the *Times* declared in April 1860, "the coolie is a slave; the subject, first of deception, and then of servitude in no degree different from that of an African slave." The nominal term of service in Cuba was eight years, but no one was obliged to take care of worn-out Chinese workers at the end of their terms. In this respect, the *Times* commented, "the Asiatic slave is more helpless than the African," since Chinese workers had to fend for themselves once their work was done. By this logic, coolies lacked both the freedom of wage labor and the paternalism of slavery. The newspaper found it "mortifying" that American captains and owners from the North were "willing to connect themselves with a trade condemned by the entire civilized world as piracy."[23]

Calling on Congress to act, the *Times* offered a definition of the coolie trade. It had nothing to do with the voluntary migration of Chinese workers to the United States, who—like Irish and German immigrants—paid for their own passage and worked either for wages or on short-term contracts. It also stood in sharp contrast to the system of Indian indentured labor supervised by the agents of the British government, which supposedly came with secure wages, decent food and medical care, and often a free return passage at the end of the term of service. The migration of South Asians to Guiana, Trinidad, and Mauritius, the *Times* claimed, "was not in any wise [*sic*] compulsory." The Indian system of labor migration was "not the ally, but the enemy of Slavery." The Chinese coolie trade, however, was "an altogether different matter." The "coolie laborer" in Cuba was "not one whit better off than the African brought there to perpetual slavery." Responsibility for ending the trade, the *Times* concluded, lay on the shoulders of the United States, "to vindicate our national reputation, by acting . . . as becomes our Christianity and our civilization."[24]

On July 11, 1860, British Foreign Secretary Lord John Russell proposed a remedy to the Cuban slave trade and coolie trade. The difficulties in suppressing the slave trade, Russell believed, arose mainly from the demand in Cuba and similar countries "for laborers suited to a hot climate." If this demand could be supplied from China through a properly regulated trade, the incentive to import slaves from Africa would be greatly diminished, as the price of a slave would increase far beyond that of a Chinese laborer. Russell proposed a three-part plan. British, Spanish, and American vessels would cruise the coast of Cuba; the Spanish authorities would introduce a system of inspection and registration to detect the importation of enslaved people contrary to the law; and agents of the European powers would cooperate with the Chinese authorities in planning emigration by contract workers.[25]

William Henry Trescot, the acting secretary of state, replied that although President Buchanan shared Russell's views on the slave trade, the president could not assent to these proposals. A systematic plan of cruising would require a treaty with Spain to enable US vessels to enter Cuban waters. Great Britain already had this right, but American ships would be subject to seizure. The United States could not ask the Spanish to introduce a registration system—and, even if the Spanish agreed, no such system could be effective given how many slave-trading companies operated in Havana. Finally, and most significantly, the president did not agree that the coolie trade could be regulated in such a way as to "relieve it of those features of fraud and violence which render the details of its prosecution scarcely less horrible than those of the middle passage." Importing Chinese labor, moreover, would have a harmful influence on every region of the United States. In the states where slavery existed, "these heathen Coolies would demoralize the peaceful, contented and orderly slaves, very many of whom are sincere Christians." In the free states, they would compete—just like free black people—with "our own respectable and industrious laborers, whether of native or foreign birth, who constitute so large a portion of our best citizens." Russell replied with muted exasperation that the British government had never contemplated the introduction of Chinese laborers into the United States, only into Cuba. There the matter ended. To regulate American involvement in the coolie trade, the United States would need to act alone.[26]

Congressional debate on regulating coolie labor spanned the Pierce, Buchanan, and Lincoln administrations. Congress first introduced legislation to prohibit American involvement in the trade in 1856, but southern congressmen opposed this effort, despite the potential threat to slavery posed by the importation of Chinese contract workers. As always, the prospect of federal intervention to regulate migration met strong resistance in the South. Slaveholders feared that the national government might use its commerce power to control the movement of free black people and perhaps even to regulate the interstate slave trade.[27]

Thomas D. Eliot, an antislavery congressman from Massachusetts, led the campaign against coolieism. Based in the abolitionist stronghold of New

Bedford, Eliot vocally opposed the Fugitive Slave Act of 1850 and the Kansas-Nebraska Act of 1854. After leaving the Whig Party, he joined the Free-Soil Party and then the Republican Party. He introduced one of the earliest bills in Congress calling for emancipation. Elliot first attempted to report a bill prohibiting American involvement in the coolie trade on March 31, 1860. This effort was unsuccessful, but when the Lincoln administration submitted a report on the coolie trade to the House in December 1861, Eliot proposed an amended bill. The Chinese coolie, he declared, was the subject "first of the meanest deception, and then of a servitude in no respect practically different from that which the African slave trade binds upon its victim." On January 15, the House passed Eliot's bill, which prohibited American involvement in the transportation of Chinese workers "against their will and without their consent."[28]

Republican Senator John Conover Ten Eyck of New Jersey moved on behalf of his chamber's Committee on Commerce to strike the phrase "against their will and without their consent." In the name of protecting Chinese migrant laborers from enslavement, Ten Eyck's amendment prohibited the immigration of all "coolies," casting Chinese contract workers as unfree by definition, regardless of whether they signed contracts voluntarily or were coerced into doing so. Coolieism was absolute; its opposite was freedom. Defining coolie labor this way had long-term consequences, justifying the eventual exclusion of all Chinese laborers on the grounds that they were enslaved. Under the 1862 act, however, Chinese workers traveling to the United States remained within the category of voluntary migration. The Senate passed the bill with Ten Eyck's amendment, the House concurred, and Abraham Lincoln signed An Act to Prohibit the "Coolie Trade" by American Citizens in American Vessels on February 19, 1862.[29]

The Coolie Trade Prohibition Act outlawed participation by American vessels in the shipment abroad of Chinese migrants who were "held to service or labor." It authorized all American ships, not just those of the US Navy, to examine and detain other American vessels suspected of transporting coolie laborers. Such vessels were forfeited to the United States and violators faced fines of up to $2,000 and prison terms of up to one year. The act drew a clear distinction between the international slave trade (including coolieism) and voluntary migration (characterized by a variety of arrangements, including the short-term contracts of Chinese workers in the American West). US consular officials abroad were tasked with screening out migrants belonging to the former category. Yet only the Chinese could fall into both categories—as coolies going to the Caribbean and Latin America, and as free migrants going to the United States. The new system of certification prior to departure laid the administrative groundwork for Chinese exclusion in the 1880s and the consular visa system of the twentieth century.[30]

Like the first laws regulating the external slave trade in 1794 and 1800, the Coolie Trade Prohibition Act was directed at Americans transporting unfree passengers to foreign ports rather than the United States. Even if congressmen from the secessionist slaveholding states had been present to object to the bill, it raised no conflict between local police power and national commerce power. Because the 1862 law classified Chinese workers in the American West as free immigrants, like those coming from Europe, it had no immediate effect on immigration to the United States. The Chinese who built the Central Pacific Railroad between 1865 and 1869 entered into contracts voluntarily, agreeing to pay off advances for their transportation and upkeep from

FIGURE 5.2 "Central Pacific Railroad—Construction." Chinese laborers at work on a bridge over the Sacramento Ravine in the Sierra Nevada Mountains, 1877. Between 15,000 and 20,000 Chinese immigrants worked on the construction of the Transcontinental Railroad. Most of them were employed to build the Central Pacific Railroad eastward from Sacramento, while Irish immigrants dominated the labor force that built the Union Pacific Railroad westward from the Missouri River. The two lines met at Promontory Point, Utah, in 1869, and construction continued in the 1870s. Photograph by Carleton E. Watkins. Courtesy of Union Pacific Railroad Museum.

their wages. These contracts did not violate the prohibition on coolie labor introduced in 1862. The workers, however, were often recruited on five-year contracts and worked for lower wages under significantly harsher conditions than their largely Irish counterparts. These exploitative conditions led many Americans to see them as inherently unfree and to denounce Chinese labor contractors for running a new system of slavery. The gradual cooliezation of Chinese migrant laborers after the Civil War would culminate in their exclusion from the United States in the 1880s.[31]

## Immigration Policy during and after the Civil War

With the antislavery Republican Party controlling the national government during the Civil War, Congress turned next to questions concerning European immigration. During the war, the question of alien suffrage became entangled with the military draft. The Militia Act of 1862 called for a nine-month enrollment by able-bodied male citizens between the ages of eighteen and forty-five, with the numbers apportioned by state population. Whereas the Militia Acts of 1792 and 1795 had restricted military service to white men, the 1862 act permitted African Americans to serve in the army (with the initial goal of deploying them as military laborers rather than in combat). Controversy arose over whether the new act applied to declarant aliens (immigrants who had filed "first papers" declaring their intention to naturalize). In August 1862, Governor Edward Salomon of Wisconsin wrote to Secretary of War Edwin M. Stanton, informing him that roughly half of his state's able-bodied men were declarant aliens. Because these men were eligible to vote in Wisconsin, Salomon urged that they be included in the draft. Stanton replied that declarations of intent did not, in themselves, make men subject to conscription, but that those who had exercised the right to vote were draftable. When Carl Wehlitz, a Prussian immigrant in Milwaukee who had voted and was duly drafted, challenged his conscription, the Wisconsin Supreme Court ruled unanimously against him. The Enrolment Act of March 1863, which introduced conscription into the Union Army for men aged between twenty and forty-five, included aliens who had filed first papers. Abraham Lincoln issued a proclamation on May 8, 1863, that all declarant aliens who had voted could be drafted immediately, and that those who had filed papers but not yet voted must either accept conscription after sixty-five days or renounce their right to residency as well as naturalization.[32]

The Constitution of the Confederate States of America, meanwhile, outlawed alien suffrage altogether. The Confederate constitutional convention in Montgomery, Alabama, in 1861 stipulated that "no person of foreign birth, not a citizen of the Confederate States, shall be allowed to vote for any officer, civil or political, State or Federal." Confederate leaders feared that naturalized British and German immigrants might oppose slavery. The Catholic Irish, although they tended to vote Democrat and support slavery, faced widespread nativist hostility in the South because of their poverty and religion. Georgia, for example, disenfranchised propertyless whites in 1860, largely in response to the growth of the Irish immigrant population in Augusta and Savannah. Only after the Civil War did declarant alien suffrage become widespread in the South, driven by the need to attract immigrants.[33]

As wartime production expanded, demand for labor increased significantly. The labor supply declined, however, due to military service and low immigration. In the South, where immigration had always been low, enslaved people were forced to support a war designed to perpetuate slavery. Toward the end of the conflict, some enslaved people were even pressed into military service as cooks, teamsters, and laborers. Immigration to the United States fell sharply in the early years of the war. Annual arrivals from Europe, which stood at 251,306 in 1857, fell to about one-third of that number in 1861 and 1862. The Homestead Act of 1862, a massive federal program for encouraging westward settlement, made freehold land available not only to citizens but also to declarant aliens. Also in 1862, Congress passed a military service act providing that immigrants honorably discharged from the Union Army did not have to submit declarations of intent and needed only one year of residency before naturalization. American consular officials publicized these measures abroad, and, partly as a result, the number of immigrants from Europe to the United States almost doubled in 1863. Nonetheless, mine operators, railroad officials, and iron manufacturers, concerned about labor shortages and high wages, looked for their own ways to import workers from Europe.[34]

Although indentured servitude disappeared in the United States after 1815, American employers had imported small numbers of skilled workers from Europe throughout the antebellum era to build wool and cotton mills, open mines, and equip factories. Most of these workers were British. They typically came to the United States on contracts of three years or more, which ensured that they would not only pay off the loans for their transportation, but also continue to perform needed labor for some time thereafter. The idea that a prospective immigrant would enter into a long-term labor contract while living abroad was not new, but the degree of cooperation between private corporations and the federal government during the Civil War was unprecedented.[35]

Business interests in the Northeast formed agencies during the war to recruit workers for employers. The American Emigrant Company, founded in Hartford in 1863 by bankers, lawyers, and politicians, rather than industrialists or merchants, initially hoped to populate some of its western landholdings with immigrants. Reorganized in 1864 as an agency for recruiting immigrant labor, the company sought to make a profit by supplying skilled European workers to American employers. The teachings of economist Henry C. Carey, who advocated high tariffs and high immigration, inspired the American Emigrant Company and similar groups, including Boston's Foreign Emigrant Society, also founded in 1863. Salmon P. Chase, William H. Seward, and other members of Abraham Lincoln's cabinet supported the idea of importing contract labor.[36]

In his annual message to Congress in December 1863, Abraham Lincoln addressed immigration at length. Many foreign-born Americans, he noted, were evading military service by denying that they had declared their intent to become citizens or had already naturalized. Lincoln called on the courts to file naturalization records and declarations of intent with the secretary of the interior and reiterated that pleas for exemption from military service should be denied if aliens had voted. He also asked Congress to craft a new policy to encourage immigration from Europe. Although "this source of national wealth and strength" was flowing into the United States at a higher level than during the early years of the Civil War, he noted, there was still a significant shortage of manpower in industry, mining, and especially agriculture. Thousands of unemployed people were "thronging our foreign consulates," seeking to emigrate to the United States "if essential, but very cheap, assistance can be afforded them." It was clear, Lincoln concluded, "that, under the sharp discipline of civil war, the nation is beginning a new life. This noble effort demands the aid, and ought to receive the attention and support of the government." The result was the Act to Encourage Immigration, the first federal law other than the Passenger Acts to regulate admissions from Europe. Significantly in the context of subsequent federal law, the intention of this act was to attract immigrants rather than to restrict or exclude them.[37]

The Senate passed a bill in March 1864 providing for the appointment of a commissioner of immigration in the Department of State and a superintendent who would direct a new US immigrant office in New York City. This bill ignored the demands of some Republicans and businessmen that the federal government should directly fund immigrants' transportation costs. The House, with the encouragement of Secretary of State Seward, who had for some time been encouraging private organizations to foster immigration, produced a bill proposing a "commercial system" whereby the government would cooperate with business interests in attracting foreign workers on short-term labor contracts (of twelve months or less). Despite their differences, both the House and the Senate rejected direct government sponsorship of immigration, partly for constitutional and fiscal reasons, but also for fear of attracting poor immigrants rather than thrifty productive laborers.[38]

In June 1864, between the passage of the Senate and House versions of the immigration bill, the Republican (National Union) Convention met in Baltimore to nominate Abraham Lincoln for a second presidential term. By this time the Republican Party had rejected most of its antebellum nativism. The National Union platform declared that "foreign immigration, which in the past has added so much to the wealth, development of resources and increase of power to this nation, the asylum of the oppressed of all nations, should be fostered and encouraged by a liberal and just policy." The Democrats, preoccupied with the slaveholders' rebellion as it approached defeat, were silent on immigration that year. Congress reconciled the two bills, and Lincoln signed the Act to Encourage Immigration on July 4, 1864.[39]

Under the new legislation, the federal government endorsed a policy of selecting and recruiting immigrants. The commissioner of immigration, appointed for a term of four years at an annual salary of $2,500, was responsible for gathering and disseminating information about American labor needs in order to encourage migration to and within the United States, arranging with American railroads and transportation companies for tickets to be sold to immigrants, and providing protection from fraud along with information and advice on destinations. To prevent undue influence by private recruiting agencies, no person involved in any corporation that transported immigrants or sold them land could fill any post created under the Act to Encourage Immigration. The act also allayed prospective immigrants' fears of conscription by clarifying that they could not be drafted unless they had announced their intention to become American citizens. Nor were they required to become citizens in order to stay in the United States.[40]

In his last annual message to Congress, in December 1864, Abraham Lincoln reflected on the new immigration policy. He expressed satisfaction that the Act to Encourage Immigration was being implemented to the extent possible, but he urged that it be amended to help government officers prevent ongoing frauds against immigrants and to emphasize that the government neither needed nor intended to conscript immigrants on arrival. Continued immigration to the United States, Lincoln concluded, was "one of the principal replenishing streams which are appointed by Providence to repair the ravages of internal war, and its wastes of national strength and health." Lincoln's belief in immigration as a source of vitality and prosperity reflected both the economic exigencies and the tragic realities of the Civil War, but it also had deeper roots in his political ideology. The self-made European immigrant, after all, was in many respects his ideal American.[41]

Although the Act to Encourage Immigration stopped short of subsidizing transportation, it recognized contracts made abroad, of twelve months or shorter, that conformed with regulations established by the new commissioner of immigration. Emigrants pledged to repay the expenses of their passage from their wages. In recognizing these contracts—as distinct from the eight-year terms of service Chinese workers endured in Cuba—Congress implicitly affirmed the migration of free Chinese workers to the American West under the broadly similar "credit-ticket" system. Yet, while the 1862 act required Chinese migrants to obtain certificates from US consular agents at their port of embarkation signifying that they were free, no such documentation was required of European immigrants under the 1864 act. The Act to Encourage Immigration took pains to emphasize that the short-term contracts it sanctioned were not "contravening the Constitution of the United States or creating in any way the relation of Slavery or servitude." If an immigrant received advances on wages, however, the contract would operate as a lien on any property acquired, whether under the Homestead Law or otherwise, until the debt was liquidated.[42]

In practice, the recruitment system was ineffective. The Act to Encourage Immigration adopted the House's plan of attracting immigrant workers through a combination of public and private efforts and lent federal support to these efforts by recognizing short-term contracts. Funding, however, was deliberately small, with only $25,000 appropriated. The government chose not to incorporate a national immigrant company, for fear that any such enterprise would look mainly to its own interests. Nonetheless, the American Emigrant Company billed itself as the "handmaid of the new Immigration Bureau." Confirming this impression, the new federal superintendent was housed in the company's office at 3 Bowling Green in New York City. The company also opened offices in England, Scotland, Wales, Belgium, France, Prussia, and the Scandinavian countries, working in tandem with US consular officials who distributed pamphlets, maps, and information. The initial plan was to advance money to employers to cover transatlantic fares, with immigrants signing contracts to redeem their debts in the United States. Lacking the funds to cover the fares, the company adopted two other methods. Employers could advance passage money directly to immigrants identified by the company for a fee. Or immigrants could pay their own way and arrange employment and transportation in New York City via letters of introduction provided by the company, again with a fee charged to the employers. In both cases, employers would reclaim their debts from the wages of contract workers. But the cost of importing labor in this way was prohibitive, and in Britain, the principal intended recruiting ground, trade union newspapers and emigrant letters exposed the company's exaggerations about wages and the cost of living in the United States. Demand for contract labor, which had never been high, dwindled in 1866 and 1867.[43]

The American Emigrant Company responded by trying to tighten the labor contracts. The lien on property provided by the 1864 act as a protection against broken contracts proved ineffective, as most of the workers were in industrial rather than agricultural jobs and were more likely to leave for similar positions than to search for a homestead. The company recommended that fugitive workers should forfeit twice the balance they owed to their employers, who would have the right to impound the workers' wages in their new jobs. This suggestion evoked the coercive labor contracts of the early nineteenth century, whereby workers and servants lost their entire wage if they absconded before serving their full term. Nineteenth-century sailors also endured exceptionally coercive labor conditions. States in the Old Northwest used similar laws in an effort to bind African Americans to servitude during the antebellum era, and southern states enacted Black Codes directly after emancipation in an effort to tie the freedmen to plantation labor. The American Emigrant Company urged the government, unsuccessfully, to amend the 1864 act to cover minors and married women. Under the principle of coverture, married women had long been prohibited not only from owning property but also from making contracts and earning wages. State passed laws relaxing some of these restrictions, though usually with the goal of protecting family finances rather than advancing the rights of women. Labor contracts recognized under federal law, the company hoped, would allow for greater control over female as well as male labor.[44]

When Congress ignored the American Emigrant Company's calls to amend the 1864 act, some states responded by passing their own laws to encourage immigration. Connecticut, for example, passed an Act to Encourage the Importation of Laborers embracing all the revisions the company suggested and allowing nonresident employers to enforce their contracts in the state's courts. Whether organized locally or nationally, these schemes to import workers through cooperation between governments and the private sector tended to be strongly antilabor. During a work stoppage in Chicago in 1867, for example, the American Emigrant Company helped iron manufacturers import 200 workers from Belgium and 800 from Prussia, prompting opposition from the Iron Molders' Union and the National Labor Union. This incident and others gave rise to an enduring hostility to immigrant contract workers over the coming decades.[45]

Some Radical Republicans were uncomfortable with the idea of importing contracted workers from Europe. When Congress considered repealing the Act to Encourage Immigration in 1866, Senator Lot Morrill of Maine, chairman of the Commerce Committee, was among those who denounced the law on antislavery grounds. The act made it clear that contracts had to be twelve months or shorter and did not resemble "Slavery or servitude." But Morrill claimed that, in contemplating the bill in 1864, the Commerce Committee "was astonished that the Senate ever gave it a moment's consideration" as it "was so closely allied to the Coolie business." Government-sponsored schemes to import foreign workers, for Morrill, were "another species of slavery." The United States, supposedly "the asylum for the downtrodden and oppressed," was implementing a policy "to go out among the peoples of Europe and purchase them in the market like cattle, and then bind them to us by penalties and conditions which would disgrace a barbarous nation." Along with his Republican colleague, John Conness of California, Morrill conceded that private companies had the right to import workers, but both men insisted that the federal government should play no role in sponsoring this trade. Most Republicans defended the Act to Encourage Immigration, however, and no action was taken in 1866.[46]

Two years later, the act was allowed to expire without fanfare. Protests by organized labor played a role here, but there were other reasons: funding was deliberately inadequate; contracts were difficult to enforce when broken; and immigration agencies in individual states allowed private employers to import labor more cheaply and effectively than through the American Emigrant Company. A Republican Party presiding over emancipation, in any case, was not likely to extend its involvement in recruiting contract labor much beyond the wartime emergency. Radical Reconstruction was underway, and it was in this context that the United States formulated a national immigration policy for the first time.

# 6

## Reconstruction

OVER THE WINTER of 1869–1870, Frederick Douglass traveled across the United States, delivering a lecture called "Our Composite Nationality." Douglass had escaped from slavery in 1838 and became one of America's most prominent abolitionists. By 1869, he had reasons to be optimistic. Over the previous four years, the Thirteenth Amendment had abolished slavery, and the Fourteenth Amendment had written the principle of birthright citizenship into the Constitution. Congress was debating another amendment, on voting rights. The United States, Douglass declared, was "the most conspicuous example of composite nationality in the world." It had the widest array of "ethnological" and religious diversity. Until recently, its treatment of African Americans had "lacked humanity and filled the country with agitation and ill-feeling, and brought the Nation to the verge of ruin." The problem, Douglass believed, was not the American system of government or the principles underlying that system, but the way "the ruling power of the country" managed relations between the different kinds of people constituting the nation. "We have for a long time hesitated to adopt and carry out the only principle which can solve that difficulty and give peace, strength and security to the Republic," Douglass declared, "and that is the principle of absolute equality."[1]

Chinese immigrants, Douglass noted, were arriving in the United States in large numbers, and they too were facing racial discrimination. He welcomed the Chinese, calling on the United States to be a home "not only for the negro, the mulatto and the Latin races" but also for the Asian immigrant, who should "feel at home here, both for his sake and for ours." Only one-fifth of the world's population was white, Douglass pointed out. Why should the remaining four-fifths be deprived of the right to come to the United States? The rights of people to migrate and to join the body politic where they settled, as Douglass put it, were founded on "the broad fact" of a common human

**FIGURE 6.1** The great abolitionist Frederick Douglass in 1870, the year he delivered his lecture "Composite Nationality," outlining a multicultural vision of American democracy. Photograph by George Francis Schreiber, 1870. National Portrait Gallery, Smithsonian Institution; gift of Donald R. Simon.

nature. "Man is man the world over," he declared. "A smile or a tear has no nationality. Joy and sorrow speak alike in all nations, and they above all the confusion of tongues proclaim the brotherhood of man." The "question of Chinese immigration," Douglass insisted, "should be settled upon higher principles than those of a cold and selfish expediency. There are such things in the world as human rights." Among these rights were "the right of locomotion; the right of migration; the right which belongs to no particular race, but belongs alike to all and to all alike." Free and open migration for all was central to the interracial democracy Douglass saw emerging from the ashes of slavery.[2]

Reconstruction had contradictory effects for immigrants. Its crowning accomplishment, the Fourteenth Amendment, extended due process and equal protection to every "person" under the jurisdiction of the United States, including foreigners who had not naturalized or were prohibited by law from doing so. On this basis, Chinese immigrants challenged state and federal laws that sought to exclude them or that discriminated against them after entry. Under the principle of birthright citizenship enshrined in the Fourteenth Amendment, moreover, the American-born children of all immigrants were automatically citizens of the United States. These egalitarian developments triggered a racial backlash against the Chinese. The newly empowered national government created by Reconstruction, once it wrested control over immigration from the states, could regulate admissions in ways that no state could hope to accomplish.[3]

## Civil Rights and Citizenship

Within a month of the abolition of slavery in December 1865, the coauthor of the Thirteenth Amendment, Senator Lyman Trumbull of Illinois, introduced the first civil rights bill in American history. Unlike more radical members of the Republican Party, Trumbull did not want the bill to address social equality or political rights. Asked in the Senate debates to explain what he meant by the term "civil rights," Trumbull replied that the first section of the proposed bill provided the answer: "The right to make and enforce contracts, to sue and be sued, to give evidence, to inherit, purchase, sell, lease, hold, and convey real and personal property, and to full and equal benefit to all laws and proceedings for the security of person and property." As distinct from political rights or social equality, these were "fundamental rights belonging to every man as a free man, and which under the Constitution as it now exists we have a right to protect every man in." Voting remained a privilege, rather than a right pertaining to citizenship.[4]

Opposition to the civil rights bill focused on two related questions. Did the federal government have the power to define and protect rights of this kind? And what sorts of people would enjoy these rights? Senator Willard Saulsbury Sr., Democrat of Delaware, denounced the bill as "one of the most dangerous ever introduced into the Senate of the United States, or to which the attention of the American people was ever invited." Citing *Gibbons v. Ogden* (1824) and *New York v. Miln* (1837), Saulsbury insisted that the framers of the Constitution had intended all the powers embraced by the proposed bill to be reserved exclusively to the states. Congressman Michael Kerr, Democrat of Indiana, warned that if Congress had the power to pass the bill, it could also force his state to admit "negroes or mulattoes, coolies or Mexicans, Hottentots or Bushmen" (derogatory terms for the Indigenous people of southern Africa, used here to describe Africans in general). The

United States, Kerr predicted, would become "substantially Africanized, Mexicanized or Coolyized."[5]

Opponents of the civil rights bill demanded to know on what basis formerly enslaved people could become United States citizens, as well as the implications for naturalizing nonwhite immigrants. Senator Peter Van Winkle, a Republican/Unionist from West Virginia who supported President Andrew Johnson, asked Trumbull, "if these Africans are not now citizens of the United States, where is the authority by law of Congress to make them citizens?" Echoing the *Dred Scott* decision, Van Winkle claimed that African Americans were not part of the American people when the Constitution was established and that extending citizenship to them would require a constitutional amendment. This question, he warned, involved "not only the negro race, but other inferior races that are now settling on our Pacific coast, and perhaps involves a future immigration to this country of which we have no conception." Trumbull replied that the naturalization clause in the Constitution gave Congress the power to establish whatever naturalization process it wished. This clause did not use the word "foreigners," Trumbull pointed out, and Congress had more than once "naturalized a whole people," including the Stockbridge Indians in 1843, the inhabitants of Florida after its acquisition in 1819, and the inhabitants of Texas after its annexation in 1845. Congress, in short, had broad and exclusive authority to declare who was a citizen of the United States.[6]

Opponents of the civil rights bill also wanted to know if Native Americans would become citizens. When Trumbull introduced a version of the bill stating that "All persons born in the United States, and not subject to any foreign Power, are hereby declared to be citizens of the United States, without distinction of color," Senator James Guthrie, Democrat of Kentucky, and Senator Jacob Howard, Republican of Michigan, objected that this language would confer citizenship on Native Americans. Trumbull explained that the United States regarded Native Americans living on tribal lands as foreigners, interacting with them by treaties, and that his bill had no intention of naturalizing them. Senator James H. Lane, Republican of Kansas, asked whether Native Americans who had "separated themselves from their tribal relations" and taken private allotments of land would be considered citizens of the United States. Trumbull explained that they already were citizens if they had left their land and incorporated themselves into local communities. The civil rights bill confirmed that Native Americans born on tribal lands were not citizens of the United States, by excluding "Indians not taxed" from its provisions. Trumbull and his fellow Republican John Bingham emphasized that extending US citizenship to Native Americans unilaterally would undermine their sovereignty. Subsequent efforts to confer citizenship in this way, which many Native Americans resisted, confirmed their prediction.[7]

With regard to immigrants, the debate over citizenship pitted proponents of racialist social contract theories against advocates of a more inclusive approach. Senator Edgar Cowan, Republican of Pennsylvania, offered the most alarmist predictions, demanding to know whether the American-born children of Chinese immigrants and "Gypsies" would be citizens. In using the term Gypsies, Cowan did not specify a particular group, but he was probably referring to an itinerant community, originating in the German Rhineland, present in York County, Pennsylvania, from the 1840s onward. The members of this community were not necessarily of Roma or Sinti descent. They traveled through the countryside in wagons during the summer selling homemade baskets and brushes. To Cowan, they were transients, unwilling or unable to assimilate into American society, and therefore deeply threatening.[8]

Cowan invoked the Gypsy threat as part of a larger objection to birthright citizenship. Certain kinds of people, he insisted, were not suited to become citizens. These included not only formerly enslaved African Americans but also Chinese immigrants and "Gypsies" and their American-born children. Trumbull explained to Cowan that "under the naturalization laws the children who are born here of parents who have not been naturalized are citizens." Any child born in the United States of immigrant parents, therefore, was a citizen. "Is not the child born in this country of German parents a citizen?" he asked Cowan, referring to the dominant ethnic group in Pennsylvania. Germans, for Cowan, evidently did not include "Gypsies," and they were superior to other groups. "Germans are not Chinese," Cowan replied, "Germans are not Australians, nor Hottentots, nor anything of the kind." Not all children of immigrants, Cowan insisted, were citizens by birthright. In Pennsylvania, he contended, "that is not the law, and never has been the law." Cowan went so far to claim that the *Dred Scott* decision had not only excluded black people from citizenship, it had also excluded "every other race but the white."[9]

Radical Republicans repudiated this racist position. "Was not America said to be a land of refuge?" Senator Lot M. Morrill of Maine asked. "Has it not been since the earliest period held up as an asylum for the oppressed of all nations? All the nations of the earth and all varieties of the races of the nations of the earth have gathered here." People of every variety—"the Irish, the French, the Swede, the Turk, the Italian, the Moor, and so I might enumerate all the races and all the variety of races"—had come to America from the beginning. It was "a fundamental mistake to suppose that settlement was begun here in the interests of any class or condition or race or interest." Where, Morrill demanded to know, was "color" or "race" in the Declaration of Independence? Even the *Dred Scott* decision, he argued, barred free black people from citizenship not strictly speaking on grounds of race or color, but on the basis of condition (i.e., their enslavement or that of their ancestors). America's foundational dictum that all men were created equal excluded "the idea of race or color or caste."[10]

On February 2, 1866, the Senate voted to approve the civil rights bill. The first section prohibited discrimination against the "inhabitants" of any state or territory on account of "race, color or previous condition of slavery." The House approved the bill on March 13 but only after changing the word "inhabitants" to "citizens." The Senate agreed to this change and the resulting Civil Rights Act declared that "all persons born in the United States, and not subject to any foreign Power, excluding Indians not taxed," were citizens of the United States. All citizens, "of every race and color, without regard to any previous condition of slavery or involuntary servitude, except as a punishment for crime," had the same right as "white citizens" to make and enforce contracts, take lawsuits, testify in court, and own property. All citizens were also subject to the same punishment for crimes, "any law, statute, ordinance, regulation, or custom, to the contrary notwithstanding." The act imposed fines of up of $1,000 or a year in prison on persons who, "under any law or custom," deprived "any inhabitant of any State or Territory" of the rights it secured, or violated the ban on inequitable punishments. While this provision did not extend the rights of citizens to alien immigrants, it did allow Chinese immigrants to challenge differences in criminal penalties in state laws regulating entry or mandating removal.[11]

To become law, the Civil Rights Act had to overcome a challenge by President Andrew Johnson, who vetoed the measure on March 27, 1866. The act, he objected, extended citizenship to "the Chinese of the Pacific States, Indians subject to taxation, the people called Gipsies, as well as the entire race designated as blacks, people of color, negroes, mulattoes, and persons of African blood." If native-born people were already citizens of the United States under the Constitution, Johnson asked, why was it necessary to pass such a measure? If they were not, was it "sound policy to make our entire colored population, and all other excepted classes, citizens of the United States" at a time when eleven of the thirty-six states (i.e., those in the former Confederacy) were unrepresented in Congress? "Can it be reasonably supposed," Johnson asked, that the 4 million former slaves who were about to receive citizenship had "the requisite qualifications to entitle them to all the privileges and immunities of citizenship of the United States?" European immigrants, by contrast, had to wait five years before they could naturalize as citizens. This would amount to discrimination, Johnson claimed, "against large numbers of intelligent, worthy and patriotic foreigners, and in favor of the negro." Congress, he alleged, was seeking not simply to impose "a perfect equality" between black and white but also to ensure that distinctions of race and color operated "in favor of the colored against the white race." It was doing so by interfering with matters that the sovereign states had previously regulated exclusively. This policy, he warned, would destroy the federal system, "break down the barriers which preserve the rights of the States," and concentrate power in the national government. In an extraordinary move, Congress responded by overriding Johnson's veto, signaling that the legislative branch would dictate the terms of Reconstruction.[12]

The Civil Rights Act, the first significant statute in American history to be passed over a president's veto, became law on April 9, 1866. By disconnecting citizenship from race and basing it on birthright, the act repudiated the *Dred Scott* decision. It also significantly increased the power of the federal government to protect the rights of citizens against actions by the states. Radical Republicans realized, however, that the Civil Rights Act would not be enough. A statute could be repealed by Congress or invalidated by the Supreme Court. Thaddeus Stevens of Pennsylvania predicted that Congress would repeal the act as soon as southern Democrats and their northern allies, known as Copperheads, regained control of the national legislature. A more fundamental definition of national citizenship and its attendant rights was needed. Passed by Congress on June 13, 1866, and ratified by the states on July 9, 1868, the Fourteenth Amendment did more than write the Civil Rights Act into the Constitution. The product of a war to end slavery, it transformed American democracy by extending equal rights to all residents of the United States, including aliens, and giving the federal government broad supervisory power over the states.[13]

As during the debates over the Civil Rights Act, opponents of the proposed amendment demanded to know if Native Americans would be citizens. The Civil Rights Act, in excluding "Indians not taxed" from citizenship, implied that Native Americans who left their tribal lands and lost their immunity from taxation were eligible for national citizenship. The Fourteenth Amendment dropped the phrase "Indians not taxed" in favor of "subject to the jurisdiction of the United States," in the understanding that Native Americans on tribal lands would not be included. Yet Senator James R. Doolittle, Republican of Wisconsin, claimed that all Native Americans, not just those in tribal relations, were subject to the US jurisdiction and would be eligible for citizenship if the phrase "excluding Indians not taxed" was omitted. Senator Jacob Howard, Republican of Michigan, explained to Doolittle that Native Americans who maintained tribal relations were not "born subject to the jurisdiction of the United States" but were regarded, and had always been treated, as members of "quasi foreign nations." The words "subject to the jurisdiction thereof," Trumbull added, meant subject to complete jurisdiction, "or not owing allegiance to anyone else." The egalitarian wing of the Republican Party intended this part of the Fourteenth Amendment, once again, to protect Native sovereignty (while excluding two other minor categories, children born in the United States to foreign diplomats and children born to enemy combatants during an invasion).[14]

If these debates helped clarify who was eligible to be a citizen, critics of the proposed Fourteenth Amendment demanded to know what citizenship meant. Senator Cowan asked Howard for a legal definition. "What does it mean?" he asked. "What is its length and breadth?" In particular, Cowan wanted to know the status of a child born to a Chinese immigrant in California or to a Gypsy in his native Pennsylvania. Cowan conceded that any traveler, whether "from Ethiopia, from Australia, or from Great Britain," was entitled to some degree of legal protection in the United States. But were the people of California "to remain quiescent," he asked, "while they are overrun by a flood of immigration of the Mongrel race?" Were they to be "immigrated out of house and home by Chinese?" Could they take no measures to protect themselves? Under the Constitution, Cowan claimed, each state had the right to forbid entry by any person who was not a citizen of one of the other states. The decision on whether to admit or exclude migrants depended on their "inherent character." There were "nations of people with whom theft is a virtue and falsehood a merit," Cowan declared, and "to whom polygamy is as natural as monogamy is with us." It was impossible "to mingle all the various families of men, from the lowest form of Hottentot up to the highest Caucasian, in the same society." Although Cowan professed, in a familiar racist refrain, to be "as liberal as anybody toward the rights of all people," he insisted on drawing the line at a certain point.[15]

Cowan was not willing to see his own state of Pennsylvania give up its right to expel a group who were invading its borders, owed the state no allegiance, and had "a distinct, independent government of their own—an *imperium in imperio*." These people paid no taxes, performed no military service or other civic duties, had no homes or settled residences, owned no land, and settled as trespassers wherever they went. Cowan was referring, once again, to Gypsies. "They wander in gangs in my State," he complained. "They follow no ostensible pursuit for a livelihood. They trade horses, tell fortunes, and things disappear mysteriously. Where they came from nobody knows. Their very origin is lost in mystery." They did not intermingle or intermarry with other groups. Were they, by a constitutional amendment, to be put beyond the power of the state where they lived? Even "Indians not taxed," for Cowan, were less dangerous than "Gypsies." Given the tiny presence of this group, even in Pennsylvania, Cowan was clearly raising this phantom threat to symbolize some deeper peril. His main concern seems to have been Chinese immigration. Would the western states, Cowan asked, lose control over immigration by "the Mongol race" in the same way?[16]

Not every Republican in California shared Cowan's anxiety. Senator John Conness, who immigrated to the United States from Ireland at the age of fifteen and had close ties with railroad interests that depended on Chinese migrant labor, stepped in to reassure Cowan. If Cowan knew as much about Chinese immigrants as he did about Gypsies, Conness explained, he would not be alarmed on California's behalf. The Chinese were "a docile, industrious people" who moved from mining into other branches of industry and labor. They were "very valuable laborers, patient and effective." Conness pointed out that all children born in California, regardless of their parentage, were citizens of the United States and entitled to equal civil rights with other citizens. The Civil Rights Act of 1866 had established that principle, and it was time now to incorporate it into the fundamental law through a constitutional amendment. As for Cowan's fears about Pennsylvania, Conness declared that "I have heard more about Gypsies within the last two or three months than I have heard before in my life." The only "invasion" of Pennsylvania he could remember had occurred during the Civil War, and on that occasion Pennsylvania had not claimed "the exclusive right of expelling the invaders." On the contrary, it had called for help from neighboring states and did not regard its sovereign rights as violated when the citizens of New York and New Jersey came to its assistance.[17]

As with any political compromise, the Fourteenth Amendment had its limits. Thaddeus Stevens wanted political and social equality, not just equality before the law. He regarded the second section of the amendment, on representation, as the most important. A state that excluded adult male citizens from the franchise would suffer a proportional reduction in its representation in Congress. Stevens regretted that the penalty was proportional rather than absolute; a version of the amendment defeated in the Senate had provided "that if one of the injured race was excluded the State should forfeit the right to have any of them represented." The final version of the amendment penalized disenfranchisement "except for participation in rebellion, or other crime," rather than explicitly prohibiting it by race. By using the word "male" in the section on suffrage, moreover, the amendment introduced a gender distinction into the Constitution for the first time. Stevens also pointed out that "the true measure of justice" would be to give "every adult freedman a homestead on the land where he was born and toiled and suffered. Forty acres of land and a hut would be more valuable to him than the immediate right to vote." Stevens was a pragmatist as well as a radical, and when the House agreed to the Senate version on June 13, 1866, with the final definition of citizenship, he voted in favor. The Fourteenth Amendment then had to be ratified. Without the votes of black men in the South, it would not have become part of the Constitution. The amendment became law on July 28, 1868.[18]

The Fourteenth Amendment provided a simple and profound definition of citizenship. "All persons born or naturalized in the United States and subject to the jurisdiction thereof," the opening sentence stated, "are citizens of the United States and of the State wherein they reside." This language, Senator Howard predicted, would settle "the great question of citizenship," removing all doubt as to which persons were and were not citizens. Enshrining birthright citizenship in the Constitution affirmed a century-long struggle for rights by African Americans. It conferred immediate citizenship on American-born children of every background, without qualification. As well as defining citizenship, the opening section stipulated that no state could "make or enforce any law which shall abridge the privileges or immunities of citizens of the United States." More fundamentally than the Civil Rights Act, the Fourteenth Amendment repudiated the *Dred Scott* decision. It re-made the American state through a constitutional revolution that bound the national government to its citizens by protecting their rights. Whereas the Bill of Rights added to the Constitution in 1789 had restricted the actions of Congress, the Fourteenth Amendment restricted the actions of states. This momentous shift set in motion the process known as "incorporation," which unfolded in the twentieth century, whereby the states as well as Congress had to abide by the Bill of Rights (or, at least, the first eight of its ten amendments, given that the last two pertained to states' rights). In this way, rights became an attribute of national citizenship rather than a matter of local discretion. The Fourteenth Amendment by no means eliminated police power, but it significantly expanded federal authority in local affairs.[19]

Significantly, the opening section of the amendment applied to resident aliens as well as citizens. The first of that section's two sentences defined who was a citizen of the United States. The second referred to the privileges and immunities of citizens, but also declared that no state could "deprive any *person* of life, liberty, or property, without due process of law; nor deny to any *person* within its jurisdiction the equal protection of the laws." As Representative John Bingham of Ohio, one of the chief architects of the amendment explained, this language was designed to protect "the absolute equality before the law of all persons, whether citizens or strangers." The Fourteenth Amendment allowed immigrants—especially the Chinese—to challenge laws that discriminated against them. Congress turned next to the related questions of voting rights and naturalization. Initially focused on the rights of African Americans, the debate over the Fifteenth Amendment developed into a broader debate about suffrage and access to citizenship.[20]

## Voting Rights and Naturalization

Radical Republicans favored a single, uniform rule for suffrage applying to the whole nation. The states, in other words, should no longer set the eligibility requirements for voting. Western Republicans, however, worried that Chinese immigrants would gain the vote through changes in the naturalization law. Nativists in the East, meanwhile, were concerned about Irish immigrants. With the Irish in mind, Rhode Island prevented foreign-born citizens from voting in state elections via a property qualification, and Massachusetts and Connecticut used literacy tests for the same purpose. In this context, Republican leaders feared that a broad amendment providing universal manhood suffrage would not pass. Such an amendment might have barred measures restricting the vote on grounds of birthplace, property, or religion, as well as race.[21]

During the debates in Congress, much of the opposition to federal control over voting rights came from western Republicans opposed to Chinese immigrants. On February 5, 1869, Senator George H. Williams of Oregon warned that, if the Constitution could be amended to abolish "all political distinctions on account of race and color," naturalization laws could also be changed on the same principle, allowing the Chinese to vote. Echoing Senator Cowan's attack on Gypsies, Williams warned that the Chinese in the United States were "a distinct and separate nationality, an *imperium in imperio*." He conceded that states could not discriminate against any person born in the United States on grounds of race, color, or previous condition of servitude, but he believed that each state should continue to regulate suffrage, subject to limited oversight by Congress. The states had a sovereign right to make their own rules on political participation by foreigners, depending on the nature of the foreigners in question, in line with their duty to promote the public good. By retaining power over suffrage, Williams hoped, they could prevent not just Chinese immigrants, but also their American-born children, from voting or holding office. Senator Doolittle also objected to "giving universal equality and political power to all the races in the United States, including the Chinese." The states must be allowed to make whatever qualifications they wished for voting.[22]

Radical Republicans rejected these antidemocratic arguments. Charles Sumner offered some practical advice. "In the construction of a machine," he explained, "the good mechanic seeks the simplest process, producing the desired result with the greatest economy of time and force." Sumner recommend that Congress take the same approach. "We are mechanics," he explained, "and the machine we are constructing has for its object the conservation of Equal Rights." Slaveowners before the Civil War, "insisting that Slavery was national and Freedom sectional," had claimed protection under the Constitution. Now, after a war to defeat slavery, "the champions of a kindred pretension" were claiming they could "deny political rights on account of race or color and thus establish that vilest of institutions, a Caste and an Oligarchy of the skin." The Civil War and Reconstruction, Sumner warned, would be in vain unless "State Rights shall yield to Human Rights, and the nation be exalted as the bulwark of all. This will be the crowning victory of the war." States could and should pass laws to protect their citizens within their own jurisdictions, but they could not interfere with "those equal rights, whether civil or political," protected by the Constitution. A state was local rather than universal in character, and what could be more universal than "the Rights of Man?" What could be less universal than the restrictions called for by the "champions of Caste and Oligarchy"? Color—whether of hair, eyes, or skin—could never be a qualification under the Constitution.[23]

Sumner's Democratic opponents objected that there was no natural right to vote. If such a right existed universally, Senator George Vickers of Maryland pointed out, all citizens—female as well as male—would possess it. Suffrage was not one of the natural and "unalienable" rights referred to in the Declaration of Independence, and, even if it had been, these rights were abstractions that did not feature in the Constitution. In practice, governments decided who had the right to vote, based on their ability to understand and participate in the political process. Naturalists and ethnographers, Vickers

FIGURE 6.2 "Uncle Sam's Thanksgiving Dinner" (1869). In Thomas Nast's utopian vision, Uncle Sam carves a turkey, surrounded by men, women, and children of all backgrounds, with the centerpiece proclaiming "self-government/universal suffrage" and the sentiments in the lower corners—"Come One Come All" and "Free and Equal"—setting the tone for the inclusive feast. Columbia, the personification of America, sits at the table opposite the host, chatting with a Chinese guest, while an African American man sits to her left. Representatives of several other nationalities and groups, including a Native American, sit around the table. As the portrait of Castle Garden suggests, all European immigrants are welcome; even the Irishman, to Uncle Sam's left, is only mildly simian by Nast's standards. *Harper's Weekly*, November 20, 1869. Library of Congress Prints and Photographs Division, LC-USZ62-85882.

claimed, had established that mankind was divided into several distinct races or varieties. Yet, according to Sumner, no distinctions could be drawn on the basis of color. Vickers agreed with Williams that "the introduction of a foreign element upon our Pacific coast" made such distinctions inevitable. The people of the individual states, who were "acquainted with the moral and intellectual character and habits of those who live in them," must retain the power to decide who was qualified to vote. When Senator William Pitt Fessenden, a moderate Republican from Maine, pressed Williams on whether states could discriminate against people of European origin, Williams replied that naturalized European immigrants would not be affected. "No distinction can be made against an Englishman or a German on account of race or color by the people of the United States," he explained. "No constitutional amendment could be adopted in a State declaring that a German should be excluded from the elective franchise or the right to hold office on account of race, for they belong to the same race that we do." States should be allowed to "discriminate against foreigners on account of race and color," but they would not—and could not—discriminate against European immigrants.[24]

Confronted with these racist arguments, Charles Sumner urged the Senate not just to confer the right to vote but also "to provide for full equality of rights in all respects." He suggested adding the words, "And there shall be no discrimination in rights on account of race or color," to the proposed Fifteenth Amendment, thereby providing not just "a guarantee of the right to vote and hold office, but a guarantee of equal rights universally." Asked by Senator Charles R. Drake, Republican of Missouri, why this revision was necessary, given that the first section of the Fourteenth Amendment guaranteed due process and equal protection, Sumner responded: "I want to make complete work and finish it so that hereafter there shall be no question." Sumner then proposed that the amendment should refer simply to the right to vote, rather than the right of citizens to vote. This version of the amendment would read: "The right to vote shall not be denied or abridged by the United States or by any State on account of race, color, or previous condition of servitude." West Coast senators and their allies objected strenuously, with Senator Oliver Morton, Republican of Indiana, demanding to know if Sumner's language would "give the right to vote and to hold office affirmatively to any man without naturalization?" Sumner responded that the point was simply to guarantee that the right to vote could not be abridged on account of race or color, but Morton objected that striking out the words "citizens" would make Chinese immigrants eligible to vote and hold office. Senator Doolittle agreed, adding predictably that Sumner's amendment would enfranchise not only the Chinese but also "the Indians in every State and Territory of the Union." Even without Sumner's revision, Doolittle warned, Congress could remove the word "white" from the naturalization laws and create a path to citizenship for Chinese residents, who could then become voters. Sumner reminded Doolittle that he had a bill for just that purpose before the Committee of the Judiciary.[25]

Radical Republicans, aware of the implications of Reconstruction not just for African Americans but also for American society as a whole, supported an egalitarian approach. Senator John Sherman, Republican of Ohio, insisted that extending the franchise only to black people was "not broad enough when we are about to change the Constitution." As the Republican Party was "about to lay the foundation for a political creed," Sherman declared, the strongest foundation would be universal male suffrage. Senator Simon

Cameron, Republican of Pennsylvania, supported Sumner's proposal to outlaw all discrimination on account of race or color "because it invites into our country everybody; the negro, the Irishman, the German, the Frenchman, the Scotchman, the Englishman, and the Chinaman." Cameron pledged that he would "welcome every man, whatever may be the country from which he comes, who by his industry can add to our national wealth." Chinese immigrants, he observed, had enriched the West through their work in the mines and on the railroads, yet they were excluded from naturalization and the franchise. By the same logic, he pointed out, one might as well say that the Irish immigrants who built America's canals and railroads should be prevented from becoming citizens. Given the extent of the opposition, however, Sumner withdrew his proposal that the Fifteenth Amendment should omit the word "citizens."[26]

The Fifteenth Amendment in its final form, approved by Congress on February 26, 1869, stated: "The right of citizens of the United States to vote shall not be denied or abridged by the United States or by any State on account of race, color, or previous condition of servitude." Notably absent from this list was sex. Susan B. Anthony, Elizabeth Cady Stanton, and other feminist leaders denounced the amendment for this reason. Rhode Island, concerned about potential implications for its property qualification for naturalized citizens, delayed ratification until January 1870. California and Oregon rejected the amendment for fear that Chinese immigrants would win the right to naturalize. Three of the four border states that had rejected secession—Kentucky, Maryland, and Delaware—refused to ratify the Fifteenth Amendment, as did the former Confederate state of Tennessee. But the six southern states that had completed their Reconstruction process ratified the amendment, and Congress required the remaining four to do so as a condition of readmission to the Union. The Fifteenth Amendment, ratified on February 3, 1870, fell short of affirming universal manhood suffrage. Its negative framing also left a loophole whereby southern states denied African Americans the vote through ostensibly neutral measures like poll taxes or literacy tests after Reconstruction. Yet its prohibition of discrimination on grounds of race, color, or previous servitude signified that black and white men belonged to the same body politic. Although southern states soon found ways to limit black suffrage, this intervention by the federal government against the states was a revolutionary achievement.[27]

Even as they crafted the Fifteenth Amendment, Republicans suspicious of immigrant and working-class voters were calling for greater federal control over naturalization. In the course of the nineteenth century, naturalization policy had become entangled with expatriation. Applicants for US citizenship were required not only to take an oath to support the Constitution but also to renounce allegiance to any foreign prince or state. When this policy was introduced in 1795, British Foreign Secretary Lord Grenville informed the US minister to the Court of St. James, Rufus King, that no British subject could "by such a form of renunciation as that which is prescribed in the American law of naturalization, divest himself of his allegiance to his sovereign." Any attempt to do so would be considered "an act highly criminal on their part." This policy of perpetual allegiance rested on the principle "once a British subject, always a subject." Congress, by contrast, both permitted and required aliens who became citizens of the United States to sever the ties binding them to other governments. As Attorney General Caleb Cushing put it in 1856, "The doctrine of absolute and perpetual allegiance, the root of the denial of any right of emigration, is inadmissible in the United States. It was a matter involved in, and settled for us by, the Revolution which founded the American Union." The right of expatriation, Cushing explained, was central to American naturalization policy, which permitted foreigners to "incorporate with its people, make its flag their own, and aid in the accomplishment of a common destiny."[28]

The Democratic Party platform of 1868, addressing immigration for the first time since before the Civil War, laid out a firm position on expatriation and naturalization. Recognizing "the questions of slavery and secession as having been settled for all time to come," the party called for "equal rights and protection for naturalized and native-born citizens at home and abroad" and for "the maintenance of the rights of naturalized citizens against the absolute doctrine of immutable allegiance and the claims of foreign powers to punish them for alleged crimes committed beyond their jurisdiction." The reference here was to Irish-American nationalists, known as Fenians, who sent men to Ireland to fight for independence. Born in the United Kingdom of Great Britain and Ireland, some of these men were naturalized American citizens. Yet, when they went on trial in Ireland, the British government claimed them as perpetual subjects. Facing pressure from the United States, the British finally abandoned the doctrine of perpetual allegiance in 1870. Parliament passed a naturalization act that year recognizing the right of British subjects (except married women, lunatics, and infants) to sever their ties and become citizens in a country of their choosing.[29]

Many Republicans, fearful that immigrants would thwart their agenda for Reconstruction, also wanted to reform American naturalization policy. Some proposed shifting control over the process from cities and states to the federal level. Congress passed a Naturalization Act on July 13, 1870. What started as a debate over European immigrants turned into an extended discussion of whether Chinese immigrants could become citizens. Charles Sumner, who wanted everyone, including Chinese immigrants and people of African origin, to have access to citizenship, proposed striking the word "white" from the naturalization laws so that "there shall be no distinction of race or color." Doing so, he declared, would "bring our laws and institutions in harmony with the Declaration of Independence." Two anti-Chinese Republican senators, George H. Williams of Oregon and William Stewart of Nevada, led the opposition. "These people are brought here under the infamous coolie contracts," Stewart exclaimed, "the same contracts that have disgraced humanity in the taking of these poor people to the West India islands and various portions of South America as slaves." When Sumner's bill failed, Lyman Trumbull proposed adding the words "persons born in the Chinese empire" to the list of those eligible for naturalization, but this version too was defeated.[30]

President Grant signed the Naturalization Act into law on July 14, 1870. The act stated simply that "the naturalization laws are hereby extended to aliens of African nativity and to persons of African descent." It did not place the naturalization process under federal control, as some nativists had initially hoped. It was not color-blind in Sumner's sense, and neither did it extend naturalization to the Chinese as Trumbull had proposed. The debate over naturalization had exposed a rift in the Republican Party between a radical minority who believed in universal equality and a majority who felt that the egalitarianism of Reconstruction had gone far enough. The Naturalization Act of 1870 was a deliberately anti-Chinese measure, the opening salvo in a campaign to restrict Chinese immigration.[31]

## Regulating Chinese Immigration

As the United States expanded its political and economic influence overseas in the mid-nineteenth century, trading opportunities in Asia became increasingly important. Secretary of State William H. Seward, in particular, saw free migration as inseparable from free trade. China, for its part, wanted to secure rights for its subjects abroad. The Burlingame-Seward Treaty of 1868 protected American commerce in Chinese ports and cities and established China's right to appoint consuls in the United States. Recognizing "the mutual advantage of the free migration and emigration of their citizens and subjects, respectively, from the one country to the other, for purposes of curiosity, of trade, or as permanent residents," the treaty affirmed the "inherent and inalienable right of man to change his home and allegiance." Citizens of either country visiting or residing in the other would "enjoy the same privileges, immunities, or exemptions in respect to travel or residence as may there be enjoyed by the citizens or subjects of the most favored nation." In line with the Coolie Trade Prohibition Act of 1862, these provisions applied only to migration defined as free. China and the United States agreed to make it a penal offense to transport subjects or citizens of either country abroad without their "free and voluntary consent." In recognizing freedom of movement, the Burlingame-Seward Treaty embodied the antislavery critique of coolieism while offering important protections to Chinese migrants. Both parties to the treaty, however, agreed that their migrants could not be naturalized as citizens.[32]

Federal legislation passed in the 1870s, building on the Civil Rights Act of 1866 and the Fourteenth Amendment, offered additional protections to alien immigrants residing in the United States. Whereas the 1866 act secured equal protection of laws to "all persons born in the United States," the Enforcement Act of 1870 (also known as the Civil Rights Act) guaranteed to "all persons within the jurisdiction of the United States" the same rights, in every state and territory, to make and enforce contracts, sue and be parties to suits, testify

FIGURE 6.3 "Chinese Emigration to America." Sketch of Chinese passengers being served and eating food on board the steamship *Alaska*, bound for San Francisco. *Harper's Weekly*, May 20, 1876. Chinese in California Virtual Collection: Selections from the Bancroft Library, University of California, Berkeley.

in court, and to enjoy the full and equal benefit of laws and security of person and property. Under the 1870 act, no person could be deprived of any of these rights by reason of being an alien or on grounds of color or race. This provision rendered California's laws prohibiting testimony by Chinese immigrants against white persons unenforceable. The 1870 Civil Rights Act also provided that no person could be punished in a manner different from that prescribed for citizens, undermining state laws that singled out Chinese immigrants. Likewise, the act prohibited selective taxation of immigrants, providing that "no tax or charge shall be imposed or enforced by any State upon any person immigrating thereto from a foreign country which is not equally imposed and enforced upon every person immigrating to such State from any foreign country."[33]

Additional measures passed in the 1870s affirmed these protections by expanding the power of the federal government to protect citizens and residents against acts of violence that deprived them of constitutionally protected rights. The Enforcement Act of 1871 (also known as the Civil Rights Act and the Ku Klux Klan Act) criminalized conspiracies to deny the right to vote, to serve on juries, or to enjoy equal protection of laws. This act referred to "any person within the jurisdiction of the United States," and "any person or class of persons," in several of its provisions. Finally, an act passed in 1875 "to Protect All Citizens in Their Civil and Legal Rights" recognized, despite its title, "the equality of all men before the law" and declared that it was "the duty of government in its dealings with the people to mete out equal and exact justice to all, of whatever nativity, race, or color, or persuasion, religious or political." This statute—the last civil rights act passed during Reconstruction—originated in a radical proposal by Charles Sumner to prohibit racial discrimination in schools, juries, and churches as well as public accommodations. As enacted, the law provided for civil and criminal penalties in public accommodations only, dropping the church and school provisions, but even in its final form it applied to "all persons," not just citizens, extending significant protections to immigrants living within the jurisdiction of the United States.[34]

The Supreme Court, however, had already begun to undermine the protections conferred by the civil rights acts and the Reconstruction amendments. In the *Slaughterhouse Cases* of 1873, a group of white butchers in Louisiana challenged a corporate monopoly granted by the state legislature that created a single slaughterhouse downstream from New Orleans and required the city's butchers to bring their animals there to be slaughtered. As a public health measure enacted under the state's police power, the law was designed primarily to prevent independent slaughterhouses from dumping refuse in the Mississippi River. The architects of the law also hoped to make the New Orleans meat-packing industry more competitive by erecting a modern facility. Arguing that they had been deprived of employment, the butchers claimed that Louisiana's law violated the guarantee of equal protection under the Fourteenth Amendment and the ban on involuntary servitude under the Thirteenth Amendment. By a majority of 5 to 4, the Court rejected these arguments.[35]

Writing for the majority, Justice Samuel Miller affirmed that the main purpose of the Fourteenth Amendment was to protect the citizenship rights of African Americans, yet he defined these rights very narrowly. A prominent member of the antebellum Republican Party in Iowa, Miller supported equality before the law. In *Slaughterhouse,* he upheld a law passed by Louisiana's biracial Reconstruction legislature against a challenge by white butchers. Yet his decision, by limiting national citizenship and augmenting state sovereignty, curtailed the rights of black people. In drafting the Fourteenth Amendment, John Bingham had emphasized that "care of the property, the liberty, and the life of the citizen" remained under the control of the states. Bingham's goal, however, was to empower Congress to compel obedience to the Constitution and to "punish all violations by State officers of the bill of rights." In *Slaughterhouse,* Miller ruled that the Fourteenth Amendment applied only to a limited set of rights derived from national rather than state citizenship (such as access to ports and navigable waterways, protection when traveling abroad, and the right to assemble peacefully to seek redress of grievances from the federal government). All other rights, he concluded, remained under the control of the states. The Bill of Rights constrained the actions of the federal government only; put another way, its protections had not yet been incorporated into the Fourteenth Amendment and therefore did not apply to actions by the states. Miller's ruling made it much more difficult to enforce civil rights in the way Bingham and other architects of the Fourteenth Amendment had intended.[36]

The Supreme Court further limited the scope of federal power in *U.S. v. Cruikshank* (1876). Following a disputed gubernatorial election in 1872, a group of black militiamen sought refuge in the courthouse in Colfax, Louisiana. On April 13, 1873, in the worst atrocity of the Reconstruction era, a white supremacist mob attacked the courthouse and killed more than one hundred African Americans, most of them as they surrendered or after they had been imprisoned. Several of the perpetrators were arrested, but only three were brought to trial. Accused of conspiring to deprive their victims of their civil rights, the defendants were prosecuted and convicted under the criminal conspiracy section of the 1870 Enforcement Act. By a majority of 5 to 4, the Supreme Court overturned their convictions on technical grounds. Even though white people had attacked and killed black people, the majority found, the indictment was invalid because it did not specifically mention race as a motivation, as required for a prosecution under the Enforcement Act. This ruling sent a signal that acts of terror against African Americans would go unpunished. The same applied to Chinese immigrants seeking legal protection against mob violence. In keeping with its decision in the *Slaughterhouse Cases*, the Court ruled in *United States v. Cruikshank* that citizens' rights remained mostly under the control of the states rather than the federal government. The federal government could prohibit states from violating certain federally protected rights (covering racially motivated violence if properly specified in an indictment), but actions by individuals—including murder and conspiracy—did not come under federal regulation. Racial terror, in short, was a matter of local sovereignty.[37]

The majority opinion in the *Slaughterhouse Cases*, however, raised the possibility that the Thirteenth Amendment might apply to a broader range of coercive relationships than chattel slavery. Although the amendment "was intended primarily to abolish African slavery," the Court suggested that "it equally forbids Mexican peonage or the Chinese coolie trade when they amount to slavery or involuntary servitude." When Congress prohibited slavery and involuntary servitude in the territories in 1862, its sole concern was African American slavery. The overlapping systems of peonage and Native American captivity in the Southwest, however, involved complex networks of debt, captivity, kinship, and religion. In 1865, President Andrew Johnson condemned Native American slavery in New Mexico and ordered an investigation. The territorial Supreme Court, invoking the Thirteenth Amendment and the Civil Rights Act of 1866, criminalized peonage in New Mexico in 1867. Congress, led by two Massachusetts Radical Republicans, Charles Sumner and Henry Wilson, passed a national anti-peonage act the same year. Strikingly, as in the Coolie Trade Prohibition Act of 1862, this law denied any distinction between bondage entered into voluntarily or involuntarily. It defined all forms of peonage, regardless of whether their origins lay in family ties or kidnapping, as inherently coercive and therefore illegal. Once again, bondage was absolute, and its implied opposite was absolute freedom.[38]

If the Thirteenth Amendment adjusted the boundaries of coercion in a way that benefited debt peons, it had the opposite effect for Chinese immigrants. Ignoring the fact that most Chinese workers arrived in the United States on short-term contracts, restrictionists argued that all of them were coolies who should be excluded on antislavery grounds. Western politicians increasingly equated Chinese laborers with coolies and coolieism with slavery. Chinese laborers, Senator William Stewart of Nevada had declared during the debates on the 1870 Naturalization Act, were brought to the United States under the same coolie contracts as those going to Cuba and Peru. Federal restriction of Chinese immigration in 1882 rested explicitly on the contention that Chinese laborers were unfree.[39]

The restriction movement originated in California, where most Chinese immigrants lived. Starting in the 1850s, California passed a series of laws designed to deter the entry of Chinese immigrants or control the lives of those already resident in the state. These laws were repeatedly challenged in the courts, initially on commerce clause grounds and then on the basis of the protections introduced during Reconstruction. Undaunted, California passed two new measures in March 1870, presented as exercises of the state's police power, to curtail immigration by Chinese laborers and women. An act to Prevent the Importation of Chinese Criminals and to Prevent the Establishment of Coolie Slavery required any "Chinese or Mongolian, born either in the Empire or China or Japan, or any of the islands adjacent to the Empire of China," to present evidence that his migration was voluntary and that he was a person "of correct habits and good character." Chinese immigrants, the law stated, were creating "a species of slavery which is degrading to the laborer and at war with the spirit of the age." An act to prevent the Kidnapping and Importation of Mongolian, Chinese, and Japanese Females, for Criminal or Demoralizing Purposes, required East Asian women to provide evidence of voluntary migration and good character. Those who imported any criminal, coolie, or woman contrary to the two laws faced fines of up to $5,000 or imprisonment for up to twelve months. An amendment to the Anti-Kidnapping Act in 1874 added the categories "convicted criminal" and "lewd or debauched woman."[40]

In August of 1874, the steamer *Japan* arrived in San Francisco from Hong Kong carrying 500 passengers, including eighty-nine women. An immigration inspector boarded the ship with his agents and examined the passengers, questioning them through an interpreter. Women with children were allowed to land, but those traveling alone came under suspicion. Finding the testimony of twenty-two female passengers unsatisfactory, the commissioner concluded that they fell into the category of "lewd or debauched." When the captain refused to post bonds, the women were confined on board the *Japan*. They petitioned for a writ of habeas corpus, but the Fourth District

Court in San Francisco ruled that exclusion of "lewd or debauched" women lay within California's police power and ordered them returned to the ship. Led by a passenger named Ah Fook, the women applied for another writ of habeas corpus, this time to the California Supreme Court. Ah Fook's attorney maintained that the California law violated the guarantees of travel and residence provided by the Burlingame Treaty of 1868. The state Supreme Court dismissed this argument. Because the California law applied to all passengers arriving by ship, the court ruled, it did not discriminate against the Chinese in particular. Nor did the law violate due process, because excluding paupers or criminals was a quarantine measure that came under the state's police power. The justices did not discuss whether the detention of the Chinese women violated the equal protection clause of the Fourteenth Amendment. California, it seemed, had finally found an effective way to exclude Chinese immigrants by targeting women outside the institution of monogamous marriage. The state Supreme Court had struck down previous exclusion measures on commerce clause grounds, but policing the entry of "lewd and debauched women" did not fall into that category.[41]

At this point, however, another of the detained women, Ah Fong, filed a writ of habeas corpus in the United States circuit court for California. Justice Stephen Field of the US Supreme Court, presiding over the case in his role as a judge on the circuit court, invalidated the state law in September 1874. A state's power to exclude foreigners, Field found, was more limited than the California Supreme Court had supposed. This power, he insisted, was based on a narrow "right to self-defense." The California statute was too broad and vague. The doctrine of states' rights, Field noted, arose from the "necessity" felt by southern slaveholding states "of excluding free negroes from their limits." The Civil War, however, had changed all that: states could no longer create their own policies on admission and exclusion. Field also held that California's immigration act of 1874 violated the federal Civil Rights Act of 1870, which prohibited the imposition of a tax or charge on any immigrant group that was not imposed on immigrants from all countries. The California statute did not impose a monetary tax but, Field insisted, it did impose a "charge," which he defined as "any onerous condition." Requiring a bond as a condition of landing passengers, he found, was "as onerous as any charge which can well be imposed." Field ordered the release of the twenty-two passengers.[42]

Field was not motivated by sympathy toward Chinese immigrants. On the contrary, he expressed sympathy with the movement to exclude them. "It is felt that the dissimilarity in physical characteristics, in language, in manners, religion and habits," Field noted, "will always prevent any possible assimilation of them with our people." California's law violated equal protection, he ruled, not because it discriminated by race or gender, but because it singled out one class of immigrants—those who arrived by sea (as distinct from those who traveled overland from Canada or Mexico or across the plains by railway)— for special treatment. Equal protection aside, Field pointed out that no state had the authority to exclude immigrants. Power over immigration, based on the commerce clause and the treaty-making clause, lay "exclusively within the jurisdiction of the General Government, and is not subject to State control or interference." If the states wanted to restrict immigration, Field advised, "recourse must be had to the Federal Government, where the whole power of this subject lies." In March 1875, just a few months after Fields's decision, Congress proceeded to pass the Page Act, a turning point in the transition to federal authority over immigration.[43]

Horace F. Page, a Republican congressman from California, had long opposed Chinese immigration. The Coolie Trade Prohibition Act of 1862 placed Chinese laborers in the same category as other free immigrants. Over the next decade, however, as restrictionists expanded the category of "coolie" to cover the Chinese in the United States as well as the Caribbean, Page repeatedly equated Chinese immigrants—both male laborers and female prostitutes— with slaves. Between 1873 and the passage of the 1875 act that bears his name, he sponsored four anti-Chinese bills and three House resolutions seeking to renegotiate the Burlingame Treaty and restrict Chinese immigration. The House Committee on Foreign Affairs rejected all of these proposals. In 1874, the Republicans, having suffered huge electoral defeats, hardened their anti-Chinese stance in a bid for greater support in the West. In his annual message to Congress in December 1874, President Ulysses S. Grant called for restrictions on Chinese immigration.[44]

Grant singled out two categories, coolies and prostitutes. The great majority of immigrants who came to the United States from China, he claimed, did not "come voluntarily, to make their homes with us and their labor productive of general prosperity." They came "under contracts with head-men, who own them almost absolutely." Chinese women were especially exploited, "brought for shameful purposes, to the disgrace of the communities where [they] settled and to the great demoralization of the youth of these localities." By targeting the two groups Grant mentioned, Page could say he was not restricting free migration by Chinese subjects generally. The Burlingame Treaty of 1868 recognized the right to free migration as an "inalienable right of man" while prohibiting migration "without free and voluntary consent." Prostitutes and laborers, for Page, fell into the latter category.[45]

Chinese prostitutes and coolies, Page insisted, were the equivalent of slaves. In laying out the case for restriction before Congress, he presented testimony from various sources, including what he claimed were prostitutes' contracts. He also presented a petition to the president of the United States signed by 17,000 "laboring men" of California, all "true and loyal citizens," lamenting the importation of Chinese laborers who worked for low wages. Writing in the midst of an economic depression, the petitioners complained that the vast sums in bonds and public lands Congress was providing for the construction of transcontinental railways were used to employ Asian labor while thousands of American workers were destitute. Noting the petitioners' "devotion to the great principles of freedom" during the Civil War, Page

FIGURE 6.4 "Uncle Sam's Thanksgiving Dinner" (1877). Eight years after Thomas Nast published "Uncle Sam's Thanksgiving Dinner" portraying an inclusive American feast, *The Wasp*, a nativist newspaper in San Francisco, responded with a vicious parody by G. Frederick Keller using the same title. Once again, people from many cultural backgrounds sit at the holiday table, but whereas Nast's cartoon included women and children, even in the Chinese case, Keller's includes only men. Reinforcing the sense that assimilation is impossible, nobody is eating the same food; each figure has his own national dish. An Englishman recoils in horror as a Chinaman begins to dine. Columbia stands resolute and disappointed in the background. An African American butler proudly carries the turkey; uncooked, it will not be needed. Uncle Sam brandishes his utensils but has no control. *The Illustrated Wasp*, November 24, 1877. Chinese in California Virtual Collection: Selections from the Bancroft Library, University of California, Berkeley.

claimed that they saw in Chinese immigration an equal or greater threat than slavery. The presence of the Chinese was accelerating the concentration of wealth and eroding republican institutions. Great corporations and monopolies prospered while the petitioners, "largely composed of the early emigrants to California and their children" who had come west in search of land, were reduced to poverty.[46]

The Page Act, crafted as an extension of the Coolie Trade Prohibition Act of 1862, criminalized the importation of prostitutes, felons, and coolies. The 1862 law, however, recognized Chinese immigrants in the United States as free migrants. Chinese laborers did not come to the United States on coolie contracts. Their right to migrate, moreover, was protected by the Burlingame Treaty. The Page Act, therefore, had little impact on immigration by male laborers. In its primary goal of restricting immigration by Chinese women, however, the act was very successful. It targeted prostitutes in general but singled out Asian women for special scrutiny. Under the Page Act, US consular officials at the ports of departure in "China, Japan, or any Oriental country" granted certificates of embarkation only to those women who could demonstrate that their migration was "free and voluntary" and not for "lewd or immoral purposes." The officials who conducted inspections abroad tended to regard all single Chinese women, except those from the wealthiest classes, as prostitutes. Women who passed the first round of consular interrogation were then examined by the harbormaster or on board ship. Only Chinese women had to obtain certificates before leaving port; European women were questioned about their intentions not at the point of departure but on arrival in the United States. Officials at the ports of arrival were authorized to inspect vessels in order to certify that Chinese women passengers were not being imported for prostitution. Even when a Chinese woman survived interrogation before departure, she could still be detained on arrival and sent back to China if the captain refused to post a $500 bond. Each woman arriving from China was required to have her own certificate and photograph, whereas the men on board carried one document for the entire group, certifying that none of them were contract laborers or criminals.[47]

The Page Act set a precedent for the federal government's use of gender and marriage as regulatory mechanisms in immigration control. There may have been some humanitarian motive to assist prostitutes, but the main effect of the act was to further reduce the number of Chinese women entering the United States. As a result, Chinese men could not start families. By 1890, Chinese males outnumbered females in the United States by 27 to 1, a disparity that remained in place until after World War II. Ironically, but inevitably, this skewed sex ratio resulted in the outcome the Page Act ostensibly wanted to avoid: increased prostitution. The Page Act marked a decisive step in the shift from state to federal control over immigration.[48]

Overall, Reconstruction had contradictory implications for immigration. The Fourteenth Amendment and the civil rights acts provided Chinese immigrants with a basis for challenging discriminatory state laws. The federal courts began to develop a jurisprudence based on the principle of equal protection. The Supreme Court eviscerated the Thirteenth and Fourteenth Amendments, significantly limiting the power of the federal government to protect the rights of African Americans, but the Court also indicated that the power to regulate immigrant admissions lay with Congress rather than the states. With local laws subject to judicial review, restrictionists realized that the federal government could exclude immigrants much more effectively than any state and pressured Congress to act. The era of national immigration control was at hand.

# 7

# *Immigration and National Sovereignty*

CHAE CHAN PING, a long-time resident of the United States, went to China for a short visit in 1887. He returned to San Francisco on the steamship *Belgic* on October 8, 1888, carrying the certificate he needed to reenter the United States. One week earlier, Congress had passed legislation discontinuing the practice of issuing these return certificates and invalidating those already issued. Denied permission to land, Chae Chan Ping filed for a writ of habeas corpus. The court refused to issue the writ, on the grounds that he had not been deprived of his liberty unlawfully, and ordered him returned to the custody of the *Belgic*. Chae Chan Ping appealed. When his case reached the US Supreme Court in 1889, his lawyers did not challenge Congress's power to control admissions. Instead, they argued that Chae Chan Ping, who had lived in San Francisco since 1875, was being expelled as a lawful resident alien. The US government, however, insisted that because he was outside the country, Congress had a clear right to bar his entry. The Court agreed, ruling unanimously against Chae Chan Ping, who was sent back to China at the expense of the shipping line that carried him.[1]

Justice Stephen Field delivered the opinion. Field did not mention Chae Chan Ping's due process argument but concentrated instead on the nature of federal authority over the admission of immigrants. The power to exclude foreigners, he wrote, was "an incident of sovereignty belonging to the government of the United States as a part of those sovereign powers delegated by the Constitution." Among those powers, he identified declaring war, making treaties, suppressing insurrections, regulating foreign commerce, and naturalizing immigrants. He did not specify how any of these powers implied or included authority to admit or exclude foreigners. The power to regulate borders, Field concluded, was inherent in national sovereignty and predated the set of rules established by the Constitution. The federal government had the right to restrict immigration whenever the interests of the country required. As a matter of national security, immigration was best left to the political branches of the federal government, with minimal interference by the judiciary. This doctrine has guided American immigration policy ever since.[2]

## The End of State Authority

Fourteen years before Chae Chan Ping brought his case, the Supreme Court ruled definitively against state immigration laws on commerce clause grounds. On June 24, 1875, the steamship *Ethiopia* arrived in New York City from Glasgow, Scotland. Both New York and Massachusetts had evaded the ruling in the *Passenger Cases* (1849) by replacing head taxes with nominally voluntary commutation fees in the same amount. Under New York law, the captain of every vessel arriving from a foreign port was required, within twenty-four hours of arrival, to report in writing the name, birthplace, last residence, and occupation of every alien passenger. For each such passenger reported, the captain had to sign a bond of $300 to indemnify against expenses for their relief or support over the next four years. Alternatively, he could commute this requirement by paying a $1.50 fee for each alien passenger within twenty-four hours of landing. John and Thomas Henderson, the owners of the *Ethiopia*, decided to challenge this law by instructing the captain to pay the fee only for passengers who intended to reside in the state of New York. The city sued to recover the funds, and the case made its way on appeal to the US Supreme Court, which considered *Henderson v. Mayor of City of New York* in conjunction with *Commissioners of Immigration v. North German Lloyd*, a case involving a Louisiana law "so very similar to, if not an exact copy of, that of New York as to need no separate consideration." Counsel for the Hendersons contended that state laws imposing bonds, taxes, or fees violated the commerce clause. New York was receiving 100,000 immigrants annually, they pointed out, which would result in $30 million worth of bond money if the law was enforced. The state's lawyers responded that the option of paying commutation money (which by the same calculation would have amounted to $150,000 in direct revenue for the state) met the objections raised in the *Passenger Cases* because it did not amount to a passenger tax.[3]

The Court concluded unanimously that the state laws under consideration were unconstitutional because they intruded on federal commerce power and on relations with foreign nations. Justice Samuel Miller, delivering the opinion of the Court, described the system of bonds and fees as dishonest. He found it "absurd" to suppose that the captain of a ship that landed hundreds of passengers every month would post a bond of $300 for each passenger, when he could pay $1.50 per passenger instead—less than the cost of preparing a bond and getting sureties approved. Ship captains, in other words, had no choice but to pay the fee, which Miller found extortionate. As its purpose was to impose a tax on vessels for the privilege of landing passengers from foreign countries, this policy violated the commerce clause. In the half century since John Marshall had declared navigation a form of commerce in *Gibbons v. Ogden* (1824), Miller noted, the transportation of passengers from Europe to the United States had become "a part of our commerce with foreign nations of vast interest to this country as well as to the immigrants who come among us to find a welcome and a home within our borders." As this form of commerce pertained to "the exterior relation of this whole nation with other nations and governments," a uniform national rule was necessary. The Constitution provided the rule. Power over immigrant admissions was a matter of foreign commerce and international relations, areas in which the federal government had exclusive authority.[4]

Miller had no patience for the argument that state sovereignty prevailed because the New York statute did not come into operation until twenty-four hours after the passengers landed. The dissenting justices in the *Passenger Cases* had argued that police laws regulating the admission of immigrants operated within the borders of the states and therefore did not intrude on federal commerce power. But Miller dismissed this argument as "a mere evasion of the protection which the foreigner has a right to expect from the federal government when he lands here a stranger, owing allegiance to another government, and looking to it for such protection as grows out of his relation to that government." The New York statute under review in *Henderson* required the ship's owner or captain to sign a bond or pay a commutation fee precisely because he was landing passengers. The operation of the law commenced "at the other end of the voyage," Miller noted, as the captain passed the commutation fee along to the passenger as part of the fare. This sum was "in effect a tax on the passenger, which he pays for the right to make the voyage—a voyage only completed when he lands on the American shore." Under the Constitution, Miller explained, Congress had the power to control "this whole subject" through legislation. The New York and Louisiana statutes, which regulated commercial matters of national and international concern, were unconstitutional and void.[5]

Miller's ruling settled the question of which branch of government controlled immigrant admissions. For a state to argue that a law taxing immigrants was legitimate under its police power was, for Miller, beside the point. Regardless of what class of legislative powers a state regulation belonged to, Congress had exclusive power over foreign and interstate commerce. Miller did not deny the power to preserve public health and welfare and to protect their residents against poverty and disease lay with the states. He left open the extent to which they could "by appropriate legislation protect themselves against actual paupers, vagrants, criminals, and diseased persons, arriving in their territory from foreign countries." But no state could exercise this power "in regard to a subject matter which has been confided exclusively to the discretion of Congress by the Constitution." This was precisely the question the Court had dodged in *New York v. Miln* in 1837 and on which it had been so badly divided in the *Passenger Cases* in 1849. Now the matter was settled.[6]

On the same day that the Supreme Court decided *Henderson*, it also delivered its decision in the case of Chy Lung, one of the twenty-two Chinese women detained when they arrived in San Francisco on the *Japan* in 1874. After Justice Stephen Field, riding circuit, had ordered the women released, Chy Lung took a suit to test the constitutionality of California's immigration law. This case differed from *Henderson* in two ways. First, Chy Lung was held prisoner because the captain of the *Japan* refused to sign a $500 bond to indemnify against expenses for her support. Second, the California statute, unlike those of New York and Louisiana, did not require a bond or fee for all alien passengers, only for certain classes, including paupers, the sick and infirm, and "lewd and debauched women." Arguing on equal protection grounds that no equivalent law would have been imposed on passengers from England or France, Chy Lung's attorney insisted that the Chinese were entitled to the same rights as other immigrants under the Fourteenth Amendment and the civil rights acts.[7]

In a unanimous decision, written once again by Samuel Miller, the Court invalidated the California law. Describing the law as "a most extraordinary statute," Miller expressed his consternation that the state of California, its commissioner of immigration, or the sheriff of San Francisco had not submitted a brief in its support. The law, he noted, authorized the commissioner of immigration to charge seventy-five cents per passenger examined, three dollars for preparing a bond, and one dollar each for both of the two sureties. In lieu of posting a bond, captains could pay a sum determined by the commissioner, who retained 20 percent of this fee for his services. "It is hardly possible," Miller wrote, "to conceive a statute more skillfully framed, to place in the hands of a single man the power to prevent entirely vessels engaged in a foreign trade, say with China, from carrying passengers, or to compel them to submit to systematic extortion of the grossest kind."[8]

California's policy, Miller feared, would lead to conflicts with foreign nations. If Chy Lung and her companions had been British subjects, he pointed out, their treatment would have given rise to international tension and probably a claim for redress. Any such claim would not have been made against the state of California, which under the Constitution could "hold no exterior relations with other nations," but against the government of the United States. If war resulted, the entire Union would suffer, not just California. If an indemnity had to be paid to end the conflict, the federal government would foot the bill. No state could determine foreign policy in this way. "The passage of laws which concern the admission of citizens and subjects of foreign nations to our shores belongs to Congress, and not to the states," Miller concluded. "It has the power to regulate commerce with foreign nations; the responsibility for the character of those regulations and for the manner of their execution belongs solely to the national government. If it be otherwise, a single state can at her pleasure embroil us in disastrous quarrels with other nations." This power allowed Congress to regulate immigration in the interest of national security.[9]

As in *Henderson*, Miller acknowledged that the states retained a police power over immigrants, but he did not seek to define that power. In the absence of legislation by Congress, he wrote, each state could protect itself "by necessary and proper laws against paupers and convicted criminals from abroad." The power to do so, however, could arise only from "a vital necessity for its exercise. The California statute, Miller concluded, so far exceeded what was necessary or appropriate as to be wholly unjustified. This decision favored Chy Lung in the short term by overturning the statute under which she had been imprisoned. It also left open the possibility that states could regulate aspects of immigration beyond entry and exit. Yet, together with *Henderson*, it marked a powerful assertion of federal authority, signaling the end of state-based legislation regulating immigrant admissions.[10]

By 1876, the Democratic and Republican Parties both supported Chinese exclusion. The Republican national platform called for a full investigation of "the effects of the immigration and importation of Mongolians on the moral and material interests of the country." As a Massachusetts delegate pointed out at the national convention, this was the first time the party had included "a discrimination of race" in its platform. The Democrats, meanwhile, demanded that Americans on the West Coast be protected against "the incursions of a race not sprung from the same great parent stock," who were denied access to naturalization and were "unaccustomed to the traditions of a progressive civilization, one exercised in liberty under equal laws." The Democratic platform denounced the Republican Party for permitting Chinese "coolies" and prostitutes to enter the United States and demanded legislation, or revisions to the Burlingame Treaty with China, to "prevent further importation or immigration of the Mongolian race."[11]

In July 1876, the Senate and House appointed a Joint Special Committee to investigate Chinese immigration. After examining 130 witnesses, the committee published a 1,250-page report the following February. Lawyers, doctors, merchants, ministers, judges, and other professionals offered a multipronged criticism of Chinese immigrants based on race, culture, religion, and marital and family practices. Ignoring the fact that Chinese immigrants were not allowed to integrate, the report complained that they were "non-assimilative with the whites," retained their distinctive food and clothing, and demonstrated no desire to learn English, intermarry, or become citizens. Chinese women, the report claimed, were "bought and sold for prostitution," "treated worse than dogs," and "held in a most revolting condition of slavery."[12]

At the heart of this wide-ranging attack on the Chinese was the labor question. The "capitalist classes," the committee's report noted, prospered by employing inexpensive Chinese labor. Employers interviewed by the committee conceded that some "social and moral evils" arose from Chinese immigration, but most of them opposed restriction. By contrast, nearly all laborers and artisans wanted Chinese workers excluded. The report cited abundant evidence claiming that Chinese immigrants reduced wages to starvation levels for white men and women and deprived white people of employment. As a result, young white men were idle, while young white women were "compelled to resort to doubtful means of support." Chinese immigrants worked for such low wages, the report contended, in part because they had no families to support. Only by gaining political power could the Chinese protect and improve themselves; yet naturalizing them, and thereby allowing them to vote, was unthinkable because they lacked "sufficient brain capacity" to be capable of self-government and had little regard for truth or oaths. The committee therefore recommended that the president take measures to modify the treaty with China and that Congress pass a law "to restrain the great influx of Asiatics to this country."[13]

In the meantime, anti-Chinese agitation continued at the state level. In July 1877, after a sympathy rally in San Francisco for striking railroad workers in the East, rioters stormed the docks of Pacific Mail Steamship line, which transported Chinese laborers to California. The mob rampaged through Chinatown for three days, killed at least four Chinese men, destroyed more than twenty Chinese laundries, and attacked the Chinese Methodist Mission. Following the riot, Denis Kearney, an Irish immigrant, organized the Workingmen's Party of California "to unite all the poor and workingmen and their friends into one political party . . . defending themselves against the encroachments of capital on the happiness of our people and the liberties of our country." The Workingmen's Party included small businessmen as well as workers, united in their opposition to monopoly power and Chinese labor. Kearney himself was a drayman rather than a laborer; he owned a small business that hauled goods throughout San Francisco. His party proposed "to wrest the government from the hands of the rich and place it in those of the people, where it properly belongs," and it pledged to "destroy the great money power of the rich by a system of taxation that will make great wealth impossible in the future." For the Kearneyites, the key to capitalist exploitation lay in Chinese immigration. The Workingmen's Party pledged "to rid the country of cheap Chinese labor as soon as possible, and by all the means in our power, because it tends still more to degrade labor and aggrandize capital." Kearney began and ended every speech with the slogan "The Chinese Must Go!"[14]

The Workingmen's Party claimed not to advocate violence, but in a series of incendiary speeches Kearney encouraged attacks on his twin enemies, Chinese laborers and corporate capitalists. He blamed the owners of large businesses and factories, and the Chinese immigrants they employed, for keeping jobs scarce and wages low. The Workingmen's Party platform stated that it would "wait upon all who employ Chinese and ask for their discharge, and it will mark as public enemies those who refuse to comply with their request." The platform claimed that the party would "encourage no riot or outrage" but also stated that it would "not volunteer to repress, or put down, or arrest, or prosecute the hungry and impatient who manifest their hatred of the Chinamen . . . or those who employ him."[15]

Twice arrested on charges of inciting a riot, Kearney organized a political movement that became a significant force both in California and nationally. In June 1878, when elections were held for delegates to the Constitutional Convention, Workingmen's Party delegates were nominated in every district and carried fifty-one of the 152 seats, including thirty in San Francisco. By this time, the California labor movement had split into factions, with another Irish immigrant, Frank Roney, advocating a racially egalitarian form of socialism. Nonetheless, the Kearneyites, by combining with farmers and some Democrats and Republicans, scored significant triumphs at the Constitutional Convention. The Committee on Chinese recommended that all Chinese immigration to the state be banned and that Chinese residents be denied access to the courts, suffrage, public employment, state licenses, and property purchases. The delegates rejected some of these measures, but the final document barred Chinese people from employment by corporations or the government, denied them the right to vote, called for exclusion laws, and authorized local authorities to expel or segregate the Chinese.[16]

California voters adopted the new Constitution by a narrow margin in 1879. The document required the legislature to take all necessary measures to protect against "the presence of aliens who are or may become vagrants, paupers, mendicants, criminals, or invalids afflicted with contagious or infectious diseases," as well as "aliens otherwise dangerous or detrimental to the well-being or peace of the State." The Constitution also called on the legislature to set the conditions for the entry, residence, and removal of such persons. "Asiatic coolieism," it declared, "is a form of human slavery, and is forever prohibited in this State, and all contracts for coolie labor shall be void." No corporation formed under the laws of California could "employ directly or indirectly, in any capacity, any Chinese or Mongolian." No Chinese person was to be employed on any public works scheme "except in punishment for crime." The Constitution required the legislature to use "all the means within its power" to discourage the immigration of "foreigners ineligible to become citizens of the United States" and to delegate to cities and towns the necessary authority to remove Chinese immigrants or place them in prescribed locations. Many of the laws enacted by the California legislature on the basis of the new Constitution, however, were ruled unconstitutional by the federal Ninth Circuit Court. Increasingly frustrated that laws passed at the state level were subject to judicial review, restrictionists looked to Congress for more sweeping and durable reforms.[17]

## Chinese Exclusion

With the 1880 presidential election approaching, both the Democrats and the Republicans courted the western vote by embracing Chinese exclusion. When Congress passed a so-called Fifteen Passenger bill in February 1879 to prevent steamships from bringing more than fifteen Chinese passengers to the United States on a single voyage, President Rutherford B. Hayes expressed sympathy with the white residents of the Pacific states, but he vetoed the proposed law as a violation of the Burlingame Treaty's guarantee of free movement between China and the United States. The Democratic Party platform in 1880 demanded that the treaty be amended and called for "no more Chinese immigration, except for travel, education, and foreign commerce, and that even carefully guarded." The Republicans called for restriction, too, through the enactment of "such just, humane and reasonable laws and treaties as will produce that result." Hayes appointed a commission to renegotiate the Burlingame Treaty. A new agreement, known as the Angell Treaty, signed in Beijing on November 17, 1880, and ratified by the Senate on May 9, 1881, cleared a path toward Chinese exclusion by allowing Congress to "regulate, limit, or suspend" immigration by Chinese laborers deemed harmful to the "good order" of the country, provided that the regulations were "reasonable" and the prohibition was not absolute. Teachers, merchants, diplomats, and tourists would be exempt, as well as laborers already in the United States.[18]

In the debates over Chinese restriction, racial nativism triumphed over the egalitarian strand of immigration jurisprudence that emerged from Radical Reconstruction. Opponents of Chinese restriction insisted that equal protection prohibited differential treatment of a group on racial grounds. Restrictionists responded with a social contract argument, reminiscent of the *Dred Scott* case, that the framers of the Declaration of Independence and the Constitution had never intended to include people like the Chinese. Senator Samuel B. Maxey, Democrat of Texas, for example, welcomed European immigrants, all "men of my own race and color" who came "to enjoy the blessings of free government, and soon become part of us." But the Constitution, he claimed, "never contemplated the bringing of all people of all colors, climes, races, and conditions into this country and making of them citizens." The only immigrants the framers intended to become naturalized citizens "were people of the Caucasian race." There were no Chinese in the United States when the Constitution was adopted, and the men who framed and ratified that compact never dreamed that there would be. Through the Constitution, the people of the United States had secured the blessings of liberty for themselves and their posterity, but the term "posterity" referred to "the pure, unmixed Caucasian race." The United States had incorporated African Americans into citizenship, but it could not do so in the Chinese case. As Maxey put it, "We can afford to work no more brick without straw into the political building."[19]

Following the ratification of the Angell Treaty, Senator John F. Miller, Republican of California, introduced a bill in February 1882 suspending immigration by Chinese laborers for twenty years. If mankind existed "in one grand co-operative society, in one universal union, under one system of laws," Miller declared, there would be no need for such a measure. "But the millennium has not yet begun," and man existed, as he had always done, "in societies called nations, separated by the peculiarities if not the antipathies of race." The history of mankind, for Miller, was for the most part a history of "racial conflicts and the struggles between nations for existence." By "a perfectly natural process," these nations had developed "distinct civilizations, as diverse in their characteristics as the races of men from which they have sprung." The two "grand divisions" of mankind, East and West, had finally met on the American shore of the Pacific Ocean. These two civilizations were "of diverse elements and character, both the result of evolution under different conditions, radically antagonistic, and as impossible of amalgamation as are the two great races who have produced them." Miller warned that a second "irrepressible conflict" was underway, comparable to the Civil War, "which shook the very foundations of American empire upon this continent." Exploiters of cheap labor and supporters of protective tariffs, he explained, opposed Chinese restriction because they wanted high prices for manufactured goods and low wages for workers. Advocating the admission of servile laborers into the country without limit, they supported "the aggrandizement of capital and the debasement of labor."[20]

Miller rejected the proposition that arguments against Chinese labor would also apply to immigrants from Europe, "particularly the Irish." European immigrants, he insisted, "are men of the like mental and physical characteristics of the American laborer. They are of the same or a kindred race, trained under a like civilization, with similar aspirations, hopes, and tendencies." They assimilated into American society and became "a part of the American people," competed with native-born workers as equals, and defended free institutions and republican government. The Pacific Coast states were populated by all kinds of immigrants and would welcome "the German, the Irishman, the Scandinavian, the Italian, and all who come from beyond the Atlantic." But, Miller declared, "of Chinese we have enough, and would be glad to exchange those we have for any white people under the sun." Every nation, he believed, had the right to protect itself against the introduction of any class of immigrants it regarded as dangerous to its peace and happiness. "Self-preservation," as international law jurists had shown, was "the foundation principle of the constitution of nations." A nation deprived of this power could not be sovereign.[21]

Along with making an argument based on national sovereignty, Miller called for exclusion based on race. The United States prevented Chinese immigrants from becoming citizens under its naturalization laws and the Burlingame Treaty, he declared, because they were "unfit for the responsibilities, duties, and privileges of American citizenship." If they were allowed to enter and remain in the United States, they would demand citizenship, and the same arguments that led to the enfranchisement of black people would be advanced in their favor. Regardless of whether they became citizens or remained "pariahs," their growing numbers posed a threat to "free government." In California, Miller claimed, the number of men capable of bearing arms was about equally divided between Chinese and white residents. Was it to be imagined, he asked, that "no race conflicts would ensue?" This was no time for soft-heartedness, he warned. Some of his colleagues had advanced "a hazy sort of theory that it is unjust or illiberal to discriminate against any race or variety of men who seek residence in this country," but national sovereignty and security demanded "an intelligent discrimination." It was "not only just and wise but humane to keep the bad sorts out." The time for "a judicious sifting process" had come. Chinese laborers must be excluded, not only because they were laborers but also because they "always were and always will be unfit for American citizenship."[22]

In Miller's opinion, the United States did not need additional immigrants of any kind. With a population of 50 million, the country was already "stocked with an intelligent, vigorous, and civilized people" who would grow though natural means. Miller noted that the political economist Thomas Malthus had calculated in his *Essay on Population* (1798) that the population of the United States was capable of doubling every twenty-five years. On this basis, Miller predicted that the population would reach 100 million by 1915 and 200 million by 1950 without immigration, "and so on in the same ratio until the increase of human life in this country should be limited only by the means of subsistence." Why not select the best from the millions who wanted to come and could assimilate? "Why not discriminate?" It was not a matter of numbers: "quality" was "more important than quantity."[23]

Yet, even judged by quantity, Miller greatly exaggerated the threat allegedly posed by Chinese laborers. Senator George Frisbie Hoar, Republican of Massachusetts, whose father Samuel Hoar had been expelled from South Carolina in 1844 for trying to initiate a lawsuit challenging South Carolina's Seamen Acts, turned Miller's point about numbers against him. The census of 1880, Hoar noted, listed only 105,000 Chinese-born people in the United States, or one five-hundredth of the total population. The total number of immigrants from all nations who entered the United States in the year 1881 was 720,045, of whom only 20,711 were Chinese. "We go boasting of our democracy, and our superiority, and our strength," Hoar declared, while failing to apply the Golden Rule "to the natives of the continent where it was first uttered." Whereas Miller articulated racial nativism in its crudest form, Hoar offered an impassioned defense of the American liberal creed as he understood it. Nothing could conflict more with "the genius of American institutions," he declared, than legal distinctions between individuals based on race or occupation. Racial prejudice—"the last of human delusions to be overcome"—had "left its hideous and ineradicable stains on our history in crimes committed by every generation" against "the negro, the Irishman, and the Indian." And now Congress, for the first time, had proposed a law "inflicting upon a large class of men a degradation by reason of their race and by reason of their occupation."[24]

Hoar found Chinese restriction doubly objectionable because it was based on class well as race. He condemned the Angell Treaty for drawing distinctions between Chinese laborers and other Chinese people, as well as between Chinese immigrants and other immigrants. Under this treaty and the proposed exclusion law it enabled, the United States could deny to the laborer what it could "not deny to the scholar or to the idler." It could also deny to Chinese people what it could "not justly deny to the Irishman." Was the doctrine of equality, which the United States had proclaimed throughout the first century of its history, "a mere empty phrase or lie?" Was the United States "to hold out two faces to the world," one to Europe and the other to Asia? The United States, Hoar believed, could never deny "the right of every man who desires to improve his condition by honest labor." The ability to work was the property of the individual alone, and he should be free "to go anywhere on the face of the earth that he pleases."[25]

Some of the arguments against the Chinese, Hoar pointed out, had been used against African Americans and Irish immigrants earlier in the nineteenth century. Advocates of Chinese exclusion invoked "the old race prejudice which has so often played its hateful and bloody part in history." Within twenty years of emancipation, African Americans had "vindicated their title to the highest privileges and their fitness for the highest duties of citizenship." Chinese Americans, Hoar predicted, would do the same. He reminded his fellow senators "how the arguments now used against the Chinese filled the American mind with alarm when used against the Irishman." According to "the honest bigotry" of the mid-nineteenth century, Irish immigrants would undermine American labor by working for low wages. Living in squalor and filth, they owed allegiance as Catholics to a foreign potentate and were considered incapable of citizenship. Yet the Irish had proceeded to build America's railroads and cities, they acquired land and deposited money in savings banks, and their sons and daughters provided the labor force for America's factories. Irish Americans had served the Union loyally in the Civil War. Year by year, the Irish ceased to be "the dupe of demagogues"— Democrats and priests—as they learned "the higher duties of citizenship." Meanwhile, the wages of American workingmen had risen, not fallen. While bettering his own condition, the Irish worker had "raised to a higher grade of social life and wealth the American laborer whose place he has taken." Hoar had no reason to believe that the long-term impact of the Chinese on American society would be any different. Miller's racial nativism, however, won the day.[26]

In April 1882, Congress passed a bill suspending immigration by Chinese laborers for twenty years. President Arthur vetoed this bill as an unreasonable restriction in violation of the Angell Treaty. When the Senate failed by five votes to override the veto, Horace Page introduced a new bill suspending immigration by Chinese laborers, both skilled and unskilled, for ten years. The bill exempted merchants, teachers, students, diplomats, and other travelers verified by the Chinese government, as well as laborers present in the United States before the Angell Treaty and those who entered within ninety days of the act's passage. Chinese laborers who arrived or remained in the United States illegally could be deported. Captains of vessels who knowingly landed laborers in violation of the law were guilty of a misdemeanor with a penalty of $500 per passenger and imprisonment for up to one year. Consistent with the Angell Treaty, the act allowed Chinese laborers already resident in the United States to leave and return if they obtained certificates before departing. The act reaffirmed the ban on courts admitting Chinese immigrants to citizenship. President Arthur signed the so-called Chinese Exclusion Act into law on May 6, 1882.[27]

Three years after the Chinese Exclusion Act, Congress introduced a bill to prohibit employers from bringing any foreigners into the United States under contract to perform labor. This time the target was European immigrants. The decision not to renew the Act to Encourage Immigration (1864) removed the imprimatur of the federal government from contract labor, but it by no means ended the practice. Consular agents continued to promote immigration by skilled workers, and private employers continued to import workers under contract. The Alien Contract Labor Act of 1885 attempted (with limited success) to prohibit this practice. Also known as the Foran Act, this legislation

FIGURE 7.1 "E pluribus unum (Except the Chinese)." In this cartoon published in *Harper's Weekly* on April 1, 1882, a month before President Arthur signed the Chinese Exclusion Act, Thomas Nast portrays the impact of the new law in stark and simple terms. At the "Temple of Liberty," protected by a drawbridge, a soldier reads from a huge document labeled "US Passport" to a forlorn Chinese immigrant in traditional garb with an exaggerated queue. The soldier's uniform and the fortress evoke imperial Europe. The caption rebukes America for abandoning its tradition as a haven of liberty and a refuge for all. Chinese in California Virtual Collection: Selections from the Bancroft Library, University of California, Berkeley.

fined employers who prepaid workers' transportation costs or assisted their migration in other ways, and outlawed work contracts made prior to departure. It exempted domestic servants, actors, artists, lecturers, and singers, as well as skilled workers in short supply. Proceeding from the assumption that all Chinese laborers and some European migrants were unfree, the Foran Act framed the free European worker—liberated from the shackles of contract by government regulation—as America's archetypal immigrant.[28]

Supporters of the Foran Act defended it as an antislavery measure. Senator John Sherman, Republican of Ohio, who had introduced the Act to Encourage Immigration in the Senate in 1864, explained the connection with Chinese

**FIGURE 7.2** "The Only One Barred Out." In this caricature of the Chinese Exclusion Act, published in *Frank Leslie's Illustrated Newspaper* on April 1, 1882, a well-dressed Chinese man with a prominent queue, sits outside the Golden Gate of Liberty. He embodies "Order" and "Industry," while the sign to his right declares "Communist, Nihilist, Socialist, Fenian & Hoodlum Welcome but No Admittance to Chinamen." Library of Congress Prints and Photographs Division, LC-DIG-ds-11861.

exclusion. The Exclusion Act of 1882, for Sherman, excluded the Chinese laborer "not on account of his race," but because he belonged to "a class of men who came to this country not the owners of themselves, but owned by others, owned by corporations, who had contracted away their liberty, their manhood, before they came here—a class who were quasi servants and serfs." The act excluded laborers "not because they were Chinese, or because their color was different from ours, but because they were not free men." They came to the United States "as slaves to work against and to compete with free men in their labor." Even so, Sherman had voted against Chinese exclusion because it departed from the American policy "to open our doors to laboring men from all lands and from all climes." Yet he supported the 1885 anti-contract measure in the name of free labor. Although no group should be excluded from the United States on grounds of "race or color," he concluded, "we may properly refuse to allow slaves to be brought into this country." Senator Henry Blair,

Republican of New Hampshire, added that the bill "aimed at slavery rather than freedom." It would prohibit the importation of "cheap and servile labor of foreign lands" at the expense of "the working people of our own country," by preventing "the cooly practices which have been initiated and carried on to considerable extent between America and Europe." But it would not disrupt "the natural flow" of immigration.[29]

Senator John Morgan, Democrat of Alabama, asked Blair whether he was placing European contract laborers in the same category as Chinese. Blair responded that if Europeans arrived on low-wage contracts, the effect upon American labor was "precisely that which we undertook to remedy and to prohibit by the anti-Chinese act." Morgan objected that the Chinese Exclusion Act had not merely protected American workers. It addressed "a social question, a question of the infusion of lower blood into the social element in this country . . . it was more a question of race than anything else." Such considerations, he insisted, could not apply to European workers. His own "relations with foreign people both by affinity and by blood" could never allow him to place European immigrants in the same category as Chinese. The immigrants excluded under the proposed anti-contract law of 1885, in short, were not coolies.[30]

Congress passed the Foran Act on February 26, 1885. Like the Coolie Trade Prohibition Act of 1862 and the Peonage Act of 1867, this law erased any distinction between voluntary and involuntary contract labor. From an antislavery perspective, any immigrant worker who signed a contract abroad, whether freely or under duress, was entering a form of bondage. Yet the Foran Act was very difficult to enforce. European immigrant workers could simply deny that they had contracts, and family members or friends, as distinct from employers, could continue to assist their migration. Whereas European immigrants could enter the United States by demonstrating that their migration was voluntary, Chinese laborers—defined as unfree by nature—no longer had this option. Dividing humanity into asymmetrical categories in this way created new mechanisms of border control. Federal regulation, in other words, produced the categories of the free and unfree immigrant through racial classification.[31]

## Sources of Federal Authority

In 1882, Congress passed the first general Immigration Act, a separate measure from the Chinese Exclusion Act passed three months earlier. Designed and implemented by officials in New York and Massachusetts who wanted the federal government to assume the burden of immigrant relief, the law levied a head tax of fifty cents on all passengers and excluded the same classes of passengers—convicts, the physically and mentally disabled, and those likely to become a public charge—targeted by earlier state laws. The previous year, New York had passed a law requiring captains to pay one dollar for the inspection of every alien passenger arriving from a foreign port. A French shipping company called Compagnie Générale Transatlantique challenged this law, and the case went to the Supreme Court in 1883. Counsel for New York argued that the statute did not impose a tax on passengers, but was intended to support an inspection law, passed by the state three days earlier, to regulate the arrival of "habitual criminals, or pauper lunatics, idiots, and imbeciles, or deaf, dumb, blind, infirm, or orphan [*sic*] persons without means or capacity to support themselves and subject to become a public charge," along with those carrying "infectious or contagious disease." Writing for a unanimous Court, Justice Samuel Miller observed that the Court had so often ruled that a state tax on passengers was a regulation of foreign commerce that the issue was no longer open for debate. The Immigration Act of 1882 covered the same ground as the New York statute, Miller observed, "and they cannot coexist." Only Congress could regulate immigrant admissions, and any state law that tried to do so violated the commerce clause.[32]

No sooner had the Court reached this decision than arguments that immigrants were articles of commerce began to lose their plausibility. The Reconstruction amendments and the Peonage Act of 1867 barred the practice of owning people as property in the United States. The Page Act of 1875, the Chinese Exclusion Act of 1882, and the Foran Act of 1885, by outlawing the importation of coolies, prostitutes, and contract workers, consolidated the emerging view that immigrants must be free and unfree migrant workers must be excluded. Yet, if passengers were not merchandise, how could the commerce clause continue to provide federal authority over immigrant admissions? To justify the exclusion of Chinese workers, a stronger claim to authority was needed. The first signs of what that claim might look like emerged in the *Head Money Cases* of 1884.[33]

On October 2, 1882, the Dutch ship *Leerdam* arrived in New York City from Rotterdam with 382 passengers who were not citizens of the United States. As required by the 1882 Immigration Act, the captain provided a list of the passengers, specifying their age, sex, occupation, intended destination, and countries of citizenship. The collector of the port of New York City, William H. Robertson, demanded the required fee of $191 (fifty cents for each alien passenger). The captain made the payment under protest, to avoid a lien being taken on his ship. In the *Head Money Cases*, the Supreme Court unanimously sustained Robertson's actions and upheld the Immigration Act on commerce clause grounds. "This act of Congress," Justice Samuel Miller noted in his opinion for the Court, "is similar in its essential features to many statutes enacted by States of the Union for the protection of their own citizens and for the good of the immigrants who land at the seaports within their borders." The purpose of these laws, Miller explained, was to help poor and vulnerable immigrants and to protect the people in whose midst they arrived. It was clear that the power to pass such laws must exist in some legislative body, and the Court had ruled several times it resided in the federal government rather than the states. For the courts to deny that Congress had power to control admissions was equivalent to saying that the power did not exist at all. Denying Congress its powers under the commerce clause implied that the framers of the Constitution had allowed all nations to send their people to the United States "without restraint or regulation," including "the entire European population of criminals, paupers, and diseased persons." Congress had exclusive authority to pass laws regulating admissions, such as the 1882 act, as part of its power to control commerce with foreign nations.[34]

Yet the most notable aspect of the *Head Money Cases* was not Miller's now familiar finding on the commerce power, but a new kind of claim by the federal government about its authority over immigration. Based on the Court's decisions over the previous decade, the government could have offered a successful argument on the basis of commerce alone. Solicitor General Samuel L. Phillips, however, did not mention the commerce clause in his brief. He claimed instead that the power to regulate borders was an inherent attribute of national sovereignty, an essential feature of any independent country. Rather than seeking to locate authority over admissions and exclusion in a specific part of the Constitution, Phillips argued that Congress's power in this domain was, in effect, extra-constitutional. Power over immigration was "implied in [the] very existence of independent government anterior to the adoption of the constitution." Defenders of the Seamen Acts and other laws controlling the mobility of free black people in the antebellum era had made a virtually identical argument with regard to state power. Regulating the entry of dangerous outsiders, they claimed, was an elementary aspect of sovereignty. In the *Head Money Cases*, the federal government applied this argument to the nation at large.[35]

The Constitution, from this perspective, recognized rather than created the sovereign power to control national borders. Any provisions in the Constitution relating to this power were "merely in recognition, and not in creation thereof." Through its system of enumerated powers, the Constitution defined the relationship of the federal government to the states, to persons born within the United States, and to foreigners with lawful permanent residence. The admission of immigrants, however, involved relations with other nations. "The Constitution," Solicitor General Phillips insisted, "is merely a *domestic* thing, whilst the nation itself has *foreign* relations, powers and duties, as well as domestic." It had no bearing on foreigners entering the United States who lacked residence there. Immigrants leaving one country for another were beyond the protection of the Constitution. Justice Miller ignored these arguments, basing his ruling on commerce clause grounds alone. The government's argument in the *Head Money Cases*, however, was an important milestone in the transition to federal authority over immigration.[36]

Policies directed against Chinese laborers were at the heart of this transition. The Exclusion Act of 1882 was a compromise measure rather than an absolute ban. Its official title, "An act to execute certain treaty stipulations with the Chinese," reflected the fact that US immigration policy toward China was still a matter of diplomacy rather than fiat. The act did not apply to non-laborers, it shortened the proposed restriction period from twenty to ten years, and it exempted laborers who arrived before the act was passed or who resided in the United States before the Angell Treaty. It also eliminated proposals for an internal registration and passport system, making it difficult to determine whether Chinese people were in the United States illegally. Registration requirements of this kind were not introduced until 1891. Nor did the 1882 act make illegal immigration a crime punishable by imprisonment or a fine. Congress appropriated only $5,000 annually, resulting in lax enforcement, especially along the Canadian border. The 1882 act, in short, had only a limited effect, in part because of the diplomatic context.[37]

Chinese immigrants already in the United States suffered an extreme backlash after the 1882 act. Anti-Chinese violence in the West reached its peak in 1885 and 1886. The Chinese government proposed a new treaty (known as the Bayard-Zhang Treaty) designed to reduce attacks on Chinese workers, which would have approved a twenty-year ban on laborers unless they had return certificates and either $1,000 in property or a wife, child, or parent in the United States. Both sides agreed to the Bayard-Zhang Treaty, but rumors soon reached Washington that the Chinese were considering backing out. By initially supporting the idea of a new treaty with a longer exclusion term for laborers, the Chinese government had revealed its weakness. No longer fearful of diplomatic and commercial repercussions, the United States determined to close the door to Chinese workers unilaterally. President Grover

Cleveland pushed forward a bill amending the exclusion laws in direct violation of treaty obligations with China.[38]

The Scott Act of 1888 barred all Chinese laborers who had left the United
States from returning, regardless of whether they held certificates. The return
certificates provided for in 1882 would no longer be issued. Certificates already issued were immediately void. In approving the Scott Act, Cleveland
issued a long signing statement. "The experiment of blending the social
habits and mutual race idiosyncrasies of the Chinese laboring classes with
those of the great body of the people of the United States," he declared, had
proved to be "in every sense unwise, impolitic, and injurious to both nations."
China's failure to ratify the Bayard-Zhang Treaty had created an "emergency,"
Cleveland claimed, in which the government of the United States was "called
upon to act in self-defense by the exercise of its legislative power."[39]

Chae Chan Ping returned to San Francisco on October 8, 1888, seven days
after the Scott Act was passed. Denied permission to land on the grounds that
his return certificate was no longer valid, Chae Chan Ping filed for a writ of
habeas corpus. When the US circuit court in California refused to issue this
writ, he challenged the Scott Act. In arguments before the Supreme Court in
1889, Chae Chan Ping's lawyers did not dispute that Congress could refuse
to admit foreigners. After all, the Court had already ruled unanimously in
*Henderson* and *Chy Lung* that admissions lay under the control of the federal
government. Pointing out that Chae Chan Ping was a long-term lawful resident of the United States, they challenged the right of Congress to expel him.
They also contended that the Scott Act could not be upheld under the treaty
power (since it abrogated US treaties with China) or the war powers (since
China was not at war with the United States and Chae Chan Ping was not a
belligerent). In addition, they claimed that the Scott Act violated Chae Chan
Ping's rights to due process as a "person," that it was an unconstitutional bill
of attainder (i.e., legislation punishing an individual without a judicial trial),
and that it was an ex post facto law retroactively imposing criminal punishment for an act committed when it was not a crime.[40]

For the US government, Solicitor General George A. Jenks responded that
because Chae Chan Ping was outside the country, Congress had a clear right
to exclude him based on the nation's sovereign power to control its borders.
In other words, Jenks saw the case as one about admission and exclusion
rather than expulsion. Jenks cited international law theorist Emer de Vattel
in support of the right of nations to exclude foreigners, just as proslavery antebellum jurists had cited Vattel in support of local sovereignty. Jenks also
pointedly quoted Vattel: "There are states, such as China and Japan, into

FIGURE 7.3 "The Chinese Question Again." In the Scott Act of 1888, Congress unilaterally discontinued the practice of issuing return certificates for Chinese laborers who left the country and tried to return, and refused to recognize certificates already issued. This image from *The Wasp* conveys the fear that, despite Uncle Sam's effort to close the door through "Scott's Exclusion Act," Chinese laborers were still finding many ways to enter the United States. Wood engraving. *The Wasp*, v. 23, July–December 1889. Chinese in California Virtual Collection: Selections from the Bancroft Library, University of California, Berkeley.

which all foreigners are forbid [*sic*] to penetrate without an express permission." In contrast to the *Head Money Cases*, the solicitor general did not make an argument for extra-constitutional power over immigration. He argued that this power was grounded in federal control of foreign affairs and implicit in the migration or importation clause (ignoring the Supreme Court's ruling the previous year, in *New York v. Compagnie Générale Transatlantique*, that the clause had always referred exclusively to the external slave trade). The state of California filed an amicus brief arguing that the ability to exclude aliens was essential to any nation's sovereignty, and locating the authority to do so in Congress's power under the Constitution to deal with aliens in time of war. California also insisted that Chae Chan Ping's residence in the United States was not a right but "a privilege permitted to be enjoyed only so long as the U.S. continued [to be] so minded."[41]

Justice Stephen Field delivered the unanimous opinion of the Court. Field had invalidated California's discriminatory law against "lewd and debauched women" in Ah Fong's case in 1874 and joined the decision invalidating that law in *Chy Lung* the following year. In neither case, however, was he concerned with the rights of Chinese immigrants. The violation of equal protection he identified in 1874 concerned discrimination between modes of migration (by sea but not by land), rather than by kinds of immigrant. That case, for Field, was about the balance between state and federal power, but he had long been hostile to the Chinese. Fear of Chinese immigrants, as he put it in *Chae Chan Ping*, was "a well founded apprehension—from the experience of years—that a limitation to the immigration of certain classes from China was essential to the peace of the community on the Pacific coast, and possibly to the preservation of our civilization there." In California, Field noted, members of the Constitutional Convention of 1878 had claimed that Chinese immigration was "approaching the character of an Oriental invasion, and was a menace to our civilization." As a judge on the California circuit court, Field was aware that the lower federal courts in San Francisco were inundated with cases brought by Chinese immigrants. Ironically, by challenging exclusionary and discriminatory laws, these immigrants were demonstrating exactly the kind of understanding of American institutions their critics claimed they could never achieve. Chae Chan Ping's was one such case. Field's decision significantly limited the role of the courts in immigration matters, in deference to the legislative and executive branches of the federal government.[42]

Field agreed with the solicitor general that the power to admit and exclude foreigners was inherent in the sovereignty of the United States as a nation-state. Under the Constitution, he explained, most local matters were controlled by local authorities, but the United States acted as one nation in its relations with foreign countries. "For local interests, the several states of the union exist," he wrote, "but for national purposes, embracing our relations with foreign nations, we are but one people, one nation, one power." For Field, the power of Congress to exclude aliens was no longer "open to controversy."

Immigration was a matter of national sovereignty and security. "Jurisdiction over its own territory," Field explained, "is an incident of every independent nation. It is a part of its independence." Every nation, to preserve its independence, had to guard against "foreign aggression and encroachment." It did not matter whether the threat came from the actions of a hostile nation "or from vast hordes of its people crowding in upon us." If Congress considered "the presence of foreigners of a different race in this country, who will not assimilate with us, to be dangerous to its peace and security," their exclusion should not be prevented simply because there were no military hostilities with the nation of which they were subjects. Contrary to Chae Chan Ping, Field saw the case as one regarding the exclusion of an alien residing outside the nation's jurisdiction rather than his expulsion. For this reason, he designated his opinion the *Chinese Exclusion Case*. Field's opinion extended to the national level the sovereign claims made by the states throughout the antebellum era to police their borders, and he drew on the same international law theorists to do so.[43]

Field also rejected the notion that the Scott Act, by revoking certificates of return, violated rights guaranteed by treaty. Certificates issued under laws or treaties, he explained, conferred no rights that could not be removed by subsequent legislation. Treaties were only the equivalent of legislative acts; they could be repealed or modified by laws, and "the last expression of the sovereign will must control." Congress had granted Chae Chan Ping the right to return under the Chinese Exclusion Act of 1882; it had revoked that right in the Scott Act of 1888. The latter act, as "a constitutional exercise of legislative power," took precedence over any previous laws or any existing treaties between the United States and China. "If there be any just ground of complaint on the part of China," Field concluded, "it must be made to the political department of our government, which is alone competent to act upon the subject." In referring to the "political" branches of the government, Field did not distinguish between the legislature and the executive, but he insisted that the judiciary—conceived as a neutral, nonpolitical interpreter of the law—should not interfere in foreign affairs, including immigration.[44]

The *Chinese Exclusion Case* clarified the nature of sovereignty and assigned control over immigrant admissions to Congress and the president. That did not mean, however, that the Supreme Court suddenly reversed an existing policy of open borders or created federal power over immigration for the first time. America's borders had never been wide open, even if most immigrants were admitted. States had regulated external and internal mobility throughout the nineteenth century. The executive branch had shaped immigration policy by making treaties, ratified by the Senate, regulating international commerce, migration, and expatriation. Fourteen years before the *Chinese Exclusion Case*, moreover, the Supreme Court unanimously affirmed Congress's power to regulate admissions under the commerce clause in *Henderson* and *Chy Lung* (a position also endorsed by the majority in the contentious *Passenger Cases* of 1849). Federal authority over immigration, in short, was already well established before the *Chinese Exclusion Case*.

At the heart of the case, however, was an important question of administrative law. The question was no longer who controlled immigration, but on what grounds the federal government claimed this authority, and who was in charge. If regulating borders was a matter of national sovereignty, which part of the federal government should control it? Justice Field's answer was that the "political" branches of the government should do so, with minimal involvement by the courts. If the Supreme Court had recognized Chae Chan Ping's residency in the United States as a right, he would have been entitled to judicial process in the form of a trial. By ruling that his residency was a privilege rather than a right, the Court indicated that immigration officials could inspect arriving passengers and order their exclusion directly without judicial intervention. The Court did not hold, by any means, that all immigration law was immune from judicial review nor that immigrants—either in the process of arriving or after entry—had no constitutional rights. It did rule that the legislative and executive branches of the federal government had a plenary power to regulate and restrict admissions.[45]

This allocation of authority rested on the assumption that the United States was the only political entity with the right to control the national territory over which it claimed sovereignty. On this basis, Congress had the power to admit, exclude, or expel immigrants as it saw fit. Yet hundreds of Native nations living within the borders of the United States also had claims to territorially bounded political status. During Reconstruction, Radical Republicans respected this sovereignty by exempting Native Americans living on tribal lands from national citizenship under the Civil Rights Act of 1866 and the Fourteenth Amendment. In 1871, however, Congress unilaterally discontinued the practice of making treaties with Native nations. In this context, conferring US citizenship on Native Americans was double-edged. In the postbellum era, on the one hand, many Native American nations—especially those that had succeeded in retaining their land against threats of dispossession and removal—resisted citizenship as a negation of their sovereignty.

Some Native American individuals, on the other hand, welcomed citizenship because it provided access to public education and the vote.[46]

One such individual was John Elk, a Winnebago born on tribal land who moved to Omaha, Nebraska, where he attempted to register for the vote in 1880. When the authorities in Omaha rejected his attempt, Elk filed a petition in the US circuit court in the District of Nebraska claiming that he was a citizen of the United States under the Fourteenth Amendment. Elk's lawyer contended that denying him the right to vote violated both the Fourteenth and the Fifteenth Amendments. In *Elk v. Wilkins* (1884), the Supreme Court rejected John Elk's claim to citizenship by a majority of 6 to 2. Justice Horace Gray explained for the majority that a Native American born a member of a tribe was not a United States citizen by birthright. Congress could, if it wished, bestow citizenship on any such individual through naturalization, but he could not become a citizen simply by living apart from his tribe or nation.[47]

If citizenship had potential benefits for certain individuals, it was also a powerful mechanism for undermining the autonomy of Native American nations. The Dawes Allotment Act of 1887 provided that any Native American born in the United States who had taken an individual plot of land under the act, or who had voluntarily moved from his tribe and "adopted the habits of civilized life," was eligible for US citizenship. Far from being an egalitarian measure, this act imposed citizenship whether it was wanted or not. The same imperialist logic lay behind the Major Crimes Act of 1885, which placed certain crimes committed by Native Americans on tribal land under federal jurisdiction. The Supreme Court upheld the constitutionality of the Major Crimes Act in *United States v. Kagama* (1886), with Justice Samuel Miller applying to Native American affairs the same kind of sovereign power claimed by the government over immigrant admissions in the *Head Money Cases* two years earlier. From the late 1880s onward, Native American policy and immigration policy developed in tandem. Underlying both was the principle that the federal government had a power, inherent in its sovereignty, to control national territory and membership. *United States v. Rogers* had set an important precedent for this kind of claim to power in 1846. After the Civil War, the expanded federal state became an instrument of control rather than liberation for Chinese immigrants and Native Americans alike.[48]

In two cases in the early 1890s, the Court consolidated federal power over immigration. *Nishimura Ekiu v. United States* (1892) involved a challenge to the Immigration Act of 1891, the second general immigration law passed by Congress. Nishimura Ekiu, an immigrant from Japan, was denied the right to land when she arrived in San Francisco in 1891. She claimed that placing authority for this decision in the hands of immigration officials alone, without the possibility of judicial review, was unconstitutional. In an 8 to 1 decision, the Court ruled against her. Justice Horace Gray, writing for the majority, cited Vattel and other authorities on international law in support of his conclusion that it was "an accepted maxim of international law, that every sovereign nation has the power, as inherent in sovereignty and essential to self-preservation, to forbid the entrance of foreigners within its dominions or to admit them only in such cases and upon such conditions as it may see fit to prescribe." In the United States, Gray explained, this power was "vested in the national government, to which the Constitution has committed the entire control of international relations, in peace as well as in war." The power belonged to "the political department of the government" and could be exercised either through treaties made by the president and Senate or through statutes enacted by Congress.[49]

The following year, In *Fong Yue Ting v. United States,* the Supreme Court considered three challenges to the Geary Act of 1892, which renewed the exclusion of Chinese laborers for ten years and required all Chinese laborers in the United States to obtain certificates of residence, with photographic identification, under penalty of deportation. The Court rejected the challenges by a majority of 6 to 3. Noting that the *Chinese Exclusion Case* and *Nishimura* had established the sovereign right of the United States to control its borders, Gray quoted Vattel: "Every nation has the right to refuse to admit a foreigner into the country, when he cannot enter without putting the nation in evident danger, or doing it a manifest injury." The United States, Gray ruled, had the same "absolute and unqualified right" to deport unnaturalized foreigners as it did to exclude them. He quoted Vattel that the nation "has a right to send them elsewhere, if it has just cause to fear that they will corrupt the manners of the citizens, that they will create religious disturbances, or occasion any other disorder, contrary to the public safety. In a word, it has a right, and is even obliged, in this respect, to follow the rules which prudence dictates." The Court also found that deportation was not a "punishment for crime" but a civil administrative procedure for removing those who violated the residency rules set by the national government. Criminal due process—"the provisions of the Constitution securing the right of trial by jury and prohibiting unreasonable searches and seizures and cruel and unusual punishments"—therefore did not apply. Justice Field, in dissent, argued against deporting Fong Yue Ting on the same principle of territorially bounded sovereignty by which he had excluded Chae Chan Ping. For Field, the nation had a perfect right

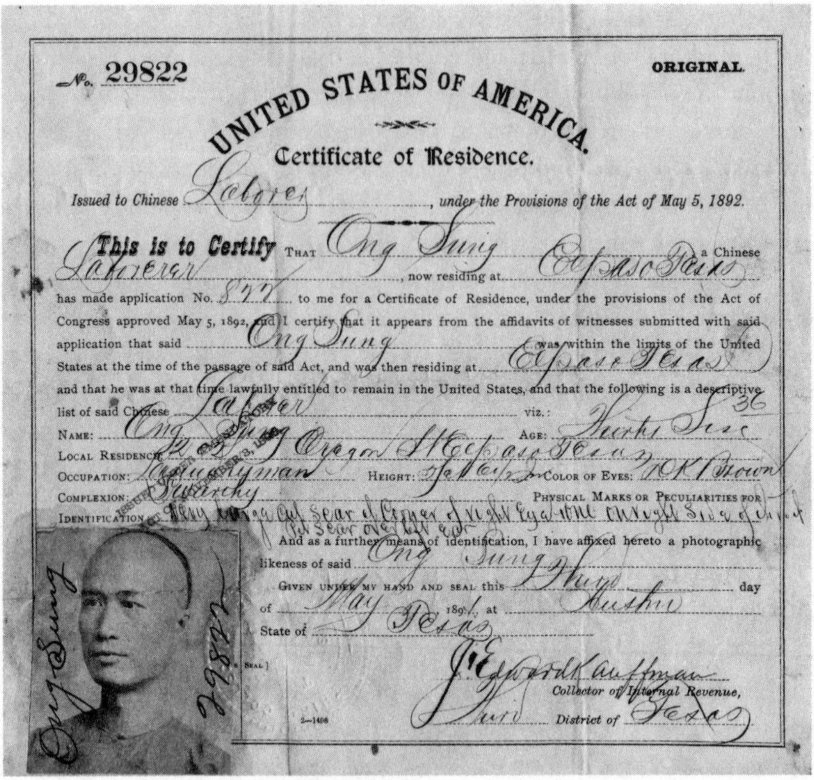

No. 29822 ORIGINAL.

UNITED STATES OF AMERICA.

Certificate of Residence.

Issued to Chinese Laborer, under the Provisions of the Act of May 5, 1892.

This is to Certify THAT Ong Sung a Chinese Laborer, now residing at El Paso Texas has made application No. 877 to me for a Certificate of Residence, under the provisions of the Act of Congress approved May 5, 1892, and I certify that it appears from the affidavits of witnesses submitted with said application that said Ong Sung was within the limits of the United States at the time of the passage of said Act, and was then residing at El Paso Texas and that he was at that time lawfully entitled to remain in the United States, and that the following is a descriptive list of said Chinese Laborer viz.:

NAME: Ong Sung AGE: Thirty Six 36

LOCAL RESIDENCE: Oregon St El Paso Texas

OCCUPATION: Laundryman HEIGHT: 5 ft 6½ in COLOR OF EYES: Dk Brown

COMPLEXION: Swarthy PHYSICAL MARKS OR PECULIARITIES FOR IDENTIFICATION: Very large cut scar at corner of right eye

And as a further means of identification, I have affixed hereto a photographic likeness of said Ong Sung

GIVEN UNDER MY HAND AND SEAL this Third day of May 1894 at Austin State of Texas

[SEAL]

J. Edward Kauffman Collector of Internal Revenue, Third District of Texas

2—1406

Ong Sung 29822

FIGURE 7.4 "Certificate of Residence of Chinese laborer Ong Sung." From 1892 onward, Chinese laborers were required to register and receive certificates of residence, under pain of imprisonment followed by deportation, in order to live in the United States. Each certificate carried a photograph of the registrant and a detailed description. Ong Sung, a laundryman residing at El Paso, received his certificate in Austin, Texas, in 1894, noting his name, occupation, and place of residence, and identifying him as thirty-six years old, five-feet six-and-a half inches tall, with dark brown eyes, a "swarthy" complexion, and a large cut at the corner of his right eye. Certificate of Residence of Chinese laborer On Sung, No. 29822, Austin, Texas, May 3, 1894. History San José Research Library.

to prevent Chae Chan Ping from reentering the national territory. At the same time, however, the United States was obliged to uphold Fong Yue Ting's rights as a legal resident within its territorial jurisdiction. The federal government, in other words, could exclude foreigners at its own discretion, but once they entered the United States they enjoyed rights under the Constitution that the government must protect.[50]

The Fourteenth Amendment was enduringly important in this respect. It extended equal protection and due process not just to citizens but also to all people living under the jurisdiction of the United States, including

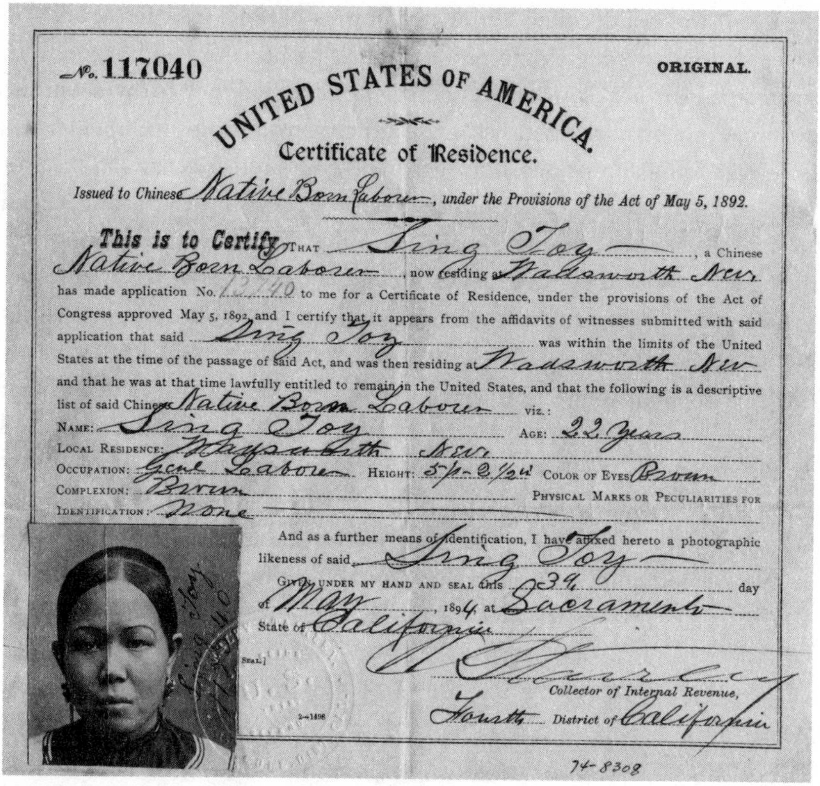

№. 117040 ORIGINAL.

UNITED STATES OF AMERICA.

Certificate of Residence.

*Issued to Chinese* Native Born Laborer, *under the Provisions of the Act of May 5, 1892.*

**This is to Certify** THAT Sing Toy, a Chinese Native Born Laborer, now residing at Wadsworth Nev. has made application No. 13740 to me for a Certificate of Residence, under the provisions of the Act of Congress approved May 5, 1892, and I certify that it appears from the affidavits of witnesses submitted with said application that said Sing Toy was within the limits of the United States at the time of the passage of said Act, and was then residing at Wadsworth Nev and that he was at that time lawfully entitled to remain in the United States, and that the following is a descriptive list of said Chinese Native Born Laborer viz.:

NAME: Sing Toy AGE: 22 years
LOCAL RESIDENCE: Wadsworth Nev
OCCUPATION: Gen Laborer HEIGHT: 5 ft 2 1/2 in COLOR OF EYES: Brown
COMPLEXION: Brown PHYSICAL MARKS OR PECULIARITIES FOR IDENTIFICATION: None

And as a further means of identification, I have affixed hereto a photographic likeness of said Sing Toy

GIVEN UNDER MY HAND AND SEAL this 3d day of May, 1894 at Sacramento State of California

[SEAL]

*Collector of Internal Revenue,*
Fourth *District of* California

74-8308

**FIGURE 7.5** "Certificate of Residence of Sing Toy." The document certifies that that Sing Toy, "a Chinese Native Born Laborer, residing at Wadsworth, Nevada" in 1894, was twenty-two years old, five-feet two-and-a-half inches tall, brown haired, with a brown complexion and no "Marks of Peculiarities for Identification." The certificate, issued in Sacramento, California, misidentifies Sing Toy as male (though generic use of the pronoun "he"), but the "photographic likeness of said Sing Toy" is that of a woman. Certificate of Residence of Sing Toy, native-born laborer, No. 117040, Sacramento, California, May 3, 1894. History San José Research Library.

unnaturalized immigrants. The Supreme Court upheld this principle in *Yick Wo v. Hopkins* (1886), which unanimously invalidated a San Francisco ordinance that discriminated against Chinese laundry operators. The guarantees of equal protection under the Fourteenth Amendment, the Court noted, "extend to all persons within the territorial jurisdiction of the United States, without regard to differences of race, of color, or of nationality." Federally protected equality before the law, in other words, prevailed over local police power. It continues to do so today.[51]

The onset of federal control did not prevent states from regulating immigration in certain ways. In *Chy Lung* (1875), Justice Miller explained that the Court was not deciding "for or against the right of a state, in the absence of legislation by Congress, to protect herself by necessary and proper laws against paupers and convicted criminals from abroad, nor to lay down the definite limit of such right, if it exist." The Constitution preempted states from regulating admissions, but they could pass protective laws in cases of "vital necessity," so long as these measures did not clash with existing federal laws. Miller made the same distinction in the *Henderson* case, noting that the Court's decision did not affect the ability of states to protect themselves against paupers, vagrants, and criminals in the absence of congressional legislation. He did not elaborate on this point, other than to say that when any such statute came before the Court, "it will be time enough to decide that question." This distinction, between national laws regulating admissions and expulsions and local laws controlling immigrants' lives after arrival, is increasingly important today. How states and cities treat immigrants depends on how they define the public good. And, just as in nineteenth century, where people live determines the rights they enjoy.[52]

# Epilogue

THE TRANSITION FROM a loosely federated state in the antebellum era to a more unified nation-state with overseas imperial ambitions after the Civil War necessarily involved a redefinition of sovereignty. The United States could not assert its international power without defining its powers as a nation-state. One of these powers, which the Supreme Court found to be inherent in national sovereignty, was control over the admission, exclusion, and deportation of foreigners. Other than filing writs of habeas corpus when denied permission to enter, foreigners had few protections against the decisions of federal immigration inspectors. Deportees were denied criminal due process on the grounds that their removal was a civil procedure rather than punishment for a crime. The doctrines laid down by the Supreme Court at the end of nineteenth century, which emerged from the abolition of slavery and Chinese exclusion, provided the basis for a national immigration policy. In *Trump v. Hawaii* (2018), the Supreme Court upheld a so-called travel ban on Muslim immigrants based on the precedent set in *Chae Chan Ping v. United States* 120 years earlier.[1]

As a result of developments in the late nineteenth century, immigration policy in the United States resides in its own special category of law. Immigrants today have some due process rights, but foreigners with irregular status can be imprisoned and deported on the basis of minor crimes, originally classified as misdemeanors under state law, which count as "aggravated felonies" under federal law. They are not entitled to government-appointed counsel during deportation proceedings. The federal government, in particular the executive branch, exercises enormous and often arbitrary power over admissions and expulsions, which the courts generally legitimize in the name of national security. Yet, while immigration to the United States often results from American foreign policy choices, the central policy issues it presents within American society—including poverty, education, public health, civil rights, and citizenship—have no evident connection to foreign affairs to justify this judicial deference. Most people migrate, as they have always done, not to threaten national security but in search of a better life for themselves and their families.[2]

Wong Kim Ark moved back and forth from California to China in pursuit of just that goal. Born in San Francisco around 1870 to Chinese immigrant parents who had lived in the United States for many years, he first visited China when he was eight years old. When his parents decided to settle in China, Wong returned to San Francisco and found work as a cook. He made two more visits to China, married a local woman, and started a family there. When Wong came back to San Francisco from China in August 1895, bearing an identity card with his photograph and the signatures of two white witnesses attesting to his birth in California, the immigration inspector denied him entry. From this official's perspective, Wong was a Chinese subject, and—as a laborer—he was barred from entering the United States (unless he carried a return certificate issued by the government). The government chose Wong Kim Ark as a test case on birthright citizenship. At the habeas corpus hearing, the US district attorney argued that Wong could not be a citizen of California or the United States because he owed the same allegiance to China as his parents, who were prohibited from naturalizing as citizens. Wong had the backing of local Chinese merchants, who also wanted to bring a test case. When the California district court ruled in Wong's favor, the government appealed to the Supreme Court, which considered the case in 1898.[3]

At stake in *United States v. Wong Kim Ark* were two conceptions of citizenship with significantly different implications for national sovereignty—the principle of *jus soli* (right of the soil, or birthright citizenship) enshrined in the Fourteenth Amendment, and the principle of *jus sanguinis* (right of blood, or law of descent), which restricted citizenship to those whose parents were citizens. For the government, Solicitor General Holmes Conrad of Virginia, who had served in the Confederate Army as a cavalry officer during the Civil War, pointed out that the dominant principle in international law was *jus sanguinis*. Under this principle, no person could be a citizen of the United States, even if born on American soil, unless one or both of his parents were citizens by birthright or naturalization. As Chinese immigrants could satisfy neither criterion, Conrad argued, their American-born children could never be citizens. Invoking the *Dred Scott* case, the solicitor general contended that the words "ourselves and our Posterity" in the Preamble to the Constitution

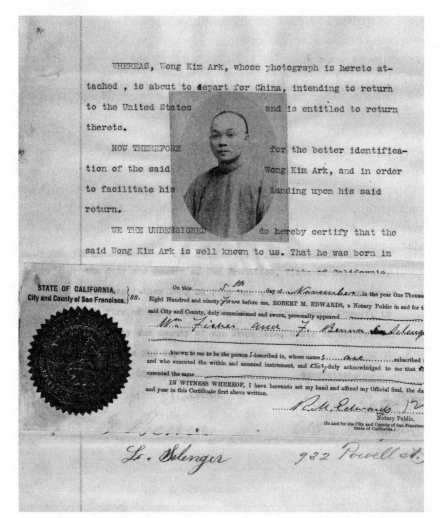

FIGURE E.1 Departure statement and photograph of Wong Kim Ark at the time he left the United States in November 1894, carrying a certificate with the signatures of two witnesses affirming that he was born in the United States. Admiralty Case Files, 1851–1966, Records of District Courts of the United States, 1685–2009, Record Group 21, National Archives at San Francisco.

covered only the original parties to the social contract that created the United States, in other words, people of European origin. Nor, by Conrad's logic, were the children of any unnaturalized immigrants—including Europeans— automatically citizens simply by virtue of birth on American soil. Like their parents, he insisted, these American-born children were not fully "subject to the jurisdiction" of the United States, as they too owed allegiance to a foreign power. If applied as policy, Conrad's position would have stripped millions of American-born people of citizenship.[4]

Two years earlier, in *Plessy v. Ferguson* (1896), the Supreme Court had upheld racial segregation in Louisiana on the principle of separate but equal. Segregated public facilities, the Court ruled, did not violate equal protection under the Fourteenth Amendment as long as the facilities were of equal quality. Nor did a state law mandating separate facilities violate the Thirteenth Amendment's ban on slavery or involuntary servitude. On the contrary, the Court found, any such law was a reasonable exercise of police power, designed to protect the public peace and promote the public good. The Reconstruction amendments, the Court ruled, protected civil and political rights, but they were not intended to legislate social equality. In the chilling words of Justice Henry Brown, writing for the 7 to 1 majority, "if one race be inferior to the other socially, the Constitution of the United States cannot put them upon the same plane." African Americans were citizens of the United States, but long before *Plessy*, the Court had stripped the Reconstruction amendments of their intended meaning, preventing the federal government from protecting black people against discrimination and racial terror.[5]

Justice John Marshall Harlan issued a famous dissent in *Plessy*. "The arbitrary separation of citizens on the basis of race while they are on a public highway," he wrote, "is a badge of servitude wholly inconsistent with the civil freedom and the equality before the law established by the Constitution." Under the Constitution, Harlan explained, "there is in this country no superior, dominant, ruling class of citizens. There is no caste here. Our Constitution is color-blind, and neither knows nor tolerates classes among citizens. In respect of civil rights, all citizens are equal before the law." The decision in *Plessy*, Harlan correctly predicted, would "prove to be quite as pernicious as the decision made by this tribunal in the *Dred Scott Case.*" The antebellum tradition of police power survived in the post-Reconstruction South, justifying white supremacy in the form of segregation. Jim Crow laws across the American South prevented African Americans from traveling freely, using public accommodations like restaurants or hotels, attending integrated schools, voting or holding office, serving on juries, or testifying in court.[6]

Harlan consistently favored rights for African Americans, but he was no friend of Chinese immigrants. The Chinese, he observed in *Plessy*, were "a race so different from our own that we do not permit those belonging to it to become citizens of the United States. Persons belonging to it are, with few exceptions, absolutely excluded from our country." Yet, under the Louisiana law, Chinese people could ride in the same passenger coaches as white citizens, while African American citizens were "declared to be criminals, liable to imprisonment." It is not surprising, given his views on Chinese immigrants, that Harlan took the government's side in *Wong Kim Ark*, concurring with a dissenting opinion written by Chief Justice Melville Fuller.[7]

Fuller argued strongly against *jus soli* as the foundational principle of American citizenship. American naturalization policy grants citizenship based on a contract in which the host society agrees to accept immigrants if they agree to comply with its basic norms and rules. In this sense, allegiance is based on mutual consent. Yet birthright citizenship, Fuller insisted, removes the need for consent by either party. Citizenship by birth rather than consent, he claimed, was a feudal relic based on the allegiance of subjects to their lord, with no place in a republican democracy. The United States, Fuller wrote, had always "rejected the doctrine of indissoluble allegiance and maintained the general right of expatriation." The whole basis of American naturalization policy was that immigrants could cast off prior allegiance rather than being bound perpetually by an accident of birth. Fuller found it ironic that the Fourteenth Amendment introduced the English common law precept of birthright citizenship into the Constitution at just the point when Britain was breaking free of this principle, allowing its subjects to renounce their allegiance to the Crown and become US citizens. He could find no evidence that birthright provided the foundation of citizenship before the Civil War. Yet African Americans had claimed citizenship throughout the antebellum period by virtue of birth on the soil, and the architects of the Civil Rights Act of 1866 and the Fourteenth Amendment wrote this principle into the law knowing that it was already standard practice in many states.[8]

Fuller agreed with the government that Chinese immigrants and their children were not fully subject to the jurisdiction of the United States. All persons born in the United States and not owing allegiance to any foreign power, he conceded, were automatically citizens under the Fourteenth Amendment. But allegiance, Fuller insisted, must be "single and not double." Chinese immigrants retained their allegiance to a foreign power, he claimed, and it was precisely to prevent the children of such immigrants from acquiring citizenship merely by birth on American soil that the phrase "not subject to any foreign power" was inserted into the Civil Rights Act. Likewise, for Fuller, the phrase "subject to the jurisdiction thereof" in the Fourteenth Amendment excluded from citizenship anyone born in the United States who owed allegiance of any kind, or was subject in any way, to a foreign power. Chinese immigrants, of course, could not demonstrate their allegiance to the United States, because they were prohibited—on racial grounds—from naturalizing. Yet Fuller presented their inability to become citizens as proof of their lack of allegiance, and he applied this twisted logic to the American-born children of Chinese immigrants as well, insisting that they remained subject to the same sovereign as their parents. "I am of opinion," Fuller concluded, "that the President and Senate by treaty, and the Congress by naturalization, have the power, notwithstanding the Fourteenth Amendment, to prescribe that all persons of a particular race, or their children, cannot become citizens."[9]

By a majority of 6 to 2, the Court rejected this reactionary position. Justice Horace Gray, writing for the majority, ruled that Wong Kim Ark was automatically a citizen under the Fourteenth Amendment because he was born in the United States. Yet the Court's endorsement of birthright citizenship did not arise from any deep commitment to racial equality. Eight of the nine justices who decided the case, after all, had upheld segregation in *Plessy v. Ferguson*. In *Wong Kim Ark*, the majority was primarily concerned about the impact on European immigrants. If the Fourteenth Amendment excluded the American-born children of Chinese immigrants from citizenship, Gray pointed out, the same reasoning could be used "to deny citizenship to thousands of persons of English, Scotch, Irish, German, or other European parentage who have always been considered and treated as citizens of the United States." The amendment, he reminded the Court, specified only two criteria for citizenship—birth or naturalization—and it applied to all persons without regard to race, religion, or nationality. The power of naturalization vested in Congress by the Constitution, Gray added, was "a power to confer citizenship, not a power to take it away." Chinese immigrants could not naturalize as citizens because no statute or treaty authorized them to do so, but the absence of legislation or treaties had no bearing on the citizenship of their children. Every person born in the United States and subject to its jurisdiction was a citizen. Wong Kim Ark was free to resume his life. Yet it was a life constrained by constant surveillance. He and his children had to prove their citizenship every time they tried to enter or reenter the United States. In 1932, Wong settled in China permanently.[10]

Each side in *Wong Kim Ark* argued that the other's approach to citizenship undermined national sovereignty. Proponents of citizenship by descent claimed that birthright citizenship would lead to "double allegiance." American-born children of immigrants, they argued, would be able to claim foreign citizenship through their parents, as most countries followed the rule

**FIGURE E.2** Photograph of Wong Kim Ark, May 19, 1904, prior to a visit to China. "Return Certificate Application Case File of Chinese Departing—Wong Kim Ark." Identification Photograph on Affidavit "In the Matter of Wong Kim Ark, Native Born Citizen of the United States" (12017/42223). Return Certificate. Application Case Files of Chinese Departing 12/24/191—12/03/1943. Records of the Immigration and Naturalization Service, 1787–2004. Record Group 85, National Archives at San Francisco.

of *jus sanguinis* rather than *jus soli*. These countries would continue to expect allegiance from, and grant citizenship to, their people abroad. If the United States followed the norm and based its citizenship policy on *jus sanguinis* rather than birthright, the government argued, immigrants and their children would remain permanently subject to a single, foreign jurisdiction. People of Chinese origin, wherever they lived, would always be subjects of China. Chinese immigrants and their children could reside in the United States but none of them, even if born there, could become citizens—thereby resolving the problem of double allegiance. Wong Kim Ark's lawyers turned this devious argument on its head, arguing that birthright citizenship was essential to national sovereignty. A universal policy based on the principle of descent, they pointed out, would force the United States to recognize people born on its soil as citizens of foreign countries. A nation that could not protect its citizenship policy against the claims of foreign jurisdictions was not an independent nation. Without control over citizenship, what would sovereignty amount to?[11]

Justice Gray agreed with Wong Kim Ark's lawyers. As the author of the majority opinion in *Fong Yu Ting* (1893), Gray had upheld Congress's plenary power to deport aliens. He applied the same logic of sovereignty in *Wong Kim Ark*. It was "the inherent right of every independent nation," Gray wrote, "to determine for itself, and according to its own constitution and laws, what classes of persons shall be entitled to its citizenship." Just as the federal government had the authority to exclude or expel immigrants, it also had the authority to grant citizenship to and compel allegiance by those it permitted to reside within its territorial boundaries. The Court's liberal conception of citizenship in *Wong Kim Ark*, in short, was also a powerful assertion of national sovereignty.[12]

———

The federal government controls immigration and citizenship in the United States today. States and cities can no longer determine whom to admit, exclude, or deport, as they did before the Civil War. They continue, however, to regulate immigrants' lives after they arrive in the country, using their police power to do so. Scholars distinguish between two kinds of law in this respect: immigration law (regulating entry, exclusion, and deportation), and alienage law (regulating immigrants' lives after they arrive, without necessarily infringing on federal power). State-level alienage laws often monitor and punish immigrants by restricting access to driver's licenses, public benefits, and education; requiring employment verification; penalizing the leasing of property to the undocumented; or prohibiting day laborers from congregating in public spaces. Measures of this kind place immigrants into a second-class category within a hierarchy of "tiered personhood" reminiscent of Jim Crow. State laws restricting access to the vote fall into a similar category.[13]

States and localities sometimes introduce anti-immigrant measures expecting that they will fail in the courts but hoping to exert pressure on the federal government to act. California's Proposition 187, introduced in 1994, attempted to deny access to public education, non-emergency healthcare, and other services to unsanctioned immigrants and required state officials to report their presence. A federal district court invalidated this measure. The verification and reporting measures, the court found, amounted to an unconstitutional regulation of immigration by a state, and the denial of education violated equal protection under the Fourteenth Amendment. Yet, although

Proposition 187 was never implemented, it succeeded in putting immigration in the national spotlight.[14]

Arizona's Support Our Law Enforcement and Safe Neighborhoods Act (SB 1070), an omnibus measure passed in 2010, is a prominent recent example of state-level anti-immigrant legislation. SB 1070 required nonresident aliens over the age of eighteen to register and carry proof of status, criminalized solicitation of work by day laborers, instructed state law enforcement officers to determine the immigration status of suspects, permitted warrantless arrests of those believed to be removable, and barred state or local officials from obstructing federal immigration laws. The US Supreme Court struck down most of these provisions, though it upheld the power of state police to investigate suspects' immigration status. Measures like Arizona's—as well as those in Alabama, Georgia, and South Carolina—blur the line between immigration law and alienage law. SB 1070 aimed not simply to regulate the lives of immigrants already present in the state but also to deter immigration. In passing the act, the legislature declared its intention "to make attrition through enforcement the public policy of all state and local government agencies in Arizona." The provisions of the act would "work together to discourage and deter the unlawful entry and presence of aliens." SB 1070 clearly intended to restrict immigration as well as to monitor immigrants after they arrived and settled.[15]

Justice Antonin Scalia, commenting approvingly on SB 1070 in his dissenting opinion in *Arizona v. U.S.* (2012), attempted to revive the antebellum tradition of state police power. "Notwithstanding 'the myth of an era of unrestricted immigration' in the first 100 years of the Republic," Scalia noted, "the States enacted numerous laws restricting the immigration of certain classes of aliens, including convicted criminals, indigents, persons with contagious diseases, and (in Southern States) freed blacks." These laws "not only provided for the removal of unwanted immigrants but also imposed penalties on unlawfully present aliens and those who aided their immigration." As a sovereign state, Arizona had "the inherent power to exclude persons from its territory," subject only to limitations set by the Constitution or imposed by Congress. If Arizona could not secure its territory, it would no longer be sovereign. Far from challenging federal immigration policies, Scalia noted, SB 1070 enforced these policies more effectively.[16]

The states' rights tradition in American history is often associated with racism and reactionary politics, yet it can also support progressive causes. Many local authorities today support federal immigration policies, cooperate with national agencies such as Immigration and Customs Enforcement (ICE), or call for more restrictive and punitive laws. Others, however, seek to protect immigrants from federal surveillance. The parallel with the antebellum era is striking. Northern states before the Civil War provided refuge for fugitive slaves and free black people in danger of being kidnapped into slavery, and they tried to protect their black citizens in southern ports. Slaveowners, meanwhile, demanded federal intervention to capture and return fugitives, while defending slavery as a local institution immune from outside interference. In *Prigg v. Pennsylvania* (1842), the Supreme Court ruled that, although Pennsylvania could not obstruct the Fugitive Slave Act, it was not obliged to enforce federal law. Pennsylvania retained sovereignty over its internal affairs and could use its police power to protect the public welfare, as long as its laws did not infringe on federal authority. In response to *Prigg* and the Fugitive Slave Act of 1850, northern states passed new personal liberty laws prohibiting public participation in the capture and return of fugitives.

While states and cities cannot defy federal immigration law, neither can the federal government order them to participate in enforcing that law. Local measures promoting immigrant integration through access to driver's licenses or public benefits today do not usually contradict federal authority. Nor does noncompliance with federal deportation policy necessarily entail violation of federal law. States and cities can decide for themselves the extent to which they cooperate with the national government on immigration policy or whether to provide a refuge for undocumented immigrants. With the executive branch playing an ever more prominent role in immigration policy, states and localities increasingly choose to protect the rights of foreigners through legislation and litigation. The sanctuary movement, operating partly within the structures of local government and partly at the grassroots level, confronts national power more directly.[17]

Although the decision in *Wong Kim Ark* became settled doctrine, recent decades have seen renewed challenges to birthright citizenship. The debate, such as it is, focuses once again on the words "subject to the jurisdiction thereof" in the Fourteenth Amendment. Opponents of birthright citizenship argue that the amendment was not meant to refer to the children of unsanctioned immigrants, as there were no "illegal immigrants" at that time. This assertion is factually wrong in two ways. First, as Scalia's opinion in *Arizona v. U.S.* affirmed, any foreigner residing in the United States in the antebellum era contrary to state immigration policies was violating the law. Second, free and enslaved black people who entered the United States despite federal statutes passed in 1803 and 1807 barring their entry were in the country illegally, albeit through no fault of their own. The architects of the Fourteenth

Amendment clearly intended the American-born children of all immigrants to be citizens, regardless of the status of their parents. With minor exceptions, anyone born on American soil is a citizen of the United States.[18]

The campaign to undermine birthright citizenship today begins at the local and state level. One proposal is to issue a certain kind of birth certificate for children of citizens and permanent residents and a different kind for the children of irregular immigrants. Another is to define state citizenship to require at least one parent to be a citizen. Like state laws denying benefits to irregular immigrants or their children, measures of this kind would not withstand judicial review. Merely proposing them, however, puts pressure on the federal government to crack down on immigration in other ways. At the federal level, legislation could try to exclude children of irregular immigrants from citizenship on the grounds that they are not subject to the jurisdiction of the United States. Any such law would almost certainly be declared unconstitutional unless the Fourteenth Amendment was amended. Such an amendment might state that a person born in the United States to immigrant parents is not a citizen unless at least one parent is either a citizen or a lawfully admitted permanent resident. This amendment would have to be passed by a two-thirds majority in both houses of Congress and would require approval by three-quarters of the states, either by their legislatures or by ratifying conventions chosen in special elections. If the amendment became part of the Constitution, it would bring American policy into line with many other countries around the world. It would also be highly reactionary. Most countries limit access to citizenship, whether by race, ethnicity, culture, religion, or parental status. In the United States, there are no such qualifications.

The most far-reaching proposals to protect immigrants today are emerging, once again, at the local level. The "New York Is Home Act" (2014) proposed extending state citizenship to noncitizens regardless of their immigration status. After a waiting period and with proof of good character, as in federal naturalization policy, all immigrants could apply for state citizenship and would have access to driver's licenses or other identification documents, public health and tuition benefits, professional licenses, protections against discrimination, and the right to vote and hold public office at the local and state level. Defining the boundaries of social and political community in this way redirects deep-rooted traditions of state sovereignty toward the integration of foreigners, at a time when Congress remains gridlocked on immigration. It also generates a significant conflict within federalism over the power to control immigration and define political membership. Local sovereignty is not simply a matter of autonomy from the federal government. It can also entail an obligation to protect all people, of every background, to enhance the general welfare. What matters is who defines the common good and how. Rights can be protected even more effectively if defined nationally and guaranteed by the federal government, but in the contemporary context cities, counties, and states have a vitally important role to play.[19]

# Chronology

1790  The first Naturalization Act, limited to free white persons, lays down the procedure whereby immigrants can become citizens after a waiting period followed by an oath of allegiance.

1793  Congress passes the first Fugitive Slave Act.

1795  Congress extends the waiting period for naturalization from two to five years.

1798  Congress passes the Alien and Sedition Acts and an act extending the waiting period for naturalization to fifteen years.
Jefferson and Madison issue the Kentucky and Virginia Resolutions.

1802  In a new naturalization act, Congress restores the waiting period to five years.

1803  Congress passes an act prohibiting the importation of enslaved or free black people into states that already forbid their entry.

1807  Congress prohibits the importation of enslaved people into the United States after 1808.

1819  The first Passenger Act sets rules for conditions on board ships.

1820  Missouri enters the Union as a slave state, with slavery prohibited in the remainder of the Louisiana Purchase north of 36° 30′.

1822  Denmark Vesey and thirty-four other African Americans are executed after rumors of a planned uprising in South Carolina.
South Carolina passes its first Seamen Act, confining free black sailors to jail for the duration of their stay in port.

1823  In *Elkison v. Deliesseline*, Supreme Court justice William Johnson rules that South Carolina's Seamen Act violates the federal government's treaty power and Congress's exclusive power to regulate foreign and interstate commerce, although his opinion has no practical impact.

1824　In *Gibbons v. Ogden*, the Supreme Court rules that that navigation is a form of commerce and that Congress controls interstate and foreign commerce.

1830　The Indian Removal Act creates the mechanism for expelling more than 80,000 Native Americans to the interior.

1836　In *Commonwealth of Massachusetts v. Aves*, the Superior Court rules that an enslaved child brought to the state is free as slavery does not exist under Massachusetts law.

1837　In *New York v. Miln*, the Supreme Court upholds a state law requiring ships arriving in New York City to furnish a report on their passengers as a legitimate use of police power.

1841　In *Groves v. Slaughter*, the Supreme Court confronts the question of whether the interstate slave trade falls under the commerce clause, but it avoids the question on a technicality.

1842　In *Prigg v. Pennsylvania*, the Supreme Court invalidates a state law that prevents any black person from being removed for the purpose of enslavement, ruling that the Fugitive Slave Act of 1793 takes precedence. The Court finds that the state must comply with, but is not obliged to enforce, federal policy, and acknowledges the state's police power to regulate public health and safety by excluding or deporting undesirable persons.

1847　Congress passes a second Passenger Act.

1849　In the *Passenger Cases*, a badly divided Supreme Court invalidates state laws imposing taxes on immigrants as a violation of federal power under the commerce clause.

1850　As part of the Compromise of 1850, Congress passes a second Fugitive Slave Act.

1854　In *People v. Hall*, the California Supreme Court rules that no person of Chinese origin can testify in court against a white person.
Congress passes the Kansas-Nebraska Act, overriding the Missouri Compromise by opening the Louisiana Purchase territories to slavery under the principle of "popular sovereignty."
The Republican Party is founded.

1855　Congress passes a third Passenger Act.
Congress passes a Naturalization Act providing that a child born outside the United States is a US citizen if their father is a US citizen and that an alien immigrant woman gains citizenship through marriage to an American citizen or the naturalization of her husband.

1857 In *Dred Scott v. Sandford*, the Supreme Court invalidates the Missouri Compromise and rules that no person whose ancestors were brought to the United States as slaves can be a citizen of the United States, thereby excluding African Americans—both enslaved and free—from citizenship.

1860 In *Lemmon v. People of New York*, the New York courts rule that enslaved people brought into the state are automatically free, as slavery does not exist under the laws of New York.

1861 The attempted secession of eleven states from the Union to protect slavery triggers the Civil War.

1862 The Coolie Trade Prohibition Act outlaws involvement by American vessels in the transportation of unfree Chinese workers to foreign ports.

1863 Abraham Lincoln issues the Emancipation Proclamation.

1864 Congress passes an Act to Encourage Immigration, lending federal recognition to short-term contracts for European workers.

1865 The Thirteenth Amendment prohibits slavery and involuntary servitude in the United States, except in cases of punishment for crime.

1866 The first civil rights act acknowledges all persons born under the jurisdiction of the United States as citizens and provides federal protection for the right to make contracts, take legal suits, testify in court, and hold property.

1868 The Fourteenth Amendment defines national citizenship at the constitutional level for the first time, establishing birth on the soil and naturalization as the criteria; protects the rights of citizens against actions by the states; and extends due process and equal protection to persons as well as citizens.

The Burlingame-Seward Treaty recognizes the right of "free and voluntary" migrants to travel from China to the United States and vice versa, but not their right to naturalize as citizens.

1870 The Fifteenth Amendment prohibits denying the right to vote on grounds of "race, color, or previous condition of servitude."

Congress extends the right of naturalization to aliens of African nativity and to persons of African descent, but not to Chinese immigrants.

1873 In the *Slaughterhouse Cases*, the Supreme Court rules that the privileges and immunities clause of the Fourteenth Amendment applies only to a limited set of rights pertaining to federal (as distinct from state) citizenship. The Court also suggests that the Thirteenth Amendment might apply to forms of servitude beyond African American slavery, including peonage and the coolie trade.

1875 The Page Act targets Chinese immigrants by prohibiting the admission of prostitutes, coolies, and criminals.

In *Henderson v. Mayor of New York* and *Chy Lung v. Freeman*, the Supreme Court unanimously invalidates state immigration laws, describing immigration as a matter of vital national concern and grounding federal authority in the commerce clause.

1876 Congress appoints a joint special committee to investigate Chinese immigration.

1880 The Angell Treaty allows Congress to regulate Chinese immigration through "reasonable" means.

1882 The Chinese Exclusion Act bans immigration by Chinese laborers for ten years. Those in violation of the law can be deported. Laborers who leave the United States may return with proper documentation.

The first general immigration act, modeled on the recently invalidated state laws and implemented by state officials, levies a head tax of fifty cents on every alien passenger, and excludes convicts, mentally or physically impaired passengers, and others deemed likely to become a public charge from entering the United States.

1884 In the *Head Money Cases*, the federal government argues that power to regulate national borders is inherent in national sovereignty. The Supreme Court upholds the Immigration Act of 1882, but on commerce clause grounds.

1885 The Alien Contract Labor Act, known as the Foran Act, prohibits any company or individual from bringing unskilled immigrants to the United States to work under contracts signed abroad.

1886 In *Yick Wo v. Hopkins*, the Supreme Court invalidates ordinances in San Francisco that discriminate against Chinese laundry businesses, on the grounds that they violate the equal protection clause of the Fourteenth Amendment.

1888 The Scott Act unilaterally discontinues the practice of issuing certificates of return for Chinese laborers and invalidates certificates already issued.

1889 In *Chae Chan Ping v. United States (The Chinese Exclusion Case)*, the Supreme Court upholds the Scott Act, finding that power over admissions is inherent in the sovereignty of the United States and assigning that power to the "political branches" of the federal government (i.e., the legislature and the executive) with minimal interference by the judiciary.

1891  A second general immigration act enlarges the federal bureaucratic structure, expands the list of excludable classes, and authorizes deportation beyond the special category of Chinese laborers.

1892  The Geary Act extends the exclusion of Chinese laborers for another ten years and requires all Chinese laborers in the United States to carry residence permits. Those found to be present illegally are subject to imprisonment at hard labor, followed by deportation.

In *Nishimura Ekiu v. United States*, the Supreme Court rules that the United States has an absolute right to exclude all foreigners, not just Chinese laborers, finding that immigration is an international matter that should be left to the political branches of government.

1893  In *Fong Yue Ting v. United States*, the Supreme Court rules that the United States has the same inherent power to deport unnaturalized foreigners as it does to exclude them. The Court also rules that deportation, as an administrative procedure rather than a form of punishment, does not require criminal due process.

1896  In *Plessy v. Ferguson*, the Supreme Court upholds segregated facilities on the principle of separate but equal.

1898  In *United States v. Wong Kim Ark*, the Supreme Court upholds the principle of birthright citizenship enshrined in the Fourteenth Amendment, ruling that persons born on American soil are automatically citizens, even if their parents can never become citizens under naturalization law.

# Notes

INTRODUCTION

1. *Henderson v. Mayor of City of New York*, 92 U.S. 259 (1875); *Chy Lung v. Freeman*, 92 U.S. 275 (1875).

2. *Chae Chan Ping v. United States*, 130 U.S. 581 (1889), known as the *Chinese Exclusion Case*.

3. U.S. Constitution, art. 4, sec. 2, cl. 3; An Act respecting fugitives from justice, and persons escaping from the service of their masters, ch. 7, 1 Stat. 302 (February 12, 1793); An Act to amend, and supplementary to, the Act entitled "An Act respecting Fugitives from Justice, and Persons escaping from the Service of their Masters," approved February twelfth, one thousand seven hundred and ninety-three, ch. 60, 9 Stat. 462 (September 18, 1850); Karla M. McKanders, "Immigration Enforcement and the Fugitive Slave Acts: Exploring Their Similarities," *Catholic University Law Review*, 61 (2012): 921–54; Daniel Kanstroom, *Deportation Nation: Outsiders in American History* (Cambridge: MA: Harvard University Press, 2007), 77–83.

4. Martha S. Jones, *Birthright Citizens: A History of Race and Rights in Antebellum America* (New York: Cambridge University Press, 2018), 37; Daniel Walker Howe, *What Hath God Wrought: The Transformation of America, 1815–1848* (New York: Oxford University Press, 2007), 260–66; Eric Foner, "Lincoln and Colonization," in Eric Foner, ed., *Our Lincoln: New Perspectives on Lincoln and His World* (New York: Norton, 2008), 137–66.

5. Claudio Saunt, *Unworthy Republic: The Dispossession of Native Americans and the Road to Indian Territory* (New York: Norton, 2020), xiii–xiv, 161–63, 279–81; An Act to provide for an exchange of lands with the Indians residing in any of the states or territories, and for their removal west of the river Mississippi, Ch. 148, 4 Stat. 411 (May 28, 1830); *Cherokee Nation v. Georgia*, 30 U.S. (5 Pet.) 1 (1831); *Worcester v. Georgia*, 31 U.S. (6 Pet.) 515, 559 (1832); *United States v. Rogers*, 45 U.S. (4 How.) 567 (1846); Bethany R. Berger, "'Power over This Unfortunate Race': Race, Politics

and Indian Law in *United States v. Rogers*," *William & Mary Law Review* 45 (April 2004): 1957–2052; Sarah H. Cleveland, "Powers Inherent in Sovereignty: Indians, Aliens, Territories, and the Nineteenth Century Origins of Plenary Power over Foreign Affairs," *Texas Law Review* 81 (November 2002): 1–284 (esp. 25–47); Maggie Blackhawk, "Federal Indian Law as Paradigm Within Public Law," *Harvard Law Review* 132 (May 2019): 1791–1877 (esp. 1829–30); *United States v. Kagama*, 118 U.S. 375 (1886). Finding the word "removal" too soft, Saunt describes the process of Indian "expulsion" as a form of "deportation" with elements of "extermination."

6. Santiago Legarre, "The Historical Background of the Police Power," *Journal of Constitutional Law* 9 (February 2007): 745–96; Harry N. Scheiber, "State Police Power," in Leonard W. Levy et al., eds, *Encyclopedia of the American Constitution*, 6 vols. (1986; New York: Macmillan Reference, 2000), 4:2505–12; William J. Novak, "Common Regulation: Legal Origins of State Power in America," *Hastings Law Journal* 45 (April 1994): 1061–97, 1082–83, 1091, 1094–95; Gerald L. Neuman, "The Lost Century of American Immigration Law (1776–1875)," *Columbia Law Review* 93 (December 1993): 1833–1901; Hidetaka Hirota, *Expelling the Poor: Atlantic Seaboard States and the Nineteenth-Century Origins of American Immigration Policy* (New York: Oxford University Press, 2017); Kunal M. Parker, *Making Foreigners: Immigration and Citizenship Law in America* (New York: Cambridge University Press, 2015), 103–13; Michael A. Schoeppner, *Moral Contagion: Black Atlantic Sailors, Citizenship, and Diplomacy in Antebellum America* (New York: Cambridge University Press, 2019); *New York v. Miln*, 36 U.S. (11 Pet.) 102, 142–43 (1837). The guiding (if sometimes incompatible) principles of police power, as Novak explains, were *salus populi suprema lex esto* (the welfare of the people shall be the supreme law) and *sic utero tuo ut alienum non laedas* (use your own property without injury to other people's). The states retained substantial police powers after the Civil War, though state actions were now subject to federal review under the Fourteenth Amendment and on freedom of contract grounds.

7. Hirota, *Expelling the Poor*, 42–69; Neuman, "Lost Century," 1846–57; Parker, *Making Foreigners*, 93–97, 103–13; Kate Masur, *Until Justice Be Done: America's First Civil Rights Movement, from the Revolution to Reconstruction* (New York: Norton, 2021), 4–6, 11–12, 14–18; Michael A. Schoeppner, "Black Migrants and Border Regulation in the Early United States," *Journal of the Civil War Era* 11 (September 2021): 317–39. On raising passenger fares to offset taxes and fees, see *Passenger Cases*, 48 U.S. (7 How.) 283, 465 (1849); *Henderson v. New York*, 259–60.

8. U.S. Constitution, art. 1, sec. 8, cl. 4; An Act to establish an uniform Rule of Naturalization, ch. 3, 1 Stat. 103 (March 26, 1790); An Act to establish an uniform rule of Naturalization; and to repeal the act heretofore passed on that subject, ch. 20. 1 Stat. 414 (January 29, 1795); An act supplementary to and to amend the act, intituled [*sic*] "An act to establish an uniform rule of naturalization," and to repeal the act heretofore passed on that subject, ch. 54, 1 Stat. 566 (June 18, 1798); An Act To establish an uniform rule of Naturalization and to repeal the

acts heretofore passed on that subject, ch. 28, 2 Stat. 153 (April 14, 1802); An Act to amend the Naturalization Laws and to punish Crimes against the same, and for other Purposes, ch. 154, 16 Stat. (July 14, 1870).

9. U.S. Constitution, art. 1, sec. 8, cl. 11; art. 1, sec. 9, cl. 1; art. 2, sec. 2, cl. 2; Anna O. Law, "The Historical Amnesia of Contemporary Immigration Federalism Debates," *Polity* 47 (July 2015): 302–19 (esp. 312–18).

10. U.S. Constitution, art. 1, sec. 8, cl. 3; *Gibbons v. Ogden*, 22 U.S. (9 Wheat.) 1 (1824), 189–90; Mary Sarah Bilder, "The Struggle over Immigration: Indentured Servants, Slaves, and Articles of Commerce," *Missouri Law Review* 61 (Fall 1996): 743–824; Charles Warren, *The Supreme Court in United States History*, 3 vols. (Boston: Little, Brown, 1922), 2:77–82.

11. *New York v. Miln*, 132, 141, 142–43; Emer de Vattel, *The law of nations, or, Principles of the law of nature, applied to the conduct and affairs of nations and sovereigns, with three early essays on the origin and nature of natural law and on luxury*, ed. Béla Kapossy and Richard Whatmore, trans. Thomas Nugent (1758; Indianapolis: Liberty Fund, 2008), Book 2, ch. VII, § 94, ch. VIII, § 100; Bilder, "Struggle over Immigration," 745–51, 799–807. The justices in the majority based their decision only on the part of the New York statute requiring a passenger report, ignoring other provisions in the law that captains must post bonds for alien passengers. Joseph Story, the lone dissenter, ruled that the statute as a whole violated the commerce clause.

12. *Passenger Cases*, 48 U.S. (7 How.) 283, 474 (1849); Vattel, *The law of nations*, Book 1, ch. XIX, § 231; Book 2, ch. VIII, §§ 93, 94, 99, 100.

13. *Passenger Cases*, 492; *Dred Scott v. Sandford*, 60 U.S. (19 How.) 393 (1857); Novak, "Legal Transformation of Citizenship," 92–94, 98, 99; Hirota, *Expelling the Poor*; Jones, *Birthright Citizens*; Masur, *Until Justice Be Done*, 55–56.

14. Eric Foner, *Reconstruction: America's Unfinished Revolution, 1862–1877*, updated edition (1988; New York: Harper Perennial Modern Classics, 2014); Eric Foner, *The Second Founding: How the Civil War and Reconstruction Remade the Constitution* (New York: Norton, 2019), 71; Laura F. Edwards, *A Legal History of the Civil War and Reconstruction: A Nation of Rights* (New York: Cambridge University Press, 2015); Richard Franklin Bensel, *Yankee Leviathan: The Origins of Central State Authority in America, 1859–1877* (New York: Cambridge University Press, 1990); Jones, *Birthright Citizens*; Martha S. Jones, "Citizenship," in Nikole Hannah-Jones et al., eds, *The 1619 Project: A New Origin Story* (New York: One World Press, 2021), 219–36; Masur, *Until Justice Be Done*; William J. Novak, "The Legal Transformation of Citizenship in Nineteenth-Century America," in Meg Jacobs, William J. Novak, and Julian E. Zelizer, eds., *The Democratic Experiment: New Directions in American Political History* (Princeton: Princeton University Press, 2003), 92.

15. *Henderson v. New York*, 259–60; *Chy Lung v. Freeman*, 276–78; Neuman, "Lost Century," 1893, 1897; Kunal M. Parker, "Citizenship and Immigration Law, 1800–1924: Resolutions of Membership and Territory," in Michael Grossberg and Christopher Tomlins, eds., *The Cambridge History of Law in America*, 3

vols, vol. 2: *The Long Nineteenth Century (1789–1920)* (New York: Cambridge University Press, 2008), 176; Cleveland, "Powers Inherent in Sovereignty," 107–9. On local pressure for national immigration control following the invalidation of state laws, see Hidetaka Hirota, "The Moment of Transition: State Officials, the Federal Government, and the Formation of American Immigration Policy," *Journal of American History* 99 (March 2013): 1092–1108. On Western pressure for Chinese exclusion, see Andrew Gyory, *Closing the Gates: Race, Politics, and the Chinese Exclusion Act* (Chapel Hill: University of North Carolina Press, 1998), 140–42, 194–95, 223–25.

16. An Act to Prohibit the "Coolie Trade" by American Citizens in American Vessels, ch. 27, 12 Stat. 340 (February 19, 1862); An Act to Encourage Immigration, ch. 246, 13 Stat. 385 (July 4, 1864); Moon-Ho Jung, "Outlawing 'Coolies': Race, Nation, and Empire in the Age of Emancipation," *American Quarterly* 57 (September 2005): 677–701; Kevin Kenny, "The Antislavery Origins of US Immigration Policy," *Journal of the Civil War Era* 11 (September 2021): 361–81; Lucy Salyer, *Laws Harsh as Tigers: Chinese Immigrants and the Shaping of Modern Immigration Law* (Chapel Hill: University of North Carolina Press, 1995), 28; Beth Lew-Williams, *The Chinese Must Go: Violence, Exclusion, and the Making of the Alien in America* (Cambridge, MA: Harvard University Press, 2018), 235–40. The Act to Encourage Immigration (1864), in sharp contrast to the 1862 anti-coolie law, gave federal recognition to short-term contracts recruiting European workers. This act generated opposition to contract labor on antislavery grounds and was allowed to expire after four years.

17. An Act to Prevent the Kidnapping and Importation of Mongolian, Chinese, and Japanese females, for Criminal or Demoralizing Purposes, ch. 230, 1870 Cal. Stat. 330 (March 18, 1870); An Act to Prevent the Importation of Chinese Criminals and to Prevent the Establishment of Coolie Slavery, ch. 231, 1870 Cal. Stat. 332 (March 18, 1870); An act supplementary to the acts in relation to immigration, ch. 141, 18 Stat. 477 (March 3, 1875); Kerry Abrams, "Polygamy, Prostitution, and the Federalization of Immigration Law," *Columbia Law Review* 105 (April 2005): 657–59, 661–63, 674–77, 690–703, 711; Lew-Williams, *The Chinese Must Go*, 235–40.

18. An Act to execute certain treaty stipulations relating to Chinese, ch. 126, 22 Stat. 58 (May 6, 1882).

19. Neuman, "Lost Century," 1871, 1872, 1873; Philip A. Kuhn, *Chinese Among Others: Emigration in Modern Times* (Lanham, MD: Rowman and Littlefield, 2008), 215; Alexander Saxton, *The Indispensable Enemy: Labor and the Anti-Chinese Movement in California* (1971; Berkeley: University of California Press, 1995), esp. 19–45; Eugene H. Berwanger, *The Frontier Against Slavery: Western Anti-Negro Prejudice and the Slavery Extension Controversy* (1967; Urbana: University of Illinois Press, 2002), ix–xi, 3–5, 59–77.

20. An act to regulate Immigration, ch. 376, 22 Stat. 214 (August 3, 1882); An act in amendment to the various acts relative to immigration and the importation of aliens under contract or agreement to perform labor, ch. 551, 26 Stat. 1084 (March

3, 1891); Hirota, "Moment of Transition," 1092–108; Hirota, *Expelling the Poor*, 191–92, 201–2.

21. An Act to execute certain treaty stipulations relating to Chinese (1882); An act a supplement to an act entitled "An act to execute certain treaty stipulations relating to Chinese" approved the sixth day of May eighteen hundred and eighty two, ch. 1064, 25 Stat. 504 (October 1, 1888); *Chae Chan Ping v. United States*.

22. *Chae Chan Ping v. United States*, 582–83; Vattel, *The law of nations*, Book 2, ch. VIII, §100; Cleveland, "Powers Inherent in Sovereignty," 124–25. The term "plenary power" can refer to any power held exclusively by one branch of government. In immigration scholarship it refers to the sweeping power exerted by the "political branches" of government (i.e., the legislature and executive) over admission, exclusion, and expulsion.

23. Elizabeth Ellis, "The Border(s) Crossed Us Too: The Intersections of Native American and Immigrant Fights for Justice," *emisférica* 14 (Fall 2018): https://hemisphericinstitute.org/en/emisferica-14-1-expulsion/14-1-essays/the-border-s-crossed-us-too-the-intersections-of-native-american-and-immigrant-fights-for-justice-2.html, paras. 2, 7–9, 14–15, 22–26, 30–31; Berger, "'Power over This Unfortunate Race,'" 1957–2052; Bethany R. Berger, "The Anomaly of Citizenship for Indigenous Rights," in Shereen Hertel and Kathryn Libal, eds., *Human Rights in the United States: Beyond Exceptionalism* (New York: Cambridge University Press, 2011), 217, 219–20, 225–26; Bethany R. Berger, "Birthright Citizenship on Trial: *Elk v. Wilkins* and *United States v. Wong Kim Ark*," *Cardozo Law Review* 37 (April 2016): 1185–258 (especially 1205–10, 1239–43, 1256–57); Blackhawk, "Federal Indian Law," 1860; Cleveland, "Powers Inherent in Sovereignty," 48–51, 54–77; Julian Lim, "Immigration, Plenary Powers, and Sovereignty Talk: Then and Now," *Journal of the Gilded Age and Progressive Era* 19 (April 2020): 217–29.

24. *Nishimura Ekiu v. United States*, 142 U.S. 651, 659 (1892), Justice Gray citing Vattel, *The law of nations*, Book 2, ch. VIII, §§ 94, 100; *Fong Yue Ting v. United States*, 149 U.S. 698, 708–9 (1893), Justice Gray quoting Vattel, *The law of nations*, Book 1, ch. XIX, §§ 230, 231; Adam B. Cox and Cristina M. Rodríguez, *The President and Immigration Law* (New York: Oxford University Press, 2020), 31.

25. F. H. Hinsley, *Sovereignty*, 2nd ed. (Cambridge: Cambridge University Press, 1986); Hent Kalmo and Quentin Skinner, eds., *Sovereignty in Fragments: The Past, Present and Future of a Contested Concept* (Cambridge: Cambridge University Press, 2010); Terry Nardin, "The Diffusion of Sovereignty," *History of European Ideas* 41.1 (2015): 89–102; Andreas Osiander, "Sovereignty, International Relations, and the Westphalian Myth," *International Organization* 55 (Spring 2001): 251–87; James J. Sheehan, "The Problem of Sovereignty in European History," *American Historical Review* 111 (February 2006): 1–15; Jewel L. Spangler and Frank Towers, eds., *Remaking North American Sovereignty: State Transformation in the 1860s* (New York: Fordham University Press, 2020), 1–17; William J. Novak, "The Myth of the 'Weak' American State," *American Historical Review* 113 (June 2008): 752–72;

Brian Balogh, *A Government out of Sight: The Mystery of National Authority in the Nineteenth Century* (New York: Cambridge University Press, 2009); Gautham Rao, "The New Historiography of the Early Federal Government: Institutions, Contexts, and the Imperial State," *William and Mary Quarterly* 77 (January 2020): 97–128.

26. Masur, *Until Justice Be Done*, xxi; Foner, *Second Founding*, xxvii; Jones, *Birthright Citizens*; Christopher James Bonner, *Remaking the Republic: Black Politics and the Creation of American Citizenship* (Philadelphia: University of Pennsylvania Press, 2020); Manisha Sinha, *The Slave's Cause: A History of Abolition* (New Haven: Yale University Press, 2016); Salyer, *Laws Harsh as Tigers*; John McNelis O'Keefe, *Stranger Citizens: Migrant Influence and National Power in the Early American Republic* (Ithaca, NY: Cornell University Press, 2021).

27. Hidetaka Hirota, "Exclusion on the Ground: Racism, Official Discretion, and the Quotidian Enforcement of General Immigration Law in the Pacific Northwest Borderland," *American Quarterly* 69 (June 2017): 347–70; Beth Lew-Williams, "Before Restriction Became Exclusion: America's Experiment in Diplomatic Immigration Control," *Pacific Historical Review* 83 (February 2014): 24–56; Kelly Lytle Hernandez, *Migra! A History of the U.S. Border Patrol* (Berkeley: University of California Press, 2010); S. Deborah Kang, *The INS on the Line: Making Immigration Law on the US-Mexico Border, 1917–1954* (New York: Oxford University Press, 2016).

28. Mae M. Ngai, *Immigration and Ethnic History* (Washington, DC: American Historical Association, 2012), 14; Rogers M. Smith, *Civic Ideals: Conflicting Visions of Citizenship in U.S. History* (New Haven: Yale University Press, 1997). Smith argues that liberal democracy in the United States was constantly under threat from inegalitarian strains of thought, resulting in periodic retrenchments rather than any linear model of progress. Resting on assumptions regarding race, gender, and religion, the "ascriptivist" tradition Smith examines resulted in the persistent belief that the people of the United States were by nature white, male, and Protestant, and that African Americans, Native Americans, women, and certain immigrants were unsuited for citizenship.

29. A. Naomi Paik, *Bans, Walls, Raids, Sanctuary: Understanding U.S. Immigration for the Twenty-First Century* (Oakland: University of California Press, 2020), 102–29, 132–34; Pratheepan Gulasekaram and S. Karthick Ramakrishnan, *The New Immigration Federalism* (New York: Cambridge University Press, 2015), 59–64, 119–50; Maeve Glass, "Citizens of the State," *University of Chicago Law Review* 85 (June 2018): 928–29.

CHAPTER 1

1. Thomas Jefferson, et al., July 4, 1776, Copy of Declaration of Independence, Library of Congress, https://www.loc.gov/item/mtjbib000159/; Thomas

Jefferson, "original rough draught" of the Declaration of Independence, Library of Congress, https://www.loc.gov/exhibits/declara/ruffdrft.html; Thomas Jefferson, *The writings of Thomas Jefferson: being his autobiography, correspondence, reports, messages, addresses, and other writings, official and private*, ed. Henry Augustine Washington, 9 vols. (Washington, DC: Taylor & Maury, 1853–1854), 1:19.

2. Thomas Paine, *Common Sense* (1776; New York: Penguin Classics, 1982), 100; Jefferson and Slavery, https://www.monticello.org/thomas-jefferson/jefferson-slavery/; George Washington to the members of the Volunteer Association and other Inhabitants of the Kingdom of Ireland, December 2, 1783, George Washington Papers, Library of Congress, https://www.loc.gov/resource/mgw3c.005/?sp=97&st=single; James Madison, August 13, 1787, in Jonathan Elliot, *The Debates in the Several State Conventions on the Adoption of the Federal Constitution, as Recommended by the General Convention at Philadelphia in 1787*, 5 vols. (Philadelphia: J. B. Lippincott; Washington, DC: Taylor & Maury, 1836–1859), 5:411.

3. J. Hector St. John de Crèvecoeur, *Letters from an American Farmer* (1782; New York: Penguin Classics, 1981), 68–69, 70, 71.

4. Thomas Jefferson, "Notes on the State of Virginia" (1787), Avalon Project: Documents in Law, History, and Diplomacy, Yale Law School (cited hereafter as Avalon Project), https://avalon.law.yale.edu/18th_century/jeffvir.asp.

5. Letters of Agrippa, *Massachusetts Gazette*, November 1787–January 1788 (Agrippa Letter IX, December 28, 1787), http://teachingamericanhistory.org/library/document/agrippa-ix/. Agrippa was the pseudonym of James Winthrop (1752–1821), scion of a prominent New England family.

6. James H. Kettner, *The Development of American Citizenship, 1608–1870*, rev. ed. (1978; Chapel Hill: University of North Carolina Press, 2005), 3–128, 131–286; Lucy Salyer, *Under the Starry Flag: How a Band of Irish Americans Joined the Fenian Revolt and Sparked a Crisis over Citizenship* (Cambridge, MA: Harvard University Press, 2018), 1–6.

7. U.S. Constitution, art. 2, sec. 1, cl. 5; art. 3, sec. 2, cl. 1; art. 4, sec. 2, cl. 2.

8. Articles of Confederation, art. 4; Alexander Hamilton, John Jay, and James Madison, *The Federalist Papers*, ed. Isaac Kramnick (1788; New York: Penguin, 1987), , 447.

9. Martha S. Jones, *Birthright Citizens: A History of Race and Rights in Antebellum America* (New York: Cambridge University Press, 2018), 10–14; Martha S. Jones, "Citizenship," in Nikole Hannah-Jones et al., eds., *The 1619 Project: A New Origin Story* (New York: One World Press, 2021), 219–36; Christopher James Bonner, *Remaking the Republic: Black Politics and the Creation of American Citizenship* (Philadelphia: University of Pennsylvania Press, 2020), 1–8.

10. U.S. Constitution, art. 1, sec. 8, cl. 4; An Act to establish an uniform Rule of Naturalization, ch. 3, 1 Stat. 103 (March 26, 1790); An Act to secure the Right of Citizenship to Children of Citizens of the United States born out of the Limits thereof, ch. 71, 10 Stat. 604 (February 10, 1855); Marian L. Smith, "'Any woman who

is now or may hereafter be married . . . .' Women and Naturalization, ca. 1802–1940," National Archives *Prologue Magazine* 30 (Summer 1998), Genealogy Notes, https://www.archives.gov/publications/prologue/1998/summer/women-and-naturalization-1.html. The 1855 law granted citizenship to any woman who had married or would marry a male citizen of the United States (but not to any man who married a female citizen), as well as to children born abroad to US citizen fathers (but not to mothers).

11. Thomas Hart Benton, *Abridgment of the Debates of Congress, from 1789 to 1856*, 16 vols. (New York: D. Appleton, 1860–1867), 1:186 ("Rule of Naturalization," House of Representatives, February 1790); An Act to establish an uniform Rule of Naturalization (1790); Kettner, *Development of American Citizenship*, 131–286.

12. An Act to establish an uniform rule of Naturalization, and to repeal the act heretofore passed on that subject, ch. 20. 1 Stat. 414 (January 29, 1795); House debate on naturalization bill, 1794–95, in Joseph Gales and William W. Seaton, *The Debates and Proceedings in the Congress of the United States*, 42 vols. (Washington, DC: 1834–1856), cited hereafter as Annals (by Congress and session number): 3rd Cong., 2nd Sess., House, 1004–9, 1021–23, 1026–27, 1028–32, 1033–38, 1064. The other Catholic signatories of the Constitution were Daniel Carroll and Charles Carroll of Maryland.

13. An act supplementary to and to amend the act, intituled [*sic*] "An act to establish an uniform rule of naturalization," and to repeal the act heretofore passed on that subject, ch. 54, 1 Stat. 566 (June 18, 1798); Gerald L. Neuman, "The Lost Century of American Immigration Law (1776–1875)," *Columbia Law Review* 93 (December 1993): 1882.

14. An Act To establish an uniform rule of Naturalization and to repeal the acts heretofore passed on that subject, ch. 28, 2 Stat. 153 (April 14, 1802); Jefferson, "Notes on the State of Virginia" (1787); Alexander Hamilton, "The Examination," nos. 7 and 8 (January 7 and 12, 1802), in Harold C. Syrett, ed., *Papers of Alexander Hamilton*, 27 vols. (New York: Columbia University Press, 1961–87), 25:491–97; Neuman, "Lost Century," 1882.

15. U.S. Constitution, art. 1, sec. 8, cl. 1. On the status of passengers as persons or imports, see Justice Philip Pendleton Barbour's majority opinion in *New York v. Miln*, 36 U.S. 102 (1837), 136–37 (discussed in Chapter 2) and Chief Justice Roger Taney's dissenting opinion in the *Passenger Cases*, 48 U.S. (7 How.) 283 (1849), 477–78 (discussed in Chapter 3). On indentured servants and other migrants as commerce in the colonial era, see Mary Sarah Bilder, "The Struggle over Immigration: Indentured Servants, Slaves, and Articles of Commerce," *Missouri Law Review* 61 (Fall 1996): 748, 761, 771.

16. U.S. Constitution, art. 1, sec. 8, cl. 11; art. 2, sec. 2, cl. 2; Michael A. Schoeppner, *Moral Contagion: Black Atlantic Sailors, Citizenship, and Diplomacy in Antebellum America* (New York: Cambridge University Press, 2019); Beth Lew-Williams, *The Chinese Must Go: Violence, Exclusion, and the Making of the Alien in America* (Cambridge, MA: Harvard University Press, 2018).

17. U.S. Constitution, art. 1, sec. 2, cl. 3; art. 1, sec. 9, cl. 1; art. 4, sec. 2, cl. 3; amend. 2; amend. 5; Sean Wilentz, *No Property in Man: Slavery and Antislavery at the Nation's Founding* (Cambridge, MA: Harvard University Press, 2018); David Waldstreicher, *Slavery's Constitution: From Revolution to Ratification* (New York: Hill and Wang, 2009); Paul Finkelman, "Slavery in the United States: Persons or Property?," in Jean Allain, ed., *The Legal Understanding of Slavery: From the Historical to the Contemporary* (New York: Oxford University Press, 2012), 105–34; Carol Anderson, "Self-Defense," in Hannah-Jones et al., eds., *The 1619 Project*, 255–57. The Second Amendment, by upholding state militias, facilitated the control of enslaved people, and the Fifth Amendment protected property rights (including property in slaves). Wilentz argues that, although the Constitution recognized slavery as created at the state level, it did not recognize the ownership of human property at the level of national law, and that it therefore opened a path for antislavery constitutionalism in the nineteenth century. Waldstreicher and Finkelman argue forcefully that the Constitution recognized human property and was a proslavery document.

18. U.S. Constitution, art. 1, sec. 8, cl. 3; Max Farrand, ed., *The Records of the Federal Convention of 1787*, 3 vols. (New Haven: Yale University Press, 1911) (cited hereafter as Farrand), 2:364. New England's economy was deeply connected to slavery through the sugar, slave, and rum trades (and later to southern cotton production), but it did not depend on continued importation of slave labor.

19. Farrand 2:371; David L. Lightner, *Slavery and the Commerce Power: How the Struggle Against the Interstate Slave Trade Led to the Civil War* (New Haven: Yale University Press, 2006), 17–18, 19, 21; David L. Lightner, "The Founders and the Interstate Slave Trade," *Journal of the Early Republic* 22 (Spring 2002): 27–28.

20. U.S. Constitution, art. 1, sec. 8, cl. 3; art. 1, sec. 9, cl. 1. The year originally proposed for ending the external slave trade, 1800, was changed to 1808, with the New England states again in coalition with the Lower South. In the *Passenger Cases*, 454, Justice McKinley argued that the migration or importation clause conferred power on Congress to regulate both free migration and the importation of enslaved persons immediately in the four new states admitted to the Union between 1789 and 1808 and in all states thereafter.

21. Farrand 2:417. George Mason held that the word "importation" was necessary to prevent the introduction of convicts.

22. Elliot, *The Debates in the Several State Conventions*, 2:452–53; 4:101, 102.

23. Farrand 3:484; Lightner, "Founders and the Interstate Slave Trade," 36, 39; Benjamin Rush to Jeremy Belknap, February 28, 1788, in John P. Kaminski, ed., *A Necessary Evil? Slavery and the Debate over the Constitution* (Madison, WI: Madison House, 1995), 147.

24. Kramnick, ed., *Federalist Papers*, 273, 275.

25. Lightner, *Slavery and the Commerce Power*, 16–36; Lightner, "Founders and the Interstate Slave Trade," 30, 32; David Brion Davis, *The Problem of Slavery in the Age of Revolution 1770–1823* (Ithaca, NY: Cornell University Press, 1975), 129;

Paul Finkelman, *Slavery and the Founders: Race and Liberty in the Age of Jefferson* (New York: M.E. Sharpe, 1996), 175 n74; Walter Berns, "The Constitution and the Migration of Slaves," *Yale Law Journal* 78 (December 1968): 198–228.

26. An Act Concerning Aliens, ch. 58, 1 Stat. 570 (June 25, 1798), known as the Alien Friends Act; An Act Respecting Alien Enemies, ch. 66, 1 Stat. 577 (July 6, 1798), known as the Alien Enemies Act; An Act in addition to the Act "An act for the punishment of certain crimes against the United States," ch. 74, 1 Stat. 596 (July 14, 1798), known as the Sedition Act; An act supplementary to and to amend the act (June 18, 1798).

27. An Act Respecting Enemy Aliens, 1798, sec.1; Annals, 5th Cong., 2nd Sess., House, 1786–87, 1789, 1795.

28. An Act Concerning Aliens.

29. Annals, 5th Cong., 2nd Sess., House, 1955, 1974, 1980, 1981.

30. U.S. Constitution, art. 1, sec. 8, cl. 1; Annals, 5th Cong., 2nd Sess., House, 1955, 1957.

31. Annals, 5th Cong., 2nd Sess., House, 1963, 1965, 1968, 1969. As a member of the Pennsylvania legislature in 1793, Gallatin wrote a committee report denouncing slavery and calling on the state to abolish it. In 1798, as a member of the House of Representatives, he supported an attempt to prohibit slavery in the Mississippi Territory west of Georgia. He was also a member of the Pennsylvania Abolition Society.

32. Annals, 5th Cong., 2nd Sess., House, 1965, 1968, 1969, 1974, 1975, 1981; Julia Rose Kraut, *Threat of Dissent: A History of Ideological Exclusion and Deportation in the United States* (Cambridge, MA: Harvard University Press, 2020), 17–23.

33. Annals, 5th Cong., 2nd Sess., House, 1969, 1985, 1986–89, 1990; Lightner, *Slavery and the Commerce Power*, 43.

34. Annals, 5th Cong., 2nd Sess., House, 1968–69, 1979, 1992, 1993; see also, Baldwin's reply to Dayton, 2003–4.

35. John C. Miller, *Crisis in Freedom: The Alien and Sedition Acts* (Boston: Little, Brown, 1951), 53, 164; Lightner, *Slavery and the Commerce Power*, 42; Anna O. Law, "The Historical Amnesia of Contemporary Immigration Federalism Debates," *Polity* 47 (July 2015): 312–18; Gregory Fehlings, "Storm on the Constitution: The First Deportation Law," *Tulsa Journal of International and Comparative Law* 10 (2002): 84–85.

36. Draft of the Kentucky Resolutions, October 1798, Avalon Project, https://avalon. law.yale.edu/18th_century/kenres.asp; Lightner, *Slavery and the Commerce Power*, 45; Kentucky Resolution—Alien and Sedition Acts, December 3, 1799, Avalon Project, https://avalon.law.yale.edu/18th_century/kenres.asp.

37. Draft of the Kentucky Resolutions; Kentucky Resolution—Alien and Sedition Acts, December 3, 1799; Kraut, *Threat of Dissent*, 23–25; Adam B. Cox and Cristina M. Rodríguez, *The President and Immigration Law* (New York: Oxford University Press, 2020), 19.

38. Cox and Rodríguez, *The President and Immigration Law*, 19, 23–30; Virginia Resolutions—Alien and Sedition Acts, Avalon Project, https://avalon.law.yale.edu/18th_century/virres.asp.

39. An Act to prohibit the carrying on the Slave Trade from the United States to any foreign place or country, ch. 11, 1 Stat. 347 (March 22, 1794); An act in addition to the act entitled "An act to prohibit the carrying on the slave trade from the United States to any foreign place or country," ch. 51, 2 Stat. 70 (May 10, 1800); An Act: To prevent the importation of certain persons into certain States, where, by the laws thereof, their admission is prohibited, ch. 10, 2 Stat. 205 (February 28, 1803); Finkelman, "Slavery in the United States: Persons or Property?," 120; Gabriel J. Chin and Paul Finkelman, "Birthright Citizenship, Slave Trade Legislation, and the Origins of Federal Immigration Regulation," *UC Davis Law Review* 54 (July 2021): 2215–65 (esp. 2227–32); Daniel Kanstroom, *Deportation Nation: Outsiders in American History* (Cambridge, MA: Harvard University Press, 2007), 76. In *Dred Scott v. Sanford* (1857), Chief Justice Roger Taney notoriously denied that any black people were US citizens at the time of the Revolution and the Constitution. I am grateful to Michael Schoeppner for his suggestion that the 1803 statute can be read as the first US immigration law. The language of this act was designed to prevent captains from claiming that enslaved persons found on their ships were servants. The act imposed fines of $1,000 for each person so misrepresented. The act exempted "seamen natives of countries beyond the Cape of Good Hope."

40. An Act to Prohibit the Importation of Slaves, ch. 22, 2 Stat. 426 (March 2, 1807); An Act in addition to the Acts prohibiting the stave trade, ch. 101, 3 Stat. 532 (March 3, 1819); An Act to continue in force "An Act to protect the commerce of the United States, punish the crime of piracy," and also make further provisions for punishing the crime of piracy, ch. 113, 3 Stat. 600 (May 15, 1820); Finkelman, "Slavery in the United States: Persons or Property?," 121–22; Chin and Finkelman, "Birthright Citizenship," 2232–38, 2250. Chin and Finkelman cite the UNESCO-funded Slave Voyages project (https://www.slavevoyages.org/assessment/estimates) that 13,151 enslaved persons embarked for the United States between 1808 and 1875, of whom 10,941 disembarked. For an argument connecting the external slave trade laws to restrictions on internal mobility and interpreting free black migration in the antebellum era as a form of involuntary illegal immigration, see Michael Schoeppner, "Black Migrants and Border Regulation in the Early United States," *Journal of the Civil War Era* 11 (September 2021): 317–39.

41. Peter Kolchin, *American Slavery: 1619–1877*, rev. ed. (1993; New York: Hill and Wang, 2003), 77–80; Anne Twitty, *Before* Dred Scott: *Slavery and Legal Culture in the American Confluence, 1787–1857* (New York: Cambridge University Press, 2016), 4–5, 31–42; M. Scott Heerman, *The Alchemy of Slavery: Human Bondage and Emancipation in the Illinois Country, 1730–1865* (Philadelphia: University of Pennsylvania Press, 2018), 2–4, 58–81; Don E. Fehrenbacher, *The Dred Scott*

*Case: Its Significance in American Law and Politics* (New York: Oxford University Press, 1978), 84–86; Wilentz, *No Property in Man*, 31–41, 103–4. Congress did not accede to requests by settlers to permit slavery or to bring enslaved people into the Northwest Territory, but neither did it seek to enforce the ordinance against slaveholders already living in the region, where slavery had long existed. Some settlers in Ohio, Illinois, and Indiana continued to hold slaves in the early nineteenth century. Others adopted forms of long-term, coercive servitude that resembled slavery.

42. Sven Beckert, *Empire of Cotton: A Global History* (New York: Vintage Books, 2015), 100–20; Adam Rothman, *Slave Country: American Expansion and the Origins of the Deep South* (Cambridge, MA: Harvard University Press, 2005); Kolchin, *American Slavery*, 22–23, 93–105, 111–15; Steven Mintz, "Historical Context: American Slavery in Comparative Perspective," Gilder Lehman Institute of American History, https://www.gilderlehrman.org/history-resources/teaching-resource/historical-context-american-slavery-comparative-perspective.

43. Lightner, *Slavery and the Commerce Power*, 15, 16, 36.

44. Annals, 15 Cong., 2 Sess., House, 1166, 1170–84 (quote 1184); Lightner, *Slavery and the Commerce Power*, 5, 6, 49–52. On prior congressional debates over slavery in the Mississippi and Orleans Territories and the Louisiana Purchase, see Rothman, *Slave Country*, 24–34.

45. David L. Lightner, "The Door to the Slave Bastille: The Abolitionist Assault upon the Interstate Slave Trade, 1833–1839," *Civil War History* 34 (September 1988): 236.

46. Farrand 3:436–37, 439; Robert Walsh, *Free Remarks on the Spirit of the Federal Constitution, the Practice of the Federal Government, and the Obligations of the Union, Respecting the Exclusion of Slavery from the Territories and New States* (Philadelphia: A. Finley, 1819), 17–18.

47. Annals, 16th Cong., 2d Sess., 549, 550; Kate Masur, *Until Justice Be Done: America's First Civil Rights Movement, from the Revolution to Reconstruction* (New York: Norton, 2021), 45–47. Barbour joined the US Supreme Court in 1836 and served until his death in 1841.

48. Annals, 16th Cong., 1st Sess., House, 1316; Masur, *Until Justice Be Done*, 47–49.

49. Masur, *Until Justice Be Done*, 53–55.

50. Lightner, *Slavery and the Commerce Power*, 58–62; Lightner, "Door to the Slave Bastille," 235–52; David L. Lightner, "The Interstate Slave Trade in Antislavery Politics," *Civil War History* 36 (June 1990): 119–36. Although neither the Free-Soil Party in the 1840s nor the Republicans in the 1850s called on Congress to prohibit the interstate slave trade, defenders of slavery remained fearful. They raised the matter prominently in discussions over the Compromise of 1850 and during the secession crisis of 1860–1861.

CHAPTER 2

1. An act for the better regulation and government of Free Negroes and Persons of Color and for other purposes (Seamen Act of 1822), December 1, 1822, in David J. McCord, ed., *The Statutes at Large of South Carolina*, 10 vols. (Columbia, SC: Printed by A. S. Johnston, 1840), 7:461–62.

2. An act the more effectually to prohibit Free Negroes and Persons of Color from entering into this State and for other purposes (December 20, 1823), in McCord, ed., *Statutes at Large of South Carolina*, 7:463–66; 27th Cong., 3rd Sess., HR Report No. 80, "Free Colored Seamen—Majority and Minority Reports" (January 20, 1843), 18–23 (including a report on *The State of South Carolina v. Daley* from the *Charleston Courier*, June 23, 1824).

3. HR Report No. 80, "Free Colored Seamen," 20–21; *Gibbons v. Ogden*, 22 U.S. (9 Wheat.) 1 (1824).

4. Santiago Legarre, "The Historical Background of the Police Power," *Journal of Constitutional Law* 9 (February 2007): 745–96; Harry N. Scheiber, "State Police Power," in Leonard W. Levy et al., eds., *Encyclopedia of the American Constitution*, 6 vols. (New York: Macmillan Reference, 2000), 4:2505–12; William J. Novak, "Common Regulation: Legal Origins of State Power in America," *Hastings Law Journal* 45 (April 1994): 1061–97, 1082–83, 1094–95; William J. Novak, "The Myth of the 'Weak' American State," *American Historical Review* 113 (June 2008): 752–72; Ariel Ron and Gautham Rao, "Taking Stock of the State in Nineteenth-Century America," *Journal of the Early Republic* 38 (Spring 2018): 61–67; Gerald L. Neuman, "The Lost Century of American Immigration Law (1776–1875)," *Columbia Law Review* 93 (December 1993): 1833–1901; Hidetaka Hirota, *Expelling the Poor: Atlantic Seaboard States and the Nineteenth-Century Origins of American Immigration Policy* (New York: Oxford University Press, 2017); Kunal M. Parker, *Making Foreigners: Immigration and Citizenship Law in America* (New York: Cambridge University Press, 2015), 103–13; Michael A. Schoeppner, *Moral Contagion: Black Atlantic Sailors, Citizenship, and Diplomacy in Antebellum America* (New York: Cambridge University Press, 2019); Julius S. Scott, *The Common Wind: Afro-American Currents in the Age of the Haitian Revolution* (New York: Verso, 2018).

5. Schoeppner, *Moral Contagion*, 20–25.

6. An act for the better regulation and government of Free Negroes and Persons of Color and for other purposes (Seamen Act of 1822); Neuman, "Lost Century," 1873, 1877; Schoeppner, *Moral Contagion*, 25–30.

7. *Calder v. Deliesseline*, 16 S.C.L. Harper 186 (1824), as discussed in Schoeppner, *Moral Contagion*, 32–34.

8. "Opinion of the Hon. William Johnson, delivered on the 7th August, 1823, in the case of the arrest of the British seaman under the third section of the State act, entitled 'An act for the better regulation of free negroes and persons of color, and

for other purposes,' passed in December last," in HR Report No. 80, "Free Colored Seamen" (January 20, 1843), 27–34; Schoeppner, *Moral Contagion*, 35, 39, 44.

9.  HR Report No. 80, "Free Colored Seamen" (January 20, 1843), 27, 28, 29, 50, 51; *Elkison v. Deliesseline*, 8 F. Cas., 493 (C.C.D.S.C. 1823) (No. 4366), 7–8, 10–11; Schoeppner, *Moral Contagion*, 40–43. The commercial treaty of 1815, extended for ten years in 1818 and made indefinite in 1827, provided for "a reciprocal liberty of commerce between the territories of the United States of America and His Britannic Majesty's territories in Europe." On this basis, Elkison's lawyer claimed that British ships with "free colored seamen on board" had the right to enter US ports without interference.

10. Michael Schoeppner, "Status Across Borders: Roger Taney, Black British Subjects, and a Diplomatic Antecedent to the Dred Scott Decision," *Journal of American History* 46 (June 2013): 52; Schoeppner, *Moral Contagion*, 31–32, 38–39, 41.

11. Act of 1822, sec. 3; HR Report No. 80, "Free Colored Seamen" (January 20, 1843), 29, 30, 31, 34.

12. HR Report No. 80, "Free Colored Seamen" (January 20, 1843), 33, 34; Schoeppner, *Moral Contagion*, 46; Kate Masur, *Until Justice Be Done: America's First Civil Rights Movement, from the Revolution to Reconstruction* (New York: Norton, 2021), 163. As well as filing a writ of habeas corpus, Elkison's attorney filed a writ of de homine replegiando, which would have freed the prisoner on bail pending a challenge to the validity of the law under which he was detained. Johnson concluded that, while he had "no right to refuse" this second writ, it was doubtful if it "could avail the party against the sheriff."

13. Essays by "Caroliensis" [Robert J. Turnbull and Isaac E. Holmes], Zeno, and Philominus [William Johnson], *Charleston Mercury*, August–October 1823, in Howard Gillman, Mark A. Graber, and Keith E. Whittington, eds., *American Constitutionalism*, 2 vols., vol. 1: *Structures of Government*, 2nd ed. (New York: Oxford University Press, 2016), supplementary material, 4–5; Schoeppner, *Moral Contagion*, 47, 50; William Johnson, *The Opinion of the Hon. William Johnson, delivered on the 7th August, 1823, in the case of the arrest of the British Seamen* . . . (Charleston, SC: A. E. Miller, 1823); Benjamin Hunt, *The Argument of Benj. Faneuil Hunt, in the case of the arrest of the Person claiming to be a British Seaman* . . . (Charleston, SC: C. C. Sebring, 1823).

14. Chief Justice John Marshall to Justice Joseph Story, quoted in Charles Warren, *The Supreme Court in United States History*, 3 vols. (Boston: Little, Brown, 1922), 2:86.

15. *The Wilson v. United States*, 30 Fed. Cas. 239 (No. 17846) (C.C.D. Va. 1820); An Act to regulate the collection of duties on imports and tonnage, ch. 22, 1 Stat. 627 (March 2, 1799); An Act: To prevent the importation of certain persons into certain States, where, by the laws thereof, their admission is prohibited, ch. 10, 2 Stat. 205 (February 28, 1803); Schoeppner, *Moral Contagion*, 56; Marshall to Story, quoted in Warren, *The Supreme Court in United States History*, 2:86. The captain of the *Wilson* recovered his vessel.

16. *Gibbons v. Ogden*; An act for enrolling and licensing ships and vessels to be employed in the coasting trade and fisheries, and for regulating the same, ch. 8, Stat. 1 (February 18, 1793); Herbert A. Johnson, Gibbons v. Ogden: *John Marshall, Steamboats, and the Commerce Clause* (Lawrence: University Press of Kansas, 2010).

17. Michael Schoeppner, "Legitimating Quarantine: Moral Contagions, the Commerce Clause, and the Limits of *Gibbons v. Ogden*," *Journal of Southern Legal History* 1 & 2 (2009): 94–96.

18. *Gibbons v. Ogden*, 189–90, 199–200, 203, 205, 216–17, 230. Justice William Johnson, concurring with the majority in a separate opinion, agreed with Marshall that the migration or importation clause not only referred to the importation of slaves but also acknowledged free immigration "as a legitimate subject of revenue."

19. *Gibbons v. Ogden*, 1, 195, 203, 204, 210, 222; U.S. Constitution, art. 4, sec. 2, cl. 2; Warren, *The Supreme Court in United States History*, 2:77–88; Maurice G. Baxter, *The Steamboat Monopoly:* Gibbons v. Ogden, *1824* (New York: Knopf, 1972), 55–57, 59; Norman R. Williams, "*Gibbons*," *NYU Law Review* (October 2004): 1398–1499.

20. *Gibbons v. Ogden*, 222–23, 227.

21. Thomas Jefferson to William B. Giles, December 26, 1825, Founders Online, National Archives, https://founders.archives.gov/documents/Jefferson/98-01-02-5771; *Gibbons v. Ogden*, 197; Annals, 18th Cong., 1st Sess., House, 2097.

22. *Gibbons v. Ogden*, 206–7; David L. Lightner, "The Supreme Court and the Interstate Slave Trade: A Study in Evasion, Anarchy, and Extremism," *Journal of Supreme Court History* 29 (November 2004): 232–34; Warren, *Supreme Court in United States History*, 2:77–79, 82 (quoting an argument by Thomas Addis Emmet in May 1824 before the New York Court of Chancery, along with southern criticisms of Marshall in the *Charleston City Gazette*, March 10, 24, 1824, and the *Richmond Enquirer*, March 16, 1824).

23. HR Report No. 80, "Free Colored Seamen" (January 20, 1843), 12–14, 25–36.

24. John MacPherson Berrien to the President of the United States, Attorney General's Office, March 25, 1831, Appendix to K. Rayner's Minority Report, HR Report No. 80, "Free Colored Seamen" (January 20, 1843), 49–58 (quotes 51, 52–53, 55).

25. HR Report No. 80, "Free Colored Seamen" (January 20, 1843), 52, 54, 55.

26. HR Report No. 80, "Free Colored Seamen" (January 20, 1843), 55.

27. HR Report No. 80, "Free Colored Seamen" (January 20, 1843), 56–57.

28. H. Jefferson Powell, "Attorney General Taney & the South Carolina Police Bill," *Green Bag* 5 (2001): 78, 80.

29. Roger B. Taney to State Department, May 28, 1832, manuscript opinion on the Seamen Act, in Powell, "Attorney General Taney & the South Carolina Police Bill," 83–89 (quotes 83–84, 85); Schoeppner, "Status Across Borders," 61, 62–63, 67; Schoeppner, *Moral Contagion*, 87–90; Martha S. Jones, *Birthright Citizens: A History of Race and Rights in Antebellum America* (New York: Cambridge University Press, 2018), 13.

30. Taney to State Department, May 28, 1832, 83–89 (quote 83); *Worcester v. Georgia*, 31 U.S. (6 Pet.) 515 (1832); Andrew Jackson, State of the Union address, December 8, 1829, Project Gutenberg Ebook, https://www.gutenberg.org/files/5016/5016-h/5016-h.htm; U.S. Constitution, art 4, sec. 3, cl. 1; Schoeppner, "Status Across Borders," 61, 62–63; Schoeppner, *Moral Contagion*, 87–90.

31. Taney to State Department, May 28, 1832, 85, 87–89.

32. Mary Sarah Bilder, "The Struggle over Immigration: Indentured Servants, Slaves, and Articles of Commerce," *Missouri Law Review* 61 (Fall 1996): 748, 754–56, 758–61, 772–74; Robert J. Steinfeld, *Coercion, Contract, and Free Labor in the Nineteenth Century* (New York: Cambridge University Press, 2001), 246; John McNelis O'Keefe, *Stranger Citizens: Migrant Influence and National Power in the Early American Republic* (Ithaca, NY: Cornell University Press, 2021), 143–45, 149–60.

33. Jonathan M. Gutoff, "Fugitive Slaves and Ship-Jumping Sailors: The Enforcement and Survival of Coerced Labor," *University of Pennsylvania Journal of Labor and Employment Law* 9.1 (2006): 87–116; Bilder, "Struggle over Immigration," 748, 760, 782–83, 787, 791; Raymond L. Cohn, *Mass Migration Under Sail: European Immigration to the Antebellum United States* (New York: Cambridge University Press, 2010); Steinfeld, *Coercion, Contract, and Free Labor*, 11.

34. An Act regulating passenger ships and vessels, ch. 46, 3 Stat. 488 (March 2, 1819); Friedrich Kapp, *Immigration, and the Commissioners of Emigration of the City of New York* (New York: Nation Press, 1870), 23, 42; Edward Prince Hutchinson, *Legislative History of American Immigration Policy, 1798–1965* (Philadelphia: University of Pennsylvania Press, 1981), 20–22.

35. Neuman, "Lost Century," 1833–1901; Adam B. Cox and Cristina M. Rodríguez, *The President and Immigration Law* (New York: Oxford University Press, 2000), 20–21, 23–26; Mae M. Ngai, *Immigration and Ethnic History* (Washington, DC: American Historical Association, 2012), 4. The restriction laws of the 1920s combined with the consular visa system and border patrol, as Ngai demonstrates, transformed a system that was "normatively open" into one that was "normatively closed" (i.e., one in which admission became the exception rather than the rule).

36. Gabriel J. Loiacono, *How Welfare Worked in the Early United States: Five Microhistories* (New York: Oxford University Press, 2021); Hirota, *Expelling the Poor*, 42–69; Neuman, "Lost Century," 1846–57; Parker, *Making Foreigners*, 93–97, 103–13; Masur, *Until Justice Be Done*, 4–6, 11–12, 14–15, 17–18, 54; Michael A. Schoeppner, "Black Migrants and Border Regulation in the Early United States," *Journal of the Civil War Era* 11 (September 2021): 317–39.

37. Hirota, *Expelling the Poor*, 45–46; Neuman, "Lost Century," 1849–50.

38. An Act concerning Passengers in Vessels coming to the Port of New-York (February 11, 1824), in *Laws of the State of New York Passed at the Forty-Seventh Session of the Legislature* (Albany: Leake and Croswell, 1824), ch. 37, 27–29; Title IV, in *Laws of the State of New York Passed at the Second Meeting of the Fiftieth Session of the*

*Legislature* (Albany: E. Croswell, 1827), 290–92; Neuman, "Lost Century," 1852–55; Hirota, *Expelling the Poor*, 46–47. The head tax in support of the marine hospital, introduced in 1797, was declared unconstitutional in the *Passenger Cases*, 48 U.S. (7 How.) 283 (1849).

39. Kapp, *Immigration, and the Commissioners of Emigration of the City of New York*, 45–60 (quotes 46, 51–52); Katherine Carper, "The Migration Business, 1824–1876," unpublished PhD dissertation, Boston College, 2020, 67–68; Katherine Carper, "The Migration Business and the Shift from State to Federal Immigration Regulation," *Journal of the Civil War Era* 11 (September 2021): 341–42.

40. An act concerning passengers in vessels coming to the port of New York (1824); *New York v. Miln*, 36 U.S. (11 Pet.) 102 (1837), 153–54; Kapp, *Immigration*, 44–45; Page, "Transportation of Immigrants," 746, 747; Carper, "Migration Business," 68–71; Kirk Scott, "The Two-Edged Sword: Slavery and the Commerce Clause, 1837–1852," *Fairmount Folio: Journal of History* 2 (1998): 43. Congress decides the number of Supreme Court justices, which was set at six, seven, nine, and ten at different times in the nineteenth century. In 1837, Congress expanded the number to nine and on his last day in office—one month after the *Miln* case—Jackson appointed John Catron of Tennessee and John McKinley of Alabama to the Court.

41. *New York v. Miln*, 131–32; Page, "Transportation of Immigrants," 747; Lightner, *Slavery and the Commerce Power*, 69, 102, 109, 113; Lightner, "The Founders and the Interstate Slave Trade," 25–26.

42. *New York v. Miln*, 132, 136–37.

43. *New York v. Miln*, 133, 134; *The Federalist Papers*, ed. Isaac Kramnick (1788; New York: Penguin, 1987), 292–97 (quotes 296).

44. *New York v. Miln*, 132, 139; Justice Barbour citing Emer de Vattel, *The law of nations, or, Principles of the law of nature, applied to the conduct and affairs of nations and sovereigns, with three early essays on the origin and nature of natural law and on luxury*, ed. Béla Kapossy and Richard Whatmore, trans. Thomas Nugent (1758; Indianapolis: Liberty Fund, 2008), Book 1, ch. VII, § 94 and ch. VIII, § 100. Nineteenth-century jurists cited Vattel frequently, but selectively, to justify sovereignty over borders. Vattel wrote that every exile had "the right to dwell somewhere on earth" (Book 1, ch. XIX, § 229–31) and that nations in which they sought refuge were obliged to welcome them, at least temporarily, unless they had "very important reasons for a refusal" (Book 2, ch. IX, § 125).

45. *New York v. Miln*, 139–40, 141, 148.

46. *New York v. Miln*, 146–48.

47. *New York v. Miln*, 142–43; *Passenger Cases*, 429–31; Tony Allen Freyer, *The Passenger Cases and the Commerce Clause: Immigrants, Blacks, and States' Rights in Antebellum America* (Lawrence: University Press of Kansas, 2014), 38–41. In the *Passenger Cases*, Justice Wayne strongly objected to Taney's reading of *Miln*, insisting that only Taney and Barbour had endorsed the opinion that passengers could not be subjects of commerce. See Chapter 3.

48. *New York v. Miln*, 154, 156, 157.

49. *New York v. Miln*, 157, 158, 159.

50. *New York v. Miln*, 154, 159, 160–61; *Brown v. Maryland*, 25 U.S. 419 (1827).

51. *New York v. Miln*, 142 (quote), 143–48; *New York v. Miln*, argument of Mr. Blount for the plaintiff, in Richard Peters, *Reports of the Cases Argued and Adjudged in the Supreme Court of the United States, January Term, 1837* 16 vols. (Philadelphia: Desilver, Thomas & Co., 1837), 10:106–10 (quote 109); Lightner, "Supreme Court and the Interstate Slave Trade," 236; Schoeppner, *Moral Contagion*, 105.

52. William Goodell, *The American Slave Code in Theory and Practice: Its Distinctive Features Shown by Its Statutes, Judicial Decisions, and Illustrative Facts* (New York: American and Foreign Anti-Slavery Society, 1835), 355–60; Ira Berlin, *Slaves Without Masters: The Free Negro in the Antebellum South* (1975; New York: Free Press, 2007), 316–40, 372–74; Jones, *Birthright Citizens*, 25; Neuman, "Lost Century," 1868, 1870–71; Kunal M. Parker, "Citizenship and Immigration Law, 1800–1924: Resolutions of Membership and Territory," in Michael Grossberg and Christopher Tomlins, eds., *The Cambridge History of Law in America*, 3 vols., vol. 2: *The Long Nineteenth Century (1789–1920)* (New York: Cambridge University Press, 2008), 175, 178–79; Barbara J. Fields, *Slavery and Freedom on the Middle Ground: Maryland During the Nineteenth Century* (New Haven: Yale University Press, 1985), 39; Elizabeth Stordeur Pryor, *Colored Travelers: Mobility and the Fight for Citizenship Before the Civil War* (Chapel Hill: University of North Carolina Press, 2016), 110, 112. Parker develops the argument in "Citizenship and Immigration Law, 1800–1924" and *Making Foreigners* that many Americans born on the soil were treated as foreign.

53. Neuman, "Lost Century," 1866–67; Masur, *Until Justice Be Done*, 2–4, 11–12, 16–18; Schoeppner, "Black Migrants and Border Regulation in the Early United States"; Paul Finkelman, "Prelude to the Fourteenth Amendment: Black Legal Rights in the Antebellum North," *Rutgers Law Journal* 17 (1986): 435–37, 432–42, 477; Pryor, *Colored Travelers*, 112–13.

54. Neuman, "Lost Century," 1867; Finkelman, "Prelude," 421–22, 439–41; Masur, *Until Justice Be Done*, 19; Schoeppner, "Black Migrants"; *Nelson v. People*, 33 Ill. 390; Act of February 12, 1853, Ill. Laws 57.

55. *Moore v. Illinois* 55 U.S. (14 How.) 13 (1852), 18; Parker, "Citizenship and Immigration Law," 179; Neuman, "Lost Century," 1880. Parker shows that "native-born free blacks remained suspended between the status of citizen and alien" and that "at least some Southern state courts formally assimilated out-of-state free blacks to the status of aliens." In *Heirn v. Bridault*, 37 Miss. 209 (1859), he notes, the Mississippi Supreme Court ruled that a free black woman from Louisiana could not inherit the property of a white man with whom she had been living in Mississippi, because—being in violation of the law against the entry of free black people—she was an alien.

56. Manisha Sinha, *The Slave's Cause: A History of Abolition* (New Haven: Yale University Press, 2016), 160–64; Jones, *Birthright Citizens*, 1, 37; Samantha Seeley, *Race, Removal, and the Right to Remain: Migration and the Making of the United States* (Williamsburg, VA, and Chapel Hill: Omohundro Institute of Early American History and Culture and University of North Carolina Press, 2021), 305–07.

57. Daniel Walker Howe, *What Hath God Wrought: The Transformation of America, 1815–1848* (New York: Oxford University Press, 2007), 260–62, 265; Brian Balogh, *A Government out of Sight: The Mystery of National Authority in the Nineteenth Century* (New York: Cambridge University Press, 2009), 146–47; Daniel Kanstroom, *Deportation Nation: Outsiders in American History* (Cambridge, MA: Harvard University Press, 2007), 85.

58. David Walker, *Walker's Appeal, in Four Articles: Together with a Preamble, to the Coloured Citizens of the World, but in Particular, and Very Expressly, to Those of the United States of America, Written in Boston, State of Massachusetts, September 28, 1829* (Boston: David Walker, 1829), 76, 77; Sinha, *The Slave's Cause*, 164–65, 168–71, 203–5, 245–46; Christopher James Bonner, *Remaking the Republic: Black Politics and the Creation of American Citizenship* (Philadelphia: University of Pennsylvania Press, 2020), 11–15, 24–25, 40, 51–52; Howe, *What Hath God Wrought*, 263–66; Eric Foner, "Lincoln and Colonization," in Eric Foner, ed., *Our Lincoln: New Perspectives on Lincoln and His World* (New York: Norton, 2008), 137–66; Seeley, *Race, Removal, and the Right to Remain*, 308–11, 322–25; Ella Forbes, "African-American Resistance to Colonization," *Journal of Black Studies* 21 (December 1990): 210–23.

59. "Rights of Our Colored Citizens," *The Liberator*, November 4, 1842, 571; Memorial of Benjamin Rich and others, HR Report No. 80, "Free Colored Seamen—Majority and Minority Reports" (January 20, 1843), 1, 7–9; Schoeppner, *Moral Contagion*, 138–40; Masur, *Until Justice Be Done*, 157, 159–60. Rich was president of the Massachusetts Humane Society, which promoted safety at sea.

60. HR Report No. 80, "Free Colored Seamen" (January 20, 1843), 2–3.

61. HR Report No. 80, "Free Colored Seamen" (January 20, 1843), 3–4, 6.

62. HR Report No. 80, "Free Colored Seamen" (January 20, 1843), 37, 38; Schoeppner, *Moral Contagion*, 142–45. Rayner appended Attorney General John M. Berrien's 1831 opinion defending the Seamen Acts to the minority report.

63. HR Report No. 80, "Free Colored Seamen" (January 20, 1843), 39, 40.

64. HR Report No. 80, "Free Colored Seamen" (January 20, 1843)," 42, 43, 44, 46, 47; *New York v. Miln*, 142.

65. Schoeppner, *Moral Contagion*, 228.

66. Georgia resolutions quoted in *Journal of the Senate of the Commonwealth of Kentucky* (Frankfort: A. G. Hodges, 1842), 165; Resolves Concerning the Treatment of Samuel Hoar by the State of South Carolina, March 24, 1845, in *Acts and Resolves Passed by the General Court of Massachusetts in the Year 1845*, chap. 111

(Boston: Secretary of the Commonwealth, 1845), 638–42; Schoeppner, *Moral Contagion*, 149–56; Masur, *Until Justice Be Done*, 176–80.

67. *Journal of the House of Representatives of the State of South Carolina, Being the Annual Session of 1844* (Columbia, SC: A. H. Pemberton, 1844), 65–66; An Act to Amend An Act Entitled "An Act More Effectually to Prevent Free Negroes and Other Persons of Color from Entering into this State, and for Other Purposes" (December 19, 1844), *Acts of the General Assembly of the State of South Carolina, Passed in December, 1844* (Columbia, SC: A. H. Pemberton, 1845), 293–94. Although art. 1 of the US Constitution prohibited suspension of the writ of habeas corpus, this ban was generally taken as applying only to Congress, which left the states to act as they pleased.

68. Resolves Concerning the Treatment of Samuel Hoar, 626–44 (quotes 629, 635); Maeve Glass, "Citizens of the State," *University of Chicago Law Review* 85 (June 2018): 866, 869, 894.

69. Resolves Concerning the Treatment of Samuel Hoar, 629, 635, 636, 643–44; *Journal of the House of Representatives of the State of South Carolina, Being the Annual Session of 1844*, 65; 29th Cong., 1st Sess., House Report No. 34, Resolutions of the Legislature of Massachusetts, in relation to Louisiana and South Carolina, December 15, 1845, passed in the Massachusetts Senate, March 26, 1845; Glass, "Citizens of the State," 911–14.

70. 29th Cong., 1st Sess., House Report No. 87, Resolutions of the Legislature of Georgia, relative to the controversy between the State of Massachusetts and the States of South Carolina and Louisiana (January 28, 1846), 1–2; 28th Cong., 2nd Sess., House doc. 128, 2, 3, Resolutions of the Legislature of Alabama relative to the proposed amendment of the constitution of the United States, by Massachusetts, &c. (February 15, 1845), 3.

CHAPTER 3

1. An Act concerning Passengers in Vessels coming to the Port of New-York (February 11, 1824), *Laws of the State of New York Passed at the Forty-Seventh Session of the Legislature* (Albany: Leake and Croswell, 1824), ch. 37; Title IV, *Laws of the State of New York Passed at the Second Meeting of the Fiftieth Session of the Legislature* (Albany: E. Croswell, 1827), 290–92; *Passenger Cases*, 48 U.S. (7 How.) 283, 284–87 (1849); Friedrich Kapp, *Immigration, and the Commissioners of Emigration of the City of New York* (New York: Nation Press, 1870); Tony Allen Freyer, *The Passenger Cases and the Commerce Clause: Immigrants, Blacks, and States' Rights in Antebellum America* (Lawrence: University Press of Kansas, 2014); Katherine Carper, "The Migration Business, 1824–1876," unpublished PhD dissertation, Boston College, 2020, 38, 113–15; Brendan P. O'Malley, "Protecting the Stranger: The Origins of U.S. Immigration Regulation in Nineteenth-Century New York," unpublished PhD dissertation, City University of New York, 2015, 39–47; Hidetaka Hirota,

*Expelling the Poor: Atlantic Seaboard States and the Nineteenth-Century Origins of American Immigration Policy* (New York: Oxford University Press, 2017), 55, 56, 64–66; Richard J. Purcell, "The New York Commissioners of Emigration and Irish Immigrants: 1847–1860," *Studies: An Irish Quarterly Review* 37 (March 1948): 29–42. Under the marine tax, no coasting vessel arriving from New Jersey, Connecticut, or Rhode Island had to pay for more than one voyage a month.

2. *Passenger Cases*, 56; David L. Lightner, *Slavery and the Commerce Power: How the Struggle Against the Interstate Slave Trade Led to the Civil War* (New Haven: Yale University Press, 2006), 84. As Lightner puts it, the justices "expressed such disparate views, that nobody then or since has been able to make overall sense of them."

3. *Commonwealth v. Aves* (1836), reported in Octavius Pickering, *Reports of Cases Argued and Determined in the Supreme Judicial Court of the Commonwealth of Massachusetts*, March Term, 1836 (Boston: Little, Brown, 1866–1870); *Groves v. Slaughter*, 40 U.S. (15 Pet.) 449 (1841); *Prigg v. Pennsylvania*, 41 U.S. (16 Pet.) 539 (1842).

4. William Blackstone, *Commentaries on the Laws of England*, 4 vols. (1765–1769; Chicago: Chicago University Press, 1992), 1:123; *Somerset v Stewart* (1772) 98 ER 499; HR Report No. 80, "Free Colored Seamen—Majority and Minority Reports" (January 20, 1843), 56; *Lemmon v. New York* (1860), reported in E. Peshine Smith, *Reports of the Cases Argued and Determined in the Court of Appeals of the State of New York* (Albany, NY: Banks and Brothers, 1860), 604–5; *Commonwealth v. Aves*; Don E. Fehrenbacher, *The Dred Scott Case: Its Significance in American Law and Politics* (New York: Oxford University Press, 1978), 53–54.

5. *Commonwealth v. Aves*, 193–94.

6. *Commonwealth v. Aves*, 198 (quote), 199–200. Curtis went on to serve as a justice on the US Supreme Court and was one of the two dissenters in *Dred Scott v. Sandford*, 60 U.S. (19. How.) 393 (1857).

7. *Commonwealth v. Aves*, 198 (quote), 201, 202, 204.

8. *Commonwealth v. Aves*, 216, 217, 218, 223 (citing *Lansford v. Coquillon*, 14 Martin's Rep. 403 and referring to *Ohio v. Carneal* (1817)); *Ohio v. Carneal* (1817), in Ervin H. Pollack, ed., *Ohio Unreported Judicial Decisions Prior to 1823* (Indianapolis: Allen Smith, 1952), 133–42 (quotes 133, 136); Kate Masur, *Until Justice Be Done: America's First Civil Rights Movement, from the Revolution to Reconstruction* (New York: Norton, 2021), 37–38. McLean served on the US Supreme Court from 1829 to 1861 and, like Benjamin Curtis, dissented in the *Dred Scott* case.

9. *Commonwealth v. Aves*, 224, 225. Shaw explained that his ruling did not apply to enslaved people who wished to return voluntarily. He did not comment on the status of those merely in transit or entering the state by accident.

10. *Groves v. Slaughter*, 40 U.S. (15 Pet.) 449 (1841).

11. *Groves v. Slaughter*, 449, 451, 452; Lightner, *Slavery and the Commerce Power*, 71–72; David L. Lightner, "The Supreme Court and the Interstate Slave Trade: A Study in Evasion, Anarchy, and Extremism," *Journal of Supreme Court History* 29

(November 2004): 237–38; Kirk Scott, "The Two-Edged Sword: Slavery and the Commerce Clause, 1837–1852," *Fairmount Folio: Journal of History* 2 (1998): 44.

12. *Groves v. Slaughter*, 489; Robert J. Walker, *Argument of Robert J. Walker, Esq., Before the Supreme Court of the United States, on the Mississippi Slave Question, at January Term, 1841. Involving the Power of Congress and of the States to Prohibit the Inter-state Slave Trade* (Philadelphia: John C. Clark, 1841), 49, 51, 58, 88; Lightner, "The Supreme Court and the Interstate Slave Trade," 238–40; Scott, "The Two-Edged Sword," 44–46.

13. *Groves v. Slaughter*, 495–503; Lightner, "The Supreme Court and the Interstate Slave Trade," 240. Thompson wrote only for himself and Justice Wayne. Chief Justice Taney and Justices McLean and Baldwin concurred with the majority, but only in the result; Justices McKinley and Story dissented; Justice Catron did not participate due to illness, and Justice Barbour had recently died.

14. *Groves v. Slaughter*, 507, 508; U.S. Constitution, art.1, sec. 2, cl. 3; art. 4, sec. 3, cl. 3; Lightner, "The Supreme Court and the Interstate Slave Trade," 240–41.

15. *Groves v. Slaughter*, 508.

16. *Groves v. Slaughter*, 515–17.

17. Justice James Wayne of Georgia joined the majority while Justices Joseph Story of Massachusetts and John McKinley of Alabama dissented.

18. *Prigg v. Pennsylvania*, 539; H. Robert Baker, Prigg v. Pennsylvania: *Slavery, the Supreme Court, and the Ambivalent Constitution* (Lawrence: University Press of Kansas, 2012).

19. U.S. Constitution, art. 4, sec. 2, cl. 3; An act respecting fugitives from justice, and persons escaping from the service of their masters, ch. 7, 1 Stat. 302 (February 12, 1793); *Prigg v. Pennsylvania*, 543–57; Paul Finkelman, "Prelude to the Fourteenth Amendment: Black Legal Rights in the Antebellum North," *Rutgers Law Journal* 17 (1986): 454. Pennsylvania's 1826 personal liberty law mandated fines of between $500 and $3,000 and prison terms of seven to twenty-one years at hard labor for violators.

20. *Prigg v. Pennsylvania*, 540, 541, 542, 615–16; Paul Finkelman, "Slavery in the United States: Persons or Property?," in Jean Allain, ed., *The Legal Understanding of Slavery: From the Historical to the Contemporary* (New York: Oxford University Press, 2012), 124; Christopher James Bonner, *Remaking the Republic: Black Politics and the Creation of American Citizenship* (Philadelphia: University of Pennsylvania Press, 2020), 106–7; Daniel Kanstroom, *Deportation Nation: Outsiders in American History* (Cambridge, MA: Harvard University Press, 2007), 80–83; Gerald L. Neuman, "The Lost Century of American Immigration Law (1776–1875)," *Columbia Law Review* 93 (December 1993): 1880. The Court issued seven separate opinions in *Prigg*. A year before *Prigg*, in *United States v. Schooner Amistad*, 40 U.S. (15 Pet.) 518 (1841), Story had freed a group of kidnapped Africans who had taken over a Spanish schooner. Although this case is sometimes celebrated as an antislavery victory, Story's ruling considered only which kinds of persons could

legitimately be held as slaves under international law and posed no threat to the institution of slavery in the United States. He set the Africans free on the grounds that they were held illegally but ordered that a cabin boy born in Cuba as a slave be returned to Cuba.

21. *Prigg v. Pennsylvania*, 541, 626–33, 650–73.

22. U.S. Constitution, art. 4, sec. 2, cl. 1, cl. 3; Maeve Glass, "Citizens of the State," *University of Chicago Law Review* 85 (June 2018): 865–66, 869–70, 894–97.

23. An Act to amend, and supplementary to, the Act entitled "An Act respecting Fugitives from Justice, and Persons escaping from the Service of their Masters," approved February twelfth, one thousand seven hundred and ninety-three, 9 Stat. 462 (September 18, 1850); Karla M. McKanders, "Immigration Enforcement and the Fugitive Slave Acts: Exploring Their Similarities," *Catholic University Law Review* 61 (2012): 921–54; Kanstroom, *Deportation Nation*, 77–83. Those who obstructed the act or assisted in the escape of fugitives were subject to fines of up to $1,000 and imprisonment for up to six months, along with civil damages to the claimant of a maximum of $1,000 for each fugitive lost.

24. *Passenger Cases*.

25. *Passenger Cases*, 409–10, 436, 439, 455, 462; *Gibbons v. Ogden*, 22 U.S. (9 Wheat.), 1, 195 (1824).

26. *Passenger Cases*, 402, 413–14, 453; *Gibbons v. Ogden*, 216, 230.

27. *Passenger Cases*, 401, 413, 453, 454.

28. *Passenger Cases*, 393–95, 400–1, 408, 409, 410; *Gibbons v. Ogden*, 189–92.

29. *Passenger Cases*, 409–10, 415, 426, 457, 458, 460. Justice Grier, likewise, acknowledged that Massachusetts could use its power to exclude undesirable immigrants, but he insisted that the law was a commercial rather than a police measure. It was "a tax on passengers *qua* passengers," imposed on the captain engaged in the commerce of transporting them. Calling this measure a police regulation to protect against paupers, for Grier, could not conceal its true character as an unconstitutional tax on the passenger trade.

30. *Passenger Cases*, 459, 461, 463.

31. *Passenger Cases*, 401, 426, 461.

32. *Passenger Cases*, 407, 440, 461, 462. Justice McLean, too, warned that if a state could impose a tax on passengers arriving from foreign countries, it could do the same for passengers entering from any state in the Union. New York City's head tax to support the Marine Hospital applied to coasting vessels as well as ships carrying alien passengers.

33. *Passenger Cases*, 426.

34. *Passenger Cases*, 464, 465, 479, 491, 508, 546, 551, 553, 558–59.

35. *Passenger Cases*, 492; *Crandall v. Nevada*, 73 U.S. (6 Wall.), 35, 38, 41, 43, 45 (1867). In *Crandall*, the Supreme Court took a significant step toward affirming the right to travel. Because the people of the United States constituted one nation, the Court ruled, the national government had the right to summon its

citizens to the capital or other locations to perform official duties, and the right to raise troops in the states and transport them across the states, while US citizens had "correlative rights" to travel throughout the country to the national capital and to federal ports, subtreasuries, land offices, revenue offices, and courts, independent of the will of the states through which they passed in pursuit of those rights. This argument rested on much the same grounds as Taney's in the *Passenger Cases* but aligned with the redefinition of national citizenship in the Civil Rights Act of 1866 and the Fourteenth Amendment, which repudiated Taney's racist position.

36. *Passenger Cases*, 474, 475, 476, 511, 540, 541, 543, 544.

37. *Passenger Cases*, 544.

38. *Passenger Cases*, 543, 544.

39. *Passenger Cases*, 470, 471, 473–74; Lightner, *Slavery and the Commerce Power*, 79.

40. *Passenger Cases*, 477, 478.

41. *Passenger Cases*, 429–31, 488.

42. *Passenger Cases*, 506.

43. *Passenger Cases*, 472, 474, 507, 508. Taney's point that states' laws constituted the laws of the United States echoed Attorney General Berrien's opinion on the Seamen Acts in 1831, in HR Report No. 80, "Free Colored Seamen" (January 20, 1843), 56–57.

44. *Passenger Cases*, 474, 508.

45. *Passenger Cases*, 546.

46. *Passenger Cases*, 284, 483, 484, 485, 486, 489.

47. *Passenger Cases*, 487, 490.

48. *Passenger Cases*, 518, 520, 521, 522, 523, 524.

49. *Passenger Cases*, 550.

50. *Passenger Cases*, 409–10, 465, 466, 467, 525.

51. *Passenger Cases*, 525, 526, 528, 529; Emer de Vattel, *The law of nations, or, Principles of the law of nature, applied to the conduct and affairs of nations and sovereigns, with three early essays on the origin and nature of natural law and on luxury*, ed. Béla Kapossy and Richard Whatmore, trans. Thomas Nugent (Indianapolis: Liberty Fund, 2008), Book 1, ch. XIX, §§ 219, 231; Book 2, ch. VII, §§ 93, 94, ch. VII, § 100.

52. *Passenger Cases*, 527, 528; Jonathan Elliot, *The Debates in the Several State Conventions on the Adoption of the Federal Constitution, as Recommended by the General Convention at Philadelphia in 1787*, 5 vols. (Philadelphia: J. B. Lippincott; Washington, DC: Taylor & Maury, 1836–1859), 4:581, 582, 586.

53. *Passenger Cases*, 528, 529. Woodbury quoted Vattel, *The law of nations*, Book 2, ch. VIII, § 99: "since the lord of the territory may, whenever he thinks proper, forbid its being entered, he has, no doubt, a power to annex what conditions he pleases to the permission to enter."

54. *Passenger Cases*, 484, 514.

55. *Passenger Cases*, 516, 517.

56. *Passenger Cases*, 542, 567; *Cooley v. Board of Wardens of the Port of Philadelphia*, 53 U.S. (12 How.) 299 (1852); Lightner, "The Supreme Court and the Slave Trade," 246–47; Freyer, *Passenger Cases*, 114–20. When Justice Woodbury died in 1851, Millard Fillmore appointed the Massachusetts Whig Benjamin Curtis to the Supreme Court. Curtis wrote the opinion in *Cooley v. Board of Wardens of the Port of Philadelphia* upholding the constitutionality of a Pennsylvania law that required vessels entering the port of Philadelphia to hire local pilots or pay a fee. According to Curtis's so-called Cooley Rule, some forms of local commerce required national regulation and others did not. Congress retained exclusive power over commerce that fell into the former category, but states retained power over most internal commerce, as well as aspects of interstate commerce like pilotage that were strictly local. Justices McLean and Wayne dissented, insisting that Congress's power over interstate commerce was exclusive. In practice, the Cooley Rule (as its alternative name, "selective exclusiveness," suggests) failed to resolve the constitutional questions of when commerce was national or local and who controlled the movement of enslaved people between states. Defenders of slavery insisted that the interstate slave trade was by definition a local rather than a national matter and that the federal government could not interfere with any aspect of the institution of slavery.

## CHAPTER 4

1. *Dred Scott v. Sandford*, 60 U.S. (19. How.) 393 (1857); Amanda Frost, *You Are Not American: Citizenship Stripping from Dred Scott to the Dreamers* (Boston: Beacon Press, 2021), 13–15; Lea S. VanderVelde, *Mrs. Dred Scott: A Life on Slavery's Frontier* (New York: Oxford University Press, 2009), 135–136; Lea S. VanderVelde, "The Dred Scott Case in Context," *Journal of Supreme Court History* 40 (2015): 263–281; Don E. Fehrenbacher, *The Dred Scott Case: Its Significance in American Law and Politics* (New York: Oxford University Press, 1978), 244–248, 251. Fort Snelling, in the Wisconsin Territory, became part of the Iowa Territory in 1838. Missouri's provision for freedom suits, Fehrenbacher points out, was based on the slave laws of Virginia and Kentucky. A second daughter, Lizzie, was born in 1846 or 1847, probably near St. Louis.

2. *Dred Scott v. Sandford*; Earl M. Maltz, *Dred Scott and the Politics of Slavery* (Lawrence: University Press of Kansas, 2007), 60–75; VanderVelde, *Mrs. Dred Scott*, 295–296; Fehrenbacher, *Dred Scott Case*, 250–257, 264–265, 270–276, 279–290, 309–314; Mark A. Graber, *Dred Scott and the Problem of Constitutional Evil* (New York: Cambridge University Press, 2006), 19–20. The Constitution (art. 3, sec. 2, cl. 1) gives the federal courts jurisdiction in cases between citizens of different states. All nine justices wrote opinions in the *Dred Scott* case. Despite disagreements among the majority, Taney's opinion is generally taken as the decision of the Court. The five southern justices, John Catron, John Campbell, Peter Daniel, Roger

Taney, and James Wayne, were proslavery Democrats—Daniel fanatically so. They were joined by two northern Democrats, Samuel Nelson and Robert Grier, who strongly opposed antislavery. Benjamin Curtis (Whig) and John McLean (a former Democrat turned conservative Republican) dissented.

3. Fehrenbacher, *Dred Scott Case*, 379, 443, 455, 490, 517, 519, 536. Douglas, the architect of the Kansas-Nebraska Act, antagonized southern Democrats by advancing a notion of residual popular sovereignty after *Dred Scott*, arguing that the decision applied only to congressional power and left territorial legislatures free to decide about slavery before admission to statehood.

4. *Dred Scott v. Sandford*, 403, 405, 407, 409, 412, 420; Fehrenbacher, *Dred Scott Case*, 329–330, 389–414. Of the seven justices in the majority, only two—Daniel and Wayne—endorsed Taney's ruling on citizenship. Campbell, Catron, Grier, and Nelson remained silent on the citizenship question, which they felt was not properly before the Court. Wayne concurred with Taney entirely; Nelson addressed neither the territory question nor the citizenship question, finding simply that Scott was a slave rather than a citizen under the laws of Missouri; Campbell, Catron, and Grier agreed with Taney on the Missouri Compromise but for various reasons. McLean and Curtis upheld the constitutionality of the Missouri Compromise and argued, on different grounds, that free black people were citizens.

5. Reed Ueda, *Postwar Immigrant America: A Social History* (New York: Bedford/St. Martin's, 1994), 11. The immigration rate (the number of arrivals per 1,000 people in the United States) reached its peak for a single decade in 1901–1910 and for a two-decade period in the 1840s and 1850s. The rate in 1891–1900 and 1911–1920 was between 5.5 and 6, compared to 11 in 1901–1910, resulting in an average two-decade rate of 8.5 per 1,000. The rate in the 1840s (8.5) and the 1850s (9.5) together give an average immigration rate of 9 per 1,000 over this twenty-year period. The corresponding figure today is less than 4 because the population is so much higher than it was a century ago, while the number of immigrants is only slightly larger.

6. Cong. Globe, 24th Cong., 1st Sess., 342 (1836); 34th Cong., 1st Sess., House Report no. 359, "Foreign Criminals and Paupers," August 16, 1856, 1–19; Edward Prince Hutchinson, *Legislative History of American Immigration Policy, 1798–1965* (Philadelphia: University of Pennsylvania Press, 1981), 25–26, 410.

7. 34th Cong, 1st Sess., House Report no. 359, "Foreign Criminals and Paupers," August 16, 1856, 19, 20, 58–73, 81–106 (quotes 101).

8. Hutchinson, *Legislative History of American Immigration Policy*, 27–29, 31, 410–411; Hidetaka Hirota, *Expelling the Poor: Atlantic Seaboard States and the Nineteenth-Century Origins of American Immigration Policy* (New York: Oxford University Press, 2017), 112–113.

9. I am grateful to Hidetaka Hirota for clarifying these details. See also Brendan P. O'Malley, "Protecting the Stranger: The Origins of U.S. Immigration Regulation in Nineteenth-Century New York," unpublished Ph.D. dissertation, City University of New York, 2015, 47–49. In 1863, Massachusetts replaced its alien

commissioners with the Board of State Charities, which administered both immigration and public welfare.

10. 34th Cong., 1st Sess., House Report no. 359, "Foreign Criminals and Paupers," August 16, 1856, 20, 22, 136–137.

11. Political Party Platforms, The American Presidency Project, http://www.preside ncy.ucsb.edu/ws/index.php?pid=2957.

12. U.S. Constitution, art. 1, sec. 2, cl. 1; art. 1, sec. 4, cl. 1.

13. Jamin B. Raskin, "Legals, Aliens, Local Citizens: The Historical, Constitutional and Theoretical Meanings of Alien Suffrage," *University of Pennsylvania Law Review* 141 (1993): 1391–1470.

14. Alexander Keyssar, *The Right to Vote: The Contested History of Democracy in the United States*, rev. ed. (New York: Basic Books, 2009), 27, 28, 65, 66; Raskin, "Legals, Aliens, Local Citizens," 1403–1405.

15. Raskin, "Legals, Aliens, Local Citizens," 1406, 1407, 1408; Gerald L. Neuman, "We Are the People: Alien Suffrage in German and American Perspective," *Michigan Journal of International Law* 13 (1992): 298–299; Robert R. Russel, "The Issues in the Congressional Struggle over the Kansas-Nebraska Bill, 1854," *Journal of Southern History* 29 (May 1963): 208; Treaty of Peace, Friendship, Limits, and Settlement Between the United States of America and the United Mexican States Concluded at Guadalupe Hidalgo, February 2, 1848, Articles VIII and IX, Yale Law School, Lillian Goldman Law Library, the Avalon Project, http://avalon. law.yale.edu/19th_century/guadhida.asp. The Treaty of Guadalupe Hidalgo gave Mexican citizens in territories acquired by the United States one year to declare if they wished to retain Mexican citizenship, failing which they became United States citizens and could vote.

16. An Act to Organize the Territories of Nebraska and Kansas, ch. 59, 10 Stat. 277 (May 30, 1854); Tyler Anbinder, *Nativism and Slavery: The Northern Know Nothings and the Politics of the 1850s* (New York: Oxford University Press, 1994); Keyssar, *Right to Vote*, 49–51, 52, 53, 66–68. Section 10 of the Kansas-Nebraska Act provided that the Fugitive Slave Act of 1850 would apply in the Territory of Nebraska. Kansas entered the Union as a free state in 1861 after a civil war between proslavery and antislavery forces in the late 1850s. Nebraska entered the Union in 1867.

17. Cong. Globe, January 25, 1855, 389; 34th Cong., 1st Sess., House Report no. 359, "Foreign Criminals and Paupers," August 16, 1856, 20, 137–138; Hutchinson, *Legislative History of American Immigration Policy*, 40–41, 411.

18. Cong. Globe, January 25, 1855, 391392.

19. 34th Cong, 1st Sess., House Report no. 124; A bill to prevent the introduction of foreign criminals and paupers (August 16, 1856); An Act to Prohibit the "Coolie Trade" by American Citizens in American Vessels, ch. 27, 12 Stat. 340 (February 19, 1862).

20. 34th Cong., 1st Sess., House Report no. 359, "Foreign Criminals and Paupers" (1856), 23–24, 146–147; Jonathan Elliot, *The Debates in the Several State*

*Conventions on the Adoption of the Federal Constitution, as Recommended by the General Convention at Philadelphia in 1787*, 5 vols. (Philadelphia: J. B. Lippincott; Washington, DC: Taylor & Maury, 1836–1859), 1:372, 2:453, 4:101; *Gibbons v. Ogden*, 22 U.S. (9 Wheat.) 1 (1824), 216–217, 230; *Passenger Cases*, 48 U.S. (7 How.) 283 (1849), 453–455.

21. 34th Cong., 1st Sess., House Report no. 359, "Foreign Criminals and Paupers" (1856), 25; *New York v. Miln*, 36 U.S. (11 Pet.) 102 (1837), 132; *Prigg v. Pennsylvania*, 41 U.S. (16 Pet.) 539 (1842), 542.

22. Abraham Lincoln to Dr. Theodore Canisius, Springfield, Illinois, May 17, 1859, in Roy P. Basler, ed., *Collected Works of Abraham Lincoln*, 9 vols. (New Brunswick, NJ: Rutgers University Press, 1953–1955), https://quod.lib.umich.edu/l/lincoln/ (quoted hereafter as CW by volume number), 3:381; Keyssar, *Right to Vote*, 69.

23. Don E. Fehrenbacher, *Prelude to Greatness: Lincoln in the 1850's* (Stanford, CA: Stanford University Press, 1962), 13; Democratic Party Platform, 1856, American Presidency Project, https://www.presidency.ucsb.edu/documents/1856-democratic-party-platform. The party added two more planks to its pro-immigrant platform in 1856, endorsing freedom of religion and condemning political crusades against Catholic immigrants.

24. U.S. Constitution, art. 4, sec. 3, cl. 2.

25. *Dred Scott v. Sandford*, 452, 490; David L. Lightner, "The Supreme Court and the Interstate Slave Trade: A Study in Evasion, Anarchy, and Extremism," *Journal of Supreme Court History* 29 (November 2004): 247–248; Fehrenbacher, *Dred Scott Case*, 383.

26. Martha S. Jones, *Birthright Citizenship: A History of Race and Rights in Antebellum America* (New York: Cambridge University Press, 2018), 128–145; Christopher James Bonner, *Remaking the Republic: Black Politics and the Creation of American Citizenship* (Philadelphia: University of Pennsylvania Press, 2020), 130–133; Jack M. Balkin and Sanford Levinson, "Thirteen Ways of Looking at *Dred Scott*," *Chicago-Kent Law Review* 82 (2007): 56–57; Fehrenbacher, *Dred Scott Case*, 341–343. Taney ignored the fact that women and children, though citizens, were not part of the "sovereign people" in the sense of voting or holding office.

27. *Dred Scott v. Sandford*, 393–394, 397, 400, 403, 407, 420–421 (quote).

28. Roger B. Taney to State Department, May 28, 1832, manuscript opinion on the Seamen Act, in H. Jefferson Powell, "Attorney General Taney & the South Carolina Police Bill," *Green Bag* 5 (2001): 83; *Dred Scott v. Sandford*, 404–405; Fehrenbacher, *Dred Scott Case*, 351.

29. *Dred Scott v. Sandford*, 394, 426–427; Balkin and Levinson, "Thirteen Ways of Looking at *Dred Scott*," 69–73, 78, 81, 87; Graber, *Dred Scott and the Problem of Constitutional Evil*, 1–89. I am grateful to Michael Schoeppner for his insights on originalism.

30. *Dred Scott v. Sandford*, 407, 409.

31. *Dred Scott v. Sandford*, 410, 412.

32. *Dred Scott v. Sandford*, 411, 419–420. Taney found further evidence to support this racially limited conception of the American people in An Act more effectually to provide for the National Defence by establishing an Uniform Militia throughout the United States, ch. 33, 1 Stat. 271 (May 8, 1792), which directed that every "free able-bodied white male citizen shall be enrolled" (thereby, in Taney's view, excluding black men); and an act for the regulation of seamen on board the public and private vessels of the United States, ch. 42, 2 Stat. 809 (March 3, 1813), which distinguished between two separate categories, "citizens of the United States, *or* persons of color, natives of the United States."

33. *Dred Scott v. Sandford*, 406, 416–417.

34. *Dred Scott v. Sandford*, 421; Elizabeth Stordeur Pryor, *Colored Travelers: Mobility and the Fight for Citizenship before the Civil War* (Chapel Hill: University of North Carolina Press, 2016), 4, 7, 104–105, 114–124; Craig Robertson, *The Passport in America: The History of a Document* (New York: Oxford University Press, 2010), 14–16, 131–134, 143–148; Edward Bates, *Opinion of Attorney General Bates on Citizenship* (Washington, DC: Government Printing Office, 1863), 12. Strictly speaking, passports were not a sign of citizenship, as the government issued them to some white residents who were not citizens. This practice, however, reinforces the point that race took priority over national origin. Attorney General Bates finally ruled in 1862 that every person born in the United States was "at the moment of birth, *prima facie* a citizen."

35. *Dred Scott v. Sandford*, 403–404.

36. John Ridge to Albert Gallatin, February 27, 1826, and Constitution of the Cherokee Nation, July 1827, both in Theda Perdue, *The Cherokee Removal: A Brief History with Documents*, 3rd ed. (Boston and New York: Bedford/St. Martin's, 2016), 34–41 (quote 41), 60–70; Andrew Jackson, State of the Union address, December 6, 1830, in Perdue, *Cherokee Removal*, 120–121; Claudio Saunt, *Unworthy Republic: The Dispossession of Native Americans and the Road to Indian Territory* (New York: Norton, 2020); Daniel Walker Howe, *What Hath God Wrought: The Transformation of America, 1815–1848* (New York: Oxford University Press, 2007), 357. As Howe observes, "the fundamental impulse" behind Jacksonian Democracy was not free enterprise, manhood suffrage, or the labor movement but "the extension of white supremacy across the North American continent."

37. An Act to provide for an exchange of lands with the Indians residing in any of the states or territories, and for their removal west of the river Mississippi, ch. 148, 4 Stat. 411 (1830); *Cherokee Nation v. Georgia*, 30 U.S. (5 Pet.) 1 (1831), 17; *Worcester v. Georgia*, 31 U.S. (6 Pet.) 515, 520, 521, 559; Maggie Blackhawk, "Federal Indian Law as Paradigm Within Public Law," *Harvard Law Review* 132 (May 2019): 1818–1823; Saunt, *Unworthy Republic*, 161–163, 279–281; Howe, *What Hath God Wrought*, 355, 356; Perdue, *Cherokee Removal*, 41, 43, 80.

38. Bethany R. Berger, "'Power Over this Unfortunate Race': Race, Politics and Indian Law in *United States v. Rogers*," *William & Mary Law Review* 45 (April

2004): 1959–1960, 1962–1965, 1970–1971, 1982–1989, 1999–2000, 2004–2007, 2042–2045; Blackhawk, "Federal Indian Law as Paradigm Within Public Law," 1829–1830; *United States v. Kagama*, 118 U.S. 375 (1886). In its eagerness to secure a ruling on Native sovereignty along the desired lines, the US government went so far as to conceal the fact that Rogers was dead when the case was heard, a fact that would have meant the Court lacked jurisdiction. Given Taney's stance on African Americans, one can see how the racialist logic in *Rogers* might have appealed to him, though legal historian Bethany R. Berger also suggests that he approved of the decision partly because it affirmed the territorial sovereignty of the United States across the North American continent at a time when war with Mexico was pending. By the time of *Dred Scott*, Taney had returned to a conception of Native sovereignty more in keeping with John Marshall's, even if it was in service of an argument denying black citizenship.

39. *Dred Scott v. Sandford*, 531, 533.

40. *Commonwealth v. Aves*, 35 Mass. 193 (1836); *Dred Scott v. Sandford*, 575, 588; Frost, *You Are Not American*, 24; Michael A. Schoeppner, *Moral Contagion: Black Atlantic Sailors, Citizenship, and Diplomacy in Antebellum* America (New York: Cambridge University Press, 2019), 140. Schoeppner notes that Curtis signed the 1842 petition and, in his dissent in *Dred Scott*, drew on Robert Winthrop's majority report on the Seamen Acts in 1843 (discussed in Chapter 2).

41. *Dred Scott v. Sandford*, 572, 573, 575, 576, 582–583, 586.

42. *Dred Scott*, 583; Fehrenbacher, *Dred Scott Case*, 318–319, 405–408. Some legal scholars have raised the possibility that the *Dred Scott* decision delayed rather than hastened the Civil War, because freeing the Scotts in 1857 and denying slaveholders constitutional protection in the territories could have triggered secession and a conflict on terms less favorable to the North. As a counterfactual proposition, this claim obviously cannot be verified. See Graber, *Dred Scott and the Problem of Constitutional Evil*, 13–14, 167–168, 237–254; Balkin and Levinson, "Thirteen Ways of Looking at Dred Scott," 67, 89–93.

43. VanderVelde, *Mrs. Dred Scott*, 320–324, 441–442; Frost, *You Are Not American*, 26–29; Fehrenbacher, *Dred Scott Case*, 568.

44. CW 2:404, 405, 406, 467; John Burt, "Lincoln's Dred Scott: Contesting the Declaration of Independence," *American Literary History* 21 (Winter 2009): 739, 740–741; Lightner, *Slavery and the Commerce Clause*, 87–88; Fehrenbacher, *Dred Scott Case*, 451–452, 487–488, 492.

45. *Lemmon v. New York*, in E. Peshine Smith, *Reports of the Cases Argued and Determined in the Court of Appeals of the State of New York* (Albany, NY: Banks and Brothers, 1860), 564; Sarah L. Gronningsater, "'On Behalf of His Race and the Lemmon Slaves': Louis Napoleon, Northern Black Legal Culture, and the Politics of the Sectional Crisis," *Journal of the Civil War Era* 7 (June 2017): 213–214, 217; Eric Foner, *Gateway to Freedom: The Hidden History of the Underground Railroad* (New York: Norton, 2015).

46. *Lemmon v. New York*, 564–565, 600–601; *New York Times*, April 16, 1860; Gronningsater, "'On Behalf of His Race and the Lemmon Slaves,'" 206.
47. *New York Times*, April 16, 1860; Gronningsater, "'On Behalf of His Race and the Lemmon Slaves,'" 213, 217, 218, 219, 220, 222, 230 n8.
48. *Lemmon v. New York*, 568, 570, 572.
49. *Lemmon v. New York*, 578–79, 581–582.
50. *Lemmon v. New York*, 583, 584.
51. *Lemmon v. New York*, 585, 590, 597, 598, 599.
52. *Lemmon v. New York*, 602, 608, 612–615. See also the opinion of Justice William B. Wright at 616–621.
53. *Lemmon v. New York*, 608, 624, 626–627, 628. In *Commonwealth v. Aves* (1836), counsel for Thomas Aves presented an unsuccessful argument on comity of the kind Wright found unprecedented.
54. *Lemmon v. New York*, 632–633 (quote, 633), 636, 637, 640, 644. Justices Comstock and Selden dissented without providing opinions. Both explained that they had been too busy to examine the case in detail but that the New York statute violated the principle of comity between the states.
55. Lightner, *Slavery and the Commerce Power*, 88; Gronningsater, "'On Behalf of His Race and the Lemmon Slaves,'" 228.
56. Alexander H. Stephens, "Corner Stone" speech, Savannah, Georgia, March 21, 1861, in Henry Cleveland, *Alexander H. Stephens, in Public and Private: With Letters and Speeches, Before, During, and Since the War* (Philadelphia: National Publishing Company, 1886), 717–729 (quotes 721).
57. Stephens, "Corner Stone," 721.

### CHAPTER 5

1. *The People v. Hall*, 4 Cal., 399 (1854), 399, 405; Act of April 16, 1850, ch. 99, 1850 Cal. Stat., 229, 230. The justices ruled 2 to 1 in Hall's favor.
2. *People v. Hall*, 401–2, 403, 404; Michael Traynor, "The Infamous Case of *People v. Hall* (1854): An Odious Symbol of Its Time," *California Supreme Court Newsletter* (Spring/Summer 2017): 2–8; Edgar Whittlesey Camp, "Hugh C. Murray: California's Youngest Chief Justice," *California Historical Society Quarterly* 20 (December 1941): 365–73; William J. Novak, "The Legal Transformation of Citizenship in Nineteenth-Century America," in Meg Jacobs, William J. Novak, and Julian Zelizer, eds., *The Democratic Experiment: New Directions in American Political History* (Princeton: Princeton University Press, 2003), 103–5; Leon R. Yankwich, "Social Attitudes as Reflected in Early California Law," *Hastings Law Journal* 10 (February 1959): 257–59 (describing *People v. Hall* as "prejudice in the form of law"). Murray was elected to a full six-year term as chief justice in 1855 with the support of the Know-Nothings and died in office in 1857.

3. An Act to Discourage the Immigration to this State of Persons who cannot become Citizens thereof, ch. 153, Cal. Stat. 194 (April 28, 1855); *People v. Downer*, 7 Cal. 169 (1857); An Act to prevent the further immigration of Chinese or Mongolians to this State, ch. 313, Cal. Stat. 295 (April 26, 1858); Kerry Abrams, "Polygamy, Prostitution, and the Federalization of Immigration Law," *Columbia Law Review* 105 (April 2005): 672–73; Hidetaka Hirota, *Expelling the Poor: Atlantic Seaboard States and the Nineteenth-Century Origins of American Immigration Policy* (New York: Oxford University Press, 2017), 89.

4. An Act to protect free white labor against competition with Chinese coolie labor, and discourage the immigration of the Chinese into the State of California, ch. 339, Cal. Stat. 462 (April 26, 1862); *Lin Sing v. Washburn*, 20 Cal. 534 (1862); Hirota, *Expelling the Poor*, 90; Abrams, "Polygamy, Prostitution, and Federalization," 673, 674, 686.

5. An Act to Prohibit the "Coolie Trade" by American Citizens in American Vessels, ch. 27, 12 Stat. 340 (February 19, 1862); An Act to Encourage Immigration, ch. 246, 13 Stat. 385 (July 4, 1864).

6. Mae M. Ngai, *The Chinese Question: The Gold Rushes and Global Politics* (New York: Norton, 2021), 33–35; Moon-Ho Jung, *Coolies and Cane: Race, Labor, and Sugar in the Age of Emancipation* (Baltimore: Johns Hopkins University Press, 2008), 5; Moon-Ho Jung, "Outlawing 'Coolies': Race, Nation, and Empire in the Age of Emancipation," *American Quarterly* 57 (September 2005): 678, 679, 699 n4; Adam M. McKeown, *Melancholy Order: Asian Migration and the Globalization of Borders* (New York: Columbia University Press, 2008), 2, 3, 7, 10; Kornel Chang, "Coolie," in Cathy J. Schlund-Vials, Linda Trinh Võ, and K. Scott Wong, eds., *Keywords for Asian American Studies* (New York: New York University Press, 2015), 37–38; Mae M. Ngai, "Chinese Gold Miners and the 'Chinese Question' in Nineteenth-Century California and Victoria," *Journal of American History* 101 (March 2015): 1084 n3. Although coolie was a pejorative term, I follow Moon-Ho Jung's practice in not placing the word between quotation marks. Doing so, he points out, can unintentionally reify the concept rather than call it into question.

7. Ngai, *Chinese Question*, 25–26; Renee C. Redman, "From Importation of Slaves to Migration of Laborers: The Struggle to Outlaw American Participation in the Chinese Coolie Trade and the Seeds of United States Immigration Law," *Albany Government Law Review* 3 (2010): 6–10; Philip A. Kuhn, *Chinese Among Others: Emigration in Modern Times* (Lanham, MD: Rowman and Littlefield, 2008), 111–14, 127, 141, 145; Adam McKeown, "Global Migration, 1846–1940," *Journal of World History* 15 (June 2004): 155–89; Adam McKeown, "Regionalizing World Migration," *International Review of Social History* 52 (2007): 134–42. The vast majority of Chinese and Indian laborers did not go to the Americas but to locations within Asia.

8. Evelyn Hu-DeHart, "Chinese Coolie Labour in Cuba in the Nineteenth Century: Free Labour or Neoslavery?," *Slavery and Abolition* 14 (April 1993): 67–86;

Evelyn Hu-DeHart and Kathleen López, "Asian Diasporas in Latin America and the Caribbean: An Historical Overview," *Afro-Hispanic Review* 27 (Spring 2008): 9–21; Jung, "Outlawing 'Coolies,'" 679; Kuhn, *Chinese Among Others*, 133, 134, 145; George Anthony Peffer, *If They Don't Bring Their Women Here: Chinese Female Immigration Before Exclusion* (Urbana: University of Illinois Press, 1999), 24; Redman, "From Importation of Slaves to Migration of Laborers," 6, 7.

9. Hu-DeHart, "Chinese Coolie Labour in Cuba in the Nineteenth Century"; Kathleen López, *Chinese Cubans: A Transnational History* (Chapel Hill: University of North Carolina Press, 2013), 15–53; Rebecca Scott, *Slave Emancipation in Cuba: The Transition to Free Labor, 1860–1899* (Pittsburgh: Pittsburgh University Press, 2000), 13–14; Kuhn, *Chinese Among Others*, 113–14. I am grateful to Michael Schoeppner for suggesting a partial analogy here with the process of *coartacion*, whereby a small number of enslaved Cubans purchased their freedom over time, gradually acquiring rights that might be protected by the courts.

10. Ngai, *Chinese Question*, 41–48, 85–87, 95–98; Ngai, "Chinese Gold Miners"; Hiroshi Motomura, *Americans in Waiting: The Lost Story of Immigration and Citizenship in the United States* (New York: Oxford University Press, 2006), 16; Peffer, *If They Don't Bring Their Women Here*, 24; Lucy Salyer, *Laws Harsh as Tigers: Chinese Immigrants and the Shaping of American Immigration Law* (Chapel Hill: University of North Carolina Press, 1995), 8, 10 n9; Jung, *Coolies and Cane*, 4, 5; Kuhn, *Chinese Among Others*, 117, 124, 212–13; Najia Aarim-Heriot, *Chinese Immigrants, African Americans, and Racial Anxiety in the United States, 1848–82* (Urbana and Chicago: University of Illinois Press, 2006), 31, 78.

11. Humphrey Marshall to Edward Everett, March 8, 1853, 34th Cong., 1st Sess., H.R. Exec. Doc. No. 105, 150–51 (1856); Jung, "Outlawing 'Coolies,'" 684.

12. *New York Times*, "Orientals in America," April 15, 1852, "Cotton, Cane, and Coolies," May 3, 1852, "The Chinaman—An Opportunity," June 14, 1852.

13. *New York Times*, "Cotton, Cane, and Coolies"; "The Chinaman—An Opportunity."

14. Letter by Mr. Parker to Mr. Webster, Legation of the United States, Canton, May 21, 1852, 34th Cong., 1st Sess., H.R. Exec. Doc. No. 105, 94–95 (with supporting correspondence, 96–149); letter by Humphrey Marshall, U.S. Commissioner, to Mr. Everett, Legation of the United States, Macao, March 8, 1853, H.R. Exec. Doc. no. 105, 151; Jung, "Outlawing 'Coolies,'" 684, 685; Ngai, *Chinese Question*, 83–84.

15. *New York Times*, comment on Proclamation by Peter Parker, April 21, 1856; *New York Times*, "The Coolie Trade," April 17, 1860; Jung, *Coolies and Cane*, 22; Jung, "Outlawing 'Coolies,'" 686, 687; 34th Cong., 1st Sess., H.R. Exec. Doc. No. 105 (1856), 71.

16. Letter from Wm. H. Robertson, Acting Consul, Havana, July 27, 1855, to William L. Marcy, Secretary of State, Washington, D.C., 34th Cong., 1st Sess., H.R. Exec. Doc. No. 105, 68–70 (quote 68); "Protest" of Francisco Antonio Pereira Silveiro (translated), in Robertson to Marcy, 34th Cong., 1st Sess., H.R. Exec. Doc. No. 105, 69–70.

17. Letter from C. D. Mudgford, Hong Kong, to Peter Parker, January 7, 1856, 34th Cong., 1st Sess., H.R. Exec. Doc. No. 105, 74–76 (1856) (quote, 74).

18. Public Notification by Peter Parker, January 10, 1856, 34th Cong., 1st Sess., H.R. Exec. Doc. No. 105, 156, 157; Proclamation issued by the scholars and merchants of Amoy, January 10, 1856, translated by M. Morrison, 34th Cong., 1st Sess., H.R. Exec. Doc. No. 105, 76–77, 79.

19. Letter from William B. Reed, U.S. Legation at Macao, concerning the coolie trade, to S. B. Rawle, Esq., U.S. Consul at Macao, January 5, 1858, in "Message from the President of the United States on the Chinese Coolie Trade," 36th Cong., 1st Sess., H.R. Exec. Doc. No. 36–88, 75 (1860); An Act to prohibit the importation of slaves, into any port or place within the jurisdiction of the United States, from and after the first day of January, 1808, ch. 22, 2 Stat. 426 (March 2, 1807); An Act in addition to "An Act to prohibit the introduction (importation) of slaves . . . from and after the first day of January, 1808," ch. 91, § 8, 3 Stat. 450 (April 20, 1818); An Act regulating passenger ships and vessels, ch. 46, 3 Stat. 488 (March 2, 1819); An Act to protect the commerce of the United States, and punish the crime of piracy, ch. 77, 3 Stat. 510 (March 3, 1819); An Act in addition to the Acts prohibiting the slave trade, ch. 101, 3 Stat. 532 (March 3, 1819); An Act to continue in force "An Act to protect the commerce of the United States, and punish the crime of piracy," and also make further provisions for punishing the crime of piracy, ch. 113, 3 Stat. 600 (May 15, 1820); An Act to Regulate the Carriage of Passengers in Merchant Vessels, ch. 16, 9 Stat. 127 (February 22, 1847); An Act to extend the Provisions of the all Laws now in Force Relating to the Carriage of Passenger in Merchant Vessels, and the Regulation thereof, ch. 111, 9 Stat. 399 (March 3, 1849); An Act to Regulate the Carriage of Passengers in Steamships and Others Vessels, ch. 213, 10 Stat. 715 (March 3, 1855); Treaty between the United States and Great Britain for the Suppression of the Slave Trade, April 7, 1862, 12 Stat. 1225 (ratified by Congress on June 7, 1862); Redman, "From Importation of Slaves to Migration of Laborers," 13. Britain signed treaties with most European nations allowing its ships to stop and search vessels suspected of engaging in the slave trade, but not until the Lyons-Seward Treaty of 1862 did the United States grant Britain a limited right to search American ships.

20. Message from the President of the United States on the Chinese Coolie Trade, 36th Cong., 1st Sess., H.R. Exec. Doc. No. 36–88, 75, 76 (1860), enclosing a letter from William B. Reed to S. B. Rawle, U.S. Consul at Macao, January 5, 1858, and a letter from William A. Macy to William B. Reed, January 8, 1858; *New York Times*, "The Ship Flora Temple," February 6, 1860.

21. Message from the President on the Asiatic Coolie Trade, December 23, 1861, 37th Cong., 2nd Sess., H.R. Exec. Doc. No. 16 (1861), 23–27, 28–35: letter from C. K. Stribling, Flag Officer, Chargé d'Affaires ad interim, Hong Kong, to J. S. Black, Secretary of State, Washington, D.C., U.S. Flag Ship "Hartford," March 26, 1861; letter from Oliver H. Perry to Mr. Stribling, U.S. Consulate, Canton, March 12,

1861; "Notes of an investigation into the riot, attended with loss of life, on board the Leonidas, which occurred on Sunday, the 24th of February, 1861, at 9 a.m."

22. Henry Anthon, Jr., to Secretary of State Lewis Cass, May 1 and May 8, 1860, 37th Cong., 2nd Sess., H.R. Exec. Doc. No. 16, 3–14, 16; Thomas Savage, U.S. Vice-Consul General, Havana, August 14, 1860, to Secretary of State Lewis Cass, 37th Cong., 2nd Sess., H.R. Exec. Doc. No. 16, 19–20; *New York Times*, "The Mutineers of the Stag-Hound," December 31, 1860. Savage reported that the *Staghound* arrived in Cuba from Swatow on August 10, 1860, with 343 coolies on board, fifty-seven having died during the passage. The *Staghound* returned to New Bedford with twenty-four prisoners on December 30.

23. *New York Times*, "The Coolie Trade," April 17, 1860; John Harris, *The Last Slave Ships: New York and the End of the Middle* Passage (New Haven: Yale University Press, 2020).

24. *New York Times*, "The American Coolie-Trade," April 21, 1860; "The Coolie Trade," July 31, 1860.

25. Lord John Russell to Lord Lyons, Foreign Office, July 11, 1860, in 37th Cong., 2nd Sess., H.R. Exec. Doc. No. 16, 17. Much of this dispatch was published in the *New York Times* on August 16, 1860.

26. 37th Cong., 2nd Sess., H.R. Exec. Doc. No. 16, 21; *New York Times*, "The Coolie-Trade," August 18, 1860; "The Slave and Coolie Trade: Official Correspondence with the British Government," August 20, 1860.

27. *New York v. Miln*, 36 U.S. (11 Pet.) 102 (1837); *Passenger Cases*, 48 U.S. (7 How.) 283 (1849).

28. Cong. Globe, 36th Cong., 1st Sess., 1441 (1860); Cong. Globe, 37th Cong., 2nd Sess., 350–51 (1862); Eric Foner, *Free Soil, Free Labor, Free Men: The Ideology of the Republican Party Before the Civil War* (1970; New York: Oxford University Press, 1995).

29. Cong. Globe, 37th Cong., 2d Sess., 355, 555–56, 581–82 (1862); An Act to Prohibit the "Coolie Trade" by American Citizens in American Vessels (1862); Jung, "Outlawing 'Coolies,'" 696; Redman, "From Importation of Slaves to Migration of Laborers," 47–48.

30. An Act to Prohibit the "Coolie Trade" by American Citizens in American Vessels (1862); Jung, "Outlawing 'Coolies,'" 698.

31. An Act to prohibit the carrying on the Slave Trade from the United States to any foreign place or country, ch. 11, 1 Stat. 347 (March 22, 1794); An act in addition to the act entitled "An act to prohibit the carrying on the slave trade from the United States to any foreign place or country," ch. 51, 2 Stat. 70 (May 10, 1800); Gordon H. Chang, *Ghosts of Gold Mountain: The Epic Story of the Chinese Who Built the Transcontinental Railroad* (New York: Houghton Mifflin, 2019), 45–46. Article V of the Burlingame-Seward Treaty of 1868 recognized the right of migration but retained the distinction between free and unfree emigration and denied Chinese immigrants the right to naturalize.

32. An Act to amend the Act calling forth the Militia to execute the Laws of the Union, suppress Insurrections, and repel Invasions, ch. 201, 12 Stat. 597 (July 17, 1862); *In re* Wehlitz, 16 Wis. 468, 468–70, 480 (1863); Enrolment Act, ch. 75, 12 stat., 731 (March 3, 1863); *Dred Scott v. Sandford*, 60 U.S. (19. How.) 393 (1857), 420 (Roger Taney citing the acts of 1792 and 1795 to support his contention that African Americans were not intended to be citizens); Roy P. Basler, ed., *Collected Works of Abraham Lincoln*, 9 vols. (New Brunswick, NJ: Rutgers University Press, 1953–55), https://quod.lib.umich.edu/l/lincoln/ (cited hereafter as CW with volume number), 6:203–4; Jamin B. Raskin, "Legals, Aliens, Local Citizens: The Historical, Constitutional and Theoretical Meanings of Alien Suffrage," *University of Pennsylvania Law Review* 141 (1993), 1410–11.

33. Confederate Constitution, art. 1, sec. 2, cl. 1 (1861), Avalon Project: Documents in Law, History, and Diplomacy, Yale Law School, https://avalon.law.yale.edu/19th_century/csa_csa.asp. Raskin, "Legals, Aliens, Local Citizens," 1414; Alexander Keyssar, *The Right to Vote: The Contested History of Democracy in the United States*, rev. ed. (New York: Basic Books, 2009), 68.

34. An Act to secure Homesteads to actual Settlers of the Public Domain, ch. 75, 12 Stat. 392 (May 20, 1862); An Act to define the Pay and Emoluments of certain Officers of the Army, and for other Purposes, ch. 200, 12 Stat. 594 (July 17, 1862); United States Department of Homeland Security, 2016 Yearbook of Immigration Statistics, Persons Obtaining Lawful Permanent Resident Status: Fiscal Years 1820 to 2016, Table 1, https://www.dhs.gov/immigration-statistics/yearbook/; Aristide R. Zolberg, *A Nation by Design: Immigration Policy in the Fashioning of America* (Cambridge, MA: Harvard University Press, 2006), 168, 169.

35. Charlotte Erickson, *American Industry and the European Immigrant, 1860–1885* (Cambridge, MA: Harvard University Press, 1957), 3–6.

36. Erickson, *American Industry and the European Immigrant*, 6–8.

37. CW 7:38, 40; An Act to Encourage Immigration (1864).

38. Heather Cox Richardson, *The Greatest Nation of the Earth: Republican Economic Policies During the Civil War* (Cambridge, MA: Harvard University Press, 1997), 165; Zolberg, *Nation by Design*, 170–71.

39. Republican Party Platform of 1864, American Presidency Project, https://www.presidency.ucsb.edu/documents/republican-party-platform-1864; CW 7:40; Erickson, *American Industry and the European Immigrant*, 11–12; Richardson, *Greatest Nation of the Earth*, 165, 167–68; Zolberg, *Nation by Design*, 170–71.

40. An Act to Encourage Immigration (1864).

41. CW 8:141; Jason H. Silverman, *Lincoln and the Immigrant* (Carbondale: Southern Illinois University Press, 2016); Barry Schwarz, *Abraham Lincoln and the Forge of National Memory* (Chicago: University of Chicago Press, 2000), 195–203.

42. Act to Encourage Immigration; Aarim-Heriot, *Chinese Immigrants*, 78, 79. With the exception of France, all the countries where the American Emigrant Company recruited were predominantly Protestant.

43. Erickson, *American Industry and the European Immigrant*, 14–28; David Montgomery, *Beyond Equality: Labor and the Radical Republicans, 1862–1872* (Urbana and Chicago: University of Illinois Press, 1981), 22–23; Andrew Gyory, *Closing the Gate: Race, Politics, and the Chinese Exclusion Act* (Chapel Hill: University of North Carolina Press, 1998), 20.

44. James W. Fox, Jr., "The Law of Many Faces: Antebellum Contract Law Background of Reconstruction-Era Freedom of Contract," *American Journal of Legal History* 49 (January 2007), 82–96, 101–9; Robert J. Steinfeld, *Coercion, Contract, and Free Labor in the Nineteenth Century* (New York: Cambridge University Press, 2001), 141–43, 147–72; Jonathan M. Gutoff, "Fugitive Slaves and Ship-Jumping Sailors: The Enforcement and Survival of Coerced Labor," *University of Pennsylvania Journal of Labor and Employment Law* 9.1 (2006): 87–116. It is not clear from the sources what kind of women's labor the American Emigrant Company had in mind. Women's ability to perform labor, with or without a contract, could be liberating; but as Eric Foner notes, all labor agreements—including those based on free choice—involve "an unequal distribution of economic power." Eric Foner, *Reconstruction: America's Unfinished Revolution, 1862–1877* (1988; updated edition, New York: Harper Perennial Modern Classics, 2014), 164.

45. Steinfeld, *Coercion, Contract, and Free Labor in the Nineteenth Century*, 23–25, 31; Erickson, *American Industry and the European Immigrant*, 28–29, 51–54; Montgomery, *Beyond Equality*, 23–24, 149, 391; Gyory, *Closing the Gate*, 21–23; Zolberg, *A Nation by Design*, 172–74.

46. Cong. Globe, 39th Cong., 1st Sess., 4040, 4041, 4043 (July 23, 1866).

CHAPTER 6

1. Frederick Douglass, "Our Composite Nationality" (lecture, Parker Fraternity, Boston, December 7, 1869), Teaching American History, https://teachingamericanhistory.org/library/document/our-composite-nationality/.

2. Douglass, "Our Composite Nationality."

3. Lacy Salyer, *Laws Harsh as Tigers: Chinese Immigrants and the Shaping of Modern Immigration Law* (Chapel Hill: University of North Carolina Press, 2000), 28; Beth Lew-Williams, *The Chinese Must Go: Violence, Exclusion, and the Making of the Alien in America* (Cambridge, MA: Harvard University Press, 2018), 235–40.

4. Cong. Globe, 39th Cong., 1st Sess., 476 (1866); Eric Foner, *Reconstruction: America's Unfinished Revolution, 1862–1877* (1988; updated edition, New York: Harper Perennial Modern Classics, 2014), 243–45; Eric Foner, *The Second Founding: How the Civil War and Reconstruction Remade the Constitution* (New York: Norton, 2019), 57–59. The Thirteenth Amendment declared that neither slavery nor involuntary servitude could exist within the United States, or any place subject to its jurisdiction, with the significant exception of "punishment for crime whereof the party shall have been duly convicted."

5. Cong. Globe, 39th Cong., 1ˢᵗ Sess., 476, 478, 1268 (1866).

6. Cong. Globe, 39th Cong., 1st Sess., 475, 497 (1866).

7. Cong. Globe, 39th Cong., 1st Sess., 498–99 (1866); Bethany R. Berger, "Birthright Citizenship on Trial: *Elk v. Wilkins* and *United States v. Wong Kim Ark*," *Cardozo Law Review* 37 (April 2016): 1198–99.

8. Cong. Globe, 39th Cong., 1st Sess., 498, 499, 507 (1866); Ann Ostendorf, "Racializing American 'Egyptians': Shifting Legal Discourse, 1690s–1860s," *Critical Romani Studies* 2 (2019): 42–59 (esp. 55–56); June Lloyd, "York's Gypsies Led a Colorful Life," *Universal York*, September 17, 2019, https://yorkblog. com/universal/yorks-gypsies-led-a-colorful-life/; June Lloyd, "Basket Making Thrived on York's Bullfrog Alley," *Universal York*, July 25, 2019, https://yorkblog. com/universal/basket-making-thrived-on-yorks-bullfrog-alley/; Pamela Reilly, "Romani in Pennsylvania," *Pennsylvania Heritage*, Spring 2017, http://paherit age.wpengine.com/article/lycoming-county-romani-pennsylvania/. Isolated individuals referred to as "Gypsies" had been transported from England, Ireland, and Scotland in the colonial era, without forming durable communities. Roma people from Eastern Europe came to the United States later, mostly in the late nineteenth and early twentieth centuries. The US Census recorded immigrants by country of birth rather than their ethnicity and did not use the term "Gypsy." I am grateful to Ann Ostendorf, Philip Erenrich, and June Lloyd for their advice on these issues. Cowan also objected that the civil rights bill would override state policies preventing aliens from purchasing land before declaring their intent to naturalize.

9. Cong. Globe, 39th Cong., 1st Sess., 498, 499, 507 (1866).

10. Cong. Globe, 39th Cong., 1st Sess., 570, 571 (1866); *Dred Scott v. Sandford*, 60 U.S. (19. How.), 393–94, 397, 400, 403, 407 (1857). In *Dred Scott*, Roger Taney always qualified his references to the "African race" with the fact of their enslavement. He did so, however, not to open up a theoretical distinction between race and condition, of the kind Morrill suggested, but because he clearly believed that slavery was the natural condition of people of African origin and descent. See Chapter 4.

11. An Act to protect all Persons in the United States in their Civil Rights and liberties, and furnish the Means of their Vindication, ch. 31, 14 Stat. 27–29 (April 9, 1866); Cong. Globe, 39th Cong., 1st Sess., 211 (1866); John Hayakawa Torok, "Reconstruction and Racial Nativism: Chinese Immigrants and the Debates on the Thirteenth, Fourteenth, and Fifteenth Amendments and Civil Rights Law," *Asian American Law Journal* 3 (1996): 77. In limiting protections to citizens rather than inhabitants, the House addressed concerns that the Senate's version might affect state laws restricting the rights of aliens to own property.

12. U.S. Senate Journal, 39th Cong., 1st Sess., 27, 279, 280, 285 (March 1866).

13. Cong. Globe, 39th Cong., 1st Sess., 2459–60 (1866); An Act to protect all Persons in the United States in their Civil Rights and liberties, and furnish the Means of their Vindication (1866); Foner, *Second Founding*, 63–67; Garrett Epps,

"Interpreting the Fourteenth Amendment: Two Dont's and Three Dos," *William & Mary Bill of Rights Journal* 16 (2007): 433–53, 457.

14. Cong. Globe, 39th Cong., 1st Sess., 2890, 2892, 2893 (1866); Berger, "Birthright Citizenship on Trial," 1198–99. Nativists in recent years have focused on the word "jurisdiction" in an effort to deny citizenship not only to irregular immigrants but also to their American-born children, on the specious grounds that they do not owe full allegiance to the United States and therefore are not fully under its jurisdiction.

15. Cong. Globe, 39th Cong., 1st Sess., 2890, 2891 (1866).

16. Cong. Globe, 39th Cong., 1st Sess., 2891 (1866).

17. Cong. Globe, 39th Cong., 1st Sess., 2891, 2892 (1866).

18. Cong. Globe, 39th Cong., 1st Sess., 2459 (1866); Foner, *Second Founding*, 81–83, 86–87, 91.

19. Cong. Globe, 39th Cong., 1st Sess., 2890 (1866); U.S. Constitution, amend. 14, sec. 1; Foner, *Second Founding*, 75–80.

20. U.S. Constitution, amend. 14, sec. 1 (emphasis added); Cong. Globe, 39th Cong., 1st Sess., 158 (1866).

21. Foner, *Second Founding*, 99–105; Alexander Keyssar, *The Right to Vote: The Contested History of Democracy in the United States*, rev. ed. (New York: Basic Books, 2009), 105–6, 183.

22. Cong. Globe, 40th Cong., 3rd Sess., 901, 938, 1011 (1869).

23. Cong. Globe, 40th Cong., 3rd Sess., 902, 903 (1869).

24. Cong. Globe, 40th Cong., 3rd Sess., 904–5, 907, 938 (1869).

25. Cong. Globe, 40th Cong., 3rd Sess., 1030, 1031, 1033 (1869).

26. Cong. Globe, 40th Cong., 3rd Sess., 1035, 1036 (1869).

27. Foner, *Second Founding*, 108, 111.

28. Grenville and Cushing quoted in *United States v. Wong Kim Ark*, 169 U.S. 649, 711, 712 (1898).

29. Democratic Party Platform of 1868, American Presidency Project, https://www.presidency.ucsb.edu/documents/1868-democratic-party-platform; Lucy Salyer, *Under the Starry Flag: How a Band of Irish Americans Joined the Fenian Revolt and Sparked a Crisis over Citizenship* (Cambridge, MA: Harvard University Press, 2018).

30. Cong. Globe, 40th Cong., 3rd Sess., 1034 (1869), 41st Cong., 2nd Sess., 5151, 5177 (July 14, 1870); An Act to amend the Naturalization Laws and to punish Crimes against the same, and for other Purposes, ch. 254, 16 Stat. (1870); Torok, "Reconstruction and Racial Nativism," 66; Salyer, *Under the Starry Flag*, 60–66, 206–8; Lucy Salyer, "Reconstructing the Immigrant: The Naturalization Act of 1870 in Global Perspective," *Journal of the Civil War Era* 11 (September 2021): 382–405; David Quigley, "Acts of Enforcement: The New York City Election of 1870," *New York History* 83 (Summer 2002): 271–92, 279; David Quigley, *Second Founding: New York City, Reconstruction, and the Making of American Democracy* (New York: Hill and Wang, 2004). Trumbull made the racialist argument that it

would be inconsistent to extend naturalization to people of African origin while denying it to the Chinese, "who [were] infinitely above the African in intelligence, in manhood, and in every respect."

31. An Act to amend the Naturalization Laws (1870); Najia Aarim-Heriot, *Chinese Immigrants, African Americans, and Racial Anxiety in the United States, 1848–82* (Urbana and Chicago: University of Illinois Press, 2006), 143–51. Although a federal court ruled in 1878 that Chinese immigrants were not eligible for naturalization because they were neither white nor of African descent, and Congress reiterated the ban on naturalization in the Chinese Exclusion Act of 1882, several hundred Asian immigrants were naturalized subsequently in state courts.

32. Treaty of July 28, 1868, U.S.-China, 16 Stat. 739–740, T.S. 48 (Burlingame Treaty), art. VI, 740; Hiroshi Motomura, *Americans in Waiting: The Lost Story of Immigration and Citizenship in the United States* (New York: Oxford University Press, 2007), 16; Mae M. Ngai, *The Chinese Question: The Gold Rushes and Global Politics* (New York: Norton, 2021), 148–49. Although China recognized the fact of overseas emigration, it remained illegal (and theoretically punishable by death) until 1893.

33. An Act to enforce the Right of Citizens of the United States to vote in the several States of the Union, and for other Purposes, ch. 114, 16 Stat. 140 (May 31, 1870); Torok, "Reconstruction and Racial Nativism," 85, 87; Gerald L. Neuman, "The Lost Century of American Immigration Law (1776–1875)," *Columbia Law Review* 93 (December 1993): 1877; Aarim-Heriot, *Chinese Immigrants, African Americans, and Racial Anxiety,* 141.

34. An Act to enforce the Provisions of the Fourteenth Amendment to the Constitution of the United States, and for other Purposes Act, ch. 22, 17 Stat. 13 (April 20, 1871); An act to protect all citizens in their civil and legal rights, ch. 114, 18 Stat. 335 (March 1, 1875); Foner, *Second Founding,* 118, 151–54; Aarim-Heriot, *Chinese Immigrants, African Americans, and Racial Anxiety,* 153–55. In the *Civil Rights Cases,* 109 U.S. 3 (1883), the Supreme Court invalidated the public accommodations sections of the 1875 Civil Rights Act on the grounds that the Fourteenth Amendment applied only to actions by states, not acts of discrimination by private individuals. This ruling, as well as hastening the onset of Jim Crow segregation, significantly broadened the range of discriminatory measures that could be taken against Chinese immigrants. Justice Harlan, the lone dissenter, pointed out that railroads and hotels were licensed by the state and performed a public service. He also interpreted the Thirteenth Amendment as a source of fundamental rights, intended not simply to abolish slavery but to outlaw all "badges and incidents" of slavery.

35. *Slaughterhouse Cases,* 83 U.S. (16 Wall.) 36 (1873); Ronald M. Labbé and Jonathan Lurie, *The Slaughterhouse Cases: Regulation, Reconstruction, and the Fourteenth Amendment,* Landmark Law Cases Abridged Edition (Lawrence: University Press of Kansas, 2005); Foner, *Second Founding,* 132–33; Foner, *Reconstruction,* 529.

36. *Slaughterhouse Cases*, 36, 37 (1873); Cong. Globe, 39th Cong., 1st Sess., 1292 (1866); Foner, *Reconstruction*, 529–30; Foner, *Second Founding*, 134–36; Torok, "Reconstruction and Racial Nativism," 69–70. Justice Field, in dissent, supported a broad interpretation of the Fourteenth Amendment but not in the name of racial equality. A Democrat and an opponent of Radical Reconstruction, he was concerned about state-level regulation of economic activity and property rights. The process of incorporating the Bill of Rights into the Fourteenth Amendment, and thereby making it applicable to the states, was not completed until the twentieth century.

37. *United States v. Cruikshank*, 92 U.S. 542 (1876); Torok, "Reconstruction and Racial Nativism," 70; Foner, *Reconstruction*, 530–31; Foner, *Second Founding*, 144–46. In the *Civil Rights Cases*, the Court ruled that the Thirteenth and Fourteenth Amendments applied only to the actions of states, not to those of individuals.

38. *Slaughterhouse Cases*, 37; Cong. Globe, 39th Cong., 2d Sess., 239–40 (1867); An Act to Abolish and Forever Prohibit the System of Peonage in the Territory of New Mexico and Other Parts of the United States, ch. 187, 14 Stat. 546 (March 2, 1867); Andrés Reséndez, *The Other Slavery: The Uncovered Story of Indian Enslavement in America* (Boston: Houghton Mifflin, 2016), 301, 303, 304; William S. Kiser, *Borderlands of Slavery: The Struggle over Captivity and Peonage in the American Southwest* (Philadelphia: University of Pennsylvania Press, 2017), 11–12, 15–16; Stacey L. Smith, "Emancipating Peons, Excluding Coolies: Reconstructing Coercion in the American West," in Gregory P. Downs and Kate Masur, eds., *The World the Civil War Made* (Chapel Hill: University of North Carolina Press, 2015), 46–57; Stacey L. Smith, *Freedom's Frontier: California and the Struggle over Unfree Labor, Emancipation, and Reconstruction* (Chapel Hill: University of North Carolina Press, 2013).

39. Cong. Globe, 41st Cong., 2d Sess., 5151 (1870); An Act to execute certain treaty stipulations relating to Chinese, ch. 126, 22 Stat. 58 (May 6, 1882); Reséndez, *The Other Slavery*, 297, 299, 300; Smith, "Emancipating Peons, Excluding Coolies," 61–67; Aarim-Heriot, *Chinese Immigrants*, 158, 159; Lew-Williams, *Chinese Must Go*, 31–36, 45–51, 239.

40. *People v. Downer*, 7 Cal. 169 (1857); *Lin Sing v. Washburn*, 20 Cal. 534 (1862); An Act to Prevent the Importation of Chinese Criminals and to Prevent the Establishment of Coolie Slavery, ch. 231, 1870 Cal. Stat. 330 (March 18, 1870); An Act to Prevent the Kidnapping and Importation of Mongolian, Chinese, and Japanese females, for Criminal or Demoralizing Purposes, ch. 230, 1870 Cal. Stat. 331 (March 18, 1870); Kerry Abrams, "Polygamy, Prostitution, and the Federalization of Immigration Law," *Columbia Law Review* 105 (April 2005): 672–74, 675–77; Lew-Williams, *The Chinese Must Go*, 43. The state of Oregon and Washington Territory passed anti-coolie laws similar to California's.

41. *Ex Parte Ah Fook*, 49 Cal. 402 (1874); *Chy Lung v. Freeman*, 92 U.S. 275, 276 (1875); Abrams, "Polygamy, Prostitution, and the Federalization of Immigration Law," 686.

42. *People v. Downer*; *Ling Sang v. Washburn*; *Ex Parte Ah Fook*; *Chy Lung v. Freeman*; In re Ah Fong, 1 F. Cas. 213, 3 Sawy. 144 (C.C.D. Cal. 1874) (No. 102), 216, 218; Abrams, "Polygamy, Prostitution, and the Federalization of Immigration Law," 686.

43. In re Ah Fong, 217, 218; Abrams, "Polygamy, Prostitution, and the Federalization of Immigration Law," 678, 690. A national law, moreover, would not be bound by the Fourteenth Amendment, which according to the *Slaughterhouse Cases* applied only to the actions of states.

44. Abrams, "Polygamy, Prostitution, and the Federalization of Immigration Law," 690–691; Foner, *Reconstruction*, 523. In the midst of an economic depression, Foner notes, the Republicans suffered "the greatest reversal of partisan alignments in the entire nineteenth century." Having held a 110-vote margin in the House of Representatives, they found themselves in the minority by sixty seats and with a much narrower majority in the Senate.

45. 3 Cong. Rec. 3 (1874), 3–4; An act supplementary to the acts in relation to immigration, ch. 141, 18 Stat. 477 (March 3, 1875); Burlingame Treaty, art. V; Abrams, "Polygamy, Prostitution, and the Federalization of Immigration Law," 643, 691.

46. 3 Cong. Rec. appx. 40–45 (1875) (quotes 44, 45); Abrams, "Polygamy, Prostitution, and the Federalization of Immigration Law," 641, 692. Most Chinese women in the United States were prostitutes or second wives, Abrams points out, but there were very few of them. Page characterized all Chinese women as prostitutes by nature and all Chinese laborers as coolies.

47. An act supplementary to the acts in relation to immigration (1875); Abrams, "Polygamy, Prostitution, and the Federalization of Immigration Law," 658, 696–703, 711; Torok, "Reconstruction and Racial Nativism," 96.

48. Abrams, "Polygamy, Prostitution, and the Federalization of Immigration Law," 701, 705–6, 711; An Act in amendment to the various acts relative to immigration and the importation of aliens under contract or agreement to perform labor, ch. 551, 26 Stat. 1084 (March 3, 1891). The 1891 act made polygamists excludable, along with many of the classes of persons previously regulated by state laws, including criminals, paupers, the insane, and people with contagious diseases.

CHAPTER 7

1. *Chae Chan Ping v. United States*, 130 U.S. 581, 581–83 (1889); Polly J. Price, "A 'Chinese Wall' at the Nation's Borders: Justice Stephen Field and the Chinese Exclusion Case," *Journal of Supreme Court History*, 43 (March 2018): 7–26.

2. *Chae Chan Ping v. United States*, 609.

3. *Henderson v. Mayor of City of New York*, 92 U.S. 259, 260–61, 275 (1875); Katherine Carper, "The Migration Business, 1824–1876," unpublished PhD

dissertation, Boston College, 2020, 250–53; Sarah Cleveland, "Powers Inherent in Sovereignty: Indians, Aliens, Territories, and the Nineteenth Century Origins of Plenary Power over Foreign Affairs," *Texas Law Review* 81 (November 2002): 107 n731 (citing brief for Appellants, *Henderson*, No. 880, 18). The Hendersons filed their appeal to the Supreme Court in December 1875 and the Court published its decision in March 1876. Both dates were part of the October–June term of 1875–1876; the case is usually cited as 1875 but sometimes as 1876. From the $1.50 commutation fee in New York City, fifty cents was to be paid to other counties in the state and the balance to the commissioners of emigration for the general expenses of administering immigration. The penalty for not paying the commutation tax was $500 for each passenger, with the vessel taken as a lien.

4. *Henderson v. New York*, 259–60, 268–69, 270–71, 273.

5. *Henderson v. New York*, 274.

6. *Henderson v. New York*, 271, 274. 275.

7. *In re Ah Fong*, 1 F. Cas. 213, 3 Sawy. 144 (C.C.D. Cal. 1874) (No. 102); *Chy Lung v. Freeman*, 92 U.S. 275, 276 (1875). See Chapter 6.

8. *Chy Lung v. Freeman*, 277–78, 280; Cleveland, "Powers Inherent in Sovereignty," 108–9 (citing brief for the Plaintiff in Error, 5–6); Kerry Abrams, "Polygamy, Prostitution, and the Federalization of Immigration Law," *Columbia Law Review* 105 (April 2005): 678–90, 703–04. Each passenger required a separate bond, the sureties had to be residents of the state, and the same sureties could not guarantee more than one bond.

9. *Chy Lung v. Freeman*, 279–80.

10. *Chy Lung v. Freeman*, 280; Abrams, "Polygamy, Prostitution, and the Federalization of Immigration Law," 703 (quote), 704, 705. In *Chy Lung*, the Court was interested in the nature of authority over immigration, not in Chinese immigrants' rights. Miller did not address Chy Lung's claim to equal protection. Justice Field had ruled in favor of the twenty-two Chinese women the previous year in the circuit court case, In re Ah Fong, on narrow equal protection grounds (finding that California's law discriminated against those who arrived by sea rather than overland), but in *Chy Lung* he joined the unanimous majority without writing a concurring opinion.

11. Republican Party Platform, 1876, American Presidency Project, https://www.presidency.ucsb.edu/node/273305; Democratic Party Platform, 1876, American Presidency Project, https://www.presidency.ucsb.edu/node/273179; Eric Foner, *Reconstruction: America's Unfinished Revolution, 1862–1877* (1988; updated edition, New York: Harper Perennial Modern Classics, 2014), 567.

12. Joint Special Committee to Investigate Chinese Immigration, S. Rep. No. 689–44, iv–vi, vii, viii (1877).

13. Joint Special Committee to Investigate Chinese Immigration, S. Rep. No. 689–44, iv–vi, vii, viii (1877).

14. Set of principles drawn up by the California Workingmen's Party on October 5, 1877, in Winfield J. Davis, *History of Political Conventions in California, 1849–1882*

(Sacramento: California State Library, 1893), 366; Andrew Gyory, *Closing the Gates: Race, Politics, and the Chinese Exclusion Act* (Chapel Hill: University of North Carolina Press, 1998), 110–31. A dray is a small cart pulled by horses. Kearney operated several such carts and hauled goods throughout the city. He ran a successful employment agency for two decades after his retirement from political activity in 1880.

15. Davis, *History of Political Conventions in California*, 367.

16. Alexander Saxton, *The Indispensable Enemy: Labor and the Anti-Chinese Movement in California* (1971; Berkeley: University of California Press, 1995), 116–37; Beth Lew-Williams, *The Chinese Must Go: Violence, Exclusion, and the Making of the Alien in America* (Cambridge, MA: Harvard University Press, 2018), 40–43; Gyory, *Closing the Gates*, 169–70.

17. 42. Cal. Constitution, art. XIX § 1–4; Najia Aarim-Heriot, *Chinese Immigrants, African Americans, and Racial Anxiety in the United States, 1848–82* (Urbana and Chicago: University of Illinois Press, 2006), 191–92.

18. Democratic Party Platform, 1880, American Presidency Project, https://www.presidency.ucsb.edu/node/273182; Republican Party Platform, 1880, American Presidency Project, https://www.presidency.ucsb.edu/node/273308; Treaty Between the United States and China Concerning Immigration, November 17, 1880, 22 Stat. 826, T. S. 49; Aarim-Heriot, *Chinese Immigrants, African Americans, and Racial Anxiety in the United States*, 197–205; Gyory, *Closing the Gates*, 136–68, 185–218; Abrams, "Polygamy, Prostitution, and the Federalization of Immigration Law," 710; Cleveland, "Powers Inherent in Sovereignty," 116.

19. Cleveland, "Powers Inherent in Sovereignty," 116; 13 Cong. Rec. S1583 (1882); see also 13 Cong. Rec. S1483, 1484, 1518–19, 1546, 1586, 1635–37, 1644–45 (1882).

20. S. 71, 47th Cong. (1882); 13 Cong. Rec. S1480, 1481, 1482, 1483, 1485 (1882).

21. 13 Cong. Rec. S1485, 1486 (1882).

22. 13 Cong. Rec. S1486 (1882).

23. 13 Cong. Rec. S1486, 1487 (1882); Thomas Robert Malthus, *An Essay on the Principle of the Future Improvement of Society, with Remarks on the Speculations of Mr. Godwin, M. Condorcet, and Other Writers* (London: J. Johnson, 1798). By 1915 the population of the United States reached 100 million, though about 26 million immigrants had arrived since Miller's speech. Immigration fell significantly after 1921 due to restriction laws. In 1950 the population was 152 million.

24. 13 Cong. Rec. S1515, 1516, 1818 (1882).

25. 13 Cong. Rec. S1517 (1882).

26. 13 Cong. Rec. S1518, 1519 (1882).

27. An Act to execute certain treaty stipulations relating to Chinese, ch. 126, 22 Stat. 58 (Act of May 6, 1882); Shirley Hune, "Politics of Chinese Exclusion," *Amerasia Journal* 9 (1982): 5–27; Gyory, *Closing the Gates*, 218–59.

28. An Act to prohibit the importation and migration of foreigners and aliens under contract or agreement to perform labor in the United States, its Territories, and

the District of Columbia (Alien Contract Labor Law, or Foran Act), ch. 164, 23 Stat. 322 (February 26, 1885), 332–33; Robert J. Steinfeld, *Coercion, Contract, and Free Labor in the Nineteenth Century* (New York: Cambridge University Press, 2001), 31; David Montgomery, *Beyond Equality: Labor and the Radical Republicans, 1862–1872* (Urbana and Chicago: University of Illinois Press, 1981); Aristide R. Zolberg, *A Nation by Design: Immigration Policy in the Fashioning of America* (Cambridge, MA: Harvard University Press, 2006), 172–74; Charlotte Erickson, *American Industry and the European Immigrant, 1860–1885* (Cambridge, MA: Harvard University Press, 1957), 28–31; Gunther Peck, *Reinventing Free Labor: Padrones and Immigrant Workers in the North American West, 1880–1930* (New York: Cambridge University Press, 2000).

29. 16 Cong. Rec. S1624 (quote), S1625 (quote), S1627, S1630, S1631, S1634 (quote), S1778, S1780–85, S1794 (1885). Sherman dismissed out of hand the idea that the 1864 act had sanctioned the principle of immigrant contract labor in American law. It was, he explained, merely a temporary wartime measure.

30. 16 Cong. Rec. S1624, 1630–31. See also 16 Cong. Rec. S1624–27, 1634, 1778–85, 1793–94.

31. An Act to prohibit the importation and migration of foreigners and aliens under contract (1885); Moon-Ho Jung, *Coolies and Cane: Race, Labor, and Sugar in the Age of Emancipation* (Baltimore: Johns Hopkins University Press, 2008); Lisa Lowe, *The Intimacies of Four Continents* (Durham, NC: Duke University Press, 2015), 1–7, 24–25; Elliot Young, "Chinese Coolies, Universal Rights and the Limits of Liberalism in an Age of Empire," *Past and Present* 227 (May 2015): 121–49; Lew-Williams, *The Chinese Must Go*, 235–40; Peck, *Reinventing Free Labor*, 85.

32. An Act to regulate immigration, ch. 376, 22 Stat. 214 (August 3, 1882); *New York v. Compagnie Générale Transatlantique*, 107 U.S. 59 (1883), 60–63; Hidetaka Hirota, *Expelling the Poor: Atlantic Seaboard States and the Nineteenth-Century Origins of American Immigration Policy* (New York: Oxford University Press, 2017), 181, 184–92; Cleveland, "Powers Inherent in Sovereignty," 110. Miller also wrote that the terms "imports," "exports," and "inspection" as used in the U.S. Constitution, art. 1, sec. 10, cl. 2, referred exclusively to personal property and never to "free human beings," and that the migration or importation clause referred only to slaves.

33. Mary Sarah Bilder, "The Struggle over Immigration: Indentured Servants, Slaves, and Articles of Commerce," *Missouri Law Review* 61 (Fall 1996): 819, 821, 822, 823; *Head Money Cases*, 112 U.S. 580 (1884).

34. *Head Money Cases*, 580, 581, 590, 591, 600; Cleveland, "Powers Inherent in Sovereignty," 112 n765.

35. Cleveland, "Powers Inherent in Sovereignty," 111 (quoting brief for the United States, *Edye v. Robertson*, No. 722, 2, one of the *Head Money Cases*). The solicitor general cited Thomas M. Cooley, *A Treatise on the Constitutional Limitations Which Rest upon the Legislative Power of the States of the American Union*, 5th ed. (Boston: Little, Brown, 1883), 197.

36. Cleveland, "Powers Inherent in Sovereignty," 110, 110 n762, 111, 112 (quoting brief for the United States, *Edye v. Robertson*, No. 722, 2, and brief for the United States, *Edye v. Robertson* No. 722, 3); Julian Lim, "Immigration, Plenary Powers, and Sovereignty Talk: Then and Now," *Journal of the Gilded Age and Progressive Era* 19 (April 2020): 7, 8.

37. Beth Lew-Williams, "Before Restriction Became Exclusion: America's Experiment in Diplomatic Immigration Control," *Pacific Historical Review* 83 (February 2014): 25, 27, 33–35, 39, 42, 46, 54–56. Counting returnees, Lew-Williams finds that more Chinese entered the United States in each of the years from 1883 to 1888 than in the year leading up to exclusion act passed in April 1882.

38. Lew-Williams, "Before Restriction Became Exclusion," 48–49.

39. An Act a supplement to an act entitled "An Act to execute certain treaty stipulations relating to Chinese," approved the sixth day of May eighteen hundred and eighty-two, ch. 1064, 25 Stat. 504 (October 1, 1888); S. Exec. Doc. 50–273 (1888); Lew-Williams, "Before Restriction Became Exclusion," 48–51; Cleveland, "Powers Inherent in Sovereignty," 123–24. During the legislative debates, a failed motion in the Senate proposed creating an exception for Chinese residents who had already left the United States with certificates of return. When President Cleveland signed the bill, he called on Congress to pass legislation creating this exception, but to no avail. Congress appropriated $50,000 for the Scott Act, compared to the $5,000 for the 1882 Chinese Exclusion Act. The number of Chinese arriving in 1889–1893 decreased by 75 percent compared to pre-1882 levels.

40. *Chae Chan Ping v. United States*, 130 U.S. 581 (1889), 581, 582; Cleveland, "Powers Inherent in Sovereignty," 124 (citing brief for the Appellant by Attorney James C. Carter, *Chae Chan Ping v. United States*, No. 1446, 3–4).

41. Cleveland, "Powers Inherent in Sovereignty," 126 (citing brief for the United States, *Chae Chan Ping v. United States* No. 1446, 5, 6–7), 128 (Argument of John F. Swift and Stephen M. White, of Counsel for Respondent Concurred in by G.A. Johnson, Attorney Gen., Cal., *Chae Chan Ping v. United States*, No. 1446, 11–12); Emer de Vattel, *The law of nations, or, Principles of the law of nature, applied to the conduct and affairs of nations and sovereigns, with three early essays on the origin and nature of natural law and on luxury*, ed. Béla Kapossy and Richard Whatmore, trans. Thomas Nugent (1758; Indianapolis: Liberty Fund, 2008), Book 2, ch. VIII, § 100; *New York v. Compagnie Générale Transatlantique*.

42. *Chae Chan Ping v. United States*, 594, 595.

43. *Chae Chan Ping v. United States*, 603–4, 606; Vattel, *The law of nations*, Book 2, ch. VIII, § 100; Adam Carrington, "Police the Border: Justice Field on Immigration as a Police Power," *Journal of Supreme Court History* 40 (2015): 20–37; Cleveland, "Powers Inherent in Sovereignty," 132; Price, "'Chinese Wall,'" 7–26; Gabriel J. Chin, "*Chae Chan Ping* and *Fong Yue Ting*: The Origins of Plenary Power," in David A. Martin and Peter H. Schuck, eds., *Immigration Law Stories* (New York: Foundation Press, 2005), 7–29.

44. *Chae Chan Ping v. United States*, 609.

45. Adam B. Cox and Cristina M. Rodríguez, *The President and Immigration Law* (New York: Oxford University Press, 2020), 31. In the *Insular Cases* (1901), the Court applied a similar principle to the territories acquired in the Spanish-American War, thereby limiting the rights of their residents to constitutional protections.

46. Bethany R. Berger, "The Anomaly of Citizenship for Indigenous Rights," in Shereen Hertel and Kathryn Libal, eds., *Human Rights in the United States: Beyond Exceptionalism* (New York: Cambridge University Press, 2011), 217, 219–20, 225–26; Elizabeth Ellis, "The Border(s) Crossed Us Too: The Intersections of Native American and Immigrant Fights for Justice," *emisférica*, 14 (Fall 2018), paras. 2, 7–9, 14–15, 22–26, 30–31, https://hemisphericinstitute.org/en/emisferica-14-1-expuls ion/14-1-essays/the-border-s-crossed-us-too-the-intersections-of-native-ameri can-and-immigrant-fights-for-justice-2.html; Lim, "Immigration, Plenary Powers, and Sovereignty Talk," 217–29; Cleveland, "Powers Inherent in Sovereignty," 48–51, 54–77.

47. *Elk v. Wilkins*, 112 U.S. 94 (1884); Bethany R. Berger, "Birthright Citizenship on Trial: *Elk v. Wilkins* and *United States v. Wong Kim Ark*," *Cardozo Law Review* 37 (April 2016): 1196–1201, 1205–10, 1208, 1232–43, 1256–57.

48. *United States v. Kagama*, 118 U.S. 375 (1886); An Act to Provide for the Allotment of Lands in Severalty to Indians on the Various Reservations, and to extend the protection of the laws of the United States and the Territories over the Indians, and for other purposes, ch. 118, 24 Stat. 388 (February 8, 1887); Major Crimes Act (part of An Act making appropriations for the current and contingent expenses of the Indian department, and for fulfilling treaty stipulations with various Indian tribes, ch. 341, 23 Stat. 385 (March 3, 1885); *United States v. Rogers*, 45 U.S. (4 How.) 567 (1846); Maggie Blackhawk, "Federal Indian Law as Paradigm Within Public Law," *Harvard Law Review* 132 (May 2019): 1798–99, 1823, 1829–33, 1843–44. On *Rogers*, see Chapter 4.

49. *Nishimura Ekiu v. United States*, 142 U.S. 651, 659 (1892): Justice Gray, citing the *Head Money Cases* (n.p.), *Chae Chan Ping v. United States*, 604–9, and Vattel's *The law of nations*, Book 2, ch. VIII, §§ 94, 100.

50. An Act to prohibit the coming of Chinese persons into the United States, ch. 60, 27 Stat. 25 (May 5, 1892); *Fong Yue Ting v. United States*, 149 U.S. 698, 707, 708–9, 730 (1893); Lew-Williams, "Before Restriction Became Exclusion," 51–52; Cleveland, "Powers Inherent in Sovereignty," 124; Mary Roberts Coolidge, *Chinese Immigration* (1909; New York: Henry Holt, 1968), 280. On the right to deport as well as exclude, Justice Gray quoted Vattel, *The law of nations*, Book 1, ch. XIX, §§ 230, 231, as well as excerpts from Théodore Ortolan, Robert Phillimore, and Ludwig de Bar. The Geary Act modified the Scott Act of 1888 by allowing Chinese immigrants, once again, to travel back and forth to China if they carried their certificates of residence. Along with the McCreary Amendment of 1893, the

Geary Act also limited the definition of exempt classes and denied bail to Chinese passengers who were not allowed to land. After 1907, all Chinese residents of the United States had to carry certificates.

51. *Yick Wo v. Hopkins*, 118 U.S. 356, 362, 366 (1886); Cleveland, "Powers Inherent in Sovereignty," 119.

52. *Chy Lung v. Freeman*, 280.

## EPILOGUE

1. *Trump v. Hawaii*, 585 U.S. (2018); *Chae Chan Ping v. United States*, 130 U.S. 581 (1889).

2. Gerald L. Neuman, "The Lost Century of American Immigration Law (1776– 1875)," *Columbia Law Review* 93 (December 1993): 1897–98.

3. *United States v. Wong Kim Ark*, 169 U.S. 649, 650, 651 (1898); Amanda Frost, *You Are Not American: Citizenship Stripping from Dred Scott to the Dreamers* (Boston: Beacon Press, 2021), 51–57; Carol Nackenoff and Julie Novkov, *American by Birth: Wong Kim Ark and the Battle for Citizenship*, Landmark Law Cases Abridged Edition (Lawrence: University Press of Kansas, 2021); Bethany R. Berger, "Birthright Citizenship on Trial: *Elk v. Wilkins* and *United States v. Wong Kim Ark*," *Cardozo Law Review* 37 (April 2016): 1185, 1226–29; Lucy Salyer, "Wong Kim Ark and the Challenge to Birthright Citizenship," in Peter Schuck and David Martin, eds., *Immigration Stories* (New York: Foundation Press, 2005), 51–85; Lucy Salyer, *Laws Harsh as Tigers: Chinese Immigrants and the Shaping of American Immigration Law* (Chapel Hill: University of North Carolina Press, 1995); Leti Volpp, "Divesting Citizenship: On Asian American History and the Loss of Citizenship Through Marriage," *UCLA Law Review* 53 (2005): 417. The Geary Act of 1892 allowed Chinese immigrants legally resident in the country to travel back and forth to China if they carried certificates proving legal residence.

4. Sarah Cleveland, "Powers Inherent in Sovereignty: Indians, Aliens, Territories, and the Nineteenth Century Origins of Plenary Power over Foreign Affairs," *Texas Law Review 81* (November 2002): 155; Frost, *You Are Not American*, 51–57.

5. *Plessy v. Ferguson*, 163 U.S. 537, 550–52 (quote 552) (1896); Williamjames Hull Hoffer, *Plessy v. Ferguson: Race and Inequality in Jim Crow America* (Lawrence: University Press of Kansas, 2012). See the discussion in Chapter 6 of the *Slaughterhouse Cases*, 83 U.S. 36 (1873), *United States v. Cruikshank*, 92 U.S. 542 (1876), and the *Civil Rights Cases*, 109 U.S. 3 (1883).

6. *Plessy v. Ferguson*, 559, 562; *United States v. Wong Kim Ark*, 705–32.

7. *Plessy v. Ferguson*, 561, 562.

8. *United States v. Wong Kim Ark*, 705–7, 711; *Plessy v. Ferguson*, 561; Salyer, "Wong Kim Ark," 52; Lucy Salyer, *Under the Starry Flag: How a Band of Irish Americans Joined the Fenian Revolt and Sparked a Crisis over Citizenship* (Cambridge, MA: Harvard University Press, 2018), 170–75, 203–5; Martha S. Jones, *Birthright*

*Citizens: A History of Race and Rights in Antebellum America* (New York: Cambridge University Press, 2018), 1–15; Martha S. Jones, "Citizenship," in Nikole Hannah-Jones et al., eds., *The 1619 Project: A New Origin Story* (New York: One World Press, 2021), 220–21, 226–33.

9. *United States v. Wong Kim Ark*, 720–22, 725, 730, 732.

10. *United States v. Wong Kim Ark*, 653, 682, 693, 694, 701, 702, 703; Frost, *You Are Not American*, 62–73. The Constitution also allows for "natural-born" citizenship, which includes children born abroad to parents who are United States citizens. In a controversial book, Peter H. Schuck and Rogers M. Smith, *Citizenship Without Consent: Illegal Aliens in the American Polity* (New Haven: Yale University Press, 1985), revived Fuller's argument, suggesting that that children of irregular immigrants were not eligible for citizenship as they were not fully under the jurisdiction of the United States. For strong rebuttals of this position, see Gerald L. Neuman, "Back to Dred Scott?," *San Diego Law Review* 24 (1987): 485–500; Gabriel J. Chin and Paul Finkelman, "Birthright Citizenship, Slave Trade Legislation, and the Origins of Federal Immigration Regulation," *UC Davis Law Review* 54 (July 2021): 2215–65.

11. Salyer, "Wong Kim Ark," 73–74.

12. *Fong Yue Ting v. United States*, 149 U.S. 698 (1893); *United States v. Wong Kim Ark*, 668; Salyer, "Wong Kim Ark," 75.

13. Karla M. McKanders, "Sustaining Tiered Personhood: Jim Crow and Anti-Immigrant Laws," *Harvard Journal on Racial & Ethnic Justice* 26 (2010): 163–210; Pratheepan Gulasekaram and S. Karthick Ramakrishnan, *The New Immigration Federalism* (New York: Cambridge University Press, 2015), 59–64.

14. California Proposition 187. Illegal Aliens Ineligibility for Public Benefits Verification and Reporting Initiative Statute (1994); Gulasekaram and Ramakrishnan, *New Immigration Federalism*, 52–53.

15. Arizona SB 1070, The Support Our Law Enforcement and Safe Neighborhoods Act (2010); *Arizona v. United States*, 567 U.S. 387 (2012); Gulasekaram and Ramakrishnan, *New Immigration Federalism*, 31, 35–36, 65–66, 123–24, 173–75; Walter Ewing, Daniel E. Martínez, and Ruben Rimbaut, *The Criminalization of Immigration in the United States* (Washington, DC: American Immigration Council, 2005).

16. *Arizona v. U.S.*, 567 U.S. 387 (2012), Justice Antonin Scalia, dissent. On the myth of open borders, Scalia cited Neuman's "Lost Century of American Immigration Law." Neuman would disagree strongly with Scalia's conclusions.

17. Gulasekaram and Ramakrishnan, *New Immigration Federalism*, 59–64, 127–50, 182–83, 202–5; A. Naomi Paik, *Bans, Walls, Raids, Sanctuary: Understanding U.S. Immigration for the Twenty-First Century* (Oakland: University of California Press, 2020), 102–29, 132–34; Mae Ngai, "A Call for Sanctuary," *Dissent Magazine*, November 22, 2016, 1–3.

18. An Act: To prevent the importation of certain persons into certain States, where, by the laws thereof, their admission is prohibited, ch. 10, 2 Stat. 205 (February 28, 1803); An Act to Prohibit the Importation of Slaves, ch. 22, 2 Stat. 426 (March 2, 1807); Chin and Finkelman, "Birthright Citizenship," 2227–32; Neuman, "Back to Dred Scott?" The Civil Rights Act of 1866 and the Fourteenth Amendment intended to exclude from citizenship only the American-born children of foreign officials, children born to enemy aliens during an occupation of the United States, and Native Americans living on tribal land.

19. Peter L. Markowtiz, "Undocumented No More: The Power of State Citizenship," *Stanford Law Review* 67 (April 2015): 869–915; Maeve Glass, "Citizens of the State," *University of Chicago Law Review* 85 (June 2018): 928–29; "New York City's Noncitizen Voting Law Is Struck Down," *New York Times*, June 27, 2022. No state citizenship law of this kind has passed yet. The New York State law remains under consideration by the legislature in Albany. The New York City Council approved legislation in December 2021 allowing legally resident noncitizens to vote in municipal elections after thirty days' residence, starting in 2023. Republican officials and voters challenged this law and, in June 2022, a New York State Supreme Court justice in Staten Island ruled that it violated the state Constitution, which granted suffrage to citizens only.

# Bibliography

PRIMARY SOURCES

*Government Documents*

Benton, Thomas Hart. *Abridgment of the Debates of Congress, from 1789 to 1856. From Gales and Seatons' Annals of Congress; from their Register of debates; and from the official reported debates, by John C. Rives. By the author of the Thirty years' view.* 16 vols. New York: D. Appleton, 1860–1867.

*Congressional Globe.*

*Congressional Record.*

Elliot, Jonathan. *The Debates in the Several State Conventions on the Adoption of the Federal Constitution, as Recommended by the General Convention at Philadelphia in 1787.* 5 vols. Philadelphia: J. B. Lippincott; Washington, DC: Taylor & Maury, 1836–1859.

Farrand, Max, ed. *The Records of the Federal Convention of 1787.* 3 vols. New Haven: Yale University Press, 1911.

Gales, Joseph, and William W. Seaton. *The Debates and Proceedings in the Congress of the United States* [otherwise known as the *Annals of Congress*]. 42 vols. Washington, DC: D. Appleton 1834–1856.

*The United States Statutes at Large.*


*Court Cases*

*Arizona v. U.S.*, 567 U.S. 387 (2012)
*Barbier v. Connolly*, 113 U.S. 27 (1885)
*Brown v. Maryland*, 25 U.S. (12. Wheat.) 419 (1827)
*Calder v. Deliesseline*, S.C.L, Harper 186 (1824)
*Chae Chan Ping v. United States (Chinese Exclusion Case)*, 130 U.S. 581 (1889)
*Cherokee Nation v. Georgia*, 30 U.S. (5 Pet.) 1 (1831)
*Chy Lung v. Freeman*, 92 U.S. 275 (1875)

*Civil Rights Cases*, 109 U.S. 3 (1883)

*Commonwealth of Massachusetts v. Aves*, 35 Mass. 193 (1836)

*Cooley v. Board of Wardens of the Port of Philadelphia*, 53 U.S. (12 How.) 299 (1852)

*Crandall v. Nevada*, 73 U.S. (6 Wall.) 35 (1867)

*Dred Scott v. Sandford*, 60 U.S. (19. How.) 393 (1857)

*Elk v. Wilkins*, 112 U.S. 94 (1884)

*Elkison v. Deliesseline*, 8 F. Cas. 493 (So. Car. Cir. Ct., 1823)

*Ex Parte Ah Fook*, 49 Cal. 402 (1874)

*Fong Yue Ting v. United States*, 149 U.S. 698 (1893)

*Gibbons v. Ogden*, 22 U.S. (9 Wheat.) 1 (1824)

*Groves v. Slaughter*, 40 U.S. (15 Pet.) 449 (1841)

*Head Money Cases*, 112 U.S. 580 (1884)

*Henderson v. Mayor of New York*, 92 U.S. 259 (1875)

*In re Ah Fong*, 1 F. Cas. 213 (C.C.D. Cal. 1874) (No. 102)

*Johnson v. M'Intosh*, 21 U.S. (8 Wheat.) 543 (1823)

*Kelly v. Owen*, 74 U.S. (7 Wall.) 496 (1868)

*Lemmon v. People of New York*, 20 N.Y. 562 (1860)

*License Cases*, 46 U.S. (5 How.) 504 (1847)

*Lin Sing v. Washburn*, 20 Cal. 534 (1862)

*Moore v. Illinois*, 55 U.S. (14 How.) 13 (1852)

*New York v. Compagnie Générale Transatlantique*, 107 U.S. 59 (1883)

*New York v. Miln*, 36 U.S. (11 Pet.) 102 (1837)

*Nishimura Ekiu v. United States*, 142 U.S. 651 (1892)

*Passenger Cases*, 48 U.S. (7 How.) 283 (1849)

*People v. Downer*, 7 Cal. 169 (1857)

*People v. Hall*, 4 Cal. 399 (1854)

*Plessy v. Ferguson*, 163 U.S. 537 (1896)

*Prigg v. Pennsylvania*, 41 U.S. (16 Pet.) 539 (1842)

*Slaughterhouse Cases*, 83 U.S. (16 Wall.) 36 (1873)

*Somerset v. Stewart* (1772) 98 ER 499

*Trump v. Hawaii*, 585 U.S. (2018)

*United States v. Cruikshank*, 92 U.S. 542 (1876)

*United States v. Kagama*, 118 U.S. 375 (1886)

*United States v. Rogers*, 45 U.S. (4 How.) 567 (1846)

*United States v. Schooner Amistad*, 40 U.S. (15 Pet.) 518 (1841)

*United States v. Wong Kim Ark*, 169 U.S. 649 (1898)

*The Wilson v. United States*, 30 Fed. Cas. 239 (No. 17846) (C.C.D. Va. 1820)

*Wong Wing v. United States*, 163 U.S. 228 (1896)

*Worcester v. Georgia*, 31 U.S. (6 Pet.) 515 (1832)

*Yick Wo v. Hopkins*, 118 U.S. 356 (1886)

## Published and Digitized Primary Materials

Agrippa (James Winthrop, pseud.). "Letters of Agrippa." *Massachusetts Gazette*, November 1878–January 1788. Letter IX, December 28, 1787, on "the intercourse between us and foreigners."

American Council of Learned Societies. Report of Committee on Linguistic and National Stocks in the Population of the United States. *Surnames in the United States Census of 1790: An Analysis of National Origins of the Population.* 1932; Baltimore, MD: Genealogical Publishing, 1969.

Blackstone, William. *Commentaries on the Laws of England.* 4 vols. 1765–1769. Chicago: Chicago University Press, 1992.

Douglass, Frederick. "Our Composite Nationality." December 7, 1869. https://teac hingamericanhistory.org/library/document/our-composite-nationality/.

Jefferson, Thomas. "Notes on the State of Virginia" (1787). Yale Law School. The Avalon Project: Documents in Law, History, and Diplomacy. https://avalon.law. yale.edu/18th_century/jeffvir.asp.

Goodell, William. *The American Slave Code in Theory and Practice: Its Distinctive Features Shown by Its Statutes, Judicial Decisions, and Illustrative Facts.* New York: American and Foreign Anti-Slavery Society, 1835.

Hamilton, Alexander. "The Examination," nos. 7–9 (1802). In *The Papers of Alexander Hamilton.* Edited by Harold C. Syrett. New York: Columbia University Press, 1961–. 25:491–501.

Hamilton, Alexander, John Jay, and James Madison. *The Federalist Papers.* Edited by Isaac Kramnick. 1788. New York: Penguin, 1987.

Hunt, Benjamin. *The argument of Benj. Faneuil Hunt, in the case of the arrest of the person claiming to be a British seaman, under the 3d section of the State Act of Dec. 1822, in relation to Negroes, &c. before the Hon. Judge Johnson, Circuit Judge of the United States, for 6th Circuit: ex parte Henry Elkison, claiming to be a subject of His Britannic Majesty, vs. Francis G. Deliesseline, sheriff of Charleston District.* Charleston, SC: A. E. Miller, 1823.

Jefferson, Thomas. *The Papers of Thomas Jefferson.* 44 vols. General editor James P. McClure. Princeton: Princeton University Press, 1950–2019.

Jefferson, Thomas. *The writings of Thomas Jefferson: being his autobiography, correspondence, reports, messages, addresses, and other writings, official and private.* Edited by Henry Augustine Washington. 9 vols. Washington, DC: Taylor & Maury, 1853–1854.

Johnson, William. *The opinion of the Hon. William Johnson, delivered on the 7th August, 1823, in the case of the arrest of the British seaman under the 3d section of the state act, entitled, "An act for the better regulation of free Negroes and persons of colour, and for other purposes," passed in December last: ex parte Henry Elkison, a subject of His Britannic Majesty, vs. Francis G. Deliesseline, sheriff of Charleston District.* Charleston, SC: C. C. Sebring, 1823.

Kaminski, John P., ed. *A Necessary Evil? Slavery and the Debate over the Constitution.* Madison, WI: Madison House, 1995.

Kapp, Friedrich. *Immigration, and the Commissioners of Emigration of the City of New York.* New York: Nation Press, 1870.

Lieber, Francis. *The Stranger in America.* Philadelphia: Carey, Lea, and Blanchard, 1835.

Lincoln, Abraham. *Collected Works of Abraham Lincoln.* Edited by Roy P. Basler. New Brunswick, NJ: Rutgers University Press, 1953–1955. https://quod.lib.umich.edu/l/lincoln/.

Lincoln, Abraham. *Lincoln: Speeches and Writings, 1832–1865.* Edited by Don E. Fehrenbacher. New York: Library of America, 1989.

Madison, James. *Debates on the Adoption of the Federal Constitution in the Convention Held at Philadelphia in 1787, with a Diary of the Debates of the Congress of the Confederation, as Reported by James Madison.* Philadelphia: J. B. Lippincott, 1866.

Madison, James. *The Writings of James Madison, comprising his Public Papers and his Private Correspondence, including his numerous letters and documents now for the first time printed.* Edited by Gaillard Hunt. New York: G.P. Putnam's Sons, 1900.

McMaster J., and F. Stone. *Pennsylvania and the Federal Constitution, 1787–1788.* Philadelphia: Historical Society of Pennsylvania, 1888.

Paine, Thomas. *Paine: Collected Writings.* Edited by Eric Foner. New York: Library of America, 1995.

Paine, Thomas. *Common Sense.* 1776. New York: Penguin Classics, 1982.

Paine, Thomas. *The Complete Writings of Thomas Paine.* 2 vols. Edited by Philip Foner. New York: The Citadel Press, 1969.

Pickering, Octavius. *Reports of Cases Argued and Determined in the Supreme Judicial Court of the Commonwealth of Massachusetts.* Boston: Little, Brown, 1866–1870.

Powell, H. Jefferson. "Attorney General Taney & the South Carolina Police Bill." *Green Bag* 5 (2001): 75–100.

Smith, E. Peshine. *Reports of the Cases Argued and Determined in the Court of Appeals of the State of New York.* Albany, NY: Banks and Brothers, 1860.

St. John de Crevecoeur, J. Hector. *Letters from An American Farmer.* 1782. New York: Penguin Classics, 1986.

Tocqueville, Alexis de. *Democracy in America.* 1835 and 1840. New York: Penguin Classics, 2002.

Vattel, Emer, De. *The law of nations, or, Principles of the law of nature, applied to the conduct and affairs of nations and sovereigns, with three early essays on the origin and nature of natural law and on luxury.* Edited with an introduction by Béla Kapossy and Richard Whatmore and translated by Thomas Nugent. 1758. Indianapolis: Liberty Fund, 2008.

Walker, David. *Walker's Appeal, in Four Articles: Together with a Preamble, to the Coloured Citizens of the World, but in Particular, and Very Expressly, to Those of the United States of America, Written in Boston, State of Massachusetts, September 28, 1829.* Boston: David Walker, 1829.

Walker, Robert J. *Argument of Robert J. Walker, Esq., Before the Supreme Court of the United States, on the Mississippi Slave Question, at January term, 1841. Involving the Power of Congress and of the States to Prohibit the Inter-state Slave Trade.* Philadelphia: John C. Clark, 1841.

Walsh, Robert. *Free Remarks on the Spirit of the Federal Constitution, the Practice of the Federal Government, and the Obligations of the Union, Respecting the Exclusion of Slavery from the Territories and New States.* Philadelphia: A. Finley, 1819.


SECONDARY SOURCES

Aarim-Heriot, Najia. *Chinese Immigrants, African Americans, and Racial Anxiety in the United States, 1848–82.* Urbana and Chicago: University of Illinois Press, 2006.

Abrams, Kerry. "The Hidden Dimension of Nineteenth-Century Immigration Law." *Vanderbilt Law Review* 62 (October 2009): 1353–1418.

Abrams, Kerry. "Polygamy, Prostitution, and the Federalization of Immigration Law." *Columbia Law Review* 105 (April 2005): 641–716.

Adelman, Jeremy, and Stephen Aron. "From Borderlands to Borders: Empires, Nation-States, and the People in Between in North American History." *American Historical Review* 104 (June 1999): 814–41.

Akenson, Donald H. "Why the Accepted Estimates of the American People, 1790, Are Unacceptable." *The William and Mary Quarterly* 41 (January 1984): 102–119.

Albion, Robert Greenhalgh. *The Rise of New York Port.* 1939. New York: Charles Scribner's Sons, 1967.

Aleinikoff, T. Alexander. *Semblances of Sovereignty: The Constitution, the State, and American Citizenship.* Cambridge, MA: Harvard University Press, 2002.

Aleinikoff, Thomas Alexander, David A. Martin, Hiroshi Motomura, and Maryellen Fullerton. *Immigration and Citizenship Process and Policy.* 7th ed. American Casebook Series. St. Paul, MN: West Academic, 2012.

Allen, Austin. *Origins of the* Dred Scott *Case: Jacksonian Jurisprudence and the Supreme Court, 1837–1857.* Athens: University of Georgia Press, 2006.

Amar, Akhil Reed. *The Bill of Rights: Creation and Reconstruction.* New Haven: Yale University Press, 1998.

Anbinder, Tyler. *Nativism and Slavery: The Northern Know Nothings and the Politics of the 1850s.* New York: Oxford University Press, 1994.

Anderson, Carol. "Self-Defense." In Nikole Hannah-Jones et al., eds. *The 1619 Project: A New Origin Story.* New York: One World Press, 2021.

Baker, H. Robert. Prigg v. Pennsylvania: *Slavery, the Supreme Court, and the Ambivalent Constitution.* Lawrence: University Press of Kansas, 2012.

Balkin, Jack M., and Sanford Levinson. "Thirteen Ways of Looking at Dred Scott." *Chicago-Kent Law Review* 82 (2007): 49–95.

Balogh, Brian. *A Government out of Sight: The Mystery of National Authority in the Nineteenth Century.* New York: Cambridge University Press, 2009.

Barnett, Randy E. "The Original Meaning of the Commerce Clause." *University of Chicago Law Review* 68 (Winter 2001): 101–47.

Baron, Frank. "Abraham Lincoln and the German Immigrants: Turners and Forty-Eighters." *Yearbook of German-American Studies.* Supplemental Issue, vol. 4 (2012): 1–254.

Barreyre, Nicolas, and Claire Lemercier. "The Unexceptional State: Rethinking the State in the Nineteenth Century (France, United States)." *American Historical Review* 126 (June 2021): 481–503.

Baseler, Marilyn C. *"Asylum for Mankind": America, 1607–1800.* Ithaca, NY: Cornell University Press, 1998.

Batzell, Rudi. "Free Labour, Capitalism and the Anti-Slavery Origins of Chinese Exclusion in California in the 1870s." *Past and Present* 225 (November 2014): 143–86.

Baxter, Maurice G. "Encouragement of Immigration to the Middle West During the Era of the Civil War." *Indiana Magazine of History* 46 (March 1950): 25–38.

Baxter, Maurice G. *The Steamboat Monopoly:* Gibbons v. Ogden, *1824.* New York: Knopf, 1972.

Beckert, Sven. *Empire of Cotton: A Global History.* New York: Vintage Books, 2015.

Bennett, Marion T. *American Immigration Policies: A History.* Washington, DC: Public Affairs Press, 1963.

Bensel, Richard Franklin. *Yankee Leviathan: The Origins of Central State Authority in America, 1859–1877.* New York: Cambridge University Press, 1990.

Benton, Lauren. *A Search for Sovereignty: Law and Geography in European Empires, 1400–1900.* New York: Cambridge University Press, 2009.

Berger, Bethany R. "The Anomaly of Citizenship for Indigenous Rights." In Shereen Hertel and Kathryn Libal, eds. *Human Rights in the United States: Beyond Exceptionalism.* New York: Cambridge University Press, 2011.

Berger, Bethany R. "Birthright Citizenship on Trial: *Elk v. Wilkins* and *United States v. Wong Kim Ark.*" *Cardozo Law Review* 37 (April 2016): 1185–258.

Berger, Bethany R. "Liberalism and Republicanism: in Federal Indian Law." University of Connecticut School of Law, Faculty Articles and Papers, 198. https://opencommons.uconn.edu/law_papers/198.

Berger, Bethany R. "'Power over This Unfortunate Race': Race, Politics and Indian Law in *United States v. Rogers.*" *William & Mary Law Review* 45 (April 2004): 1957–2052.

Berger, Bethany R. "Race, Descent, and Tribal Citizenship." *California Law Review* 4 (2013): 23–37.

Berlin, Ira. *The Long Emancipation: The Demise of Slavery in the United States.* Cambridge, MA: Harvard University Press, 2013.

Berlin, Ira. *The Making of African America: The Four Great Migrations.* New York: Penguin, 2010.

Berlin, Ira. *Slaves Without Masters: The Free Negro in the Antebellum South.* 1975. New York: Free Press, 2007.

Berns, Walter. "The Constitution and the Migration of Slaves." *Yale Law Journal* 78 (December 1968): 198–228.

Berwanger, Eugene H. *The Frontier Against Slavery: Western Anti-Negro Prejudice and the Slavery Extension Controversy.* 1967. Urbana: University of Illinois Press, 2002.

Bilder, Mary Sarah. "The Struggle over Immigration: Indentured Servants, Slaves, and Articles of Commerce." *Missouri Law Review* 61 (Fall 1996): 743–824.

Billington, Ray Allen. *The Protestant Crusade, 1800–1860: A Study of the Origins of American Nativism.* New York: Macmillan, 1938.

Blackett, R. J. M. *The Captive's Quest for Freedom: Fugitive Slaves, the 1850 Fugitive Slave Law, and the Politics of Slavery.* New York: Cambridge University Press, 2018.

Blackhawk, Maggie. "Federal Indian Law as Paradigm Within Public Law." *Harvard Law Review* 132 (May 2019): 1787–877.

Bonner, Christopher James. *Remaking the Republic: Black Politics and the Creation of American Citizenship.* Philadelphia: University of Pennsylvania Press, 2020.

Breuilly, John. "Modern Empires and Nation States." *Thesis Eleven* 139.1 (2017): 11–29.

Brooks, Jennifer. "'John Chinaman' in Alabama: Immigration, Race, and Empire in the New South." *Journal of American Ethnic History* 37 (Winter 2018): 5–36.

Burin, Eric. *Slavery and the Peculiar Solution: A History of the American Colonization Society.* Gainesville: University Press of Florida, 2005.

Burt, John. "Lincoln's Dred Scott: Contesting the Declaration of Independence." *American Literary History* 21 (Winter 2009): 730–51.

Calavita, Kitty. *U.S. Immigration Law and the Control of Labor: 1820–1924.* Orlando, FL: Academic Press, 1984.

Camp, Edgar Whittlesey. "Hugh C. Murray: California's Youngest Chief Justice." *California Historical Society Quarterly* 20 (December 1941): 365–73.

Campbell, Stanley W. *The Slave Catchers: Enforcement of the Fugitive Slave Law, 1850–1860.* Chapel Hill: University of North Carolina Press, 1970.

Carper, Katherine. "The Migration Business, 1824–1876." Unpublished PhD dissertation, Boston College, 2020.

Carper, Katherine. "The Migration Business and the Shift from State to Federal Immigration Regulation." *Journal of the Civil War Era* 11 (September 2021): 340–60.

Carrington, Adam. "Police the Border: Justice Field on Immigration as a Police Power." *Journal of Supreme Court History* 40 (2015): 20–37.

Carwardine, Richard. *Lincoln: A Life of Purpose and Power.* New York: Alfred A. Knopf, 2006.

Carwardine, Richard, and Jay Sexton, eds. *The Global Lincoln.* New York: Oxford University Press, 2011.

Chang, Gordon H. *Ghosts of Gold Mountain: The Epic Story of the Chinese Who Built the Transcontinental Railroad.* New York: Houghton Mifflin, 2019.

Chang, Kornel. "Coolie." In Cathy J. Schlund-Vials, Linda Trinh Võ, and K. Scott Wong, eds. *Keywords for Asian American Studies.* New York: New York University Press, 2015.

Chang, Kornel. *Pacific Connections: The Making of the U.S.-Canada Borderlands.* Berkeley: University of California Press, 2012.

Chin, Gabriel J. "*Chae Chan Ping* and *Fong Yue Ting*: The Origins of Plenary Power." In David A. Martin and Peter H. Schuck, eds. *Immigration Law Stories.* New York: Foundation Press, 2005.

Chin, Gabriel J. "The *Plessy* Myth: Justice Harlan and the Chinese Cases." *Iowa Law Review* 82 (1996): 151–82.

Chin, Gabriel J. "Segregation's Last Stronghold: Race Discrimination and the Constitutional Law of Immigration." *UCLA Law Review* 46 (1998): 1–74.

Chin, Gabriel J., and Paul Finkelman. "Birthright Citizenship, Slave Trade Legislation, and the Origins of Federal Immigration Regulation." *UC Davis Law Review* 54 (July 2021): 2215–65.

Cleveland, Sarah. "Powers Inherent in Sovereignty: Indians, Aliens, Territories, and the Nineteenth Century Origins of Plenary Power over Foreign Affairs." *Texas Law Review* 81 (November 2002): 1–284.

Cohn, Raymond L. *Mass Migration Under Sail: European Immigration to the Antebellum United States.* New York: Cambridge University Press, 2010.

Coolidge, Mary Roberts. *Chinese Immigration.* New York: Henry Holt, 1909.

Cox, Adam B. "Three Mistakes in Open Borders Debates." In Jack Knight, ed. *Immigration, Emigration, and Migration.* New York: New York University Press, 2017.

Cox, Adam B., and Cristina M. Rodríguez. *The President and Immigration Law.* New York: Oxford University Press, 2020.

Daniels, Roger. *Asian America: Chinese and Japanese in the United States Since 1850.* Seattle: University of Washington Press, 1988.

Daniels, Roger. *Coming to America: A History of Immigration and Ethnicity in American Life.* 2nd ed. New York: HarperCollins Perennial, 2002.

Davis, David Brion. *Inhuman Bondage: The Rise and Fall of Slavery in the New World.* New York: Oxford University Press, 2006.

Davis, David Brion. *The Problem of Slavery in the Age of Emancipation.* New York: Alfred A. Knopf, 2014.

Davis, David Brion. *The Problem of Slavery in the Age of Revolution 1770–1823.* Ithaca, NY: Cornell University Press, 1975.

Davis, David Brion. *The Problem of Slavery in Western Culture.* Ithaca, NY: Cornell University Press, 1966.

Davis, David Brion. *The Slave Power Conspiracy and the Paranoid Style.* Baton Rouge: Louisiana State University Press, 1969.

Davis, David Brion. *Slavery and Human Progress.* New York: Oxford University Press, 1984.

DeGooyer, Stephanie. *Before Borders: A Legal and Literary History of Naturalization.* Baltimore, MD: Johns Hopkins Universtiy Press, 2022.

DeLay, Brian. "Indian Polities, Empire, and the History of American Foreign Relations." *Diplomatic History* 39 (November 2015): 927–42.

Dodson, Howard, and Sylvian Diouf. *In Motion: The African-American Migration Experience.* New York: Schomburg Center for Research, 2015.

Donald, David Herbert. *Lincoln.* New York: Simon & Schuster, 1995.

Downs, Gregory P., and Kate Masur, eds. *The World the Civil War Made.* Chapel Hill: University of North Carolina Press, 2015.

Dubber, Markus Dirk. *The Police Power: Patriarchy and the Foundations of American Government.* New York: Columbia University Press, 2005.

Edling, Max M. *National and State Authority in the US Constitution.* New York: Oxford University Press, 2021.

Edling, Max M. *A Revolution in Favor of Government: Origins of the U.S. Constitution and the Making of the American State.* New York: Oxford University Press, 2008.

Edwards, Laura F. *A Legal History of the Civil War and Reconstruction: A Nation of Rights.* New York: Cambridge University Press, 2015.

Efford, Alison Clark. "Civil War-Era Immigration and the Imperial United States." *Journal of the Civil War Era* 10 (June 2020): 233–53.

Efford, Alison Clark. *German Immigrants, Race, and Citizenship in the Civil War Era.* New York: Cambridge University Press, 2013.

Ellis, Elizabeth. "The Border(s) Crossed Us Too: The Intersections of Native American and Immigrant Fights for Justice." *emisférica* 14 (Fall 2018), https://hemisphericin stitute.org/en/emisferica-14-1-expulsion/14-1-essays/the-border-s-crossed-us-too-the-intersections-of-native-american-and-immigrant-fights-for-justice-2.html.

Epps, Garrett. *Democracy Reborn: The Fourteenth Amendment and the Fight for Equal Rights in Post-Civil War America.* New York: Henry Holt, 2006.

Epps, Garrett. "Interpreting the Fourteenth Amendment: Two Dont's and Three Dos." *William & Mary Bill of Rights Journal* 16 (2007): 433–63.

Epps, Garrett. "Second Founding: The Story of the Fourteenth Amendment." *Oregon Law Review* 85 (2006): 895–911.

Erickson, Charlotte. *American Industry and the European Immigrant, 1860–1885.* Cambridge, MA: Harvard University Press, 1957.

Ernst, Robert. "Economic Nativism in New York City during the 1840's." *New York History* XXIX (1948): 170–86.

Ewing, Walter, Daniel E. Martínez, and Ruben Rimbaut. *The Criminalization of Immigration in the United* States. Washington, DC: American Immigration Council, 2005.

Fehlings, Gregory. "Storm on the Constitution: The First Deportation Law." *Tulsa Journal of International and Comparative Law* 10 (2002): 63–114.

Fehrenbacher, Don E. *The Dred Scott Case: Its Significance in American Law and Politics.* New York: Oxford University Press, 1978.

Fehrenbacher, Don E. *Prelude to Greatness: Lincoln in the 1850's.* Stanford, CA: Stanford University Press, 1962.

Feldman, David. "Was the Nineteenth Century a Golden Age for Immigrants? The Changing Articulation of National, Local and Voluntary Controls." In Andreas Fahrmeir, Olivier Faron, and Patrick Weil, eds. *Migration Control in the North Atlantic World: The Evolution of State Practices in Europe and the United States from the French Revolution to the Inter-War Period.* New York: Berghahn Books, 2003.

Fields, Barbara J. *Slavery and Freedom on the Middle Ground: Maryland During the Nineteenth Century.* New Haven: Yale University Press, 1985.

Fields, Barbara J. "Whiteness, Racism, and Identity." *International Labor and Working-Class History* 60 (Fall 2001): 48–56.

Fields, Karen E., and Barbara J. Fields. *Racecraft: The Soul of Inequality in American Life.* London: Verso, 2014.

Finkelman, Paul, ed. *Defending Slavery. Proslavery Thought in the Old South: A Brief History with Documents.* Bedford Series in History and Culture. Boston: Bedford/St. Martin's, 2003.

Finkelman, Paul, ed. *Dred Scott v. Sandford: A Brief History with Documents.* Bedford Series in History and Culture. Boston: Bedford/St. Martin's, 1997.

Finkelman, Paul. *An Imperfect Union: Slavery, Federalism, and Comity.* Chapel Hill: University of North Carolina Press, 1991.

Finkelman, Paul. "Prelude to the Fourteenth Amendment: Black Legal Rights in the Antebellum North." *Rutgers Law Journal* 17 (1986): 415–82.

Finkelman, Paul. *Slavery and the Founders: Race and Liberty in the Age of Jefferson.* New York: M.E. Sharpe, 1996.

Finkelman, Paul. *Slavery in the Courtroom: An Annotated Bibliography of American Cases.* Washington, DC: Library of Congress, 1985.

Finkelman, Paul. "Slavery in the United States: Persons or Property?" In Jean Allain, ed. *The Legal Understanding of Slavery: From the Historical to the Contemporary.* New York: Oxford University Press, 2012.

Finkelman, Paul. *Supreme Injustice: Slavery in the Nation's Highest Court.* Cambridge, MA: Harvard University Press, 2018.

FitzGerald, David Scott, and David Cook-Martín. *Culling the Masses: The Democratic Origins of Racist Immigration Policy in the Americas.* Cambridge, MA: Harvard University Press, 2014.

Fogelman, Aaron. "Migrations to the Thirteen British North American Colonies, 1700–1775: New Estimates." *Journal of Interdisciplinary History* 22 (Spring 1992): 691–709.

Foner, Eric. *Battles for Freedom: The Use and Abuse of American History.* New York: I.B. Taurus/The Nation, 2017.

Foner, Eric. *The Fiery Trial: Abraham Lincoln and American Slavery.* New York: Norton, 2011.

Foner, Eric. *Free Soil, Free Labor, Free Men: The Ideology of the Republican Party before the Civil War.* 1970. New York: Oxford University Press, 1995.

Foner, Eric. *Gateway to Freedom: The Hidden History of the Underground Railroad.* New York: Norton, 2015.

Foner, Eric, ed. *Our Lincoln: New Perspectives on Lincoln and His World.* New York: Norton, 2008.

Foner, Eric. *Reconstruction: America's Unfinished Revolution, 1862–1877.* 1988. Updated edition. New York: Harper Perennial Modern Classics, 2014.

Foner, Eric. "Rights and the Constitution in Black Life During the Civil War and Reconstruction." *Journal of American History* 74 (1987): 863–83.

Foner, Eric. *The Second Founding: How the Civil War and Reconstruction Remade the Constitution.* New York: Norton, 2019.

Foner, Eric. *Tom Paine and Revolutionary America.* New York: Oxford University Press, 1976.

Forbes, Ella. "African-American Resistance to Colonization." *Journal of Black Studies* 21 (December 1990): 210–23.

Ford, Lisa. *Settler Sovereignty: Jurisdiction and Indigenous People in America and Australia, 1788–1836.* Cambridge, MA: Harvard University Press, 2010.

Fox, James W., Jr. "The Law of Many Faces: Antebellum Contract Law Background of Reconstruction-Era Freedom of Contract." *American Journal of Legal History* 49 (January 2007): 61–112.

Franklin, Frank G. *The Legislative History of Naturalization in the United States: From the Revolutionary War To 1861.* 1906. New York: Augustus M. Kelley, 1971.

Freund, Ernst. *The Police Power: Public Policy and Constitutional Rights.* Chicago: Callaghan, 1904.

Freyer, Tony Allen. *The Passenger Cases and the Commerce Clause: Immigrants, Blacks, and States' Rights in Antebellum America.* Lawrence: University Press of Kansas, 2014.

Frost, Amanda. *You Are Not American: Citizenship Stripping from Dred Scott to the Dreamers.* Boston: Beacon Press, 2021.

Gabaccia, Donna. *Foreign Relations: American Immigration in Global Perspective.* Princeton: Princeton University Press, 2012.

Gillman, Howard, Mark A. Graber, and Keith E. Whittington, eds. *American Constitutionalism.* 2 vols. 2nd ed. New York: Oxford University Press, 2016.

Glass, Maeve. "Citizens of the State." *University of Chicago Law Review* 85 (June 2018): 865–934.

Goodman, Adam. "Nation of Migrants, Historians of Migration." *Journal of American Ethnic History* 34 (Summer 2015): 7–16.

Gordon, Jennifer. "Immigration as Commerce: A New Look at the Federal Immigration Power and the Constitution." *Indiana Law Review* 93 (2018): 653–712.

Graber, Mark A. *Dred Scott and the Problem of Constitutional Evil.* New York: Cambridge University Press, 2006.

Green, Michael S. *Freedom, Union, and Power: Lincoln and His Party During the Civil War.* New York: Fordham University Press, 2004.

Green, Nancy L. "Expatriation, Expatriates, and Expats: The American Transformation of a Concept." *American Historical Review* 114 (2009): 307–28.

Green, Nancy L. "Tocqueville, Comparative History, and Immigration in Two Democracies." *French Politics, Culture & Society* 26 (Summer 2008): 1–12.

Gronningsater, Sarah L. H. "'On Behalf of His Race and the Lemmon Slaves': Louis Napoleon, Northern Black Legal Culture, and the Politics of the Sectional Crisis." *Journal of the Civil War Era* 7 (2017): 206–41.

Gross, Ariela. "Beyond Black and White: Cultural Approaches to Race and Slavery." *Columbia Law Review* 101 (April 2001): 640–90.

Gross, Ariela. *What Blood Won't Tell: A History of Race on Trial in America.* Cambridge, MA: Harvard University Press, 2010.

Gulasekaram, Pratheepan, and S. Karthick Ramakrishnan. *The New Immigration Federalism.* New York: Cambridge University Press, 2015.

Guterl, Matthew, and Christine Skwiot. "Atlantic and Pacific Crossings: Race, Empire, and 'the Labor Problem' in the Late Nineteenth Century." *Radical History Review* 91 (Winter 2005): 40–61.

Gutoff, Jonathan M. "Fugitive Slaves and Ship-Jumping Sailors: The Enforcement and Survival of Coerced Labor." *University of Pennsylvania Journal of Labor and Employment Law* 9.1 (2006): 87–116.

Gyory, Andrew. *Closing the Gates: Race, Politics, and the Chinese Exclusion Act.* Chapel Hill: University of North Carolina Press, 1998.

Hadden, Sally E. *Slave Patrols: Law and Violence in Virginia and the Carolinas.* Cambridge, MA: Harvard University Press, 2001.

Hahn, Stephen. *A Nation Without Borders: The United States and Its World in an Age of Civil Wars, 1830–1910.* New York: Penguin, 2016.

Hahn, Steven. "The United States from the Inside Out and the Southside North." In Jewel L. Spangler and Frank Towers, eds. *Remaking North American Sovereignty: State Transformation in the 1860s.* New York: Fordham University Press, 2020.

Hamer, Philip. "British Consuls and the Negro Seamen's Acts, 1850–1860." *Journal of Southern History* 1 (1935): 138–68.

Hamer, Philip. "Great Britain, the United States and the Negro Seamen Acts, 1822–1842." *Journal of Southern History* 1 (1935): 3–28.

Hannah-Jones, Nikole et al., eds. *The 1619 Project: A New Origin Story.* New York: One World Press, 2021.

Harris, John. *The Last Slave Ships: New York and the End of the Middle Passage.* New Haven: Yale University Press, 2020.

He, Fang, "'Golden Lilies'" Across the Pacific: Footbinding and the American Enforcement of Chinese Exclusion Laws." In Catherine Ceniza Choy and Judy Tzu-Chun Wu, eds. *Gendering the Transpacific World.* Vol. 1. Online publication. https://brill.com/view/book/edcoll/9789004336100/B9789004336100_015.xml. Leiden: Brill, 2017.

Heerman, M. Scott. *The Alchemy of Slavery: Human Bondage and Emancipation in the Illinois Country, 1730–1865*. Philadelphia: University of Pennsylvania Press, 2018.

Hernandez, Kelly Lytle. *Migra! A History of the U.S. Border Patrol*. Berkeley: University of California Press, 2010.

Hester, Torrie. "'Protection, Not Punishment': Legislative and Judicial Formation of U.S. Deportation Policy, 1882–1904." *Journal of American Ethnic History* 30 (Fall 2010): 11–36.

Higham, John. *Strangers in the Land: Patterns of American Nativism, 1860–1925*. 1955. Rev. ed. New Brunswick, NJ: Rutgers University Press, 2002.

Hinsley, F. H. *Sovereignty*. 2nd ed. Cambridge: Cambridge University Press, 1986.

Hirota, Hidetaka. "Exclusion on the Ground: Racism, Official Discretion, and the Quotidian Enforcement of General Immigration Law in the Pacific Northwest Borderland." *American Quarterly* 69 (June 2017): 347–70.

Hirota, Hidetaka. *Expelling the Poor: Atlantic Seaboard States and the Nineteenth-Century Origins of American Immigration Policy*. New York: Oxford University Press, 2017.

Hirota, Hidetaka. "'The Great Entrepot for Mendicants': Foreign Poverty and Immigration Control in New York State to 1882." *Journal of American Ethnic History* 33 (Winter 2014): 5–32.

Hirota, Hidetaka. "The Moment of Transition: State Officials, the Federal Government, and the Formation of American Immigration Policy." *Journal of American History* 99 (March 2013): 1092–108.

Hixson, Walter L. *American Settler Colonialism: A History*. New York: Palgrave Macmillan, 2013.

Holt, Michael F. *The Political Crisis of the 1850s*. New York: Wiley, 1978.

Holt, Michael F. "The Politics of Impatience: The Origins of Know Nothingism." *Journal of American History* 60 (1973): 309–31.

Holt, Michael F. *The Rise and Fall of the American Whig Party: Jacksonian Politics and the Onset of the Civil War*. New York: Oxford University Press, 1999.

Horwitz, Morton J. *The Transformation of America Law, 1780–1860*. Cambridge, MA: Harvard University Press, 1977.

Howe, Daniel Walker. *What Hath God Wrought: The Transformation of America, 1815–1848*. New York: Oxford University Press, 2007.

Hu-DeHart, Evelyn. "Chinese Coolie Labour in Cuba in the Nineteenth Century: Free Labour or Neoslavery?" *Slavery and Abolition* 14 (April 1993): 67–86.

Hu-DeHart, Evelyn, and Kathleen López. "Asian Diasporas in Latin America and the Caribbean: An Historical Overview." *Afro-Hispanic Review* 27 (Spring 2008): 9–21.

Huebner, Timothy S. "Roger B. Taney and the Slavery Issue: Looking Beyond—and Before—*Dred Scott*." *Journal of American History* 97 (June 2010): 17–38.

Hull Hoffer, Williamjames. *Plessy v. Ferguson: Race and Inequality in Jim Crow America*. Lawrence: University Press of Kansas, 2012.

Hune, Shirley. "Politics of Chinese Exclusion." *Amerasia Journal* 9 (1982): 5–27.

Huntington, Clare. "The Constitutional Dimension of Immigration Federalism." *Vanderbilt Law Review* 61 (2008): 787–853.

Hutchinson, Edward Prince. *Legislative History of American Immigration Policy, 1798–1965*. Philadelphia: University of Pennsylvania Press, 1981.

Innis, Lolita K. Buckner. "Tricky Magic: Blacks as Immigrants and the Paradox of Foreignness." *DePaul Law Review* 49 (Fall 1999): 85–137.

John, Richard. "Governmental Institutions as Agents of Change: Rethinking American Political Development in the Early Republic." *Studies in American Political Development* 11 (Fall 1997): 347–80.

Johnson, Herbert A. Gibbons v. Ogden: *John Marshall, Steamboats, and the Commerce Clause*. Lawrence: University Press of Kansas, 2010.

Johnson, Kevin R. "Race Matters: Immigration Law and Policy Scholarship, Law in the Ivory Tower, and the Legal Indifference of the Race Critique." *University of Illinois Law Review* 2 (2000): 525–57.

Jones, Martha S. *Birthright Citizens: A History of Race and Rights in Antebellum America*. New York: Cambridge University Press, 2018.

Jones, Martha S. "Citizenship." In Nikole Hannah-Jones et al., eds. *The 1619 Project: A New Origin Story*. New York: One World Press, 2021.

Jones, Reece. *White Borders: The History of Race and Immigration in the United States from Chinese Exclusion to the Border Wall*. Boston: Beacon Press, 2021.

Jung, Moon-Ho. *Coolies and Cane: Race, Labor, and Sugar in the Age of Emancipation*. Baltimore: Johns Hopkins University Press, 2008.

Jung, Moon-Ho. "Outlawing 'Coolies': Race, Nation, and Empire in the Age of Emancipation." *American Quarterly* 57 (September 2005): 677–701.

Kagan, Michael. "Is the Chinese Exclusion Case Still Good Law? (The President Is Trying to Find Out)." *Nevada Law Journal Forum* 1 (Spring 2017): 80–91.

Kalmo, Hent, and Quentin Skinner, eds. *Sovereignty in Fragments: The Past, Present and Future of a Contested Concept*. Cambridge: Cambridge University Press, 2010.

Kang, S. Deborah. *The INS on the Line: Making Immigration Law on the US-Mexico Border, 1917–1954*. New York: Oxford University Press, 2016.

Kanstroom, Daniel. *Deportation Nation: Outsiders in American History*. Cambridge, MA: Harvard University Press, 2007.

Kenny, Kevin. "Abraham Lincoln and the American Irish." *American Journal of Irish Studies* 10 (2013): 39–64.

Kenny, Kevin. "The Antislavery Origins of US Immigration Policy." *Journal of the Civil War Era* 11 (September 2021): 361–81.

Kenny, Kevin. "Mobility and Sovereignty: The Nineteenth-Century Origins of Immigration Restriction." *Journal of American History* 109 (September 2022): 284–97.

Kenny, Kevin. "Nativism, Labor, and Slavery: The Political Odyssey of Benjamin Bannan, 1850–1860." *Pennsylvania Magazine of History and Biography* 118 (October 1994): 325–61.

Kens, Paul. *Justice Stephen Field: Shaping Liberty from the Gold Rush to the Gilded Age.* Lawrence: University Press of Kansas, 1997.

Kerr-Ritchie, Jeffrey. *Rebellious Passage: The Creole Revolt and America's Coastal Slave Trade.* New York: Cambridge University Press, 2019.

Kettner, James H. *The Development of American Citizenship, 1608–1870.* Rev. ed. 1978. Chapel Hill: University of North Carolina Press, 2005.

Keyssar, Alexander. *The Right to Vote: The Contested History of Democracy in the United States.* Rev. ed. New York: Basic Books, 2009.

Kiser, William S. *Borderlands of Slavery: The Struggle over Captivity and Peonage in the American Southwest.* Philadelphia: University of Pennsylvania Press, 2017.

Klebaner, Benjamin J. "The Myth of Foreign Pauper Dumping in the United States." *Social Science Review* 35 (Sept. 1961): 302–9.

Klebaner, Benjamin J. "State and Local Immigration Regulation in the United States Before 1882." *International Review of Social History* 3 (1958): 269–95.

Knight, Jack, ed. *Immigration, Emigration, and Migration.* New York: New York University Press, 2017.

Kohler, Max J. *Immigration and Aliens in the United States: Studies of American Immigration Laws and the Legal Status of Aliens in the United States.* New York: Bloch, 1936.

Kolchin, Peter. *American Slavery: 1618–1877.* 1993. Rev. ed. New York: Hill and Wang, 2003.

Kramer, Paul A. "Power and Connection: Imperial Histories of the United States in the World." *American Historical Review* 116 (December 2011): 1348–91.

Krasner, Stephen D. *Sovereignty: Organized Hypocrisy.* Princeton: Princeton University Press, 1999.

Kraut, Julia Rose. *Threat of Dissent: A History of Ideological Exclusion and Deportation in the United States.* Cambridge, MA: Harvard University Press, 2020.

Krull, Andrew. *The Color-Blind Constitution.* Cambridge, MA: Harvard University Press, 1992.

Kuhn, Philip A. *Chinese Among Others: Emigration in Modern Times.* Lanham, MD: Rowman and Littlefield, 2008.

Labbé, Ronald M., and Jonathan Lurie. *The Slaughterhouse Cases: Regulation, Reconstruction, and the Fourteenth Amendment.* Abridged edition. Lawrence: University Press of Kansas, 2005.

Law, Anna O. "The Historical Amnesia of Contemporary Immigration Federalism Debates." *Polity* 47 (July 2015): 302–19.

Law, Anna O. *The Immigration Battle in American Courts.* New York: Cambridge University Press 2010.

Law, Anna O. "Lunatics, Idiots, Paupers, and Negro Seamen—Immigration Federalism and the Early American State." *Studies in American Political Development* 28 (October 2014): 107–28.

Lee, Erika. *At America's Gates: Chinese Immigration During the Exclusion Era, 1882–1943*. Chapel Hill: University of North Carolina Press, 2003.

Lee, Erika. "The Chinese Exclusion Example: Race, Immigration, and American Gatekeeping, 1882–1924." *Journal of American Ethnic History* 21 (Spring 2002): 36–62.

Lee, Erika. "Enforcing the Borders: Chinese Exclusion Along the U.S. Borders with Canada and Mexico, 1882–1924." *Journal of American History* 89 (June 2002): 54–86.

Lee, Erika. "Orientalisms in the Americas: A Hemispheric Approach to Asian American History." *Journal of Asian American Studies* 8 (October 2005): 235–56.

Legarre, Santiago. "The Historical Background of the Police Power." *Journal of Constitutional Law* 9 (February 2007): 745–96.

Legomsky, Stephen H. "Immigration Law and the Principle of Plenary Congressional Power." *Supreme Court Review* (1984): 255–307.

Legomsky, Stephen H. and David B. Thronson. *Immigration and Refugee Law and Policy*. 7th ed. St. Paul, MN: Foundation Press, 2018.

Levine, Bruce. "Conservatism, Nativism, and Slavery: Thomas R. Whitney and the Origins of the Know-Nothing Party." *Journal of American History* 88 (September 2001): 455–88.

Levine, Bruce. "'The Vital Element of the Republican Party': Antislavery, Nativism, and Abraham Lincoln." *Journal of the Civil War Era* 1 (December 2011): 481–505.

Lew-Williams, Beth. "Before Restriction Became Exclusion: America's Experiment in Diplomatic Immigration Control." *Pacific Historical Review* 83 (February 2014): 24–56.

Lew-Williams, Beth. "'Chinamen' and 'Delinquent Girls': Intimacy, Exclusion, and a Search for California's Color Line." *Journal of American History* 104 (December 2017): 632–55.

Lew-Williams, Beth. *The Chinese Must Go: Violence, Exclusion, and the Making of the Alien in America*. Cambridge, MA: Harvard University Press, 2018.

Lightner, David L. "The Door to the Slave Bastille: The Abolitionist Assault upon the Interstate Slave Trade, 1833–1839." *Civil War History* 34 (September 1988): 235–52.

Lightner, David L. "The Founders and the Interstate Slave Trade." *Journal of the Early Republic* 22 (Spring 2002): 25–51.

Lightner, David L. "The Interstate Slave Trade as an Issue in the Secession Crisis." *Southern Studies* 9 (Summer/Fall 1998): 1–35.

Lightner, David L. "The Interstate Slave Trade in Antislavery Politics." *Civil War History* 36 (June 1990): 119–36.

Lightner, David L. *Slavery and the Commerce Power: How the Struggle Against the Interstate Slave Trade Led to the Civil War*. New Haven: Yale University Press, 2006.

Lightner, David L. "The Supreme Court and the Interstate Slave Trade: A Study in Evasion, Anarchy, and Extremism." *Journal of Supreme Court History* 29 (November 2004): 229–53.

Lim, Julian. "Immigration, Plenary Powers, and Sovereignty Talk: Then and Now." *Journal of the Gilded Age and Progressive Era* 19 (April 2020): 217–29.

Lim, Julian. "Mormons and Mohammadens: Race, Religion, and the Anti-Polygamy Bar in US Immigration Law." *Journal of American Ethnic History* 41 (Fall 2021): 5–49.

Lindsay, Matthew J. "Immigration as Invasion: Sovereignty, Security, and the Origins of the Federal Immigration Power." *Harvard Civil Rights-Civil Liberties Law Review* 45 (Winter 2010): 1–56.

Litwack, Leon F. *North of Slavery: The Negro in the Free States, 1790–1860.* Chicago: University of Chicago Press, 1961.

Lloyd, June. "Basket Making Thrived on York's Bullfrog Alley." *Universal York*, July 25, 2019. https://yorkblog.com/universal/basket-making-thrived-on-yorks-bullfrog-alley/.

Lloyd, June. "York's Gypsies Led a Colorful Life." *Universal York*, September 27, 2019. https://yorkblog.com/universal/yorks-gypsies-led-a-colorful-life/.

Loiacono, Gabriel J. *How Welfare Worked in the Early United States: Five Microhistories.* New York: Oxford University Press, 2021.

Lonn, Ella. *Foreigners in the Union Army and Navy.* Baton Rouge: Louisiana State University Press, 1951.

Lopez, Ian Haney. *White by Law: The Construction of Race.* New York: New York University Press, 1996.

López, Kathleen. *Chinese Cubans: A Transnational History.* Chapel Hill: University of North Carolina Press, 2013.

Lowe, Lisa. *The Intimacies of Four Continents.* Durham, NC: Duke University Press, 2015.

Magee, Rhonda V. "Slavery and Immigration?" *University of San Francisco Law Review* 44 (September 2009): 1–33.

Maltz, Earl M. *Dred Scott and the Politics of Slavery.* Lawrence: University Press of Kansas, 2007.

Markowtiz, Peter L. "Undocumented No More: The Power of State Citizenship." *Stanford Law Review* 67 (April 2015): 869–915.

Martin, David A., and Peter H. Schuck, eds. *Immigration Law Stories.* New York: Foundation Press, 2005.

Masur, Kate. "State Sovereignty and Migration Before Reconstruction." *Journal of the Civil War Era* 9 (December 2019): 588–611.

Masur, Kate. *Until Justice Be Done: America's First Civil Rights Movement, from the Revolution to Reconstruction.* New York: Norton, 2021.

McClain, Charles J. *In Search of Equality: The Chinese Struggle Against Discrimination in Nineteenth-Century America.* Berkeley: University of California Press, 1994.

McDonald, Forrest, and Ellen Shapiro McDonald. "The Ethnic Origins of the American People, 1790." *The William and Mary Quarterly* 37 (April 1980): 179–99.

McKanders, Karla M. "The Constitutionality of State and Local Laws Targeting Immigrants." *University of Arkansas at Little Rock Law Review* 31 (2009): 579–600.

McKanders, Karla M. "Federal Preemption and Immigrants' Rights." *Wake Forest Journal of Law & Policy* 3.2 (2013): 333–65.

McKanders, Karla M. "Immigration Enforcement and the Fugitive Slave Acts: Exploring Their Similarities." *Catholic University Law Review* 61 (2012): 921–54.

McKanders, Karla M. "Sustaining Tiered Personhood: Jim Crow and Anti-Immigrant Laws." *Harvard Journal on Racial & Ethnic Justice* 26 (2010): 163–210.

McKeown, Adam. "Global Migration, 1846–1940." *Journal of World History* 15 (June 2004): 155–189

McKeown, Adam M. *Melancholy Order: Asian Migration and the Globalization of Borders*. New York: Columbia University Press, 2008.

McKeown, Adam. "Regionalizing World Migration." *International Review of Social History* 52 (2007): 134–42.

McPherson, James. *Abraham Lincoln*. New York: Oxford University Press, 2009.

McPherson, James, ed. *We Cannot Escape History: Lincoln and the Last Best Hope of Earth*. Champaign: University of Illinois Press, 2001.

Michael, Jerrold M. "The National Board of Health: 1879–1883." *Public Health Reports* 126 (January–February 2011): 123–29. https://www.ncbi.nlm.nih.gov/pmc/articles/PMC3001811/.

Miller, John C. *Crisis in Freedom: The Alien and Sedition Acts*. Boston: Little, Brown, 1951.

Montgomery, David. *Beyond Equality: Labor and the Radical Republicans, 1862–1872*. Urbana and Chicago: University of Illinois Press, 1981.

Moran, Rachel F., and Devon W. Carbado, eds. *Race Law Stories*. New York: Foundation Press, 2008.

Morel, Lucas E. "The *Dred Scott* Dissents: McLean, Curtis, Lincoln, and the Public Mind." *The Journal of Supreme Court History* 32 (2007): 133–51.

Morris, Thomas D. *Southern Slavery and the Law, 1619–1860*. Chapel Hill: University of North Carolina Press, 1996.

Motomura, Hiroshi. *Americans in Waiting: The Lost Story of Immigration and Citizenship in the United States*. New York: Oxford University Press, 2006.

Motomura, Hiroshi. "Immigration Law After a Century of Plenary Power: Phantom Constitutional Norms and Statutory Interpretation." *Yale Law Journal* 100 (December 1990): 545–613.

Motomura, Hiroshi. *Immigration Outside the Law*. New York: Oxford University Press, 2014.

Nackenoff, Carol, and Julie Novkov. *American by Birth: Wong Kim Ark and the Battle for Citizenship*. Abridged edition. Lawrence: University Press of Kansas, 2021.

Nardin, Terry. "The Diffusion of Sovereignty." *History of European Ideas* 41.1 (2015): 89–102.

Nelson, William E. *The Fourteenth Amendment from Political Principle to Judicial Doctrine*. Cambridge, MA: Harvard University Press, 1988.

Neuman, Gerald L. "Back to Dred Scott?" *San Diego Law Review* 24 (1987): 485–500.

Neuman, Gerald L. "Habeas Corpus, Executive Detention, and the Removal of Aliens." *Columbia Law Review* 98 (May 1998): 961–1067.

Neuman, Gerald L. "The Lost Century of American Immigration Law (1776–1875)." *Columbia Law Review* 93 (December 1993): 1833–1901.

Neuman, Gerald L. *Strangers to the Constitution: Immigrants, Borders, and Fundamental Law.* Princeton: Princeton University Press, 1996.

Neuman, Gerald L. "We Are the People: Alien Suffrage in German and American Perspective." *Michigan Journal of International Law* 13 (1992): 259–335.

Ngai, Mae M. "The Architecture of Race in American Immigration Law: A Reexamination of the Immigration Act of 1924." *Journal of American History* 86 (June 1999): 67–92.

Ngai, Mae M. "A Call for Sanctuary." *Dissent Magazine*, November 22, 2016, 1–3.

Ngai, Mae M. "Chinese Gold Miners and the 'Chinese Question' in Nineteenth-Century California and Victoria." *Journal of American History* 101 (March 2015): 1082–105.

Ngai, Mae M. *The Chinese Question: The Gold Rushes and Global Politics.* New York: Norton, 2021.

Ngai, Mae M. *Immigration and Ethnic History.* Washington, DC: American Historical Association, 2012.

Ngai, Mae M. *Impossible Subjects: Illegal Aliens and the Making of Modern America.* Princeton: Princeton University Press, 2004.

Novak, William J. "Common Regulation: Legal Origins of State Power in America." *Hastings Law Journal* 45 (April 1994): 1061–97.

Novak, William J. "The Legal Transformation of Citizenship in Nineteenth-Century America." In Meg Jacobs, William J. Novak, and Julian E. Zelizer, eds. *The Democratic Experiment: New Directions in American Political History.* Princeton: Princeton University Press, 2003.

Novak, William J. "The Myth of the 'Weak' American State." *American Historical Review* 113 (June 2008): 752–72.

Novak, William J. *The People's Welfare: Law and Regulation in Nineteenth-Century America.* Chapel Hill: University of North Carolina Press, 1996.

Oakes, James. *The Crooked Path to Abolition: Abraham Lincoln and the Constitution.* New York: Norton, 2021.

Oakes, James. "Natural Rights, Citizenship Rights, States' Rights, and Black Rights: Another Look at Lincoln." In Eric Foner, ed. *Our Lincoln: New Perspectives on Lincoln and His World.* New York: Norton, 2008.

Oates, Stephen B. *With Malice Toward None: A Life of Abraham Lincoln.* New York: Harper Perennial, 1994.

O'Keefe, John McNelis. *Stranger Citizens: Migrant Influence and National Power in the Early American Republic.* Ithaca, NY: Cornell University Press, 2021.

O'Malley, Brendan P. "Protecting the Stranger: The Origins of U.S. Immigration Regulation in Nineteenth-Century New York." Unpublished PhD dissertation, City University of New York, 2015.

Osiander, Andreas. "Sovereignty, International Relations, and the Westphalian Myth." *International Organization* 55 (Spring 2001): 251–87.

Ostendorf, Ann. "Contextualizing American Gypsies: Experiencing Criminality in the Chesapeake." *Maryland Historical Magazine* (Fall/Winter 2018): 192–222.

Ostendorf, Ann. "Historians, or Scholars of History. On the 'Ahistoriography' of Romani American History." Paper presented at Romani History: Methods, Sources, Ethics, Workshop of the Prague Forum for the Romani Histories, June 9, 2022.

Ostendorf, Ann. "Racializing American 'Egyptians': Shifting Legal Discourse, 1690s–1860s." *Critical Romani Studies* 2 (2019): 42–59.

Page, Thomas W. "The Transportation of Immigrants and Reception Arrangements in the Nineteenth Century." *Journal of Political Economy* 19 (November 1911): 732–49.

Paik, A. Naomi. *Bans, Walls, Raids, Sanctuary: Understanding U.S. Immigration for the Twenty-First Century*. Oakland: University of California Press, 2020.

Parker, Kunal M. "Citizenship and Immigration Law, 1800–1924: Resolutions of Membership and Territory." In Michael Grossberg and Christopher Tomlins, eds. *The Cambridge History of Law in America*. 3 vols. Volume 2: *The Long Nineteenth Century (1789–1920)*. New York: Cambridge University Press, 2008.

Parker, Kunal M. "From Poor Law to Immigration Law: Changing Visions of Territorial Community in Antebellum Massachusetts." *Historical Geography* 28 (2000): 61–85.

Parker, Kunal M. *Making Foreigners: Immigration and Citizenship Law in America*. New York: Cambridge University Press, 2015.

Parker, Kunal M. "State, Citizenship, and Territory: The Legal Construction of Immigrants in Antebellum Massachusetts." *Law and History Review* 19 (Autumn 2001): 583–643.

Peck, Gunther. *Reinventing Free Labor: Padrones and Immigration Workers in the North American West, 1880–1930*. New York: Cambridge University Press, 2000.

Peffer, George Anthony. *If They Don't Bring Their Women Here: Chinese Female Immigration Before Exclusion*. Urbana: University of Illinois Press, 1999.

Perdue, Theda. *The Cherokee Removal: A Brief History with Documents*. 3rd ed. Boston and New York: Bedford/St. Martin's, 2016.

Price, Polly J. "A 'Chinese Wall' at the Nation's Borders: Justice Stephen Field and the Chinese Exclusion Case." *Journal of Supreme Court History* 43 (March 2018): 7–26.

Pryor, Elizabeth Stordeur. *Colored Travelers: Mobility and the Fight for Citizenship Before the Civil War*. Chapel Hill: University of North Carolina Press, 2016.

Purcell, Richard J. "The New York Commissioners of Emigration and Irish Immigrants: 1847–1860." *Studies: An Irish Quarterly Review* 37 (March 1948): 29–42.

Quigley, David. "Acts of Enforcement: The New York City Election of 1870." *New York History* 83 (Summer 2002): 271–292.

Quigley, David. *Second Founding: New York City, Reconstruction, and the Making of American Democracy*. New York: Hill and Wang, 2004.

Rao, Gautham. "The New Historiography of the Early Federal Government: Institutions, Contexts, and the Imperial State." *William and Mary Quarterly* 77 (January 2020): 97–128.

Rao, Gautham. "*The People's Welfare* and the Early Federal State." *American Journal of Legal History* 57 (June 2017): 226–31.

Raskin, Jamin B. "Legals, Aliens, Local Citizens: The Historical, Constitutional and Theoretical Meanings of Alien Suffrage." *University of Pennsylvania Law Review* 141 (1993): 1391–470.

Redman, Renee C. "From Importation of Slaves to Migration of Laborers: The Struggle to Outlaw American Participation in the Chinese Coolie Trade and the Seeds of United States Immigration Law." *Albany Government Law Review* 3 (2010): 1–55.

Reilly, Pamela. "Romani in Pennsylvania." *Pennsylvania Heritage*, Spring 2017, http://paheritage.wpengine.com/article/lycoming-county-romani-pennsylvania/.

Reséndez, Andrés. *The Other Slavery: The Uncovered Story of Indian Enslavement in America*. Boston: Houghton Mifflin, 2016.

Richardson, Heather Cox. *The Greatest Nation of the Earth: Republican Economic Policies During the Civil War*. Cambridge, MA: Harvard University Press, 1997.

Robertson, Craig. *The Passport in America: The History of a Document*. New York: Oxford University Press, 2010.

Rodríguez, Cristina M. "The Significance of the Local in Immigration Regulation." *Michigan Law Review* 106 (February 2008): 567–642.

Ron, Ariel, and Gautham Rao. "Taking Stock of the State in Nineteenth-Century America." *Journal of the Early Republic* 38 (Spring 2018): 61–67.

Rosenberg, Norman L. "Personal Liberty Laws and Sectional Crisis: 1850–1861." *Civil War History* 17 (March 1971): 25–44.

Rothman, Adam. *Slave Country: American Expansion and the Origins of the Deep South*. Cambridge, MA: Harvard University Press, 2005.

Russel, Robert R. "The Issues in the Congressional Struggle over the Kansas-Nebraska Bill, 1854." *Journal of Southern History* 29 (May 1963): 187–210.

Saito, Natsu T. "The Plenary Power Doctrine: Subverting Human Rights in the Name of Sovereignty." *Catholic University Law Review* 51 (2002): 1115–76.

Salyer, Lucy. *Laws Harsh as Tigers: Chinese Immigrants and the Shaping of American Immigration Law*. Chapel Hill: University of North Carolina Press, 1995.

Salyer, Lucy. "Reconstructing the Immigrant: The Naturalization Act of 1870 in Global Perspective." *Journal of the Civil War Era* 11 (September 2021): 382–405.

Salyer, Lucy. *Under the Starry Flag: How a Band of Irish Americans Joined the Fenian Revolt and Sparked a Crisis over Citizenship*. Cambridge, MA: Harvard University Press, 2018.

Salyer, Lucy. "Wong Kim Ark and the Challenge to Birthright Citizenship." In Peter Schuck and David Martin, eds. *Immigration Stories*. New York: Foundation Press, 2005.

Samito, Christian G. *Becoming American Under Fire: Irish Americans, African Americans, and the Politics of Citizenship during the Civil War Era*. Ithaca, NY: Cornell University Press, 2009.

Saunt, Claudio. *Unworthy Republic: The Dispossession of Native Americans and the Road to Indian Territory*. New York: Norton, 2020.

Saxton, Alexander. *The Indispensable Enemy: Labor and the Anti-Chinese Movement in California*. 1971. Berkeley: University of California Press, 1995.

Saxton, Alexander. *The Rise and Fall of the White Republic: Class Politics and Mass Culture in Nineteenth-Century America*. New York: Verso, 1990.

Scheiber, Harry N. "State Police Power." In Leonard W. Levy et al., eds. *Encyclopedia of the American Constitution*. 6 vols. Vol. 4. 1986. New York: Macmillan Reference, 2000.

Schoeppner, Michael A. "Black Migrants and Border Regulation in the Early United States." *Journal of the Civil War Era* 11 (September 2021): 317–39.

Schoeppner, Michael A. "Legitimating Quarantine: Moral Contagions, the Commerce Clause, and the Limits of *Gibbons v. Ogden*." *Journal of Southern Legal History*, 81 (December 2009): 81–120.

Schoeppner, Michael A. *Moral Contagion: Black Atlantic Sailors, Citizenship, and Diplomacy in Antebellum* America. New York: Cambridge University Press, 2019.

Schoeppner, Michael A. "The Seamen Acts and Regulatory Authority in the Antebellum South." *Law and History Review* 31 (August 2013): 559–58.

Schoeppner, Michael A. "Status Across Borders: Roger Taney, Black British Subjects, and a Diplomatic Antecedent to the Dred Scott Decision." *Journal of American History* (June 2013): 46–67.

Schuck, Peter H. "Taking Immigration Federalism Seriously." *Yale Law School Faculty Scholarship Series* Paper 1675 (2007): 57–92.

Schuck, Peter H. "The Transformation of Immigration Law." *Columbia Law Review* 84 (January 1984): 1–90.

Schuck, Peter H., and Rogers M. Smith. *Citizenship Without Consent: Illegal Aliens in the American Polity*. New Haven: Yale University Press, 1985.

Schwarz, Barry. *Abraham Lincoln and the Forge of National Memory*. Chicago: University of Chicago Press, 2000.

Scott, Julius S. *The Common Wind: Afro-American Currents in the Age of the Haitian Revolution*. New York: Verso, 2018.

Scott, Kirk. "The Two-Edged Sword: Slavery and the Commerce Clause, 1837–1852." *Fairmount Folio: Journal of History* 2 (1998): 41–55.

Scott, Rebecca. *Slave Emancipation in Cuba: The Transition to Free Labor, 1860–1889*. Pittsburgh: Pittsburgh University Press, 2000.

Seeley, Samantha. *Race, Removal, and the Right to Remain: Migration and the Making of the United States*. Williamsburg, VA, and Chapel Hill: Omohundro Institute of Early American History and Culture and University of North Carolina Press, 2021.

Sheehan, James J. "The Problem of Sovereignty in European History." *American Historical Review* 111 (February 2006): 1–15.

Silverman, Jason H. *Lincoln and the Immigrant*. Carbondale: Southern Illinois University Press, 2016.

Sinha, Manisha. *The Slave's Cause: A History of Abolition*. New Haven: Yale University Press, 2016.

Skowronek, Stephen. *Building a New American State: The Expansion of National Administrative Capacities, 1877–1920*. New York: Cambridge University Press, 1982.

Smith, Marian L. "'Any woman who is now or may hereafter be married . . . .' Women and Naturalization, ca. 1802–1940." National Archives *Prologue Magazine* 30 (Summer 1998). Genealogy Notes. https://www.archives.gov/publications/prologue/1998/summer/women-and-naturalization-2.html.

Smith, Rogers M. "The 'American Creed' and American Identity: The Limits of Cultural Citizenship in the United States." *Western Political Quarterly* 41 (June 1988): 225–51.

Smith, Rogers M. "Beyond Tocqueville, Myrdal, and Hartz: The Multiple Traditions in America." *American Political Science Review* 87 (September 1993): 549–66.

Smith, Rogers M. *Civic Ideals: Conflicting Visions of Citizenship in U.S. History*. New Haven: Yale University Press, 1997.

Smith, Rogers M. "The Inherent Deceptiveness of Constitutional Discourse: A Diagnosis and Prescription." *Nomos* 40 (1998): 218–54.

Smith, Stacy L. "Emancipating Peons, Excluding Coolies: Reconstructing Coercion in the American West." In Gregory P. Downs and Kate Masur, eds. *The World the Civil War Made*. Chapel Hill: University of North Carolina Press, 2015.

Smith, Stacy L. *Freedom's Frontier: California and the Struggle over Unfree Labor, Emancipation, and Reconstruction*. Chapel Hill: University of North Carolina Press, 2013.

Song, Sarah. "Why Does the State Have the Right to Control Immigration?" In Jack Knight, ed. *Immigration, Emigration, and Migration*. New York: New York University Press, 2017.

Spangler, Jewel L., and Frank Towers, eds. *Remaking North American Sovereignty: State Transformation in the 1860s*. New York: Fordham University Press, 2020.

Sparrow, Bartholomew H. *The Insular Cases and the Emergence of American Empire*. Lawrence: University Press of Kansas, 2006.

Spiro, Peter J. "The States and Immigration in an Era of Demi-Sovereigns." *Virginia Journal of International Law* 35 (1995): 121–78.

Stanley, Amy Dru. *From Bondage to Contact: Wage Labor, Marriage, and the Market in the Age of Slave Emancipation*. New York: Cambridge University Press, 1998.

Steinfeld, Robert J. *Coercion, Contract, and Free Labor in the Nineteenth Century.* New York: Cambridge University Press, 2001.

Steinfeld, Robert J. *The Invention of Free Labor: The Employment Relation in English and American Law and Culture, 1350–1870.* Chapel Hill: University of North Carolina Press, 1991.

Steinfeld, Robert J. "Subjectship, Citizenship, and the Long History of Immigration Regulation." *Law and History Review* 19 (Autumn 2001): 645–53.

Stovall, Tyler. "White Freedom and the Lady of Liberty." *American Historical Review* 123 (February 2018): 1–27.

Stovall, Tyler. *White Freedom: The Racial History of an Idea.* Princeton: Princeton University Press, 2021.

Swisher, Carl B. *Stephen Field: Craftsman of the Law.* Washington, DC: The Brookings Institution, 1930.

Swisher, Carl B. *The Taney Period, 1836–64.* New York: Macmillan, 1974.

Takaki, Ronald. *Iron Cages: Race and Culture in 19th-Century America.* 1979. Rev. ed. New York: Oxford University Press, 2000.

Takaki, Ronald. *Strangers from a Different Shore: A History of Asian Americans.* 1898. Rev. ed. Boston: Little, Brown, 1998.

Tichenor, Daniel J. *Dividing Lines: The Politics of Immigration Control in America.* Princeton: Princeton University Press, 2002.

Torok, John Hayakawa. "Reconstruction and Racial Nativism: Chinese Immigrants and the Debates on the Thirteenth, Fourteenth, and Fifteenth Amendments and Civil Rights Law." *Asian American Law Journal* 3 (1996): 55–103.

Traynor, Michael. "The Infamous Case of *People v. Hall* (1854): An Odious Symbol of Its Time." *California Supreme Court Newsletter,* Spring/Summer 2017, 2–8.

Tsiang, I-Mien. *The Question of Expatriation in America Prior to 1907.* Baltimore: Johns Hopkins Press, 1942.

Twitty, Anne. *Before* Dred Scott: *Slavery and Legal Culture in the American Confluence, 1787–1857.* New York: Cambridge University Press, 2016.

Urofsky, Melvin, and Paul Finkelman. *A March of Liberty: A Constitutional History of the United States.* 2 vols. Vol. 1: *From the Founding to 1900.* 3rd ed. New York: Oxford University Press, 2011.

Ural, Susannah J., ed. *Civil War Citizens: Race, Ethnicity, and Identity in America's Bloodiest Conflict.* New York: New York University Press, 2010.

VanderVelde, Lea S. "The *Dred Scott* Case in Context." *Journal of Supreme Court History* 40 (2015): 263–81.

VanderVelde, Lea S. *Mrs. Dred Scott: A Life on Slavery's Frontier.* New York: Oxford University Press, 2009.

Volpp, Leti. "Divesting Citizenship: On Asian American History and the Loss of Citizenship Through Marriage." *UCLA Law Review* 53 (2005): 405–83.

Vorenberg, Michael. *Final Freedom: The Civil War, the Abolition of Slavery, and the Thirteenth Amendment.* New York: Cambridge University Press, 2001.

Waldstreicher, David. *Slavery's Constitution: From Revolution to Ratification.* New York: Hill and Wang, 2009.

Warren, Charles. *The Supreme Court in United States History.* 3 vols. Boston: Little, Brown, 1922.

Weiner, Mark S. *Black Trials: Citizenship from the Beginnings of Slavery to the End of Caste.* New York: Vintage Books, 2006.

Wiecek, William. *The Sources of Anti-Slavery Constitutionalism in America, 1760–1848.* Ithaca, NY: Cornell University Press, 1977.

Wilentz, Sean. *No Property in Man: Slavery and Antislavery at the Nation's Founding.* Cambridge, MA: Harvard University Press, 2018.

Williams, Norman R. "*Gibbons.*" *NYU Law Review* 79 (October 2004): 1398–499.

Witgen, Michael John. *Seeing Red: Indigenous Land, American Expansion, and the Political Economy of Plunder in North America.* Chapel Hill: Omohundro Institute and University of North Carolina Press, 2022.

Witgen, Michael John. "Seeing Red: Race, Citizenship, and Indigeneity in the Old Northwest." *Journal of the Early Republic* 38 (Winter 2018): 581–611.

Xu, Tian Atlas. "Immigration and Chinese Exclusion Law Enforcement: The Case of San Francisco." *Journal of American Ethnic History* 41 (Fall 2021): 50–76.

Yankwich, Leon R. "Social Attitudes as Reflected in Early California Law," *Hastings Law Journal* 10 (February 1959): 250–70.

Young, Elliot. *Alien Nation: Chinese Migration in the Americas from the Coolie Era Through World War II.* Chapel Hill: University of North Carolina Press, 2014.

Young, Elliot. "Chinese Coolies, Universal Rights and the Limits of Liberalism in an Age of Empire." *Past and Present* 227 (May 2015): 121–49.

Yun, Lisa. *The Coolie Speaks: Chinese Indentured Laborers and African Slaves in Cuba.* Philadelphia: Temple University Press, 2009.

Zolberg, Aristide R. "The Archaeology of Remote Control." In Andreas Fahrmeir, Olivier Faron, and Patrick Weil, eds. *Migration Control in the North Atlantic World: The Evolution of State Practices in Europe and the United States from the French Revolution to the Inter-War Period.* New York: Berghahn Books, 2003.

Zolberg, Aristide R. *A Nation by Design: Immigration Policy in the Fashioning of America.* Cambridge, MA: Harvard University Press, 2006.

# Index

*For the benefit of digital users, indexed terms that span two pages (e.g., 52–53) may, on occasion, appear on only one of those pages.*

Note: Page numbers followed by *f* indicate a figure on the corresponding page.